Soundscapes

Kay Kaufman Shelemay

W·W·Norton & Company
New York · London

Soundscapes

EXPLORING MUSIC IN A CHANGING WORLD · EXPLORING MUSIC IN A CHANGING WORLD · EXPLORING MUSIC IN A CHANGING WORLD · EXPLORING MUSIC IN A CHANGING WORLD · EXPLORING MUSIC IN A CHANGING WORLD

For my students, from whom I have learned so much.

To assist in the important work of the American Folklife Center
at the Library of Congress in preserving America's musical heritage,
the author and publisher are jointly donating to the center a
percentage of the net proceeds from this edition of *Soundscapes*.

Copyright © 2001 by W. W. Norton & Company, Inc.

Editor: Michael Ochs
Associate Managing Editor—College: Jane Carter
Director of Manufacturing—College: Roy Tedoff
Manuscript Editor: Barbara Gerr
Editorial Assistants: Jan Hoeper, Claire McCabe

The text of this book is composed in Fairfield
with the display set in Bossanova and Spire
Composition by TSI Graphics
Manufacturing by Quebecor/World
Book and cover design by Antonina Krass
Page makeup by Carol Desnoes

Library of Congress Cataloging-in-Publication Data

Shelemay, Kay Kaufman.
Soundscapes / Kay Kaufman Shelemay.
    p. cm.
Includes bibliographical references (p.), discographies, and index.
ISBN 0-393-97536-3 (pbk.)
    1. Music appreciation. 2. World music—Analysis, appreciation.
3. Ethnomusicology—Cross-cultural studies. 4. Music—North America—
History and criticism. I. Title.

MT90 .S53 2001
780′.9—dc21   00-067565

W. W. Norton & Company, Inc., 500 Fifth Avenue, New York, N.Y. 10110
                        www.wwnorton.com
W. W. Norton & Company Ltd., Castle House, 75/76 Wells Street, London W1T 3QT

1 2 3 4 5 6 7 8 9 0

Soundscape *n*. The distinctive settings, sounds, and significances of a musical culture.

Contents

Listening Guides

Preface

Music is on the move, traveling across national and geographic boundaries to reach new and broader audiences. Most places today support an international range of musics of different styles and histories. This book offers a fresh approach to the complex world of musical action and interaction, introducing and interpreting a cross-section of musical domains, called *soundscapes*.

The term *soundscape* plays a special role in this book, providing an inclusive framework for all musical traditions. This term allows us to bring together, rather than separate, musics that exist side by side in the lives and imaginations of so many people. A soundscape is flexible, accommodating local detail while allowing for translocal connections. The word *soundscape* also captures the multidimensional, dynamic nature of music as it moves across time and space.

Nowhere is a greater range of musical traditions more prominently represented than in North America. Centuries of immigration to the United States and Canada have resulted in an increasingly multiethnic population that has sustained and transformed the musical traditions of its homelands, often resulting in new styles. *Soundscapes* examines these musical traditions by exploring their transmission "at home" in North America. From the rousing presence of bagpipe bands to the calming strains of lullabies, musical traditions reflect and shape the North American settings in which they are performed.

In order to guide our exploration of music, the individual chapters of *Soundscapes* are organized around familiar cultural themes. These include processes that shape music, such as memory, migration, and bodily motion; local contexts and shared settings; and overarching social factors such as belief, identity, and political action, enacted through the musical performance. All of these topics have porous boundaries, and most are interrelated. For instance, we will find that migration is involved in virtually every soundscape we encounter. Dance, too, will appear in many discussions.

In sum, *Soundscapes* seeks to demonstrate how music is an indispensable part of the widest array of cultural and cognitive processes: music is the language through which we pray and protest, remember and relax. At the same time, music provides a vantage point from which we can understand the most deeply felt aspects of the human experience.

Each chapter—with the exception of Chapter 9, which features Native American music—includes a major case study drawn from a musical tradition that has migrated to North America from abroad. Two or more much shorter case studies complement and contrast with this primary case study. Each chapter also contains at least five "capsules" that expand on their subjects through time lines, charts, or short narratives. Capsules deal with voices and instruments ("Sound Sources"); historical background ("Looking Back"); the lives and contributions of important musicians ("Individual Portraits"); closeups of special musical events, places or subjects ("Snapshots"); and guidelines for further musical exploration ("Studying Music").

Soundscapes is an introduction to a variety of musical traditions; its flexible framework allows instructors to incorporate personal expertise, students' backgrounds and interests, and the resources of the community. Despite this book's breadth of coverage, the world of musical experience that *Soundscapes* examines inevitably remains a partial one. Readers are encouraged to fill in the gaps they perceive and to compare the materials discussed here with those from their own background and experiences.

Because different musics coexist in everyday life, *Soundscapes* intentionally juxtaposes diverse musical traditions. Whenever possible, *Soundscapes* avoids disputed terminology, such as "world music." For decades, ethnomusicologists have taken a geographical approach to the study of music, viewing selected musics primarily within their historical homelands. This foreign-cultures perspective has provided a rich cultural setting, but it has also both distanced and made exotic musical practices that can be studied next door or across town.

This book also avoids the old and tired oppositions, such as classical/vernacular, art/folk, traditional/popular, and Western/non-Western, that have for too long separated musical experiences and their study. In particular, *Soundscapes* seeks to dissolve the long-standing practice in musical pedagogy of separating the study of so-called Western and non-Western musics. All of the musical traditions discussed in these pages are today geographically "Western" in that, whatever their historical points of origin, they are today transmitted and performed in North America.

It is particularly problematic to separate the study of Western classical music from that of the rest of the world, given the extraordinary spread of Western musical styles and sounds worldwide. Throughout *Soundscapes*, these connections constantly reappear and are discussed. Conversely, the marked influence of various musical traditions on the Western classical tradition has led to the inclusion of a Western classical supplement to this book. The supplement sets forth a brief survey of the Western classical tradition, paralleling the topics of the ten chapters of the book. In this way, *Soundscapes* seeks both to collapse conventional boundaries and to trace cross-cutting musical currents.

Finally, *Soundscapes* shifts the emphasis from musical styles to the cultural processes that people construct by and through music making as it actually takes place within a multiethnic society. Approaching diverse musical languages requires a method for listening; therefore, *Soundscapes* extends discussion beyond the usual "characteristics of sound." It presents a social framework for evaluating the characteristics of a soundscape and for interpreting a musical tradition. It explores a cross-section of international musics while keeping the local styles in clear view. In this way, music becomes an anchor for understanding diverse human settings. Through constant dialogue with the present and the past, *Soundscapes* maps the diverse musical traditions of North America. What emerges is a narrative that accommodates many musical styles within an inclusive, interactive context.

Acknowledgments

In many ways, the seeds for *Soundscapes* were sown at the very beginning of my academic career, when I traveled to Ethiopia to do fieldwork on musical traditions found only there. Not long after my arrival back home several years later, I noticed that the Ethiopian musical world had begun to migrate and was settling in all around me in North America. The realization that so many musics once found only in distant places have through the vagaries of migration, tourism, and sound recordings come to be located next door slowly transformed my own research and teaching agendas. *Soundscapes* emerged over a long period of time and draws on almost everything I have read or heard.

The first acknowledgment here should by any measure be extended to the students, both undergraduates and graduates, whom I have taught over the years at Columbia, New York University, Wesleyan, and Harvard. It is to them that this book is dedicated. They have challenged me through their curiosity, introduced me to new worlds of sound, shared unforgettable moments in the field at home, and dazzled me with their own ambitious research agendas. A number of them have contributed in important ways to *Soundscapes*, whether through research collaboration and assistance, through our work together in the classroom, or by giving me access to materials otherwise unavailable.

Once I began writing *Soundscapes* in 1995, I gained a clearer understanding of why most textbooks are collaborative ventures by several authors. Although a single-author text permits one to conceptualize and shape the materials in new ways as well as to establish continuities of theme and style difficult to achieve otherwise, no single individual could possibly carry out all the primary research necessary to address a sufficiently wide range of musical materials. As a result, I have intellectual debts to many and have taken particular care to provide documentation of the sources I consulted. Here I provide an overview of the individuals who have offered advice, lent materials, or extended important critical feedback. Footnotes scattered throughout the text identify the sources of quotations or important ideas that helped me organize that section in significant ways. The bibliographies for each chapter, which contain a detailed listing of all the sources I or my research assistants consulted, are preceded by brief summaries of the research process and acknowledgments to those on whose work I have drawn.

I could not have completed *Soundscapes* without abundant assistance from many individuals and organizations. I would like to express very special thanks to:

The Bogliasco Foundation and the Liguria Study Center for the Arts and Humanities for an unforgettable residency, during which several chapters of this book were written;

Samantha Chaifetz and Mike Bortnick for tango lessons and insights into ballroom dance culture;

Jocelyn Clark and family for introducing me to Juneau, Alaska, and its rich musical life;

Nicola Cooney, Monica Devens, Lucia Faria, Vinelde Faria, Ahmed Jebari, Thomas Kane, Navin Khaneja, Takashi Koto, David Lyczkowski, Andrea Malaguti, Meley Mulugetta, Iman Roushdy, Gurmukh Singh, Rajwinder Singh, and Patricia Tang for helping to transcribe and translate song texts;

Caprice Corona and Norma Cantú for discussions of the *quinceañera;*

Virginia Danielson and Millard Irion for advice and guidance in the Eda Kuhn Loeb Music Library at Harvard University;

Beverley Diamond for assistance with Native American materials;

The Eskowitz family and Asmara Tekle for helping me map Houston's complex musical life;

James Farrington and Alec McLane for locating archival recordings in the Olin Library at Wesleyan University;

Stuart Feder for an introduction to the accordion;

Mickey Hart and the Society for Gyuto Sacred Arts for Tibetan Buddhist materials;

The Harvard-Radcliffe Office for the Arts for aid in obtaining illustrations;

Hailegebriot Shewangizou for information concerning Ethiopian Christian music in the United States;

Robert Hogan for materials on bagpipes;

Theodore Levin for information on *khoomii* and an update on the Harmonic Choir;

Jim Metzner for unearthing and sharing clips of "You're Hearing Boston";

Ezra Mtshotshi, Counsellor, and Juan A. Henriquez, Information Officer, of the South African Embassy, Washington, D.C., for assistance;

Pham Duy for exceptional generosity in supplying recordings, videotapes, and scores;

Ankica Petrovics and Saint Mary's Ethiopian Tewahedo Church for providing videotapes of Ethiopian Christian rituals in Los Angeles;

Ronald Radano for information on the spiritual;

Anne Rasmussen for sharing the wonderful Bunai photograph she uncovered and for help with recordings of Middle Eastern music in North America;

Adelaida Reyes, Deborah Wong, Terry Miller and Andrew Talle for supplying recordings, materials, and advice related to Vietnamese music;

Gil Rose, the Boston Modern Orchestra Project, and Reza Vali for help with Mr. Vali's Flute Concerto;

Joshu Skaller for preparing the overtone example and for technical assistance at many junctures;

Judith Vander for sharing materials and an unforgettable fieldtrip to the Shoshone Wind River Reservation;

María Teresa Vélez for advice and information on Santería;

Lee Warren of Harvard University's Bok Center for cogent suggestions on pedagogical concerns;

Su Zheng for materials on and recordings of Sheung Chi Ng;

Evan Ziporyn for assistance with gamelan recordings; and

Reece Michaelson and Galen Malicoat during their tenures at the Harvard Music Department for a full measure of support in all aspects of my work during the years this project was in development.

Many staff members at W. W. Norton have offered excellent support and advice. Michael Ochs first approached me to write this book and then faithfully guided the project over the course of six years; dozens of his insightful suggestions are realized in the following pages. Neil Ryder Hoos lent a sharp eye and deep knowledge of visual sources to bring life and color to these pages. Barbara Gerr's expert manuscript editing greatly enhanced the text. The creative design by Antonina Krass captures the spirit of this venture. Steve Hoge pushed the project into technological domains that would otherwise have remained unexplored. Roby Harrington offered wise counsel. And throughout, Jan Hoeper and Claire McCabe kept this complex project on track and on schedule.

A series of superb research assistants provided help without which this project would never have been completed. David Lyczkowski worked on every aspect from the very beginning and contributed immeasurably by locating sources, volunteering ideas, supplying technological savvy, and preparing drafts; he also researched and drafted materials for the *Soundscapes* classical supplement. Sarah Morelli located many wonderful illustrations and gathered materials for the dance chapter. Roe-Min Kok, Charles Starrett, and Andrew Talle researched and drafted the segments regarding musical instruments. Reece Michaelson assisted with several biographies. Elizabeth Kessler checked sources in the bibliography, helped organize recordings, prepared timelines, and aided with research. Patricia Tang supplied materials for the Instructor's Manual. Charles Starrett devoted many hours to developing the Web site and glossary, building on earlier efforts by Jennifer Baker Kotilaine. Suzanne Fatta provided invaluable research assistance during the publication process. The graduate students who helped teach *Soundscapes* during its first two iterations at Harvard in 1999 offered many cogent suggestions: they include head teaching fellows Patricia Tang and Charles Starrett, as well as Judah Cohen, Roe-Min Kok, Sarah Morelli, and Julie Rohwein.

Many colleagues have contributed greatly by offering advice. To the anonymous readers of the manuscript for W. W. Norton I am exceedingly grateful for useful feedback on the book's strengths and shortcomings. In particular, I thank Timothy Cooley and the members of his seminar at the University of California, Santa Barbara, for a penetrating reading. General discussions about the manuscript-in-progress with colleagues and graduate students during visits to the University of California, San Diego, and Florida State University provided useful suggestions. Jocelyne Guilbault, who class-tested a draft of the book during fall 1999 at the University of California, Berkeley, provided deeply appreciated constructive criticism. Ellen Harris read the entire manuscript and not only gave perceptive suggestions and corrections, but outlined an entire "Western" syllabus to accompany the book that became the basis of the *Soundscapes Classical* supplement. I am grateful to the many colleagues who read manuscript sections in which I cite their materials and who offered important corrections and commentary. I, however, take full responsibility for all interpretations and conclusions, especially those that differ from the original sources.

The expression *soundscapes* illustrates the challenge of making these acknowledgments comprehensive. My use of the term began after I read a 1991 article by the anthropologist Arjun Appadurai, who coined *ethnoscapes* to capture the shifting and nonlocalized quality of group identities in the late twentieth century. I transposed Appadurai's term to a musical context and reimagined *soundscape* in a more defined setting than his parent term *ethnoscape* might have allowed. Yet another source, which does not use the word *soundscape,* influenced me indirectly:

Mark Slobin's extended 1992 essay "Micromusics of the West: A Comparative Approach," revised and reissued in 1993 as *Subcultural Sounds: Micromusics of the West* (Hanover, N.H.: Wesleyan University Press). There Slobin briefly explores Appadurai's concept of *ethnoscapes* in relation to present-day musical life. Other appearances of the word *soundscapes* have emerged over the last several years. The most generative use in the musical arena has been that of the Canadian composer R. Murray Schafer, who in the late 1960s employed *soundscape* as a cover term for his inclusive definition of music. The word can be found in many other contexts as well—such as in the music historian Reinhard Strohm's writings about the broader sonic environment of late medieval Bruges—if only fleetingly and usually as a musical corollary to a panoramic landscape. Thus, although I did not invent the term *soundscape* and acknowledge a wide array of precedents, I have used it in a new and expanded way.

I could not have completed this large-scale project without a special measure of help and support from family and friends. Jack Shelemay was once again my supportive companion in the field and at home, and, as always, Raymond and Lillian Kaufman encouraged this work. A special group of friends aided and buoyed me in many ways throughout this project. For their intellectual companionship and advice, I am indebted to Adrienne Fried Block, Stuart Feder, Tomie Hahn, Ellen Harris, Jane Bernstein, Steven Kaplan, Ingrid Monson, Jessie Ann Owens, Adelaida Reyes, Nancy Risser, Judith Tick, and Su Zheng.

In closing, but foremost in importance, I would like to acknowledge the musicians whose creativity gives life and meaning to these pages. I hope that this book conveys my concern for the important issues at stake in their music's conception, transmission, and performance, as well as the complex questions raised by its study.

A Note on the Spelling of Foreign Language Texts and Terms

Texts and terms from more than twenty-five different languages are found in *Soundscapes*. Terms are spelled consistent with common usage, accompanied when necessary by tips for pronunciation in parentheses. In many cases, the most straightforward alternative of several possibilities has been selected. Song texts follow their presentation in the original sources credited; in general, however, diacritical markings used to indicate tonal levels or otherwise to mark sounds distinctive to indigenous scripts are not reproduced.

Soundscapes

CHAPTER

ONE ONE ONE ONE ONE ONE ONE ONE ONE ONE ONE ONE ONE ONE ONE ONE ONE ONE ONE ONE ONE

*Fireworks cascade over the musical extravaganza at the Lincoln Memorial in Washington, D.C.,
on January 1, 2000. President Clinton hosted the entertainment event to ring in the new millennium.*

OVERVIEW

MAIN POINTS

• A soundscape is the distinctive setting, sound, and significance of a musical culture.

• The characteristics of sound include quality, pitch, duration, and intensity.

• Introduction to the Tuvan throat-singing (*khoomii*) soundscape.

Introduction

From New York to Seattle, a flurry of activity surrounded the three-week-long concert tour in the spring of 1997. Feature articles appeared in newspapers several days in advance of each performance, announcing special events at local schools and universities. On their arrival in a city, the musicians were interviewed on local radio stations. The sold-out concerts were covered by area television stations and reviewed enthusiastically in the press. The activities surrounding this concert tour would not be surprising if the musicians were a well-known rock group or a world-famous string quartet. What is remarkable and what reflects our changing musical environment is that the tour encompassed a series of concerts by a group of throat singers of Tuva known as Huun-Huur-Tu. With a fifth visit to North America in 1998 and another in 1999, along with concert and festival performances in nearly every country of Europe, Huun-Huur-Tu has emerged as the foremost international representative of Tuva's remarkable musical culture.

CASE STUDY: THE THROAT SINGERS OF TUVA

What are we to make of this brief encounter with Tuvan music in North America and what can we take away from it? Most listeners are immediately startled and engaged by the Tuvans' novel vocal style, in which an individual singer produces what sounds like more than one melody at a time. The musical instruments used to accompany the singers include a graceful fiddle decorated on top with a carved horse's head. Some song lyrics tell of life among nomadic peoples in the arid plains and rugged mountains of Inner Asia, while others speak of events in the modern cities of that area. Some songs have no words at all, with

LISTENING GUIDE 1

CD 1
TRACK
1

Artii-Sayir ("The Far Side of a Dry Riverbed"; Kargyraa Khoomii)

PERFORMED BY Vasili Chazir

This excerpt provides a fine example of the throat singer's sound.

LISTEN FOR two separate layers of sound. One is a low, rough, sustained tone, the other a higher, flutelike line that moves actively at a faster rate of speed.

the singer vocalizing melodies that range from an extraordinarily low bass up to the stratosphere.

What can we learn from this exposure that could broaden our understanding of the world in which we live and the musical traditions that help give it shape and meaning? First, let's consider this: musics from around the globe surround us and are readily accessible, if only for an evening. If we want to hear a particular music, we can probably find a possibility nearby. To expand our musical horizons, we need to keep an eye open for flyers advertising concerts, call up a community arts organization or nearby campus for information, scan the local newspaper for listings, flip on a TV or radio program sponsored by a particular ethnic community, ask an interest group for an events calendar, or search for a music or performing group on the World Wide Web. If live performances are not readily available, the "World

The members of the Tuvan ensemble Huun-Huur-Tu pose with traditional stringed and percussion instruments. The musicians include Anatoli Kuular (top left), Sayan Bapa (top right), Kaigal-ool Khovalyg (bottom left), and Alexei Saryglar (bottom right).

Music" section of a local record shop stocks virtually any music anyone might wish to hear.

Even when we do not actively seek out these new musical experiences, they come to us anyway, clamoring for our acknowledgment and attention. They intrude uninvited into our most private spaces through various media. They enter casually into our perception through recordings played in restaurants and stores, and as background music for television commercials. They catch our eye and ear with the color and vibrancy of their performances as we stroll through local street fairs and arts festivals or watch newly released films. They insistently demand our attention and spare change as we walk down the street on an errand or descend into the subway on our way to work. Performers entice us to participate by attending their concerts and often by lending support to the causes for which they perform.

Two musicians play violin and cello at Pike Place Market, Seattle, Washington.

The burgeoning practice of multiple musics in familiar places is a reality of life in the twenty-first century. Their inescapable presence reminds us that we all make choices in the sights and sounds we surround ourselves with, adopting some and rejecting others. Just as we decorate our living spaces for comfort and enjoyment, choose clothes for the style, color, and image we wish to convey, and prepare food according to habit and taste, so we shape much of our sound environment to please, stimulate, inspire, and console us. We cannot help but choose and incorporate several contrasting musical styles in constructing our own sonic space at home, in social interaction, during worship, and in the course of everyday life.

But much more is at stake than simply enjoying a kaleidoscope of sound. If music is an integral part of so much of life, it has unsuspected power as well. When we encounter the variety of musics that surround us, we are given a chance to move into different worlds of experience, to travel beyond their surface in order to explore the complex of meanings hidden there. This type of inquiry is undertaken by *ethnomusicologists*, scholars who seek to document and interpret music as an integral part of cultural life (see "**Studying Music: A Definition**" and "**Looking Back: Important Moments in Ethnomusicology**"). We can begin our ethnomusicological studies by paying attention to and delving into the moment of a musical performance in whatever form we encounter it. In this way, we can begin to uncover the soundscape of which any single musical event is a small but telling part.

STUDYING MUSIC

A Definition

Ethnomusicology is a field of study that joins the concerns and methods of anthropology with the study of music. This process depends on observation of and participation in musical events.

Working in an academic discipline founded in the late nineteenth century, ethnomusicologists tended through much of the twentieth century to move outside the Western classical traditions and focus on music that was transmitted by oral tradition and associated with nonelites. Today, ethnomusicologists are involved with the widest range of musical phenomena, usually living and working with the people whose music they study. By the last two decades of the twentieth century, many ethnomusicologists had begun carrying out research not just abroad but in their home environments as well, in order to better understand the music around them. The growing number of specialized subfields includes research on virtually any living tradition. Some ethnomusicologists engage in applied work that contributes to the musical activities of libraries, museums, and other local, state, or national arts organizations.

LOOKING BACK

Important Moments in Ethnomusicology

1879	Founding of Bureau of American Ethnology, for studies of Native American Culture
1883–1898	Publication of five-volume collection titled *The English and Scottish Popular Ballads*, by Frances James Child; these collected songs thereafter termed the "Child ballads"
1885	Founding of comparative musicology, the forerunner of ethnomusicology, by Philipp Spitta, Friedrich Chrysander, and Guido Adler in Europe
1885	A. J. Ellis innovates method to compare different scales

1889	Walter Fewkes makes first cylinder recording of Passamaquoddy Indian music
1893	World's Fair Columbian Exposition in Chicago displays living musicians
1900	Founding of Phonogramarchiv (Recorded Sound Archive) in Berlin
1904	Composer Béla Bartók begins research in Eastern European folk music
1907	Frances Densmore studies medicine ceremony at White Earth Chippewa Reservation
1910	John Avery Lomax publishes *Cowboy Songs and Other Frontier Ballads*
1914	New classification system for musical instruments proposed by Erich von Hornbostel and Curt Sachs
1916–1918	Cecil Sharp and Maud Karpeles discover English ballads still being transmitted in the United States
1928	Founding of American Folksong Archive at U.S. Library of Congress
1931–1934	John and Alan Lomax's field trip to southern U.S. includes recording blues singer Leadbelly (Huddie Ledbetter)
1937	Curt Sachs leaves Europe and begins teaching at New York University
1939	Moses Asch founds record company that later becomes Folkways Records
1950	Dutch scholar Jaap Kunst first suggests the word "ethno-musicology"
1951	Development by Charles Seeger of electronic device ("melograph") for automatic transcription of music
1953	Beginning of "Ethnomusicology Newsletter," followed in 1958 by the journal *Ethnomusicology*
1960	Publication of *The Anthropology of Music* by Alan Merriam
1960	Theory of bimusicality proposed by Mantle Hood
1976	Alan Lomax's "cantometrics" first published by University of California Press
1976	Founding of American Folklife Center, Library of Congress, with permanent funding in 1998
1978	World Music Institute, presenters of cross-cultural music events, founded in New York City
1987	Folkways Records becomes Smithsonian Folkways
1998	First volume of *The Garland Encyclopedia of World Music* published

What Is a Soundscape?

The term *soundscape* as used in this book refers to one of the many musical traditions that combine to make up the broader musical landscape of our daily lives. The music of a soundscape is performed in places with which the sound then becomes associated. Each soundscape has its own characteristic sounds and has many meanings for performers and listeners.

A soundscape can have local characteristics as well as global connections because people migrate and resettle; then they remember and re-create these important events through musical performances. This musical activity can be centered in towns and cities or in rural areas.

A soundscape consists not only of a series of musical events but also the time and place within which the events take place and to which they lend both form and significance. Though we may encounter a soundscape at a given time and in a given site, it is rarely static: music and its performance are flexible, changeable, and often on the move.

Locating a Soundscape

We can locate a soundscape most easily through a specific encounter with a musical performance. The music may be part of a larger encompassing scene, such as a parade, festival, or religious ritual. Wherever it occurs, a soundscape signals its presence through a live or even a recorded musical performance.

The choir of Mount Pilgrim Church of Christ, Scranton, North Carolina, sings to the accompaniment of a piano.

A brief encounter with a single musical event rarely yields more than a preliminary entry into the totality of a soundscape. To better understand a soundscape, we need to attend repeated events and to gather a range of additional information about its *setting*, *sound*, and *significance*. It is easiest to start with the setting.

SETTING

Musical sound is not conceived, performed, or taught in a vacuum. The setting of a musical event includes everything from the *venue* (place of performance) to the behavior of those present. Therefore, the setting determines to a great extent what we will hear and see. Any musical event, too, is influenced by others that have come before it, whether the performers are part of a tradition or are trying out a new style for the first time. Many factors can influence a musical performance. The number of musicians may vary, and the absence of an important singer requires musical adjustments that change the nature of the sound. The performance space may be unusually large; performers who are not accustomed to microphones may have to adapt quickly. Performers may make changes on purpose to communicate better with a particular audience, and so on. All such factors force music makers to be creative in adapting their traditions to the situation. Finally, each soundscape has many meanings for both performers and listeners.

A band performs before a large crowd on a summer evening at the Chicago Blues Festival in Grant Park.

To take a familiar example: When we hear a symphony orchestra play in a North American concert hall, we experience the music in its intended setting. However, when we encounter a range of cross-cultural musics in the same concert hall, questions necessarily arise about the relationship of the setting to the music being performed. In many cases—in part because the Euro-American concert hall has become a common venue for many kinds of musical presentation—many musical traditions from elsewhere have become "at home" there, whatever their performance settings were in the past. In other instances, traditional venues and those faced by musicians performing abroad are dramatically different. Usually, musicians must undertake a translation process for their listeners by changing aspects of their traditional performances and by explaining in some way what they have changed.

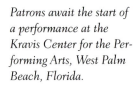

Patrons await the start of a performance at the Kravis Center for the Performing Arts, West Palm Beach, Florida.

When Tuvan singers perform in a concert hall in Seattle, Washington, or Cambridge, Massachusetts, the issues are complex. In the deep historical past, throat singing was a largely outdoor, rural musical practice; really, though, we don't know as much as we would like about the place of throat singing in the full range of Tuvan life and customs. In the last quarter of the twentieth century, increasing urbanization and the opening of conservatories created new opportunities for teaching and transmitting Tuvan music in Inner Asian cities. Throat singing, once a part of everyday life, began to appear in formal concerts. Ethnomusicologists also introduced and cultivated throat-singing techniques around the world through research and recordings. Clearly, the relationship of music to its performance settings is not always simple or straightforward. Both the performers and the listeners must adapt.

Kaigal-ool Khovalyg, a cofounder of Huun-Huur-Tu, sings khoomii and plays the igil, a two-stringed bowed instrument with a carving of a horse's head on top. As a child, Khovalyg worked as a herder before studying traditional and classical Tuvan music and performing with the Tuvan State Ensemble.

Musicians performing abroad accommodate a new performance setting by adjusting the length of the music they perform, altering the construction of their instruments (perhaps by adding amplifiers), and providing oral or written explanations of their actions. These changes are often made whether the performance setting is a formal concert hall, a street fair, or a religious ceremony.

Likewise, most listeners adjust their own perceptions in some way. Outsiders to a tradition might try to frame what they see and hear in terms of what they know and understand. Yet even when we are familiar with a tradition, we still look at it through our own knowledge and past experience. However when we experience unfamiliar music in a familiar place we may sense a marked discrepancy between what we see and what we are accustomed to seeing.

If we are careful in our observation and description—if we employ *critical listening*—we can narrow the distance between a musical event and its unusual performance setting (**see "Studying Music: Participating and Observing"**). And focusing our observations while considering the available information about past

STUDYING MUSIC

Participating and Observing

The process of identifying a musical scene and studying the soundscape of which it is a part is termed *musical ethnography*. We can employ this process in our encounters with music wherever we are. When we attend a concert or witness a musical event, it is important to listen and observe attentively. An unusual musical experience will appear at first fresh and new; on repeated encounters, the event inevitably becomes more familiar and we likely find ourselves being more selective, noticing some things and ignoring others. Being purposefully aware of our changing perceptions through focused observations and through detailed records we keep in a journal forms part of the ethnographic process.

Keeping a journal helps students of culture observe various events and later describe and interpret what they have heard and seen. This process is often called *participant observation*, because as we observe, we also become participants. Participation can be deepened by studying with a musician or by interviewing someone expert in the tradition we are studying. The participant-observer process is also called *fieldwork* and is the primary way that ethnomusicologists study music at home or abroad. Like all research processes that involve human subjects, ethnography carries with it opportunities for special insights and meaningful human relations, but it also entails heavy responsibilities. A concern with the ethics of interpersonal relations and respect for individuals and their traditions is a critical part of this discipline.

During the first decade of the twentieth century, Alice Fletcher (1838–1923) studied and wrote about music of the Omaha and other Native American communities under the sponsorship of the Bureau of American Ethnology at the Smithsonian Institution.

traditions can help us fully appreciate both the current setting of a musical event and what the music represents.

To talk about different music traditions and to compare them with other musics, we use two types of vocabulary: One uses *cross-cultural* terms, basic concepts that can be applied to any music tradition. The other seeks to understand the special terms used by insiders of a particular tradition to discuss and describe their own musical styles and ways of making music.

The sound of church bells ringing is a familiar one in North America that has deep European roots. Here the Luton Parish Bellringers of Luton, Bedfordshire, England, ring bells suspended high above them out of sight.

SOUND

Although soundscapes engage several of the senses, they imprint themselves most definitely on the ear. We can learn how to listen critically if we understand something about how sound is produced. Appreciating music means learning to hear it in a way that is appropriate to its soundscape. Many musical traditions, such as Tuvan throat singing, use voices and musical instruments in distinctive ways.

Music, the purposeful organization of sound, falls in the sensory category of hearing. Sound can be said to have four cross-cultural acoustical characteristics: *quality*, *pitch*, *duration*, and *intensity*.

Quality   Different sources of sound, whether voices or instruments, are identified by their distinctive qualities, which ultimately arise from their acoustical properties. Each pitch produced by a voice or an instrument does not consist of a single sound but of a fundamental tone—the tone our ear perceives as the basic pitch of the sound—and a series of harmonics, also called overtones. A string, for example, vibrates along its entire length when plucked, producing the fundamental pitch. At the same time, the string also vibrates independently at various subdivisions—at half the length of the string, one third the length, one fourth the length, and so on—each at a different, higher pitch and a different volume. The combination of these harmonics with the fundamental creates the characteristic tone colors of different instruments. (By gently placing a finger in the middle of the string, on a guitar for example, we can stop the fundamental from vibrating and hear the first harmonic clearly.) Although in most cases it is difficult to separate the harmonics from the fundamental tones by ear (throat singing being a striking exception), the presence and relative prominence of particular harmonics give an instrument or voice its special tone quality or "color," and makes it possible for us to distinguish between, say, a guitar and a clarinet playing the same note (see **"Sound Sources: Voices and Instruments"**).

LISTENING GUIDE 2

ON WEB SITE

Overtone Demonstration

CREATED BY Joshu Skaller

This example explains and demonstrates the importance of overtones in determining sound quality.

LISTEN FOR the difference between tones in which harmonics are present and tones in which harmonics have been filtered out.

SOUND SOURCES

Voices and Instruments

As we begin to think about the nature of musical sound, it is important to pause and consider its primary sources: the human voice and musical instruments.

Although most vocal sound is produced by the passage of air through the vocal chords, a remarkable number of vastly divergent styles can result. In Chapter 1, we encounter singing styles of Inner Asian and northern Italian origin; in subsequent chapters we will discover many other distinctive styles. There is no such thing as a "natural" singing voice.

Musical instruments exist in myriad shapes and forms. Instruments and the materials of which they are made reflect both the natural resources and the technologies of the peoples who produce them. Musical instruments also have a great deal of social and symbolic meaning within their communities. For example, flutes, trumpets, and other wind instruments are often ascribed a phallic significance and in many cultures are played mainly by men.

The diversity of musical instruments has challenged scholars, who have given a great deal of thought to describing and classifying them. Instruments of the same construction may carry different names, whereas others may have similar names but little else in common. As we explore various soundscapes in this book, we will include "insider" terms for musical instruments and indigenous systems of classification. But we will also utilize the most common system for classifying musical instruments of any culture. The system divides musical instruments into five categories that are based on how the sound is produced. The categories are: idiophones (self-sounding, such as cymbals or woodblocks), chordophones (stringed instruments, whether plucked or bowed), membranophones (drums), aerophones (vibrating air, such as flute), and electrophones (synthesizer). It is named the *Sachs-Hornbostel system* (after its originators, the scholars Curt Sachs and Erich von Hornbostel; see Appendix: Classifying Musical Instruments).

Voices and instruments usually produce quite different sounds: instruments ordinarily cover a greater range of pitch and variety of sounds than voices. However, we can hear similarities in some traditions between vocal and instrumental production. Particularly interesting are those traditions that imitate instrumental sounds through song, as in the "mouth music" with which Scottish and Irish singers duplicate the sound of bagpipes, as we will see in Chapter 2.

The sound of a bugle—or as seen here, a trumpet—playing "Taps," marks the lowering of the U.S. flag at sunset.

Every musical sound is produced by the vibration of some substance: for example, a string (violin, guitar), a column of air (saxophone, organ), a membrane (drum), or a piece of metal (vibraphone, triangle). In the case of the human voice, the vocal cords are set vibrating. The number of vibrations per second—the frequency—determines the pitch of a tone: the slower the vibration, the lower the pitch.

How do fundamentals, harmonics, and frequency apply to throat singing? By manipulating the mouth cavity and the position of the tongue, the singer causes one harmonic to be heard quite distinctly in addition to the fundamental, giving the impression that two separate pitches are being sung at once. The higher of the two pitches heard in the throat-singing example is the harmonic. Translating the example into Western notation displays both the fundamental and the precise harmonics sounded in this recording.

This example (termed a transcription) represents in Western staff notation the fundamental pitch and harmonics heard in Listening Guide 1.

Even if you can't read the notation, you can follow the number of the harmonic above the individual noteheads. There are also other musical traditions whose vocal styles or musical instruments render harmonics audible. Common examples are the Jews' (or jaws') harp, heard in North America, and the musical bow, in southern Africa.

Although we may hear throat singing as audible harmonics, the singers do not think of it that way. Moreover, there are several types of throat singing, which are collectively referred to as *khoomii*, from the Mongolian word for "throat." Other styles are called by different names in different regions and have different sound characteristics. Also, some accomplished singers develop their own personal styles, which may vary sometimes according to the pitch of the fundamental, in the loudness or softness of the sound, the position of the mouth, and the emphasis on specific harmonics.

Some of the most important *khoomii* styles are named within the Tuvan tradition, including *sygyt*, which is sung in high *register*—that is, using high pitches—

with clear harmonics that sound like whistling. *Sygyt* and related styles are most commonly referred to by outsiders as *khoomii*. *Kargyraa*, the example we heard, and other related styles are sung in a very low register and often have a text. A third type is *ezengileer* (from the Tuvan word for "stirrup"), said to reflect its roots in being sung on horseback. Other styles include those considered to reflect the contours of the Tuvan landscape, termed "steppe" and "mountain"; "nose" and "chest" *khoomii*; and those related to particular moods.

Pitch   As we have just learned, the fundamental of the harmonic series is perceived by most listeners as a pitch. When the frequency of the fundamental is doubled, the ear perceives the same pitch but at a higher level, called an *octave*. And when the frequency is halved, the pitch drops an octave. Put differently, when a low voice and a high voice sing the same tune, they are singing the same pitches but they are singing them an octave or two apart. This set of equivalent pitches at regular distances, the octave, is recognized in most musical traditions, although it is called by different names.

Certain musical traditions use fixed tunings, such as the Western classical tradition in which orchestras and ensembles tune their instruments in accordance with the international standard of 440 vibrations per second. Most other musics of the world use what is called *relative tuning*. In these cases, music is sung and/or played at a pitch level comfortable for the singer or instrumentalist, just as we might begin singing a tune on any pitch that is convenient. However, all musical traditions, whether they use fixed or relative tunings, select particular sets of pitches for regular use. Here what is important is not an absolute, standard pitch level but the distances between pitches, which are called *intervals*. The size and arrangement of these intervals vary among music systems. Listeners familiar with one system, such as that shared by much of Western classical and popular music, for example, often notice when a different set of intervals is heard, perceiving say, the music of India, as "out of tune." In the *khoomii* examples above, the pitches of the musical system are selected from those of the harmonic series.

Some musical systems have their own special terms for describing and prescribing the set of pitches they use, and by extension, the distance of the interval between any two adjacent pitches. However, in other musical traditions the individual pitches are not separated out or named; we will encounter one such example in our study of Ethiopian chant in Chapter 5. Other traditions have no special vocabulary for describing pitch, or the musical system has not been sufficiently studied to provide this information.

This notation shows a fundamental pitch along with its harmonics. The note heads in red are the harmonics actually performed by the singers, producing a five-note (pentatonic) scale.

PATRICIA C. WYNNE (drawing); LISA BURNETT (chart)

<u>Duration</u>   Just as music organizes pitch, it also organizes time. Within a musical performance, the duration of sounds can be regular, or repetitive, and it can also be episodic, irregular, or free. The *khoomii* example in Listening Guide 1 uses a regular division of time. As noted above, certain types of *khoomii* reflect rhythms drawn from the immediate environment, including galloping.

Durational elements often fall under the term *rhythm* in musical discussion, and the presence of a single, regular element may be referred to by the biological term *pulse*. Many musical traditions have special vocabularies that describe and prescribe the manner in which time is conceived and performed. Much of Western classical music is thought of and heard as having an ongoing, underlying pulse—usually with repeated and regular groupings of twos, threes, or fours—that is termed *meter*. Within the Western context, the rate of speed is called *tempo* and is specified by a variety of Italian terms. Music intended for dancing usually has rhythmic patterns that correspond to body movements, as we will see in a study of the tango in Chapter 6. Other musical traditions are based on rhythmic cycles that may be asymmetrical and are subdivided in complex and constantly changing ways; prominent examples are the rhythmic systems in South and Southeast Asian musics, as well as music originating in much of the Middle East.

<u>Intensity</u>   Although the loudness or softness of music can be measured, the human ear does not quantify intensity in the same way. However, the ear is quick to sense changes in intensity, or volume, and to perceive relative levels of loud and soft sounds.

The volume levels, or *dynamics*, in a given musical event are often determined by the construction of instruments or the techniques used by voices. Certain musical instruments, such as many types of bagpipes, were originally intended for outdoor performance. Their high level of intensity insures that they will be heard over considerable distances. Some vocal styles, such as Swiss yodeling, are also outdoor styles, as throat singing likely was in the lives of nomadic peoples. When a large number of instrumentalists or singers are performing, more contrasts in volume are possible. The use of amplification greatly complicates any generalizations we might make about intensity, given that the dynamic level of any singer, player, or musical event can be raised instantaneously.

Throughout *Soundscapes* we will draw on these cross-cultural characteristics of quality, pitch, duration, and intensity to anchor and lend detail to our discussions of sound elements. At the same time, we will take into consideration which aspects of musical sound are considered important within a given tradition and what other special concepts might be present. We will pay special attention to insider

Instruments with a penetrating quality and loud volume, such as Swiss alphorns, are often intended for outdoor use. Here a family in traditional Swiss dress poses on a hillside in Murren, Berner Oberland, Switzerland, with their alphorns.

Insider and Outsider Perspectives

When studying music, or other aspects of expressive culture, we can borrow a distinction from linguistics, between phonemic sounds, those that are meaningful within the particular language studied, and phonetic sounds, which are used by the outsider to categorize sounds without regard to their meaning. The phonemic and phonetic aspects of language have been extended to musical and other aspects of culture. In studying these, the corresponding terms *emic* and *etic* are used to stand for insider and outsider perspectives, respectively.

We must, however, keep in mind that there is no single insider perspective and that many seemingly cross-cultural approaches have, in fact, been shaped by Western cultural sensibilities. Yet those who study musics of cultures other than their own usually remain committed to uncovering insider, or emic, perspectives by trying to understand each musical tradition they study from an indigenous point of view. At the same time, ethnomusicologists compare different musical traditions in order to learn from their remarkable variety.

Outsiders can become accomplished performers in a once-unfamiliar musical style. The award-winning documentary Genghis Blues *traces the experience of Paul Pena, a blind American blues singer of Cape Verdean extraction, who taught himself throat singing and then traveled to Tuva.*

words, or craft terms, that are used to explain and understand a musical style (**see "Studying Music: Insider and Outsider Perspectives"**).

SIGNIFICANCE

Music means different things to performers and listeners of different backgrounds and experiences. Sometimes musicians can convey musical meanings clearly, expressing through commentary or action during a performance, the significance of music in their lives. In other cases, music carries meanings that are hidden, or at least hard to describe. Music can even convey information that cannot be transmitted otherwise in the face of political pressure or active repression, as we will see in Chapter 9.

The Huun-Huur-Tu musician Kaigal-ool Khova-lyg is shown singing and playing outdoors at home in Tuva, while a man sitting nearby taps his stomach to the rhythm of the music. The Tuvan grasslands, visible in the background, provided the inspiration for the name Huun-Huur-Tu. Translated as "sun propeller," the name refers to the refraction of the sun's rays that occurs at dawn and dusk on the Tuvan landscape, a phenomenon that is said to be similar to the separating or refracting of sound achieved in throat singing.

The *khoomii* style we have explored throughout this introductory discussion is an example of a soundscape with multiple meanings for performers and listeners alike. For Tuvan musicians, *khoomii* may embody and convey their deeply felt attachment to the terrain of Inner Asia. By imitating or depicting the sounds of nature, the performers link themselves to the environment of Inner Asia and to the elements of wind, water, and light, transforming natural sounds into musical representations. Besides sounds from the natural world, such as running water, Tuvans seem to map the physical landscape as well, describing it in their song texts as well as through certain vocal articulations, such as the *khoomii* styles described above. Tuvan music, unlike much of Western instrumental music, is not considered by its musicians to be abstract, but is "radically representational."[1]

Outsiders who first encounter *khoomii* music in concert may be overwhelmed by the sheer strangeness of the harmonics made audible before having a chance to comprehend the sound's significance. Repeated exposures and consideration of Tuvan points of view, however, can help outsiders become more sensitive to insider meanings.

The Ever-Changing Nature of Soundscapes

Knowing how a music tradition brought to North America has changed and the ongoing connections the music has with other places (including its original homeland) can deepen and broaden our understanding of a soundscape. The musical world of the twenty-first century has many layers and many voices. Different peo-

Visiting students from Moscow play music in front of a church on a crowded New York City street.

ple and places may reshape it further. In some cases, a music moves from one place to another because of economic, political, or other such forces. In other instances, an entire community in motion may transplant and, eventually, transform their music.

Many soundscapes have resulted from such human migrations. Although most of this book will be devoted to exploring what has happened to music transplanted into North America, you should keep in mind that migration also affects the music of the people left behind. Migrants out of a community are often young and vital members whose departure can disrupt transmission of long-standing musical practices. The anxiety and pain of separation also leave their mark on existing musical repertories.

CASE STUDY: VOCI D'ALPE

The impact of emigration can still be heard in Liguria, a region along the northwestern Italian coast. There, songs continue to be sung about migrations to America that occurred around the turn of the twentieth century. The song *Vuoi tu venire in Merica* tells of a young couple from Trentino who travel to the port of Genoa, where the husband embarks for America.

The song was recorded by the Santa Margherita Ligure Voci D'Alpe, an all-male amateur choir active in Liguria today (**see "Snapshot: Hearing Voci D'Alpe in**

SNAPSHOT

Hearing Voci D'Alpe in Concert

The church of St. Anthony is a small one, perched up the hill from the main church in the little Italian town of Piave Alta, which lies less than an hour south of Genoa, overlooking the Ligurian Sea. Built privately, the church is open for mass only once every four weeks, as well as on St. Anthony's feast day and for special events such as a pre-Christmas concert in mid-December. At one such concert, in 1997, the audience nearly fills the center pews in the church as well as the double row of benches along either side.

Other than a large crucifix mounted on the front left wall alongside the altar, all the other processional crosses, some six or seven, are covered with blue and green cloths that are securely tied down. (I am told that the covers protect the crosses from any bawdy lyrics.) A number of chandeliers hang over the altar, and at the front of the church, three small ship models are suspended from the ceiling. Behind the altar stands a statue of St. Anthony, with a cherub on one side and a pig on the other. A painting of St. Anthony, a pig standing behind him with its snout poking out beside the saint's leg, also adorns the ceiling above the nave. The elaborate wall paintings, or frescoes, are all painted in *trompe l'oeil*, that is, to "fool the eye" into thinking it is seeing three-dimensional forms.

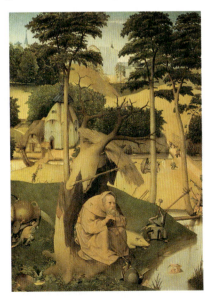

The audience becomes quiet as the choir marches in—twenty men with their conductor. The men all wear identical green-checked shirts and dark corduroy pants, and they range in age from thirty to sixty. The choir is divided into four parts: first and second tenors, baritones, and basses. (A choir of thirty-two is heard on our recording.)

One singer serves as spokesman. In his introduction to the program, he notes that making a good song is like cooking and then summarizes what each song is about. The choir sings unaccompanied while arranged in a semicircle, with the conductor in the center, his back to the audience. He gives the singers the opening pitch with a pitch pipe, and they sing a major chord to tune up.

Saint Anthony's humble life, commemorated in many churches, is also portrayed in paintings, such as this one by Hieronymus Bosch.

The repertory is a mix of traditional Italian songs and newly composed pieces. The first half of the program includes a group of songs about World War II, including one about the Russian front in 1942–1943. Other songs are about mountaineers, one from the perspective of a mother whose son joins the army. The members of the choir are deeply engaged, as is the audience; indeed, several male spectators sing along on some of the songs.

Intermission, during which everyone is offered spiced wine and cake, affords a chance to discuss the program with the conductor, Paolo Secci, who speaks some English. He tells me that the choir, was founded in 1968. He has been its conductor for ten years and learned some of the songs in the army, where he also conducted a choir. Neither he nor any members of the choir are professional musicians, and they use no notated music. Most work in a variety of professions—Secci himself works for the automobile company Fiat.

The second half of the concert features songs of love and some Christmas music, including a song of praise for St. Anthony. As an encore, the choir sings *Go Tell It on the Mountain*—in English!

After the concert, the audience may purchase copies of the choir's CD, which their proud spokesman announces has sold five thousand copies. (I first heard *Vuoi Tu Venire in Merica*, which almost everyone in Liguria knows well, on Voci D'Alpe's CD.)

Concert"). The piece is a good example of a *strophic* folk song, a musical form in which each verse is sung to the same music. Songs in this form are relatively easier to remember, an aspect of music we will consider at length in Chapter 7.

Although *Vuoi tu venire in Merica* has lived on in Italy, other Italian songs moved with Italian immigrants to the New World and crossed boundaries into other soundscapes, as we will see in Chapter 7. This song, with its invitation to come to America, could well be an anthem for *Soundscapes:* through an exploration of many musics at home in North America, we can arrive at a deeper understanding of that new world as perceived through musical discourse within and between different musical traditions.

The emergence of a broader American musical landscape is our subject in the following chapters. We will trace the paths of creative individuals and communi-

LISTENING GUIDE 3

Vuoi tu venire in Merica ("Do You Want to Come to America"; Ligurian folk song)

PERFORMED BY Voci D'Alpe

LISTEN FOR the way in which the voices sing together on different pitches. The manner in which simultaneous musical sounds relate to each other is termed *texture*. Here, several pitches are sung at the same time (called harmony), but unlike in the *khoomii* example, each singer contributes only one pitch at any one time. Note that all the singers—several on each pitch—sing in the same rhythm, enabling us to hear the words clearly. This type of texture—singing in harmony in the same rhythm—is called *homophony*.

Vuoi tu venir, Giulietta?	Do you want to come, Giulietta,
Vuoi tu venire con me?	Do you want to come with me?
Vuoi tu venire in Merica?	Do you want to come to America?
Vuoi tu venire in Merica?	Do you want to come to America?
Vuoi tu venir, Giulietta?	Do you want to come, Giulietta,
Vuoi tu venire con me?	Do you want to come with me?
Vuoi tu venire in Merica	Do you want to come to America
a travagliare con me?	And work with me?
Mi sì che vegnirìa	I would certainly come
se fus da chi a Milan,	If it were just to Milan,
ma per andare in Merica,	But all the way to America,
ma per andare in Merica . . .	But all the way to America . . .
Mi sì che vegnirìa	I would certainly come
se fus da chi a Milan,	If it were just to Milan,
ma per andare in Merica,	But all the way to America,
l'è masse mia luntan?	Is it not a little bit too far?
L'ho compagna' a Genova.	I went with him to Genoa.
M'ha di' de stalo a speta'.	He told me to wait for him.
L'era sul bastimento,	He was on the ship,
l'era sul bastimento.	He was on the ship.
L'ho compagna' a Genova.	I went with him to Genoa
M'ha di' de stalo a speta'.	He told me to wait for him.
L'era sul bastimento	He was on the ship
col fazzoletto bagna'.	With his handkerchief wet.

—Translated by Andrea Malaguti

ties who have played—and continue to play—important roles in establishing diverse soundscapes.

We will begin by exploring in Chapter 2 the soundscapes that we encounter in the course of everyday life.

IMPORTANT TERMS

acoustics
critical listening
cross-cultural
duration
dynamics
ethnomusicology
fundamental
homophony
intensity
interval
meter
musical
   ethnography

octave
overtones/
   harmonics
pentatonic scale
pitch
pulse
quality
register
relative tuning
Sachs-Hornbostel
   system
scale
setting

significance
sound
strophic form
tempo
texture
throat singing/
   khoomii
transcription

CHAPTER

TWO TWO TWO TWO TWO TWO TWO TWO TWO TWO TWO TWO TWO TWO TWO TWO

A woman listens to a portable CD player as she skates down a path on the Esplanade, a riverbank park along the Charles River in Boston.

OVERVIEW

Robert J. Hogan

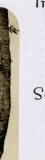

MAIN POINTS

This unit explores music:

- as it is lived and performed in settings common to everyday life

- as it takes on new meanings in each new setting

The Music of Everyday Life

Introduction

Think about the role of music in your own daily life. You may awaken to the sound of the radio tuned to your favorite station, listen to a familiar cassette on a Walkman as you go for a morning run, and then hum or sing as you take a shower. During the day you could attend a noontime concert offered somewhere near your home or campus, or hear music during a service sponsored by a local place of worship. In the evening, you might go out to a club or concert hall, perhaps buying a ticket to hear a favorite singer. If the day is a holiday or a special civic occasion, you might choose to watch a parade celebrating the event, complete with marching bands. All of these examples represent music that you might bring into your own life through your own active choice—whether by selecting a radio station, playing a recording, or attending a concert or parade.

Some musical experiences, in contrast, are not meant to be in the foreground of our perception or to capture our active interest. A notable and common example of music that is intended primarily as background is Muzak—customized, recorded music that since 1934 has established "audio architecture" in various public spaces. Muzak is designed to remain below the threshold of focused attention—that is, it should be heard passively, not listened to actively—drawing on

A saxophonist earns his living by playing in New York City's Columbus Circle subway station.

simple arrangements of music familiar to most Western listeners.[1] Muzak can be said to have formed, over time, a super-soundscape. Through its targeted use of familiar repertories from rock to jazz to classical symphonies, Muzak often seeks to convey customized meanings, such as enhancing a patron's experience while shopping. Listeners themselves can impose meanings on the music, which in turn familiarize a public space.

Other musics enter into our consciousness through accidental encounters in everyday life; these capture our attention to the extent that they become a subject of ongoing listening interest, bringing new soundscapes into our active range of experiences. For instance, one writer describes in vivid detail her first encounter with Andean musicians playing in a subway station beneath Queens in New York City and her feeling of being "transported" by their music. Her experience in "one of the dingiest urban spaces" with the unfamiliar sounds of the Andean flute not only led her to explore this music and its meaning, but inspired her to look more closely at subway musicians in general and to write an entire book on music in the subways of New York.[2]

In this unit we will focus on music that we choose to listen to as an active part of everyday life. We will spend most of our time on soundscapes that grow out of local and personal experiences and are sometimes termed "vernacular musics" (see **"Studying Music: Thinking about 'Western' Music"**).

Most definitions of vernacular culture link its origins to the commonplace aspects of life in contrast to the elite culture of major institutions or mass-produced phenomena, but there is some debate on this topic. Rather than establishing categories that are increasingly difficult to defend, we will look at the processes of

The dance troupe Stomp, seen here performing at the sixty-eighth annual Academy Awards ceremony in Los Angeles on March 26, 1996, is a striking example of how seemingly nonmusical everyday objects can be adapted for musical performance.

Thinking About "Western" Music

Any discussion of different soundscapes must take into account the varying impact of Euro-American musical sounds, repertory, ensembles, and concepts—often lumped together under the general cover term "Western music"—on many aspects of musical life in North America. In terms of their geographical location, all of the musics we are studying in *Soundscapes* have by the twenty-first century themselves become "Western." However, "Western" is most commonly used to describe European and American "art" music of the eighteenth to twentieth centuries. Also, "Western music" actually consists of many different styles of musical expression from many parts of Europe, rather than a single musical style.

Western musics of the eighteenth and nineteenth centuries can be said to share a musical vocabulary termed *tonal music*, in which a single pitch or tone serves as the point of departure and return in any given piece of music. The Western tonal system divides the octave (see Chapter 1) into twelve pitches, each of which can serve as the first and last pitch—the center of gravity—for groupings of pitches into *major* and *minor scales*.

Western music shares with the other musics the aspects of duration and quality. It has a durational framework with a regular, underlying pulse subdivided into groupings of equal length, a rhythmic system known as *meter*. In terms of quality, the stringed instruments of the orchestra—the signature ensemble of Western music—use an intentional and regular fluctuation of pitch called *vibrato* in their playing (see Chapter 8). Similarly, the use of vibrato extends throughout Western vocal music, becoming an important characteristic of Western vocal quality. Finally, many of the important philosophical concepts surrounding Western music today had their roots in the late eighteenth and nineteenth centuries, including a perspective that credited musical creativity to individual genius and the notion that music is beautiful and has the power to edify and inspire.

Initially, Western music traveled to different locales along with European missionaries and

The pitches of the Western musical system can most easily be understood by looking at a piano keyboard, where each octave is divided into twelve pitches an equal distance apart. Each pitch is sounded by pressing a white or black key. The seven white keys have letter names and are arranged in the order C–D–E–F–G–A–B. A black key can be called by the letter name of either adjacent white key, along with the sign of a sharp (#) or a flat (b): the black key between C and D can be named C-sharp or D-flat, depending on the musical context. Each of the twelve keys in the octave has its own subset of seven pitches that is a scale. These scales are the basis for the major/minor musical language of Western music.

colonists. In North America, this imported musical tradition quickly established deep roots, supported by an elite that until the late nineteenth century was led mainly by people of European descent. The international domination by the United States in twentieth-century economic and political life, along with the growth and international spread of the North American recording industry, also served to disperse "Western" musical sounds worldwide.

Initially, Western music traveled to different locales along with European missionaries and colonists. In North America, this imported musical tradition quickly established deep roots, supported by an elite that was dominated until the late nineteenth century by people of European descent. The international domination of the United States in twentieth-century economic and political life, along with the growth and international spread of the North American recording industry, also served to disperse "Western" musical sounds worldwide.

While European repertories such as the symphony and opera were transplanted and taken in innovative directions in the New World, other new American musical idioms also interacted with elements of the Western musical system. The extraordinary panoply of African American musics that emerged in the late nineteenth and early twentieth centuries—including ragtime, blues, and jazz—drew selectively on some aspects of the Western musical system, transforming them to create new genres.

Throughout North America in the twentieth century, exposure to the Western musical system in primary and secondary schools was widespread. Shared musical experiences in school and the pervasive presence of radio account for the reason most North Americans—as well as many others around the globe—have at least a passing familiarity with Western tonal music.

everyday life and the manner in which they are carried out and given meaning through music making.

CASE STUDY: THE LULLABY

Music is embedded in our memories from the earliest moments of childhood and is strongly connected to many moments—insignificant and important—in the life cycle. Hearing a lullaby sung by a parent or caretaker each evening before sleep is one of the first musical experiences for most of us. The lullaby's melody—a sequence of pitches that gives a sense of having a beginning, middle, and end—leaves an indelible mark. Beyond the almost universal use of song as a gateway to sleep, lullabies appear to share some common features. A recent study of maternal singing in several cultures suggests that the higher pitch, simple repeating patterns, and slower pace commonly used in speech to babies (so-called baby talk) also characterize lullabies.[3]

Yet, although lullabies share aspects of *quality*, *repetitive patterns*, and slow *pace*, each reflects traditions transmitted through individual families. These traditions are in turn shaped by broader patterns of a particular soundscape. Lullabies are almost always set in languages spoken in everyday life; many also include nonsense syllables, called *vocables*.

<u>Bengali Lullaby</u>   This Bengali lullaby originated in the region that today is divided between Bangladesh and northeastern India.

The moderate pace, low volume, and extensive repetition within both the instrumental and vocal parts are typical of the lullaby genre and calming in their effect (**see "Studying Music: The Effect of Music"**).

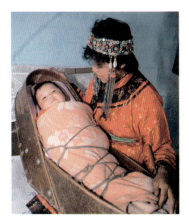

Lullabies are sung in most societies. Here a woman in Shibazhan, China, sings to her son, who is secured in a traditional wooden cradle.

STUDYING MUSIC

The Effect of Music

The lullaby is just one example of music performed purposefully to effect a change of mood or consciousness, in this case to calm a child and induce sleep. Many studies of music have noted its apparent ability to alter mental states or induce trance. Some researchers have hypothesized that the repetitive nature of musical sound, particularly when performed by drums or other percussive instruments, causes brain waves to trigger the altered state. One theory holds that intermittent sounds at certain frequencies are capable of changing brain-wave patterns.[4] Others strongly suggest that trance is a culturally conditioned response based on long-time association between a particular musical event and the expectation that it will produce a particular state of mind.[5]

Thus, although music is acknowledged universally for its power to influence emotions and its healing properties, scholars have not fully explained how music is perceived and processed within the brain. New technologies and recent advances in psychological research should provide new perspectives on the interaction between the cultural and physiological dimensions of music.

LISTENING GUIDE 4

COME, O SLEEP (Bengali Lullaby)

PERFORMERS not identified.

LISTEN TO the interaction of the instruments, which are divided into two groups. The first, which includes a flute and a bowed lute, doubles and then echoes the vocal melody; the second group—a drum, a plucked lute, and piano—sets up a repeated pattern known in cross-cultural terminology as an *ostinato*. The ostinato pattern consists of a four-beat drum rhythm, a descending melody in the piano and plucked lute, and two strokes on the small brass bells. The ostinato, with its shifting emphasis between the drum beat and the descending melody, seems to mimic the rocking motion of a mother's arms or a baby's cradle.

Aae Ghoom, aae Ghoom!	Come, O Sleep . . . O tender Sleep!
Ghoomer Mago ektukhani ghoom dye jao.	Mother of Sleep, come and lull my child.
Ghoomer deshe aache je she Golpo Dadur bari,	In your country, O Sleep, there lives in a house Grandfather, the teller of tales.
Rajar chele rajar konnar shethae tchora tchori;	In that land there are many many princes and princesses,
Koto ghora koto hati koto rajar kotha	And many many horses and elephants, kings and their palaces,
Koto bidesh koto desher golpo aache shetha.	And stories of many many lands.
Aae Ghoom, aae Ghoom!	Come, O Sleep. . . O tender Sleep.
Ghoomer Mago esho aajke moder bari jaio,	O Mother of Sleep, come today, and pay a visit to our house,
Shanjer belae khokonke more shethae nye jaio.	And take my child this evening to the house of Grandfather, the teller of tales.
Khokoner joto khelar shathi tarao jabe shathe;	Along with my child will also go all his little playmates,
Aaere Pootool, aaere Tchobi, aaere shobai joote.	Come on Pootool, come on Chobi, come along all of you.
Aae Ghoom, aae Ghoom!	Come, O Sleep . . . O tender Sleep.
Ghoomer Mago ghoom dite khajna nebe koto?	O Mother of Sleep, what would you like as a reward?
Sonar moto ranga saree debo aache joto,	I shall give you all colourful sarees that shimmer with red and gold.
Chal debo, dal debo, aaro debo haari,	I shall give you rice and grains and even earthenware to cook in.
Noder kole rekhe kheyo, theko moder baari.	You are welcome to come and eat in our house on the bank of the beautiful river.
Aae Ghoom, aae Ghoom!	Come, O Sleep . . . O tender sleep.

The recurring line (termed a *refrain*) "Come, O Sleep" begins and ends the song, and marks the divisions between the verses.

<u>All the Pretty Little Horses</u>   Lullabies are often maintained over the course of generations and contain images with culturally specific significance, especially since they tend to be transmitted orally within particular ethnic or linguistic communities.

Many lullabies that originate within one ethnic environment may, over the years, travel beyond the boundaries of community and locale. One lullaby that began among African Americans in the southern United States is today sung by Americans of many backgrounds. Known by several different titles, including *Go ter Sleep*, *Hush-a-bye*, and, perhaps most commonly, *All the Pretty Little Horses*, this lullaby has been transmitted from generation to generation through the *oral tradition*. As a result, it exists today in a number of different versions. Like those of many other lullabies, the soothing melody of *All the Pretty Little Horses* belies the deeply disturbing text. The second verse refers to the tragic situation of the black women who first sang this song as slaves, forced to neglect their own babies while caring for their masters' children.

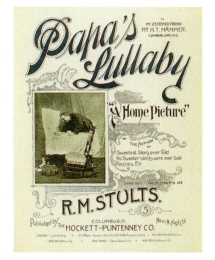

Although many lullabies have their beginnings in the oral tradition transmitted within families and ethnic communities, others, such as "Papa's Lullaby" from 1897, have been created by individual composers and published as sheet music.

During the twentieth century *All the Pretty Little Horses* has been transcribed and published by folklorists and ethnomusicologists. One such arrangement, published by the ethnomusicologists John and Alan Lomax in 1934, draws on multiple recordings they made during their fieldwork. The Lomaxes' version of *All the Pretty Little Horses* has been a popular source for later performances by folk singers and also served as the basis for a concert version with orchestra accompaniment by the American composer Aaron Copland. However, Copland and many others who recomposed or performed this song have sometimes chosen to omit the deeply unsettling second verse.

Lullabies also can be newly composed by an especially creative singer or adapted from songs popular in a particular time and place. Some lullabies serve other functions, such as holiday or religious songs.

<u>Comanche Lullaby</u>   Throughout *Soundscapes*, we will confront the problem of how to classify music that can be and is used for different occasions. One way to resolve this issue is to use terms and categories that grow out of human experience, highlighting the manner in which the same music can carry different meanings, depending on its setting and the listener's interpretation. Musical form

LISTENING GUIDE 5

CD 1
TRACK
4

All the Pretty Little Horses (African American lullaby)

PERFORMED BY Odetta

LISTEN FOR the repetitions of the melody (marked "A" in the text below). A contrasting melody ("B"), is heard only at the text "Blacks and bays." The song is sung softly at a relatively slow rate of speed, with the regular rhythm serving to lull the baby.

A: Hush-a-bye
       Don't you cry,
       Go to sleepy, little baby.

A: When you wake,
       You shall have
       All the pretty little horses.

B: Blacks and bays,
       Dapples and grays,
       All the pretty little horses.

A: Way down yonder,
       In the meadow,
       Lies my poor little babe.

A: Bees and butterflies,
       A peckin' out its eyes,
       Poor little thing is crying "Mammy!"

B: Blacks and bays,
       Dapples and grays,
       All the pretty little horses.

A: Mmm . . .
       Mmm . . .
       Go to sleepy, little baby.

A: When you wake,
       You shall have,
       All the pretty little horses.

alone does not define a musical category, or *genre*. Rather, music is adaptable and assumes different significances when it is performed on different occasions.[6]

Here is one such example: this Comanche lullaby recorded in 1988 is actually a hymn whose text is based on Psalm 71. Originally part of the Eastern Shoshone nation, the Comanche separated from the Shoshone when they were forced to migrate south in the early eighteenth century. Introduced to Christianity by missionaries, Native Americans blended Christian traditions with indigenous beliefs and translated psalms—such as the one in our recording—into their own languages.

According to the collector of this song, the singer—mother of twenty-two children—perpetuates a rich repertory of Comanche lullabies and prayer songs. This

LISTENING GUIDE 6

CD 1
TRACK
5

Comanche lullaby

PERFORMED BY Myra Burgess of Anadarko, Oklahoma

LISTEN TO the way in which the melody follows the parallel poetic structure of each psalm verse. On a larger scale, the melody of verses 1 and 2 contrasts with that for verses 3 and 4. Although only the first four psalm verses (two pairs) are heard here, the complete twenty-four verses of the psalm—sung softly without any instrumental accompaniment—offer, through simple repetition, a very effective lullaby.

1. In thee, O Lord, do I put my trust: let me never be put to confusion.
2. Deliver me in thy righteousness, and cause me to escape: incline thine ear unto me, and save me.
3. Be thou my strong habitation, whereunto I may continually resort: thou hast given commandment to save me; for thou [art] my rock and my fortress.
4. Deliver me, O my God, out of the hand of the wicked, out of the hand of the unrighteous and cruel man.

song therefore leads an interesting double life: as a psalm with religious content, it also implicitly conveys this religious significance when sung to lull a child to sleep.

Think of the lullabies you know and see if you can identify the different soundscapes they represent. Are the melodies repetitive in their structure, with one verse similar to the next? Are these songs sung at a muted dynamic level so as to provide the constant sonic environment appropriate to lulling a baby to sleep?

Compare the lullabies you know with those familiar to classmates and see if you share any songs. What other songs, such as Christmas carols or folk songs, do you know that are also used as lullabies?

Songs of the Life Cycle

The entire life cycle is marked by musical occasions. Childhood years are enriched by music and singing, with songs and dances providing both fun and a pathway to social and cultural knowledge. Birthdays are celebrated in many cultures, with rousing renditions of the song "Happy Birthday to You" being associated with that occasion in North America since at least the 1920s. (The song, you may be surprised to know, is still under copyright.) Other special moments, ranging from religious milestones to school graduations, are marked by celebrations filled with music.

The passage through puberty into adulthood is one of the critical transitions celebrated by rituals in virtually every society. All life-cycle moments entail a change of status of some sort, but the rites surrounding the physical and social transformations that mark stages of development in the teenage years are particularly significant because they celebrate the future potential—social, cultural, physical—of a community. These events tend to include performance of music and dance, which provide important opportunities for education and celebration.

CASE STUDY: THE QUINCEAÑERA

A notable example of a life-cycle celebration with strong musical content is the *quinceañera* (pronounced "keen-see-a-nye-ra"), a tradition celebrated in Latino communities in North America and abroad that marks the passage of teenage girls into adulthood. Usually held within a few days of the girl's fifteenth birthday, the *quinceañera* celebrates a chronological passage while acknowledging a particular cultural or ethnic identity and religious affiliation.

The central event marking the *quinceañera* is a party or ball given by the family of the young woman. Although the event is not a religious occasion, the ball is often held in a church, and most Latina celebrants have either prepared for or recently received the Roman Catholic sacrament of Confirmation, marking them as adults in the eyes of the Church. Some young women complete short preparatory courses before the *quinceañera*.

Traditionally, a group of friends act as attendants, escorting the young woman into church to receive Communion and then dancing with and around her at the subsequent festive celebration. Color symbolism, while often important, varies according to family, local, and ethnic traditions: for example, the celebrant might

The quinceañera *is said to date back to indigenous Mexican life-cycle traditions in which boys were honored as warriors and girls as future mothers. Later merged with influences from the Catholic church, the* quinceañera *is today celebrated in Latino communities across the United States. Several important stages of a 1994* quinceañera *celebrated by two friends are shown here. After participating in a Mass at their local church, they don traditional crowns (diadems) for a short ceremony marking their coming of age. Afterward, they celebrate with family and friends at a festive party (fiesta) with food, music, and dancing.*

wear a white gown and a crown of white flowers on her head, while her attendants wear red dresses and the young men black tuxedos.

In addition to marking a young girl's coming of age, the *quinceañera* has strong social and economic significance, mirroring the debutante balls in certain circles of Anglo-American society. But besides displaying social status and presenting a daughter approaching marriageable age, the *quinceañera* holds great significance for celebrating and reasserting a strong ethnic identity.

In the musical content of the celebration, ethnic identity comes into its fullest display, the music depending on whether the family is of Mexican, Puerto Rican, Dominican, or other Hispanic background. Although recorded music is often used for dancing at *quinceañeras* on more modest budgets, live *mariachi* bands are hired by members of the Mexican-American community whenever possible. The dances proceed in a set order, with a waltz usually played first, when the girl and her father take the floor.

The bands typically heard at *quinceañeras* are urban mariachi ensembles common throughout Mexico and the southwestern United States. A mid-twentieth-century descendant of nineteenth-century rural Mexican groups, the mariachi ensemble is increasingly widespread throughout North America, where bands can be heard at local Mexican restaurants, community events, and increasingly, on college campuses (**see "Sound Sources: The Mariachi"**). A mariachi band can include as few as three players to more than a dozen musicians playing various Mexican guitars, violins, trumpets, and a harp.

SOUND SOURCES

The Mariachi

Mariachi is the name for a Mexican (and Mexican-American) instrumental ensemble combining plucked and bowed instruments of various types with trumpets. The ensemble originated in the mid-nineteenth century in the areas around Guadalajara. After the Mexican Revolution (1910–1917), mariachi musicians arrived in Mexico City as part of a massive migration from rural villages. As a result, mariachi music became urbanized, taking on characteristics of the commercialized country music then popular in the radio and film industry. In present-day usage, *mariachi* can mean a single musician, a type of musical ensemble, or a style of music.[7]

The mariachi ensemble commonly seen today became standardized in the early 1950s. The Mexican *guitarrón* (a large, plucked four-or five-string bass guitar with a large belly) and the *vihuela* (a small, strummed folk guitar), alone or with a harp, are the rhythm instruments in the ensemble. Two trumpets and three or more violins usually supply the melody. Although most mariachi groups comprise from seven to eleven players, smaller or larger ensembles are also common, depending on the needs and financial resources of their patrons.

A mariachi band performs outdoors on a footbridge in San Antonio, Texas.

At the core of the mariachi repertory are traditional dances with lively rhythms, mostly in triple meters (consisting of groupings of three pulses, or beats). Today, many types of music are played by mariachi, from folk songs to novelty pieces to bilingual adaptations of pop tunes. Mariachi musicians may be hired to accompany a variety of life-cycle events, such as birthdays, intimate dinners, and religious services, including funerals; this chapter shows their use in the *quinceañera*.

When performing, mariachi musicians most often dress like *charros*, the Mexican horsemen or cowboys, or more rarely they wear regional dress. The mariachi identity is closely associated with the *charro* costume: the *sombrero* (wide-brimmed hat), short jacket, large bow tie, and the tight trousers trimmed with rows of *botonaduras* (silver buttons).

In the United States, mariachi has spread through Mexican-American communities and has been quickly adopted into school curricula and university programs. Mariachi has also infiltrated Disney World, Hollywood, and the pop music scene, through stars such as Linda Ronstadt and the late Selena Quintanilla Pérez. Although mariachi bands were traditionally all-male ensembles, women have begun to participate in the United States, a trend that has also been taken up in Mexico. Dozens of mariachi festivals and workshops are mounted every year in numerous places across North America.

The music played at the *quinceañera* is not, however, exclusive to this particular occasion, as it is also performed on the *día de las madres* (Mother's Day), another musical occasion in honor of women that provides bands with regular employment. The mariachi band, by also playing regularly at baptisms and weddings, provides a further, important link between the *quinceañera* and other life-cycle occasions.

Through its broad participation in life-cycle occasions, the mariachi may play the same songs in an outdoor plaza and at a party in a home. There is also a long-standing tradition that mariachi musicians perform at funerals, singing over the dead. Given the mariachi's presence at so many joyous life-cycle events, it is not surprising that many people want it to help mark the final passage from life. In the words of one mariachi performer from Los Angeles: "People say, 'If I die, I want to hear mariachi for the last time at my funeral.'"

The music of the mariachi is not alone in its association with many occasions throughout the year and within the life-cycle. It can help us appreciate that the meaning—and shape—of music at any particular moment may be defined by the musical occasion at hand. The same song can be sung at moments of joy or sorrow, gaining with each rendition an ever-expanding collection of associations for individuals and the community.

A closer look at yet another soundscape can help us understand that many musics celebrate the life cycle with similar flexibility. As such musics transcend any single moment, they can achieve even deeper meanings. A particularly rich example can be found in the complex world of bagpipe traditions.

LISTENING GUIDE 7

CD 1
TRACK
6

Linda Quinceañera

PERFORMED BY Los Dandys

A most popular song for the *quinceañera* in families of Mexican-American descent is *Linda Quinceañera*, which takes the name of the event and sets forth its significance in the text. The song mentions the waltz, a dance traditionally performed at the party celebrating the *quinceañera*.

LISTEN FOR the strophic form of the song with the voices and stringed instruments moving in the same rhythms but on different pitches, a homophonic texture we first heard in Chapter 1. This song provides a good example of how eighteenth- and nineteenth-century European styles influenced New World musics of the former colonies.

Ha llegado el día	The day has come
que tanto esperabas	which you've been waiting for,
la fecha bendita	the blessed day
que no olvidaras.	you'll never forget.
Hoy cumples quince años	Today you turn fifteen,
dulce muñequita	sweet doll,
tus sueños dorados	your golden dreams
ya son realidad.	are now a reality.
Antes eras niña	Before, you were a girl,
mi niña chiquita	my little darling,

CASE STUDY: BAGPIPE MUSIC

Of the many musical instruments (and their associated musical styles) that play important roles in a range of life-cycle events, one of the most versatile and ubiquitous is the bagpipe. The bagpipe is a wind instrument whose basic parts are an air reservoir (the "bag") that is squeezed under one arm, a blowpipe through which the player supplies air for the reservoir either from the mouth or a set of bellows held under the other arm, and one or more sounding pipes fitted with reeds that vibrate to produce the sound. Most wind instruments cannot sustain the sound while the performer takes a breath, but the bagpipe's air reservoir allows the player

hoy ya señorita	today you're a young lady
de la sociedad.	in society.
No hay nada en el mundo	There is nothing in the world
cosa más bonita	that is more beautiful
que ver tu carita	than seeing your dear expression
de felicidad.	of happiness.
Y recuerda siempre	And always remember
estos quince años	those fifteen years
que a tu vida	which, in your life,
nunca jamás volverán.	will never return.
Y recuerda siempre	And always remember
que todos gosamos	that we all rejoiced
cuando tu bailaste	when you danced
al compás de este vals.	to the beat of this waltz.
Eres una niña	You are a girl,
eres una diosa	you are a goddess,
eres tan hermosa	you are so pretty,
tan angelical.	so angelic.
Al cielo pedimos	We ask heaven
tan solo una cosa	for just one little thing:
que seas muy dichosa	that you may be so happy
una eternidad.	for an eternity.

—Translation by David Lyczkowski

to keep the sound going continuously. Indeed, most sets of bagpipes are not capable of stopping the sound between pitches. Thus, repeated pitches must be played in ways peculiar to the bagpipe.

The history of the bagpipe extends well beyond its Scottish and Irish roots of recent centuries, with archeological evidence of bagpipes in the ancient Middle East (see "Looking Back: The Scottish Highland Bagpipes").

The first known mention of a bagpipe by name, however, occurred during the reign of the Roman emperor Nero in the first century C.E. The emperor vowed that if the gods saved him from those plotting against him, he would mount a mu-

The Scottish Highland Bagpipe

This early sixteenth-century engraving of a bagpiper by Albrecht Dürer has been thought by some to be an Irish piper who served in Europe with the forces of Henry VIII. The pipes may be Irish war pipes, which were known to have two drones of unequal length and a long chante and which the player held in front of him.

1300 B.C.E.	Earliest Middle Eastern carvings of bagpipes
First century C.E.	Roman Emperor Nero (died 68 C.E.) linked to bagpipes
1200s	Possible beginnings of bagpipe playing in Scotland
1549	First written evidence of the use of the bagpipe by the highlanders as a battle instrument
Late 1500s	First pibrochs composed by Donald Mór MacCrimmon
1700s	The Irish *pìob mhór* (great pipe; pronounced "peeb for") dies out and is replaced by the bellows-blown indoor pipe that would become the uilleann pipes
1747	The Disarming Act outlaws the great highland bagpipe, considered an instrument of war
1757	First of many highland regiments raised in the British army; these regiments were allowed pipers
1765	Earliest known order for a set of great highland bagpipes (for one of the MacCrimmons in Skye)
1781	The first pibroch competition held in Falkirk and run by the Highland Society of London
1782	Repeal of the Disarming Act
Late 1700s–1800s	Flourishing of the ceilidh
Mid-1800s	Possible start of reel and "dance music" competitions at rural highland games
1854	Drums added to pipe bands, resulting in the term "pipes and drums"
1882	Edinburgh city police establish the first police pipe band in Scotland
1914	The Vancouver police establish the first pipe band in North America
1930	The Royal Scottish Pipe Band Association established, with one of its primary duties the regulation of band competitions
1966	The Simon Fraser University Pipe Band established

Different types of bag-pipes share principles of construction, although their shapes and sounds vary widely. Here we see Italian pipes played at a Christmas celebration in Rome, Italy.

sical festival and perform on the *utricularius*. Since this Latin word refers to a bag of skin, it is thought that this may be the first reference to a real bagpipe, filled with air and used to sound musical pipes.

Currently, many cultures of Western and Eastern Europe as well as the Balkans and parts of India have one or more unique types of bagpipes with widely varying characteristics. The differences in construction result in significantly different sound quality and volume. Some bagpipes can hardly be heard even if played alone; others can overwhelm any other instrument. In the twentieth century, bag-pipe makers have introduced synthetic materials for the bags, pipes, and reeds, mostly to reduce the difficulty of maintaining and tuning the bagpipes. These changes in materials have changed the sound of the bagpipes.

Although the Roman connection has been suggested by many as a source for bagpipes in the British Isles, the pipes may have been invented independently in the Scottish highlands.[8] Whatever their history, Scottish and Irish bagpipes as-sumed distinctive forms by the Middle Ages, certainly by the twelfth or thirteenth centuries, when their use in official ceremonies and military affairs began. One of the most famous early literary references to the bagpipe occurs in the prologue of *The Canterbury Tales*, where Geoffrey Chaucer (1340?–1400) describes one pil-grim, the Miller, in the following manner:

> A baggepipe well cowde [could] he blowe and sowne [sound],
> And therewith he brought us out of town.

In recent years, Scottish and Irish bagpipe ensembles have proliferated world-wide. One site on the World Wide Web lists well over two hundred pipe bands not just in Great Britain or its former colonies but in such far-flung locations as Fin-land and Uruguay. Indeed, the largest number of active pipe bands is not in Eng-

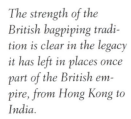

The strength of the British bagpiping tradition is clear in the legacy it has left in places once part of the British empire, from Hong Kong to India.

land, Scotland, or Ireland, but in North America. Some dozens of Canadian bands and more than one hundred United States bands are active, ranging from the small-town West Eden Highlanders of Bar Harbor, Maine, to the Red Hackle Pipes and Drums in the city of Cleveland, Ohio. The ubiquitous presence of bagpipes in North American cities and towns dates primarily to the late nineteenth and twentieth centuries.

<u>Sound</u>   The instrument most widely played today in Irish and Scottish bagpipe bands around the world is the *Scottish highland bagpipe*, which is quite complicated in its construction (**see "Sound Sources: The Scottish Highland Bagpipe"**).

A number of bagpipe tunes are played in both Scottish and Irish traditions, but they are called by different names. The following Scottish bagpipe tune, *Scotland the Brave*, is known in the Irish tradition as *The Irishman's Toast*.

"Scotland the Brave" is played for a variety of occasions. Its regular pulse allows it to serve as a vigorous march at festive parades, and when played at a slower tempo, as a majestic memorial during solemn processions.

Ireland had its own *pìob mhór* ("great pipes") until the early 1700s, when they were redesigned for indoor playing. The distinctive Irish bagpipes are smaller than the Scottish highland pipes, and the air that fills the bag is supplied by a bellows rather than a blowpipe. The distinguishing features of the great highland bagpipe are those that make it most suitable for outdoor use and marching: its loud chanter, additional drones to balance the chanter, and the long blowpipe that allows the player to stand upright. The Irish bagpipe's softer sound was more suited to indoor playing. The "union" or "uilleann" (literally, "elbow") pipes, as Irish pipes are known, declined in popularity until a renaissance of Celtic music during the 1960s and 1970s revived the instrument in both Ireland and the United States.

The Scottish Highland Bagpipe

The Scottish bagpipe has an airtight bag that in the past was made out of the skin of an animal, such as a sheep or goat, but today is more often made of rubber or rubberized cloth. Three kinds of pipes made of wood are inserted into the bag: one is called the *chanter*; the second is the *blowpipe*; and the third kind, of which there are usually three, are termed *drone* pipes. All the pipes are fastened securely into short wooden sockets called "stocks" that are sewn into openings of the skin or rubber bag, which serve to protect the *reeds* at the end of the pipes.

Each kind of pipe attached to the instrument has a different function. The most important is the chanter pipe, with eight finger holes that play the melody. The chanter of the highland bagpipe can play only nine pitches. A chanter can be made of wood, metal, or other materials, and it has a *double reed* that is concealed from view at the end that fits inside the bag.

In contrast, the drone pipes have no finger holes and sound a single, continuous pitch; in some cases, the pitch has such strong harmonics that a listener may think that extra pipes are being sounded.

The blowpipe, by which the player continuously blows air into the bag, has a nonreturn valve to prevent air from leaking out. Once the bag is filled with air, the player compresses it with an arm motion, forcing the air through the reeds of the chanter and drone pipes, causing the reeds to vibrate and the bagpipe to sound. (The Scottish highland pipes have a loud, piercing sound, appropriate for their customary use out of doors.)

Playing the bagpipes is a complicated affair, since one person must blow (or pump) the air, squeeze the bag, and finger the chanter. In the Scottish tradition, in an attempt to isolate the fingering from the other actions, a "practice chanter" has been introduced for both new students of the instrument and experienced pipers learning new tunes. The practice chanter mimics the chanter of the full bagpipes while a cap with a short blowpipe is placed over the chanter reed, allowing the practice chanter to be blown directly without the bag or drones. This arrangement allows the piper to learn the tunes without filling and squeezing the bag. Bands of great highland

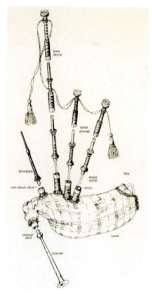

This exploded diagram of Scottish highland bagpipe clarifies aspects of bagpipe construction otherwise hidden from view.

bagpipes will often begin rehearsals with their drones "corked"—with stoppers placed in the ends of the drones so that they will not sound—so they can practice the tunes while hearing the chanters more clearly and without worrying about the tuning and blending of the drone pipes.

Pipe bands must often practice indoors, but the *pìob mhór* ("great pipes") are clearly an outdoor instrument. Even though there are indoor venues that could accommodate these bands, competitions continue to be held outdoors regardless of the weather, testing not only the players' musical skill but also their physical endurance.

The tuning of each bagpipe is fixed, since the player's lips do not touch the reed nor is the chanter blown into directly. In the past, tunings were determined by traditions of a given locality or region. Today, because most bagpipes are manufactured, tunings are fixed according to an international standard.

LISTENING GUIDE 8

CD 1
TRACK
7

Scotland the Brave (march)

PERFORMED BY The Simon Fraser University Pipe Band

Through careful fingering, an adept piper can separate and accentuate pitches with *ornaments* called *grace notes*, very short pitches that embellish the otherwise continuous sound of the chanter and drones. This process is called *gracing*, with the special term *cutting* used to refer to grace notes that divide or decorate two notes of the same pitch.

LISTEN CAREFULLY TO this recording for these distinctive articulations and ornaments, which give bagpipe music its individuality.

Indoor pipes are often distinguished by the term "smallpipes," while the term "bagpipes" generally refers to the Scottish *pìob mhór*. During the mid-nineteenth century, interest in Ireland in the *píob mhór* resurfaced. By this time, however, the native tradition had been broken and so the Irish adopted the Scottish bagpipes. Some pipe makers modified the Scottish bagpipes, basing their designs on early descriptions of Irish pipes, including the two-drone *pìob mhór*. However, only standard, Scottish-style *pìob mhór* are allowed in international competitions; thus, competition Irish bands play the three-drone Scottish pipes.

An interesting musical development, along with the revival of performance on the Irish

A street musician plays the uillean pipes in Cork, Ireland. Note that the bellows pumping air to the pipes fits under the player's arm.

LISTENING GUIDE 9

CD 1
TRACKS
8–9

The Rambling Pitchfork and The Bride's Favorite (Irish jigs)

PERFORMED BY Mattie Connolly (uilleann pipes) and Deidre Connolly (flute)

In this musical example, Mattie Connolly plays the uilleann pipes, and his daughter, Deidre, the flute. They perform two old *jigs*, lively dance tunes popular among Irish Americans.

Both of these jigs have been transmitted by oral tradition and printed notation in twentieth-century Irish music editions.[9] The musical style in this recording represents not just new trends in the Irish diaspora, but the continuing close links between Irish and Irish-American musical communities, nurtured through travel and exchange of recordings in both directions.

LISTEN FOR the rhythms organized in groups of threes or sixes.

LISTENING GUIDE 10

CD 1
TRACK
10

Canntaireachd (Irish mouth music)

PERFORMED BY Miss Mary Morrison

The distinctive sound of the bagpipes carries over into many domains of music in the Scottish and Irish traditions. Among the most interesting is a vocal style that imitates the pipes, called "mouth music" (*canntaireachd,* pronounced "CAN-ter-racht").

In the following example, LISTEN FOR the way in which the voice mimics the distinctive bagpipe articulations and ornaments with vocables.

pipes, is the emergence of father-daughter musical duos among Americans of Irish descent. In the past, the Irish musical tradition was dominated mainly by men—the women largely being restricted to Irish step dancing—but by the 1970s and 1980s, more women were encouraged to take up instrumental music and to perform in public.

The Connolly father-and-daughter team also provides an example of the way in which family networks continue to transmit musical traditions in the diaspora. Mattie Connolly, who was born in New York City in 1940, learned Irish music from his mother, who was a fiddler, but began playing the uilleann pipes only when he visited Ireland as a child. When he returned to the United States, it was difficult to find a good set of Irish pipes, so he took up bass guitar instead, performing at local Irish clubs with a band. In the 1970s, Mattie again visited Ireland and was inspired to resume playing the pipes. Subsequently, Mattie's daughter Deidre learned to play the Irish flute from local New York musicians, picking up tunes from them and her father by oral tradition.

Setting   Here we will explore three main settings in which bagpipe music is performed: occasions related to death and commemoration, occasions of entertainment and the dance, and competition and concerts.

DEATH AND COMMEMORATION

In many North American cities, bagpipes are common at funerals and other ceremonies of commemoration. When a police officer dies in the line of duty, a group of bagpipers often plays at the funeral. In fact, some police bagpipe bands were formed expressly for such solemn occasions.

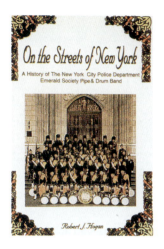

Bagpipes have been linked with warfare and death since 1549, when a French military officer observed that "while the French prepared for combat . . . the wild Scots encouraged themselves to arms by the sound of their bagpipes."[10] As early as the mid-seventeenth century, highland military companies normally included a piper. Later, small bands of eight or twelve pipers were added to regiments. At war trials following the failed 1745 uprising against England, the bagpipe was called "an instrument of war."

Many bagpipers held positions in the service of important officials or were hired by towns to play at civic functions. Many towns also employed a piper to walk through the streets of town each morning, playing the bagpipe in order to wake people up, and to make a second round in the evening at bedtime.[11] Other duties of the piper included performing at the town's horse races and fairs, playing to honor the election of magistrates, and playing at weddings and harvest festivals. For their services, pipers received a salary and a free house, called the Piper's Croft.

As early as the sixteenth century, a repertory of compositions called *pio-baireachd* (pronounced "PEE-ber-rekht"), usually shortened to *pibroch* (pronounced "PEE-brakh") emerged through the creativity of a famous group of pipers, the MacCrimmons (see "**Individual Portrait: The MacCrimmons**").

As many individuals of Irish or Scottish descent became police officers, bagpipe bands, such as the Emerald Society Pipe and Drum Band of New York City pictured here, became closely associated with North American police departments. Founded in 1960, the Emerald Society Pipe and Drum Band follows the Irish tradition of wearing solid-colored uniforms, in this case the blue and gold of the New York City Police Department.

This painting by J. Prinsep Beadle shows Piper James Richardson, V.C., playing the pipes at Regina Trench, Vimy Ridge, as part of the 16th Canadian Scottish Regiment during World War I. The abbreviation V.C. indicates that Richardson received the Victoria Cross, Great Britain's highest military award, underscoring the importance of musicians in battle.

INDIVIDUAL PORTRAIT

The MacCrimmons

What we know about the history of the MacCrimmons, a renowned family of great highland bagpipers on the Scottish Isle of Skye, is based largely on oral traditions. As with most oral traditions, the facts surrounding the family's colorful history as performers, teachers, and composers of the pibroch are clouded by contradictory tales and dubious written sources.

In the early 1500s, the MacCrimmons were appointed hereditary pipers to the chiefs of Clan MacLeod at Dunvegan Castle, which was located across Loch Dunvegan from Boreraig, the MacCrimmons' ancestral home. Members of the MacCrimmon family retained their post for two hundred fifty years. During this time they conceived the pibroch, the classical music of the bagpipe. They also began the system of *canntaireachd* ("mouth music"), whereby one could sing the instrumental pibroch with syllables representing various notes and gracings; it was through this system that new pibrochs were taught and memorized. Most of the MacCrimmon pibrochs are either commemorations or laments for particular people and events, and their attributions and titles have been used to document the MacCrimmons' history. The MacCrimmons also established a college of piping and music at Boreraig, to which chiefs of other clans sent their best pipers for seven years of study to perfect their skills. The college was closed down in 1770, around the time the position of hereditary piper to the clan ended.

How has this information about the MacCrimmons come down to us? The colorful blend of oral and written sources is worth detailing here.

The first book said to have been written about the MacCrimmons was by a Captain Neil MacLeod of Gesto in 1826. This book was probably based on accounts related orally to MacLeod by his friend Iain Dubh MacCrimmon, one of the last two MacCrimmons. However, MacLeod's book was apparently withdrawn; the only known copy disappeared in Canada in 1936. All that survives today of MacLeod's volume are various oral accounts of its contents.

Most of the "facts" concerning the MacCrimmon genealogy and the authorship of particular tunes come from another source: *A Collection of Ancient Piobaireachd*

Six-year-old Andrew Warburton of Marion, North Carolina, plays bagpipes alongside the Grandfather Mountain Highland Pipe Band at the forty-fourth annual Grandfather Mountain Highland Games and Gathering of Scottish Clans, near Linville, North Carolina, July 10, 1999.

or Highland Pipes Music written by the piper Angus MacKay in 1838. MacKay was Queen Victoria's first household piper; the accounts in his book are considered absolute truth by some and pure fabrication by others. MacKay left no record of his sources, so it is impossible either to defend or to refute his claims. To confuse matters further, much of MacKay's book conflicts with what we think MacLeod wrote in his book of twelve years before. The history of the MacCrimmons, in short, survives in several conflicting versions.

Particularly disputed is the ancestry of the MacCrimmons, which contains tantalizing possibilities of connections to other piping traditions outside Scotland. One history names a native of Scotland (Finlay of Plaid, who begat Iain Odhar MacCrimmon), as the founding father of the MacCrimmons. However, two other tales relate that Iain Odhar came from abroad—either from a family of Norse invaders of Ireland, or from Cremona, Italy. The Italian theory, probably advanced in MacLeod's 1826 book, is supported by the story that Iain Odhar was also known as "John of the Sallow Face," an apparent reference to his Italian blood. We know more certainly that around 1570, Iain Odhar's son Donald Mór was born. The first known composer and possible inventor of pibroch, Donald Mór studied with his father and also in Ireland. Donald Mór's son was the composing genius Patrick Mór (born approximately 1595), who was the father of the great piping teacher Patrick Og. Patrick Og had two sons, Malcolm and Donald Bàin, who were pipers during the 1745 rebellion against Britain. Acting on a premonition, Donald Bàin composed the famous lament *MacCrimmon Will Never Return* a few days before he was killed in a skirmish. Malcolm's sons Iain Dubh and Donald Ruadh were the last of the line; with them died the piping secrets of the MacCrimmons.

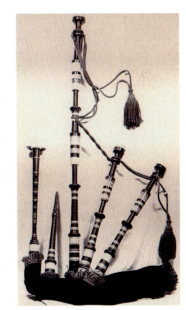

Today, the MacCrimmon Piping Heritage Centre is maintained at the site of the MacCrimmons' old school in Boreraig. There, visitors can see exhibitions, training sessions, daily performances, and workshops, and an annual "Silver Chanter" competition, begun in 1966, in which pibrochs attributed to the MacCrimmons are performed.

The chanter and top sections of the drones are thought to be all that survive of the pipes that Patrick Mór Mac-Crimmon played in the seventeenth century. The other parts are replacements.

The MacCrimmons are said to have transformed bagpipe music over the course of two hundred years, perfecting its playing style, composing and adding new forms such as the pibroch to its repertory, and raising the status of the bagpipe from a rustic instrument to an artistic venture at the heart of Scottish cultural life.[12]

The pibroch consists of an *air*, or melody, with subsequent variations. The air, termed "ground" in English, is always slow and is much longer than a march or dance tune. The melodies are usually simple, and many of them use fewer than the nine pitches available on the chanter.

ENTERTAINMENT AND DANCE

Social occasions provide another common venue for bagpipe performance. Often the pipes are heard at a *ceilidh* (pronounced *"KAY-lee"*), a festive gathering that usually includes music, socializing, and dancing (**see "Snapshot: The Ceilidh"**).

A repertory of dances became popular and associated with the ceilidh, including such numbers as *The Highland Scottische* (which entered the bagpipe repertory very early), *The Dashing White Sergeant,* and *The Strathspey and Reel.*[13]

New dances were introduced by creative dance masters throughout the twentieth century, including regional entries such as "The Swedish Masquerade," "The Virginia Reel," and "The Mississippi Dip." A variety of tunes can be used to accompany the different dances, and the selection may depend on personal taste or traditions wherever the dance is performed.

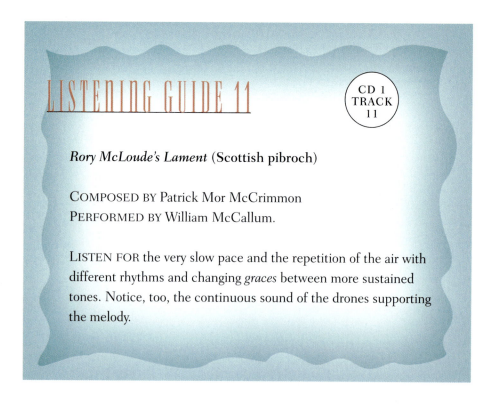

LISTENING GUIDE 11

CD 1
TRACK
11

Rory McLoude's Lament (**Scottish pibroch**)

COMPOSED BY Patrick Mor McCrimmon
PERFORMED BY William McCallum.

LISTEN FOR the very slow pace and the repetition of the air with different rhythms and changing *graces* between more sustained tones. Notice, too, the continuous sound of the drones supporting the melody.

The Ceilidh

The ceilidh is said to be rooted in public dances that flourished in the eighteenth century, following the Church of Scotland's lifting of decrees that had prohibited public dancing.[14] In 1723, the Edinburgh Assembly began to sponsor musical evenings for the gentry to raise money for the poor. These dances, to the accompaniment of the bagpipe or fiddle, at first consisted of basic reels and later gave rise to other forms of country dance. (A *reel* is a type of dance music commonly played on the bagpipe.)

During the late eighteenth and nineteenth centuries, the ceilidh and its associated dance culture flourished. Professional dance masters, known as "Dancie" plus their surnames, plied their trade. Many became itinerant teachers who played the fiddle and taught dances throughout the Scottish countryside.

The term *ceilidh* can now be used to name any sort of social-musical event associated with Scottish or Irish traditions. In North America, we can attend ceilidhs held at Irish taverns in many cities or attend a gathering held at a Scottish arts weekend at a convention hotel in New Jersey.

COMPETITION AND CONCERTS

William Cummings, the piper depicted in the painting reproduced on page 56 (and who supposedly composed several pibrochs) is said to have died as the result of a wager between his chief at Castle Grant and a local rival at MacIntosh as to which had the lustiest piper. The two pipers started from the MacIntosh seat at Moy Hall, playing their pipes, and walked to Castle Grant, some hours away. After several hours, the MacIntosh piper was exhausted, but Cummings managed to continue playing until he reached home—whereupon he collapsed, threw his pipes into the fire, and died shortly thereafter.

Although the bagpipe's volume and ability to sustain a melody allow it to be played effectively as a solo instrument, bagpipe bands (or pipe

An electrician from 103 Pipe and Drum (IBEW Local 103) plays the pipes during his lunch break.

LISTENING GUIDE 12

CD 1
TRACKS
12–13

Strathspey and Reel

PERFORMED BY the Simon Fraser University Pipe Band

The strathspey, which is set in a slightly slower tempo than the reel, has more elaborate melody and ornamentation and is characterized by a long-short rhythm termed a *dotted rhythm* because of the manner in which it is notated. (♩. ♪)

LISTEN FOR the way the low rumble of the bass drum marks the first of every four beats, accenting the beginning of every grouping, termed a *measure*. In contrast, snare drums play almost continuously, emphasizing and subdividing every beat.

bands, as they are often called) had become a common setting for bagpipe performance by the twentieth century. Each pipe band in North America has its own story and distinctive history. Some bands have close ties to either the Scottish or the Irish ethnic tradition, although very few such bands arrived in the New World by migration from Ireland or Scotland. The examples of bagpipe music we hear reflect an eclectic combination of long-time tradition, recent innovation, and the diverse occasions associated with bagpipe music.

The versions of *Scotland the Brave* and *The Strathspey and Reel* you have heard were performed by the Simon Fraser University Pipe Band of Burnaby, British Columbia, Canada. The band was formed in 1966, during the university's inaugural year. Since Simon Fraser University was named after a nineteenth-century explorer of western Canada—who was born in Vermont of Scottish ancestry—the band was founded to give the university "a kind of instant tradition." Today the Simon Fraser pipers consist of a self-described "family" of five distinct bands encompassing over one hundred fifty members. Three are junior bands with players who are under nineteen years of age, organized expressly to train new members.

The world-champion Simon Fraser bagpipe band has since 1966 been a symbol of the Simon Fraser University in Burnaby, British Columbia.

The junior bands range from a "starter" band through two graded ensembles that play increasingly difficult repertory.

The main band heard on these recordings comprises experienced players who have demonstrated professional achievement as both ensemble and solo players and who have won solo medals in competition, an increasingly important aspect of pipe-band culture. Twice in the late 1990s, the Simon Fraser Pipe Band was named World Pipe Band Champions at competitions in Glasgow, Scotland.

Dressing to honor the Fraser clan by wearing Scottish tartans with decorative belt pouches known as sporrans (**see "Snapshot: Scottish Dress"**), the pipe bands are a source of great pride for Simon Fraser University, which markets their videos and recordings and sponsors their concerts at prominent venues such as Carnegie Hall in New York City. These performances, which include examples of all the compositions named above, are occasions for school pride and boosterism, for alumni reunions, and for fundraising.

The bagpipe still sustains a large musical repertory in Scotland and Ireland. Just as its settings and sounds are varied, so are its meanings.

<u>Significance</u>   Clearly a wide range of meanings is connected to the soundscapes of Scottish and Irish piping, meanings attached to the musical sound (such as the playing of a lively march or the plaintive strains of the pibroch to signal lament or mourning) and determined by the setting. Thus, we can differentiate between a vigorous march played in a St. Patrick's Day parade from the same march played at a slower pace at a civic funeral.

Bagpipe bands often perform at civic events. The Boston Gaelic Fire Brigade marches in South Boston's annual St. Patrick's Day Parade, March 14, 1999.

SNAPSHOT

Scottish Dress

Just as bagpipes are associated with occasions ranging from funerals to battles to dances, and with musical repertories as distinctive as the pibroch and the reel, they are also linked to styles of highland dress, most notably the kilt.

Like the bagpipe, the kilt is the subject of considerable folklore and provides an excellent example of the "invention of culture" over time.[15] Although the kilt and the association of certain patterns, or tartans, with particular clans are popularly thought to be of great antiquity, in fact both emerged in the mid-eighteenth century. Before that time, people tended to wear plaids of many colors—especially browns that were the color of heather, in order to disguise themselves when they needed to bed down outdoors. The sporran, a small leather purse worn suspended from the hips, sometimes decorated with tassels, likely originated as a receptacle for a soldier's provisions while traveling.

The painting at right of the Grant Piper William Cummings illustrates early eighteenth-century formal dress. In addition to his kilt with golden yellow, red, and gray stripes, the piper wears a short coat and vest. The bagpipes he holds are quite elaborate, decorated with cord, tassels, and a white banner with red and white fringes.

Both the bagpipe and highland dress were the subject of debate, and both were banned as symbols of defiance—notably by the Disarming Act of 1746, not repealed for thirty-six years. Highland dress today thus draws on and reinvents styles popularized two centuries earlier.

The tartan worn by the Grant Piper William Cummings, painted by Richard Waitt in 1714, is unlike any Grant tartan worn today.

The pipes, too, have proven flexible and amenable to new meanings. They can be used to perform traditional reels and strathspeys for entertainment at a party or to play the same selections on a concert stage for a college pep rally.

So powerful is the voice of the bagpipe and so strong its associations with death and commemoration that it has entered into American popular culture,

Dancers from the Annapolis Valley Highland Dance Association perform at festivals and competitions throughout Nova Scotia and other Canadian maritime provinces. The dancers are also tested yearly by examiners from the Scottish Dance Teachers Alliance, Scotland, and have consistently achieved high marks.

carrying these meanings to a wide cross-section of the population. One notable example can be viewed in the 1979 film *The Onion Field*, based on Joseph Wambaugh's book of the same title. The sound of the pipes is used as a central symbol to tell the story of Iain Campbell, a police officer of Scottish descent who is murdered in an onion field by thugs. A bagpipe lament, a funeral pibroch, carries powerful yet different meanings when played at four pivotal points in the film: in the first scene, Campbell himself plays the lament on the pipes, as an expression of his Scottish heritage; the lament is next heard in the background just before Campbell is murdered, as an omen of death; a lone piper then plays the same pibroch as a commemorative lament at Campbell's funeral. In the final scene, Campbell's mother encounters a young piper playing the lament at the local highland games, as a symbol of nostalgia and continuity, both poignant and hopeful.

Guests dance to the music of the bagpipes following Bess and Jan's wedding in Lars von Trier's 1996 film Breaking the Waves. *During the wedding party, the piper plays tunes ranging from "Scotland the Brave" to "Blowin' in the Wind."*

Because the sound of the bagpipe immediately signals its presence, the instrument appears in a variety of settings, and the pieces in its large musical repertory can be fitted to many different occasions. The significance of bagpipe music stems from the particular combination of the instrument's sound, the music it plays, and the setting in which it is heard.

Conclusion

Music is woven through the fabric of our everyday lives. These case studies have demonstrated that musical sound does not stand alone but is enlivened and given meaning by its connections to many aspects of everyday life. From lullabies to bagpipe laments, musical sound assumes its significance from its settings and from its presence as lived experience.

If we are to understand how music becomes a part of everyday life and simultaneously infuses its many settings with meaning, we must look back to the process of travel and migration that brought so many different soundscapes to North America. We will examine this subject in our next chapter, Music and Migration.

What role does music play in your everyday life? Keep a journal, noting each day the soundscapes you encounter.

How many musical traditions do you come into contact each week? Which soundscapes did you intentionally incorporate and which entered your experience through an accidental exposure or serendipity?

Have you encountered any new or unfamiliar soundscapes recently? If so, try writing a brief description.

IMPORTANT TERMS

air and variations	major and minor	refrain
bagpipe	scales	Scottish highland
blowpipe	mariachi	bagpipe
ceilidh	measure	strathspey and reel
chanters	melody	strophic form
dotted rhythm	meter	texture
drones	Muzak	tonal music
genre	ornaments	uilleann pipes
gracing	oral tradition	vernacular music
homophony	ostinato	vibrato
lullaby	pibroch	vocable
	reed	

CHAPTER

THREE THREE THREE THREE THREE THREE THREE THREE THREE THREE THREE THREE THREE THREE

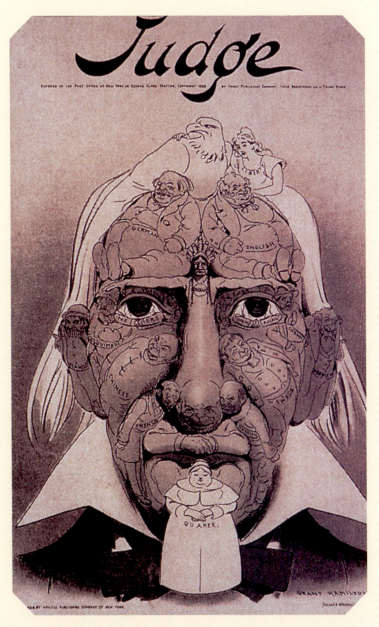

This 1898 illustration of Uncle Sam represented the
increasingly diverse American population in a novel manner.

OVERVIEW

MAIN POINTS

- Music travels easily because it exists in time, is portable, and can be transmitted in the oral tradition.

- Some musical styles are maintained when transplanted; others are transformed or discarded.

- Music making itself can embody and reenact the migration process.

Music and Migration

Introduction

As we have seen, the course of everyday life brings us into contact with a complex landscape of competing sounds and musical practices. In this chapter, we will explore the processes that bring musics to new places and establish them there. We will examine how some musical styles are maintained after they are transplanted, and how others are transformed (see "**Studying Music: Migration and the City**).

The central role of music in migration is due to three important factors: music exists in time; it is portable; and it can be sustained in the oral tradition. In the past, music traveled with human migration, as people—alone or in groups—moved to new places. Migration has always been an integral part of human experience, although sophisticated forms of modern transportation have allowed mass movements to occur much more quickly. Recording and communication technologies also transmit music of the present and past over huge distances of both time and space. For the first time in history, we can preserve performances and replay them long after they were recorded.

Although most migrations have been perceived as either long-term or permanent, improved communications and opportunities for travel have in recent years made possible the increasingly common movement back and forth between a new home and the homeland. (The possibility of return, of course, is an option only if the historical homeland still exists or is accessible to expatriates abroad.)

The stories behind migrations are rarely simple or straightforward, in part because people move for different reasons and remain settled for varying lengths of

STUDYING MUSIC

Migration and the City

Although circumstances of immigration vary widely, and migrants come from both rural and urban areas in their homelands, most have ended up entering and relocating in major North American urban centers. It is ironic, given the city's importance in immigrant musical life, that ethnomusicologists and folklorists were so slow to acknowledge it as an appropriate site for study.

In 1968, the folklorist Richard Dorson carried out one of the first studies to show that immigrants in cities have not always abandoned their traditions. Before Dorson's research, most scholars assumed that ethnic groups adapted to American culture as quickly as possible, leaving behind their original language and customs, especially any that would clearly mark them as "foreign." In studying the effect of life in an urban, industrial center on "imported cultures," Dorson charted patterns of musical and cultural continuity and change among a number of ethnic groups settled in one metropolitan area: Gary, Indiana. Dorson surveyed cultural life among immigrant communities of African, Serbian, Greek, Mexican, and Puerto Rican descent. To his surprise, he found rich musical traditions actively performed in churches and at various civic celebrations and rites of passage. He considered these urban musical traditions primarily as re-creations of those in their original homelands. At the same time, he was aware that these traditions had undergone some changes in the New World as well as maintained a lively and interactive relationship with their respective homelands.

Although Dorson emphasized ethnic separatism, he also provided evidence of how different urban communities shared common experiences of urban life. Dorson then began to document what he termed a new "lore of the city." In the thirty years since Dorson's landmark study, other ethnomusicologists have redefined our approach to the music of and among ethnic groups in urban areas. We are keenly aware that ethnic conditions of communities change, cross boundaries, and differ from life in their homelands.

time. Immigrant communities outside the historical homeland are often called *diaspora* communities, from the Greek word meaning "dispersion." Although voluntary migration is commonly assumed to be the norm, forced migration, in which circumstances compel relocation, is in fact much more common.

As we explore the musical results of voluntary and forced migration, we should be aware that these two categories are not always mutually exclusive. For instance, one group of people may undergo both voluntary and forced migration at different times in their history. Additional variables—such as the historical period of immigration; the conditions under which an individual traveled and arrived; age; ethnic or religious identity; economic situation; and educational background—all influence the *setting, sound,* and *significance* of immigrant musical life for its subsequent history.

A boatful of immigrants to the United States, musicians among them, sight land after a long and difficult voyage.

Voluntary Migration

Voluntary migration is the movement of people into a new region. Almost inevitably, migration produces new cultural and musical forms as people react to their new surroundings. For example, many migrants came to the New World on a voluntary basis, seeking new opportunities. The number of migrants increased dramatically in the second half of the nineteenth century, when the changeover from sailing ships to steamships around 1860 made ocean crossings faster, safer, and cheaper. Encouraging to those considering emigration were the provisions of the Immigration Act of 1864 and the many opportunities waiting in the New World (see "Looking Back: Immigration to the United States").

During the 1850s some 2.6 million immigrants arrived in the United States; by the 1880s the number had doubled to 5.2 million, and it reached its peak in the first decade of the twentieth century at 8.8 million people. Faster travel allowed migration from areas beyond Europe as well, and during the late nineteenth and early twentieth centuries North America saw the arrival of increasing numbers of people from the Middle East and various other places.

Each wave of migration to North America has had its musical impact. The musical heritage of the Spanish in the American Southwest was felt substantially from the late fifteenth century. British migrants carried with them *ballads,* strophic songs that tell a story, that found a permanent home in the mountains of Virginia and Kentucky, where they are remembered long after they had been forgotten in the British Isles.

Jean Ritchie, a native of Viper, Kentucky, in the Southern Appalachian Mountains is an influential singer and dulcimer player who performs ballads handed down from her Scottish, English, and Irish ancestors. "I believe that old songs have things to say to the modern generation, and that's why they've stayed around," says Ritchie, who has released more than thirty albums and has performed throughout the United States.

Immigration to the United States

August 1619	First ship carrying African slaves sails into Jamestown, Virginia
1808	Congress outlaws the international slave trade
1849–1882	First wave of Chinese immigrants begins shortly after gold rush in California and ends with Chinese Exclusion Act of 1882
1845–1850	"Great hunger" potato famine in Ireland spurs emigration
1850	Turning point in U.S. immigration: increasing numbers from Latin America, China and Scandinavia instead of from Great Britain, Ireland, and Germany
1864	Immigration Act of 1864 encourages immigration to United States; act establishes Commissioner of Immigration; immigrants can apply to U.S. government for financial aid
1865	Thirteenth Amendment to the U.S. Constitution abolishes slavery
1875–1918	First wave of Arabic-speaking immigrants arrives, mainly from Greater Syria
1882	Chinese Exclusion Act of 1882, limiting the number of Chinese who can enter the United States
Late 1880s	European immigration shifts from northern and western Europe to southern and eastern Europe (Russia, Poland, Greece, Italy)
1892	Gentry Act extends provisions of Chinese Exclusion Act of 1882 for ten additional years
1904	Chinese Exclusion Act is extended indefinitely
	Dissolution of Ottoman Empire fuels latter part of "first wave" of Arab immigration
1917	Immigration Act of 1917 excludes all Asians and encourages skilled laborers and professionals only if no unemployment in the United States
1921	Quota Act establishes yearly immigration quotas at 3 percent of foreign-born population as of 1910 census
1924	Immigration Act of 1924 makes national quotas permanent and limits yearly immigration to 2 percent of the U.S. population as of 1890 census; eastern and southern European immigration is sharply decreased, while Asian aliens are banned
1943	Chinese Exclusion Act is repealed and Chinese residents are allowed to become citizens; Chinese quota set at 105 immigrants per year
1948	Displaced Persons Act of 1948 defines those who between September 1, 1938, and January 1, 1948, were victims of Nazi

	persecution as "eligible displaced persons" qualified for permanent residence in United States
1950s–1960s	"Second wave" of Arab immigrants, primarily Muslims displaced by 1948 Arab-Israeli War
1952	Immigration Act of 1952 provides first fundamental revision of initial Immigration Act of 1864 and revises the quota system, now one-sixth of 1 percent of number of inhabitants in continental United States in 1920
1953	Refugee Relief Act of 1953 provides nonquota visas for refugees, escapees, and German expellees, allowing four thousand special visas granted to orphans under age ten; also establishes new category of persons who were persecuted because of political beliefs
1960s–present	"Third wave" of Arab immigration—skilled professionals and unskilled workers—fleeing political instability in Middle East
1962	Migration and Refugee Assistance Act of 1962 provides appropriations to UN High Commission for Refugees, to assist refugees with transportation, training, and employment
1964	Civil Rights Act of 1964 restores basic rights previously denied to Chinese-Americans
1965	Immigration and Nationality Act of 1965 amends Immigration Act of 1924; discontinues national-origin quota systems, places a numerical limit on visas (170,000), and establishes the Select Commission on Western Hemisphere Immigration to study trends and consequences of immigration to United States
1965	Immigration and Nationality Act of 1965 ushers in third wave of Chinese immigrants
1975	President Ford authorizes entry of 130,000 refugees from three countries of Indochina after fall of South Vietnam; over 125,000 are Vietnamese from urban areas of South Vietnam
1978	Second wave of Vietnamese refugees, so-called boat people, begin to enter United States in response to Vietnam's implementation of anti-Chinese policies; primarily rural people with minimal education funneled through refugee camps in Southeast Asia, peaking in 1980–1981
1980	Refugee Act of 1980 amends Immigration and Nationality Act of 1952 and Migration and Refugee Assistance Act of 1962 to establish a more uniform basis for assistance to refugees; Office of Refugee Assistance and coordinator of Refugee Affairs established in Department of Health and Human Services

1986	Immigration Reform and Control Act of 1986 amends basic Immigration and Nationality Act of 1952 to improve control of aliens in United States and increase border control
1988	Immigration Amendment of 1988 makes additional visas available to immigrants from underrepresented countries to enhance diversity
1990	Immigration Act of 1990 amends 1986 legislation and establishes present-day immigration regulations; comprehensive revision of immigration laws since 1952 act restructures immigrant selection system and narrows groups that can be excluded

LISTENING GUIDE 13

CD 1
TRACKS
14–15

Barbara Allen (Anglo-American ballad, two partial performances)

PERFORMED BY Mrs. T. M. Bryant, Evansville, Indiana, 1938, unaccompanied

PERFORMED BY Monroe Gevedon, West Liberty, Kentucky, with fiddle

Barbara Allen is one of the best-loved English ballads to survive widely in North America. The origin of the ballad is unclear, although it may have been a parody of a traditional Scottish ballad, with its text changed to mock—in veiled terms—the well-known but hated mistress of King Charles II, Barbara Villiers, who died in 1680.[1]

Here are two partial versions of *Barbara Allen* recorded in the 1930s, the second accompanied by a fiddle. Both are in strophic form. Each syllable of text is sung to one pitch, resulting in what is termed a *syllabic text-setting.* But there are also differences within both texts and tunes. Apparently, four basic versions of the text have spread and generated new versions—some influenced by printed English ballad texts called *broadsides,* others transformed as they were transmitted orally in the eastern United States.

CASE STUDY: THE CHINESE MIGRATION

Some individuals and communities migrated voluntarily in order to seek better lives and economic opportunities. However, the idea of the immigrant as spurred on by a sense of exploration and a desire for profit is mostly a romantic myth. The decision to immigrate was actually full of conflict and intensely difficult. One important example in North American history is the large wave of Chinese immigrants who began arriving on the West Coast around 1850 to participate in the gold rush and later to build the transcontinental railroad.

Migration from China was largely voluntary, in part because of the attraction, or "pull," that the United States (called Gamsaan, the "Gold Mountain") held for many. However, political anarchy, famine, and economic crisis in mid-nineteenth century China were strong "push" (negative) factors that persuaded most to migrate, even though moving to a new country was arduous. Thousands of Chinese borrowed money for their fares against wages to be earned on arrival, often result-

Although ballads were often sung without instrumental accompaniment, it was also common to play along with a fiddle (as heard in the second rendition), banjo, or guitar.

LISTEN FOR the difference between the two versions. In what ways do the texts and melodies differ?

Mrs. T. M. Bryant:

It was in the merry month of May,
And the buds on the trees were swelling.
Sweet William on his death bed lay,
For the love of Barby Allen.

He sent his servant into town,
To the place where she was dwelling.
Saying, "My master sent me here for you,
If your name be Barby Allen."

Monroe Gevedon (with fiddle):

Was early in the month of May,
When the May buds they were swelling.
Sweet William on his death bed lay,
For the love of Barby Allen.

He sent his servant to the town,
The place where she was dwelling.
My master say, "Can you come to quick?
If your name be Barby Allen."

This portrait of a Chinese immigrant musician from Canton, along with his family, female student, and interpreter, is the earliest surviving image related to Chinese music in America. By the second half of the nineteenth century, a growing fascination with people from faraway places gave rise to a series of public exhibitions. The individuals in this portrait were under contract to and displayed by Phineas T. Barnum.

ing in years of indentured servitude in the New World. Soon after their arrival, Chinese migrants also encountered serious discrimination and intolerance both in everyday life and in a series of exclusionary laws such as the 1882 Exclusion Act and the Immigration Law of 1924, which severely limited Chinese immigration. Only in 1943 was this Act repealed, and in the 1950s and 1960s was this situation redressed through the Refugee Relief Acts. Thus, any discussion of the Chinese-American community and its musical life at the turn of the twenty-first century must take into account a long, episodic, and painful migration history. Similar factors shadow the immigration history of many other communities as well.

Many voluntary Chinese immigrants, particularly those from the first half of the twentieth century, considered themselves to be only temporary sojourners in the United States. Most were motivated by economic gain, intending to return home prosperous. For this reason, many sojourners were strongly motivated to maintain the cultural traditions of their homeland, since they fully expected to return eventually. Nevertheless, the triumphant homecoming was a dream that most never realized, and many intended sojourners spent the rest of their lives in North America. Since the 1960s, most Chinese immigrants have come to settle permanently.

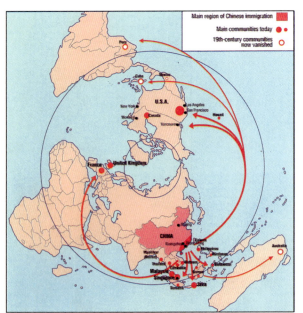

Subsequent waves of Chinese migration to North America and major concentrations of Chinese in San Francisco, Toronto, and New York should be seen in the context of the flow of Chinese people to other places around the globe, with this flow constituting the world's biggest diaspora.

The song *Ng baak loi gamsaan* ("Uncle Ng Comes to the Gold Mountain") is a fine example of how the Chinese migration process was recalled in musical performance. This song belongs to a traditional southeastern Chinese musical *genre* called *muk'yu*. Ranging in length from a few dozen lines to lengthy compositions which can take days to perform, *muk'yu* are both transmitted as an oral tradition and written down in songbooks.

Immigration is the subject of five of the twenty *muk'yu* songs known and sung by Sheung Chi Ng (affectionately known to his friends as Ng Bok, or Uncle Ng), who migrated to the United States in 1979 at the age of sixty-nine. Even though he arrived as an elderly man, "Uncle Ng" continues to sing of his dream: becoming rich and making enough money to return to his hometown. *Ng Baak Loi Gamsaan,* which he composed in 1982, traces his experience as an American immigrant.

Muk'yu can be sung by men or women and are performed on a variety of occasions, both public and private. *Muk'yu* texts, like those of other related Chinese song genres, tell of concerns of everyday life. Given the large numbers

Sheung Chi Ng (Uncle Ng), who in China sang muk'yu *at events ranging from weddings to political meetings, has since his arrival in New York performed on the streets, at a senior citizens center, and in a local park.*

of Chinese who migrated from the Guangdong region of southeast China to the United States, it is not surprising that many such songs from that region reflect the experience of immigrants. That *muk'yu* have been very popular over the course of Chinese migration to North America is confirmed by surviving nineteenth-century advertisements for *muk'yu* songbooks.[2]

Muk'yu songs divide into sections according to the course of their story lines. In *Uncle Ng Comes to the Gold Mountain,* we find the following divisions:

Introduction	lines 1 to 5
Life in Toison	lines 6 to 18
Arriving in Hong Kong	lines 19 to 26
Life in the United States	lines 27 to 51
Returning to Toison (imagined)	lines 52 to 57

Written *muk'yu* have a *fixed form*—seven syllables per line of text, usually divided 2 + 2 + 3, and often rhymed. When performing, the singer often adds extra meaningless syllables to the text, called *vocables.* Generally, the text setting is *syllabic,* but *ornaments* can be added so that each syllable is prolonged over three or more pitches (termed *melismatic* text setting).

The relationship between the text and its *melody* is further complicated in *muk'yu* and other Chinese songs because of the presence of linguistic *tones,* varying inflections that distinguish words, in the spoken Chinese language. For instance,

Ng Baak loi gamsaan ("Uncle Ng Comes to the Gold Mountain"; Chinese _muk'yu_)

PERFORMED BY Sheung Chi Ng

LISTEN TO the manner in which a simple and repetitive melody help sustain a detailed narrative. What aspects of American life are new to Uncle Ng?

1. At this leisure time I have many thoughts,
2. Once _muk'yu_ has come to my mind, I start singing;
3. This piece of _muk'yu_ is about nothing else
4. But to recall my hometown again.
5. This is a long story, hard to tell in a few words.

6. Forty years ago my hometown was liberated.
7. A new dynasty came with a new emperor.
8. Many other things I'll not talk or sing about,
9. But we worked very hard to build reservoirs.

10. Once the irrigation works were completed, we produced excellent crops.
11. The granaries were bursting with sweet potatoes and rice.
12. How many people in the world believe
13. That life gets easier when there is money and rice.

14. Yet there were struggles on the political orientation between the two lines.
15. Who wouldn't want to go overseas?
16. I thought during the nights and hoped during the days,
17. On what terms I could go to Hong Kong,
18. It seemed to me just like a mortal wanting to enter the paradise.

19. Arrived in Hong Kong, I raised my head looking around.
20. The skyscrapers were majestic and splendid.
21. Good luck makes one happy and full of vigor;
22. I hurried myself on the road going to the Gold Mountain.

23. People say that America is paradise.
24. Everybody makes money and becomes rich.
25. If I could reach my destination,
26. It might not be too late for me to have good luck and become rich.

27. On the streets I see so many beautifully dressed people.
28. They are in suits and wear ties.
29. They walk on the streets wearing high-heeled shoes.

30. I believed I could enjoy life in America.
31. How could I expect that I would still have to endure such hardship at my age?
32. Two meals everyday at irregular times.
33. At night I lodge in the *Kangning* Building on the twelfth floor.

34. Every day I walk around wandering in the streets.
35. I wouldn't want to tell my living conditions,
36. Because Uncle [I] doesn't have money to deposit in the bank.

37. New York City is so prosperous.
38. Traffic is so convenient, and crowds come and go.
39. There are everywhere skyscrapers and factories.
40. One has to watch the red and green lights when crossing streets.
41. When the green light is not on, one can't cross streets.

42. In the morning women go back to the factories,
43. And men go to work as waiters and cooks.
44. Each week they are given a salary, but there is no place to keep the money,
45. So they open an account and deposit the money in the bank.

46. Streets and alleys are full of restaurants and teahouses.
47. They are brilliantly illuminated and open until daybreak.
48. Uncle [I] has no money in his purse, I can't help it.
49. If I had money in my purse, I would go several times a day to the teahouse.

50. If I had the opportunity to return to my hometown, Toishun County, Sijiu Wushi District, Jinbeilang Township.
51. How glorious and impressive would I be as the returned *jinshan ke* (the guest from the Gold Mountain).
52. Brothers from my village would come to welcome me and visit me.
53. Brothers would be so joyful in meeting each other again.

54. At that time I would no longer be the same person as before.
55. I would first distribute money, then the sesame candies.
56. Between brothers we would have so many loving sentiments to tell that the gatherings would be endless.
57. Thus I am back to my home and see the members of my family again.

—Translated by Su Zheng

three kinds of linguistic tones can appear at the end of any given line of *muk'yu* text; correspondingly, each line can end on one of three different *cadential* (ending) musical pitches. However, the five main divisions of the song end on the same distinctive pitch, known as a *cadence*.

Uncle Ng's *muk'yu* contains information about the modern process of immigration, with detailed descriptions of late-twentieth-century buildings and cityscapes. At the same time, the song conveys ideas about immigration that reflect the older goal of the sojourner, who wishes to return home prosperous and respected (**see "Snapshot: Diaspora vs. Homeland"**).

CASE STUDY: ARAB MIGRATION FROM THE MIDDLE EAST

Some lively North American soundscapes have their roots in migrations that began as voluntary movements but at some later point included forced migration. For example, emigration from the Middle East began as a voluntary movement in the late nineteenth century. It has been suggested that immigrants from Greater Syria (which incorporated what is now Lebanon) discovered an "entrepreneurial Eden" in America in the late 1870s. Political and economic instability in the Middle East provided an impetus for what is often called the "first wave" of Arab emigrants to depart the region. The economic downturn caused by the opening of the Suez Canal in 1869—which disrupted overland trade routes—and the breakup of the Ottoman empire in 1917 were the final precipitating events. In contrast, the "second wave" of Arab immigrants included some who were forced to migrate after being dislocated during the Arab-Israeli conflict in 1948.[3]

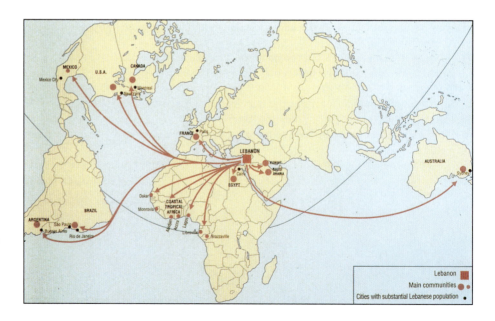

Over the course of the twentieth century, the large Lebanese diaspora has established major communities in North and South America, West Africa, France, and Australia.

SNAPSHOT

Diaspora vs. Homeland

One of the ironies of twenty-first-century musical life is the vitality of many musical traditions far from their historical homelands: for instance, it has been reported that there are more regular performances of Chinese operas in New York City than anywhere in China. Since 1990, the performance of Chinese opera has flowered in New York City, invigorated by the immigration of a number of famous Chinese opera stars to the United States, where they struggle to make a living while sustaining their art. There are frequent live performances of Chinese opera in both public auditoriums and private community gatherings. Anna Yip, who since arriving in New York from Hong Kong, has sponsored opera performances featuring both local talent and Chinese opera stars from abroad, gives this simple reason: "I'm an opera nut. You come to America and you start to get homesick."

Song Yang as Madame Du in a dress rehearsal of Episode 1 of The Peony Pavilion, *the Chinese opera finally presented at the Lincoln Center Festival in 1999.*

But the revival and performance of music across boundaries of time and space can also be the source of great controversy between diaspora communities and the authorities in their historical homeland, especially when American notions of artistic innovations collide with Chinese traditions and notions of official control. A notable case was the planned American production of *The Peony Pavilion,* a classical Chinese opera composed by Tang Xianzu in 1598. It was originally to be presented by the Shanghai Kunqu Opera Company at New York City's Lincoln Center during the summer of 1998. The performance was blocked by Chinese authorities, who denounced the avant garde production directed by Chen Shi-Zheng, a 1987 immigrant to the United States, as "feudal, pornographic, and superstitious."[4]

As a result of this cancellation and the surrounding controversy, *The Peony Pavilion* was subsequently presented in several competing versions in both the United States and China. The New York Kunqu Society, which agreed with the criticism and cancellation of the 1998 Lincoln Center production, mounted its own traditional, condensed version of the opera. A second, quite untraditional version with new music was directed in March 1999, by Peter Sellars in Berkeley, California. Lincoln Center finally succeeded in mounting the opera in its own lavish production in July 1999, with plans for additional performances in Europe and Australia. And in November 1999, a traditional, Chinese-approved version of *The Peony Pavilion* was presented in Shanghai, a postscript to an international artistic controversy debated by journalists and scholars alike.

Whether Muslims, Christians, or Jews, many Middle Eastern immigrants of the first wave had the support of extended personal and family networks in a process called "chain migration." Many Arab-American communities, such as those in Detroit and New York, were established by individuals who, on arrival, sent for other family members and encouraged close friends to join them as well. The constant

Russel Bunai and Amer Khadaj stand in front of Alamphon Arabic Records around 1950. This store in Brooklyn, New York, sold records imported from the Middle East as well as releases by Arab-Americans.

flow of people (at least until the 1924 immigration restrictions) kept connections with the homeland alive. Immigrants from the Middle East enhanced the connections by importing sound recordings of the latest musical styles. Thus musical styles traveled across great distances between the new home in North America and the historical homeland, whether modern Syria, Lebanon, Egypt, or elsewhere.

Although a variety of musical styles—including popular music for Middle Eastern nightclubs—have been invented and sustained by Arab-Americans, music performed at community events tends to be traditional, maintaining the repertories, instruments, and aesthetic values of the historical Middle East. American communities from the Middle East tended to maintain the older musical styles with which they were familiar. Many of the innovations that found their way into music in the Middle East—such as large instrumental ensembles combining Middle Eastern and Western instruments, popular in Egypt by the mid-twentieth-century—have not been widely used in North America (**see "Sound Sources: The '*Ud* and the *Qanun*"**).

Arab-Americans continue to have close ties to their homelands, and many of these connections are symbolized through song. Live concerts of Arab music are often mounted, some featuring famous musicians from the Middle East. The

This car features the traditional Hand of Fatimah, a Middle Eastern symbol for good luck and a talisman against the evil eye.

LISTENING GUIDE 15

CD 1 TRACK 17

Wakef 'ala shat baher ("Standing on the Shore"; Arab song)

PERFORMED BY Hanan and ensemble

COMPOSED BY Zaghlul al-Damnour. Featuring Hanan, vocalist; Joe Bedway, *'ud*; Yacoub Ghannim, *qanun*; Hakki Obadia and Naim Karakand, violins; drum, wood blocks, and chorus.

This traditional-style song refers to the process of immigration. Titled *Wakef 'ala shat baher*, ("Standing on the Shore") it is performed by the well-known singer Hanan, an immigrant of Lebanese descent who settled in New York in the 1940s. You will hear classical Middle Eastern instruments—the *'ud* (lute) and *qanun* (a Middle Eastern *zither* with seventy-two strings; (see "Sound Sources: The *'Ud and the Qanun*")—as well as the Western violin, which has been played in the Middle East since the nineteenth century. Hanan's vocal style is also typical of her former home, with a *nasal quality* and many ornaments. The melody that Hanan sings and that played by the instruments sound together in a near-unison texture termed *heterophony*. The melody is set in the Arab musical system of *maqam*, which we will explore in Chapter 7. The text refers to migration, describing the process of people traveling back and forth, carrying news between new home and historic homeland of a community in motion.

LISTEN FOR the form of the song as it alternates between sections in *free rhythm* sung by the soloist and verses with regular rhythm performed by the chorus. The violins, *'ud*, and *qanun* can be heard clearly during the instrumental interludes. In the solo sections, they accompany the voice in a heterophonic style. Note how drums—including a frame drum with metal disks attached—sustain the regular rhythm during the verses.

Wa'if 'ala shatt il-bahr bakkani s-safar Min mitli tlawwa' wa addi natar?	I stand at the seashore, travel made me cry. Who like me has suffered and waited as much as I did?
Ma' kill mawjih rayihah bib'at salam Ma' kill mawjih raji'ah bintur khabar Bintur khabar	With each going wave I send regards With each returning wave I wait for news I wait for news —Translated by John Eisele and Ali Jihad Racy

The 'Ud and the Qanun

The *'ud* is the principal plucked *chordophone*—stringed instrument—used in the Arab world. It has a short neck and a large body with a rounded back. Some players describe the shape of the instrument as half an egg. The rounded sound box is constructed of sixteen to twenty-one ribs made of lightweight wood. Up to three sound holes may be carved into the flat soundboard, which supports the bridge and, in turn, the strings. The length of the *'ud*'s neck varies, with tuning pegs anchoring the strings attached at the end of the neck. The *'ud*'s ten strings are paired, two to each pitch. A *plectrum,* or pick, sometimes made of an eagle feather, is used to pluck the strings.

Simon Shaheen, a Palestinian-American living in New York City who is widely admired as a virtuoso player of and composer for the 'ud, *also plays the violin. His* 'ud *was made in Damascus, Syria, by a renowned instrument maker.*

Stories about the origins of the *'ud,* which go back to the ninth and tenth centuries, credit Lamak, a descendant of the biblical Cain, with inventing the instrument. According to myth, Lamak's son had died, and when the boy's remains were hung on a tree, they suggested the original form of the *'ud.* The instrument is believed to bring health benefits to its players and audiences, and its strings are traditionally associated with cosmological elements such as the seasons and the zodiac. The *'ud* spread east and west through its use in religious and secular music; it was particularly important as the instrument that accompanied secular songs.[5]

Preferences for different types of *'ud,* with different numbers of strings, vary by geographic location. The highly popular five-stringed (that is, five double-strung) Egyptian *'ud* has a range of over two octaves. A four-stringed *'ud* is used in Morocco, whereas a six-stringed model is favored from Istanbul to Baghdad. By way of Islamic Spain, the *'ud* also entered Europe, where it was the ancestor of the lute (*l'ud*).

Different schools of *'ud* performance have contributed to the establishment of solo repertories, freeing the instrument from its traditional function of accompanying vocal music. Standardized method books for studying the *'ud* incorporating Western theoretical approaches have been available since the beginning of the twentieth century. These books depart from the traditional method of instruction by oral transmission through individual study with a master.

Another chordophone often heard in Middle Eastern music is the *qanun,* having a trapezoidal shape and twenty-six courses (sets) of three strings each. The *qanun* player attaches a plectrum to the index finger of each hand to produce a polyphonic texture. Many *'ud* and *qanun* are decorated with mother-of-pearl inlay, giving the instruments extraordinary beauty.

John Sarweh has toured Canada and the United States as a master qanun *player since 1960. The only* qanun *maker in North America, Sarweh takes several months to complete each instrument.*

most important of these events attract audiences of thousands from all over North America and receive major press coverage, such as the appearance in May 1999 of the famous Lebanese singer Fairuz at the Garden Arena of the MGM Grand in Las Vegas.

In her Las Vegas concert, Fairuz was accompanied by ten backup singers and an ensemble that included Middle Eastern instruments (among them, the *'ud*) and Western instruments, including nine violins. Such an event reconnects the Lebanese and broader Arab communities abroad with their Middle Eastern homelands, evoking deep emotion with songs such as *Take Me (And Plant Me in the Land of Lebanon)*. In the words of a woman (quoted in the *New York Times*) who had traveled from Michigan to Las Vegas to hear Fairuz sing: "My grandmother had a fig tree and grapes, and Fairuz reminded me of that. She sings about things that people used to take for granted: the walls we used to live in, the smell of the air we used to breathe. We just have memories now, and she brought them all back."

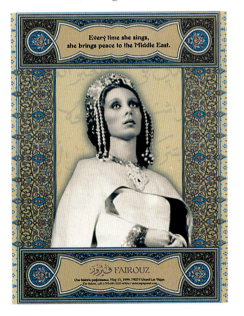

This poster advertising a 1999 Las Vegas concert by Fairuz (also spelled Fairouz) links diaspora music making to homeland politics.

LISTENING GUIDE 16

Ya ana ya ana ("*I am, I am*"; Arab song)

PERFORMED BY Fairuz; other performers are not identified.

Traditional musical styles such as that heard in *Standing on the Shore* still survive in the Middle East, but singers such as Fairuz reflect newer international trends. Just as many Middle Eastern instrumental ensembles combined traditional Arab instruments with Western violins, cellos, and even, guitars, other innovations took place. Singing styles, including that of Fairuz, became more Westernized. A number of Middle Eastern composers, following the lead of the Egyptian 'ud player and composer Muhammad Abd 'al-Wahhab, also began to borrow melodies from Western classical composers to use in their popular songs. *Ya ana ya ana*, a song with an Arabic text, is a fine model of these modern trends in Arab music, as it borrows for its melody the main theme from Mozart's Symphony No. 40 in G minor.

LISTEN TO the way Mozart's melody has been transformed by Fairuz.

Oh, when I am with you
We became strange stories on the tongue of gossipers.
Oh, when I am with you
And my letters are stolen
And they knew you are my beloved
And they knew you are my beloved.

Oh, when summer escaped
The grapes decorating the yards also escaped
And if one summer love makes me get lost
You'll find me in your heart
You either hide me, or you forget about me
You either hide me, or you forget about me.

Your nights in my eyes, are like lighted windows
Make me travel, oh my beloved, make me travel in your nights
And I say, "Don't forget"
All the time, "Don't forget"
And your eyes take me, and promise me your nights
Your nights.

They left, they left, and the mind was at peace
And the lover gathered his wing
They left their names in the mind
In the books of tears, and left themselves
They forgot each other, and now they are relieved
They forgot each other, and now they are relieved.

Oh, Oh, When I am with you . . .

—Translated by Iman Roushdy

Forced Migration

In contrast to voluntary migration, where "pull" factors are an attraction that motivates people to move, forced migration is set into motion by "push" factors beyond individual or community control. Migrations of this sort often result from violent or disastrous events.

There have been many forced migrations throughout history, such as the mass exodus to North America by many hundred thousands of Irish in the 1850s as a result of the terrible 1845 famine known as the "great hunger." Because people forced from their homes are often nostalgic for the past and maintain musical traditions as part of their shared identity, the study of *musical diasporas* has emerged as a rich and important area of present-day musical scholarship. (**See "Studying Music: Musical Diasporas."**)

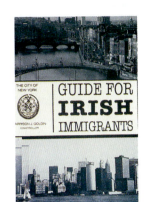

Government publications such as this one targeted to specific immigrant communities seek to make the immigration process clearer and easier.

CASE STUDY: AFRICAN MIGRATIONS

Two causes of forced migration—conquest and slavery—continue to reverberate in the background of North American life and musical styles. The periods of North American conquest—such as the impact of European settlement in colo-

STUDYING MUSIC

Musical Diasporas

Americans of Arab, Chinese, and Vietnamese origin and descent differ in their immigration histories and in their settlement patterns within the United States. Their musical lives also reflect different blends of creativity and conservatism. However, all are people living in North America who have deep connections to an ancestral homeland to which they are strongly attached and to which—in varying degrees—they wish to return. Although late-twentieth-century writers often referred to all of these groups as diaspora communities, the term *diaspora* was originally used to refer to the forced exile of the Jews to Babylon in 586 B.C.E. and, in later periods, to many places around the world.

Many soundscapes are examples of music in diaspora, soundscapes that result from voluntary or forced movements from a homeland and resettlement in two or more foreign locales. Most of the soundscapes we will study are the result of migrations, past and present. Although most are maintained by individuals who share kinship and history,

A major center of the Caribbean diaspora, New York City sustains lively traditions of Caribbean music and dance. Here girls in colorful regalia dance at the Brooklyn Labor Day Carnival, said to be the largest Caribbean event in North America with an annual attendance of over one million people.

others—as we will see—are not. In recent decades, too, the term *diaspora* has been applied to a wider variety of population movements, some of which may not involve travel from foreign locales.

As we will see throughout *Soundscapes*, people keep and sustain their musical practices and values in many ways, from preservation to creative transformation. The musicians who perform the music are expressing these values, and as a result, represent them in a particular way to outsiders as well. In all cases we should remember that music and the boundaries it constructs come from a combination of internal factors—including past experiences and values—and external influences.

nial America and the subsequent expansion to the western part of the continent—are often celebrated in American popular culture. However, they entailed the forced movement of millions of Africans through the slave trade. Also, the native North American population was severely reduced through warfare and disease; survivors often found themselves uprooted and their cultures damaged. In North America, the period of conquest that commenced in the early sixteenth century began an ongoing process that directly shaped the soundscapes of today. New social and legal systems based on those in Europe reshaped the cultural and musical landscape of North America. Throughout this book, we will explore the effects of forced migration on musical styles, how they are performed, and what they mean to performers and listeners.[6]

Many important musical genres show traces of the painful experiences of African Americans during the slave era that followed their forced movement to North America. Among the earliest and most influential of these is the black spiritual. Spirituals emerged from the musical expression of slaves converted to New World Christianity, a process that began during the eighteenth century but reached its peak in the early nineteenth. A now-lost collection of spirituals may have been compiled as early as 1819, but most of our knowledge of these songs dates from the period around and after the Civil War.[7] In 1867, the first collection

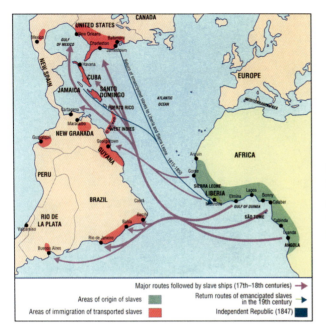

The slave ships that forcibly removed Africans from the West African coast delivered their human cargo to widely scattered places in North and South America and the Caribbean, tearing apart families and fracturing ties to their places of origin.

of spirituals was published under the title *Slave Songs of the United States*. Collections such as *Slave Songs* both preserve and romanticize the memory of the slaves' music.[8]

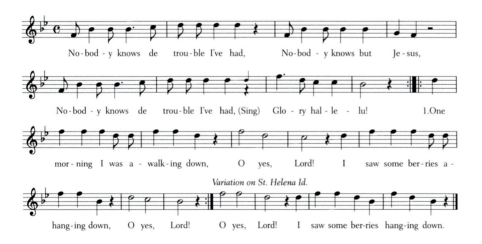

The editors of *Slave Songs of the United States* comment in their introduction that written notation alone could not convey either the spiritual's distinctive vocal style or the subtle variations in intonation and pitch of the oral renditions. Furthermore, the early descriptions of black spiritual singing, such as that in an 1839 slave owner's diary, mentioned that the spirituals were originally sung in unison. However, Allen's commentary suggests that some spirituals might have been sung

The Jubilee Singers of Fisk University in Nashville, Tennessee, many of whom were former slaves, became famous in the late 1860s and 1870s for the powerful concert versions of slave songs they performed.

Paul Robeson rehearses for a performance at Memorial Theatre in London, 1955.

in a heterophonic texture or with a soloist and chorus alternating in what is usually termed *call and response* style.

> I despair of conveying any notion of the effect of a number singing together. . . . There is no singing in parts, as we understand it, and yet no two appear to be singing the same thing—the leading singer starts the words of each verse, often improvising, and the others, who "base" him, as it is called, strike in with the refrain, or even join in the solo, when the words are familiar.

The texts, tunes, and performance styles associated with spiritual singing were transformed in the late nineteenth and early twentieth centuries to a style influenced by the Western classical music of the dominant society. The spiritual moved to the concert stage by the late nineteenth century, when the Fisk University Jubilee Singers began to travel internationally and included spirituals in their public performances. By the early twentieth century, many black concert artists were performing spirituals all over the world.[9]

CASE STUDY: THE VIETNAMESE MIGRATION

All cases of forced migration involve a traumatic break with the homeland. Today, forced migrations most commonly occur when people relocate to escape physical, political, or religious persecution. These refugees, who number in the millions, are forced to resettle in unfamiliar, and in some cases, undesired places. Their migration is the result not of the positive "pull" of a new place, but of the "push" factors of fear or suffering.

LISTENING GUIDE 17

CD 1
TRACK
19

Nobody Knows the Trouble I've Seen (African American
spiritual)

PERFORMED BY Paul Robeson, baritone, with Lawrence
Brown, pianist and arranger

One of the most famous interpreters of the spiritual was the
singer Paul Robeson (1898–1976). The son of a minister,
Robeson attended Rutgers University and later received a law
degree from Columbia University. During his student years,
Robeson began acting, and when he was unable to find a job
in the law because of racial discrimination, made a career in
the theater. This recording of *Nobody Knows the Trouble I've
Seen* was accompanied by Lawrence Brown, a musician who
worked closely with Paul Robeson. The performance was
recorded live in New York City on December 29, 1945, at the
Greenwich Village Theatre.

LISTEN TO the text and melody of this recording and compare it to that seen above in the 1867 transcription from
Slave Songs of the United States. What are the differences
between the two?

We will examine the forced migration of Vietnamese to North America to find
out how their music was affected by both the circumstances of their departure
from the homeland and the paths they followed.

Even in the late twentieth century migration was not always accomplished by
sophisticated means of transportation. The Vietnamese provide a striking example: although the 1975 air evacuation on the eve of the fall of South Vietnam to
the Communists was one of the fastest movements of a large number of people
from a single place, the later waves of Vietnamese migration were mainly in small
boats and makeshift rafts (see **"Snapshot: The Vietnamese Diaspora"**).

The Vietnamese Diaspora

The history of the present-day Vietnamese diaspora began with the entry of French missionaries in the mid-seventeenth century and culminated with French colonial control of the entire country by the 1880s. The declaration of Vietnamese independence by Ho Chi Minh in 1945 and the subsequent fighting led to the defeat of the French and the division of Vietnam in 1954, with Ho Chi Minh in control in the North and a French-supported ruler, Ngo Dinh Diem, installed in the South. Because of continued conflict between North and South Vietnam, the first American advisors arrived in the South in 1961, followed in 1965 by U.S. ground troops. American involvement in the ensuing war was largely ended by the 1973 peace talks in Paris. However, when in March and April 1975 Saigon (the South Vietnamese capital) fell to the North Vietnamese, two hundred thousand South Vietnamese sought refuge in the United States and other countries. Soon afterward, North and South Vietnam were reunited, and Hanoi became the national capital.

The first wave of Vietnamese immigrants to North America were the urban elite, many of whom settled in Orange County, California, in Washington, D.C., in New York City, and on the east coast of New Jersey. By 1978, at least one thousand people a month—the "boat people"—were leaving Vietnam by sea. Many of this "second wave" of immigrants were less-educated farmers and fishermen, and most ended up in refugee camps in the Philippines and elsewhere in Asia for interim periods ranging from several months to years. Over time, individuals filtered through the camps to the United States and eventually started new Vietnamese enclaves in places such as Houston, Texas, and Washington, D.C. Between 1978 and 1985, half a million people left Vietnam; by the mid-1990s, the Vietnamese diaspora was estimated to number 1.3 million, 70 percent of whom resided in the United States.

Members of the Garden City (Kansas) Vietnamese dragon dancers group celebrate the Vietnamese New Year, Tet, at a Garden City elementary school. The community Tet festivities for the year 2000 welcomed the lunar year of the dragon.

Among Vietnamese peoples in North America, the Vietnamese language is widely spoken; it is written in a distinctive romanized version marked with diacritics that indicate its six tones. Many of the immigrants maintain their Buddhist religion and most make a special effort to observe Tet, the holiday that in late January or early February marks both the beginning of the lunar new year and the advent of spring. A traditional ceremony on the afternoon before Tet is followed at midnight by fireworks and traditional dances.

This photograph records the plight of the Vietnamese "boat people" near the shores of Hong Kong in the late 1970s. Refugees such as these have been turned away from Hong Kong as illegal immigrants since 1988.

The Vietnamese migration provides striking examples of how music is influenced by forced migration. Vietnamese refugees were traumatized both by their harrowing escape from Vietnam and their subsequent enforced stay in camps of asylum in Hong Kong and the Philippines while they awaited resettlement abroad. Most surprising, perhaps, was the presence in refugee camps of many different musical styles, ranging from Buddhist chant to Vietnamese folk and chamber music to Western popular and classical music. Although people performed and enjoyed music of both the Western and Vietnamese musical systems—Western music more often being heard in public performances and traditional Vietnamese music played in private settings—*any* song with a Vietnamese text, whatever its musical style, was considered to be Vietnamese music. Thus, musical style itself was not the only factor that determined music's identity—and in the camps, boundaries between formerly distinctive musical categories were blurring.

Finally, people in the camps of asylum sang mainly "sad songs" and "love songs," which seemed—at first encounter—not such surprising choices. However, further investigation showed that love songs and sad songs nostalgic for pre-1975 Vietnam had in fact been prohibited by the Communist regime when it reunified the country in 1975; thus, the singing of these songs in the refugee camps was an expression of political ideology and an act of resistance. In fact, the distinction between pre- and post-1975 Vietnam, with the incorporation of South Vietnam into the communist north, became a major factor in the choice and continuation of musical genres both in the camps and afterward.[10]

Some of the music heard in the camps was that of the composer Pham Duy (pronounced "fam zwee") (**see "Individual Portrait: Pham Duy"**). Many of his songs were described as "patriotic songs." Pham Duy's music had long been popular in Vietnam because of his role in fighting French colonial forces in the late 1940s and early 1950s, but was banned in 1975. It is not surprising that since his resettlement in California in 1975, his music has been performed as an expression of patriotism for pre-1975 South Vietnam.

INDIVIDUAL PORTRAIT

Pham Duy

Pham Duy was born in Hanoi in 1921 and began his
career as a member of a traveling musical troupe in the
1940s. Although he studied music in Paris in
1954–1955, most of Pham Duy's musical education
and experience took place in his homeland, Vietnam.
A few years before the country was divided, Pham Duy
settled in the south and became a prolific composer.

As he explains on his Web site, the composer
divides his career into several periods:

The composer Pham Duy, who
lives in California, during a visit
to Paris in 1989.

- folk songs, which recorded the images of the
  Vietnamese during the struggle for independence;
  these songs culminated in his song cycles, which
  combine several folk tunes to proclaim the greatness
  of the Vietnamese people
- heart songs, which aimed to awake humanity's
  conscience, to protest against violence and inhumanity
- spiritual songs, with a Zen character, which aimed to seek the truth
- profane songs, which tackled head on hypocritical attitudes and phony virtues
- children's songs, young women's songs, and peace songs, which were songs of joy

In 1975, Pham Duy immigrated to Midway City, California, where he continues to
compose and perform new music. Pham Duy describes his new works as "refugees' songs"
and "prisoners' songs," and he continues to rework and recast older compositions. In the
last decade, the composer has adopted Western compositional and orchestration
techniques and has increasingly made use of new multimedia technology to enrich and
supplement his music.

<u>The National Road Song Cycle</u>   *Con Duong Cai Quan* (pronounced
"gon duwang gai gwan"), which is known in English as *The National Road: A Voyage through Vietnam,* is a series of songs, termed *song cycle,* incorporating several
different streams of musical influence. As Pham Duy first conceived it in 1954

and completed it in 1960, *The National Road* tells of a traveler's journey through Vietnam from north to south. The text celebrates the cultural diversity and regional differences in the country and traces aspects of its history. Its musical style reflects the composer's varied musical background and experience: the influences of traditional Vietnamese music, popular Vietnamese song, and the Western classical tradition.

Perhaps most surprising to the Western listener is the hybrid musical language with both Vietnamese and Western elements. Western and Vietnamese musical styles interacted throughout nineteenth- and twentieth-century Vietnam under the French colonial presence. A Westernized Vietnamese popular song tradition emerged between 1920 and 1940, near the end of the French colonial period. Called *tan nhac* (pronounced "dan nyac"), this style combined Western instruments and Vietnamese lyrics; occasionally it drew on Vietnamese folk melodies. Popular among young people, *tan nhac* continued to be performed in Vietnam's urban areas. *Tan nhac* features *duple* and *quadruple meters,* that is, regular groups of two or four beats. Performers are free to improvise in *tan nhac,* especially in the introductory sections of a song.[11]

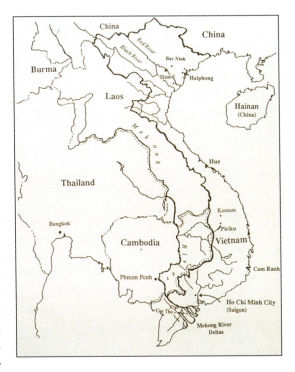

Although *The National Road* is shaped in part by the Western music system as funneled through *tan nhac,* many of its songs draw on traditional Vietnamese melodies. Most of the melodies in *The National Road* are set within the pentatonic scales widely used in traditional Vietnamese music. Drawing on traditional Vietnamese musical principles, the composer provides a "skeleton" to be varied and embellished by the performer.

The three regions of the country described in The National Road *can be located through their major cities: Hanoi in the north, Hue in Central Vietnam, and Ho Chi Minh City (formerly Saigon) in the south.*

The Perfume River Traditional Ensemble from Hue, Vietnam (see Listening Guide 18), performs in Lowell, Massachusetts, a city with many Vietnamese immigrants.

LISTENING GUIDE 18

CD 1
TRACK
20

A Thousand Miles from Home (Vietnamese song)

PERFORMED BY the Perfume River Traditional Ensemble

The Perfume River Traditional Ensemble, which is from the city of Hue, made its first visit to the United States for a two-week tour during August 1995. The ensemble performs court, chamber, and folk music of Central Vietnam. This recording is provided so that you can compare the musical language of *The National Road* and its representation of music from Central Vietnam with a performance by a traditional ensemble from that area.

The song *A Thousand Miles from Home* is a type of chamber music (*ca hue* [pronounced "ga way"]) performed for connoisseurs. The song begins with a long prelude in free rhythm. The main portion is based on an eight-beat cycle. The text refers indirectly to the mythological princess Tran Huyen Tran (pronounced "chan huyen chan"), who is also mentioned in *The National Road*.

The singer, Thu Hang, is famous for performing this repertory. She is accompanied by an ensemble of traditional Vietnamese instruments including a long-necked, "moonshaped" lute with two strings (*dan nguyet* ["dan nyuyet"]), a sixteen-stringed zither (*dan tranh* ["dan chang"]), a monochord (*dan bau* ["dan boe"]), a two-stringed fiddle (*dan nhi* ["dan yee"]), a double-reed aerophone (*ken* ["gen"]), and percussion (**see "Sound Sources: Vietnamese Instruments"**).

LISTEN FOR clear examples of traditional Vietnamese use of vibrato, along with sliding between the pitches in both string instruments and the voice. Each pitch of a given scale must be given its distinctive sound through ornaments such as these.[12]

Prelude:

In the evening, who is sitting at Van Lau harbor?
Who is fishing? Who is sad? Who loves the country? . . .

A thousand miles from her homeland, she traveled.
Her sorrow is masked by makeup to make things appear happy.
For O and Ly districts she leaves.
It is bitter, because she is in the fullness of youth like the spring.
Or is this her fate? . . .

SOUND SOURCES

Vietnamese Instruments

Musical instruments have a wide range of significance and symbolic meanings, which can vary over time and change according to the contexts in which they are played. Take as an example the Vietnamese *dan bau*, seen in the upper left-hand corner of the photograph of the Perfume River Ensemble (page 87) and here.

The *dan bau* (literally "musical instrument of the people") consists of a single string, a resonating chamber, and a small bamboo shaft used to bend the pitch. The player produces sound by plucking the string with the right hand while moving the bamboo element with the left hand to determine the pitch. It has been said that the instrument can render all possible sounds, even an imitation of the human voice. A standard textbook used by students at the Hanoi Conservatory describes the *dan bau* as being "like two brothers of the same house." That is, it represents the spirit of solidarity and kinship between two ethnic groups, the majority Kinh and the minority Muong, who are regarded as the ancestors of the Kinh. According to legend, the *dan bau* and the *khen*, a panpipe used by the Muong, have a common origin: each is made from half of the same gourd.

The dan bau *produces a delicate but resonant sound. Here it is played by Bui Huu Nhut, a native of Saigon who immigrated to the United States in 1989.*

What is your favorite musical instrument? How is it classified within the Sachs-Hornbostel system? How is it defined within its "native" cultural context, whether in the Western orchestra or an ensemble from another tradition? Does the instrument carry any special significance? Is it played in special circumstances (as, for example, the bagpipe signifies mourning or death on certain occasions)? Who plays the instrument? Mainly men, women, or individuals of particular background or training?

LISTENING GUIDE 19

Two songs from *The National Road: Come to Hue, Come* and *Who Is Walking on the Endless Road*

COMPOSED BY Pham Duy
PERFORMED BY the Ngan Khoi Chorus

These renditions of songs 8 and 9 from Part Two of *The National Road* are drawn from live performances recorded in the early 1990s by the Ngan Khoi ("Vast Ocean") Chorus, a southern California-based organization founded to promote choral singing among Vietnamese in America. The compact disc from which these excerpts are taken is sold in Vietnamese record stores throughout the United States. The notes accompanying the recording say that its producers hope to "bring you a taste of Vietnamese music through choral works sung by Vietnamese refugees in memory of their homeland."

LISTEN TO these polished performances of two songs from *The National Road*. Below we will compare them with the other performances to follow.

Song 8 is described as "a mother singing a lullaby." The text translates:

The Mother:

Aaoaaaaoi
Come to Hue, come
Don't be afraid of the wilds of Nha Ho and the rapids of Tam Giang
A a o a a a a o i
Toward father's village, the road is so long, the river so wide
Toward mother's village the mountains are so high, the passes so steep
A a o a a a a o i

The National Road consists of nineteen songs divided into three sections. The first represents the north; the second, Central Vietnam; and the final part, southern Vietnam.

On his Web site, the composer writes of his intentions in composing *The National Road*:

But sleep well, my child
'Cause there's someone
Walking to repair the bridges
A a o a a a a o i

Song 9, *Who Is Walking on the Endless Road,* is described as a "rice pounding song" that the traveler overhears as he walks through a village during harvesttime. The text reads as follows:

The Villagers:

Ho ho ho ho o i ho
Who is walking there on the endless road
Why are you hurrying thus
Ho ho ho khoan
Ho ho ho ho o i ho
Please join us, my friend
In our celebrations tonight
Ho ho ho khoan.

The Traveler:

That year when spring came
I set out in the footsteps of Princess Huyen Tran
On this road built on bones and full of sorrow
She exchanged her beauty for land
I follow in the footsteps of a love
To ensure the peace and prosperity of many
On the hills the wind blows
Bringing her perfume to the capital city.

The People of the Center:

Ho ho ho ho o i ho
You who walk on the bumpy road
Hurry, the country's task remains to be done
Ho ho ho khoan.
Ho ho ho ho o i ho
Hurry, or you'll be late
For the love story of yore
Ho ho ho khoan.

I wanted to make a musical journey. What can be more pleasurable than traveling through one's country with song cycles? *Con Duong Cai Quan* . . . was conceived in 1954, when Vietnam was divided by the world powers into a nationalist and a communist zone at Geneva. I was then studying music in Paris, and this song cycle was my protest. The work was completed in 1960.

The Ngan Khoi Choir of Garden Grove, California (see Listening Guide 19), performed its debut concert in 1989. The group, which promotes choral singing among Vietnamese-Americans, founded a children's choir in 1994. In addition to issuing recordings and videotapes of Vietnamese music, the group performs selections by American composers such as Randall Thompson's Frostiana—settings of poems by Robert Frost—and excerpts from Aaron Copland's opera The Tender Land.

We will focus on the middle section: Part Two: "Through the Central Regions." Vietnam's central region, with its capital city Hue, is well known for its distinctive musical styles. We will also discuss Pham Duy's compositions in light of the traditional songs that inspired them. However, it is both useful and interesting to include an example of the traditional music of Hue (see Listening Guide 18), a chamber music composition performed internationally by musicians from that city.

Here are two songs from the middle section of *The National Road* (see Listening Guide 19). We will first focus on the sound of the songs from a cross-cultural perspective.

SOUND

This soft song for solo female voice is sung at a relatively slow speed, in a free rhythm. The song never establishes a regular pulse, leaving its pace to the interpretation of the singer.

The melody of the song is based on a pentatonic scale, with a brief shift (*modulation*) in the middle of the second verse, at "Toward father's village," to a second, higher pentatonic scale. Almost immediately, the song shifts back to its original pentatonic scale. The *harmony* supports the pentatonic sound by moving in intervals of fourths and fifths. The overall form of the song is quite simple, with the opening phrase returning four times, with the three verses in between each repetition.

Song 8 is adapted from lullabies of Central Vietnam called *ru* (pronounced "roo"). The rhythm of each traditional lullaby is determined by the meter of its poem, and lines are frequently extended with vocables. *Ru* are also commonly sung in a pentatonic scale.

Song 9 is sung by a chorus, with a solo for the traveler in the second verse; the song is a duet between the villagers, who are pounding harvested rice to separate the grains, and the traveler, who passes them in their fields as he is hurrying through the area. The rhythm of the song depicts its text, establishing a strong quadruple meter appropriate to both the regular pounding of the rice and the quick pace of the traveler. This song is performed quite enthusiastically by both chorus and soloist, in contrast to the subdued lullaby that preceded it.

Song 9 has three main sections. The first, which we will call "A," returns after the contrasting second section, which we will call "B." Section A also reverses the order of the pentatonic scales heard in the lullaby. That is, Section A of *Who is Walking on the Endless Road* begins with a pentatonic scale starting on the pitch D and moves briefly to a scale beginning on the pitch A, and then back to D pentatonic.

The B section of Song 9 presents a contrast in texture to the A section, with a duet between the male traveler and a female soloist. Here the male voice centers around the pentatonic scale starting on A, while a competing melody, called a *countermelody,* sung by the woman rests on D pentatonic. The result is an interesting, multivoiced *(polyphonic) texture.*

Who is Walking on the Endless Road immediately signals its traditional origin in its first line with the combination of the word *ho* (pronounced "haw"), which means "to raise the voice," joined with vocables. In traditional Vietnamese music, *ho* are popular songs sung by workers to sustain themselves through hard manual labor. The songs are sung loudly to the rhythm of the work.

However, the lyrics of *ho* often also refer to love, as in Song 9 with its reference to the mythological princess Tran Huyen Tran, who sacrificed herself to unite Vietnam. Thus, the combination of a work song and a love song is a traditional element that Pham Duy has maintained.

Another aspect of Song 9 that is based on tradition is the division between male and female voices in the B section. In folk practice, the *ho* is usually sung loudly by a group in call-and-response style. The one who sings the main verse is the lead caller (or "mother"), while the rest are known as chorus callers (or "children"). In traditional *ho* performance, the call is divided into parts: a male part sung by a leader and a female part sung by a chorus. Note that Pham Duy has incorporated male-female alternation, perhaps reflecting the fact that when *ho* songs of this type have more recently been sung at festivals, boys and girls are divided into two groups to sing in call and response style as they compete for prizes.[13]

SETTING

Two additional recordings illustrate the different *settings* in which songs from *The National Road* have been performed (see Listening Guides 20 and 21).

SIGNIFICANCE

This work has a quite powerful significance for the composer and other diaspora Vietnamese. *The National Road* grew out of the specific experience of the composer, who devoted much of his life to efforts to reunify his country following its partition in 1954, only to be forced to emigrate when Saigon fell in 1975. Although the music of Pham Duy is universally known and sung by Vietnamese peo-

Come to Hue, Come (amateur performance)

COMPOSED BY Pham Duy
PERFORMED LIVE in New Jersey, early 1980s

This recording is from an amateur performance of the lullaby, *Come to Hue, Come,* taped at a New Jersey Tet celebration in the early 1980s. Pham Duy's song cycle was at the center of the Tet celebration, which also featured a fashion show choreographed to recordings and dancing to popular music played by a live combo with electric guitars, keyboards, drum set, and singer.

LISTEN TO this performance by an amateur singer accompanied by a piano, and compare it with the Song 8 recording in Listening Guide 19.

ple in the diaspora, it is not performed openly today in Vietnam. *The National Road,* which he intended as a musical realization of a unified, independent Vietnam, survives abroad as an important musical symbol of the continuing divide between Vietnamese at home and those in the diaspora. Pham Duy recalls that he had walked the route traced in *The National Road* four times, first as a singer with a drama and music troupe, and later in various political or military contexts. Pham Duy has used music as a form of resistance since the 1940s, when he broadcast songs about a free Vietnam from a cave outside Hanoi. Pham Duy recalls: In Vietnam, everything—music, poetry—has to do with politics. You cannot avoid it."[14]

Conclusion

The musical progress of the traveler through Vietnam evokes memories both of the sounds and of the scenes of different regions. Every time it is performed, it also reenacts the composer's journey through Vietnam. Today, *The National Road* also is an ironic symbol of the longer process of forced migration and scattering

LISTENING GUIDE 21

CD 1
TRACK
24

Who Is Walking on the Endless Road (synthesizer version)

COMPOSED BY Pham Duy
ARRANGED AND PERFORMED BY Duy Cuong

This rendition of Song 9 from *The National Road* is a synthesizer arrangement prepared in the California sound studio of the composer Pham Duy's son Duy Cuong.

LISTEN TO how this rendition of Song 9—a synthesized symphonic version without the vocal parts—is clearly influenced by the technoculture of the late–twentieth-century United States. Here we also see evidence of the Vietnamese interest in multiple versions of the same work, with the composer allowing rearrangements of his composition.

shared by the Vietnamese community abroad. In *The National Road,* we hear sounds and styles of traditional Vietnamese music transformed within a framework of modernization, whether through the piano accompaniment played at the Tet celebration in New Jersey, or in a recorded synthesizer version. Although the musical sound has changed and is adaptable, it still carries a great deal of traditional meaning.

The National Road is an example of music from a homeland that has been transformed through the process of migration. The musical vocabulary of *The National Road* reflects its dual traditional and Western background of both Western influence in Southeast Asia and traditional Vietnamese values in the United States. It is not surprising that *The National Road* has led a continued life abroad among Vietnamese expatriates. Wherever it is performed and in any arrangement, *The National Road* is highly charged with meaning, its seemingly Westernized musical sound masking a meaning that is intensely Vietnamese.[15]

Diaspora communities bring their soundscapes to a wider public in celebrations of important holidays, parades, and festivals. Many of these events are part of a broad spectrum of musical activities found in many localities, whereas others may be unique to a particular place. How a given place is marked by its own special blend of soundscapes—and the way in which these soundscapes define a place—are the focus of Chapter 4.

What immigrant communities live in your area? Check newspaper listings to see what musical events they sponsor.

IMPORTANT TERMS

ballad	*ho*	*qanun*
broadside	*maqam*	quadruple meter
cadence	melismatic text	*ru*
call and response	setting	song cycle
countermelody	melody	spiritual
diaspora	modulation	syllabic text
duple meter	*muk'yu*	*tan nyac*
heterophony	polyphonic texture	*'ud*

CHAPTER

FOUR FOUR FOUR FOUR FOUR FOUR FOUR FOUR FOUR FOUR FOUR FOUR FOUR FOUR FOUR FOUR FOUR FOUR FOUR FOUR FOUR FOUR FOUR FOUR FOUR FOUR FOUR

Music of the Mediterranean

Boston Early Music Festival & Exhibition
8–13 JUNE 1999

The 1999 Boston Early Music Festival, which had as its theme
"Music of the Mediterranean," included groups such as
Ensemble Sarband, which performs music drawing on
European, Islamic, and Jewish traditions. The festival program
cover featured costume designs by Robin Linklater for
Ercole Amante ("Hercules in Love"), a seventeenth-century
opera composed by Francesco Cavalli.

OVERVIEW

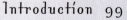

MAIN POINTS

- Every city, town, and village has its own distinctive combination of soundscapes

- Soundscapes existing side by side in one place often interact

- Closely related soundscapes—those that share sounds, settings, and significances—can be termed "soundscape clusters"

The Study of
Local Musics

Introduction

To understand music at home in North America, we could begin just about any-where. Every city, town, and village has its own distinctive musical life, its own special combination of soundscapes. Surprisingly, only in the last quarter of the twentieth century did scholars begin to explore the richness of urban musics and musical life. These valuable studies, many of which we will draw on throughout *Soundscapes,* have centered mainly on musical traditions cultivated by individual ethnic communities, or on musical events accessible to anyone in a wide variety of public places (**see "Studying Music: Mapping the City"**).

Very few attempts have been made to chart all musical life in a single place. No doubt individuals have been reluctant to attempt more than they could accomplish easily through the hands-on approach of participant observation. Yet soundscapes exist side by side in cities and towns, often sharing performance spaces as well as music, musicians, and audiences. As we begin our exploration, we will see how individual soundscapes fit within their broader urban contexts, appreciating the ways in which these separate musical worlds can occasionally interact and even overlap.

Our focus is on music in and of the city rather than more rural places for two main reasons. First, according to a report of the United Nations Population Fund,

STUDYING MUSIC

Mapping the City

Ethnomusicologists were slow to discover the rich musical life of cities, recognizing the potential for ethnographic research and carrying out fieldwork there only in the last quarter of the twentieth century. In developing a new subfield known as urban ethnomusicology, scholars in cities began by focusing on individual ethnic communities and their music. By the mid-1980s, ethnomusicologists were giving increasing attention to various kinds of music (such as rock, rap, and country) that are found in urban and rural areas in the United States and abroad.

In this chapter, we will include music performed in local ethnic communities, as well as some styles that have worldwide popularity through recordings. But we will also focus on the widest variety of soundscapes to discover whether we can draw a distinctive musical profile of a city. We will, in effect, "map" the city's musical landscape.

There are few models to guide us in this enterprise. The most detailed and large-scale study of music in and of a single city is Ruth Finnegan's book *The Hidden Musicians,* a study of amateur music making in her hometown of Milton Keynes, England. Finnegan took a close look at what she called the "musical worlds" of her community, very similar to our soundscapes. The musical worlds for which Finnegan provides an overview are of European or American heritage, including classical music, brass band, folk music, musical theater, jazz, country and western music, and rock and pop. Finnegan focused on amateur musical life and practices, observing that they are often "hidden" from both the community at large as well as from other musicians who are not involved in them. We can learn a great deal from Finnegan's work, including her concept of "musical pathways," a term she uses to summarize the known and regular routes of musical practice that characterize local music making.

by the year 2005, the majority of the world's population will live in cities. Thus, cities—and increasing numbers of "megacities" with populations greater than ten million—will increasingly predominate as settings for musical activity. Second, even small towns are more and more complex in their musical lives; therefore we can apply the same methods to study them as we do to study larger urban areas.

In this chapter, we will explore a cross-section of musics in one city, with briefer examination of two contrasting centers. Our overview will incorporate ethnic musical traditions previously explained by ethnomusicologists, but will also extend to some other musics that ethnomusicologists have less frequently studied—notably those usually labeled "classical" and "folk." All of these very different musical styles are important to a particular local music scene, and it is unfortunate that in the past they have not been surveyed in relation to each other. As participant observers, we will begin by looking at the broadest range of soundscapes as they are practiced within the life of one urban area. The city is Boston.

CASE STUDY: MUSIC IN AND OF BOSTON

Why Boston?   One of the oldest North American cities, Boston provides both a long music history and exceptional musical diversity (**see "Looking Back: A Boston Retrospective"**). Music had not always been Boston's primary artistic concern. Its first preoccupation, as noted in a recent biography of the Boston composer Amy Beach, was with "the word, as taught at Harvard and as preached from Boston's pulpits."[1] Only in the nineteenth century did music flower in Boston, thanks to the thinking among upper-class Bostonians that music had the power to uplift, educate, and refine.

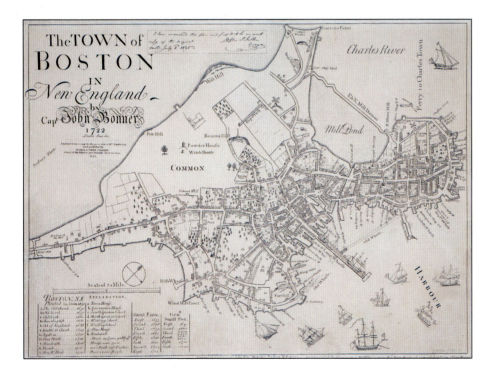

This early map of Boston shows landmarks that have not survived as well as those that still mark the landscape, including the Common, Beacon Hill, and Long Wharf.

LOOKING BACK

A Boston Retrospective

1630	English colonists from Salem, Massachusetts found the city of Boston
1636	Harvard University established by Great and General Court of the Massachusetts Bay Colony
1786	Musical Society founded in Boston (lasted only until 1789)
1790	Haitian immigrants flee to Boston as a result of revolt against French government in Haiti and set up French-speaking community
1808	Pierian Solidarity founded at Harvard as the first organization dedicated to the performance of instrumental music
1815	Handel and Haydn Society founded by a group of merchants
1832	Boston Academy of Music founded
1838	Music adopted as part of curriculum in Boston public schools
1847	Thirty-seven thousand Irish immigrants come to Boston as a result of famine
1852	Tufts University founded
	Dwight's Journal of Music appears
1861	Massachusetts Institute of Technology founded
1864	Boston College opens its doors
1867	Founding of New England Conservatory of Music, the oldest independent school of music in the United States
1869	Boston University founded
1870	Portuguese immigrants begin to arrive in Boston
1872	The great Boston fire destroys forty acres of the city
1873	John Knowles Paine becomes the first professor of music at an American university (Harvard)
1881	Boston Symphony Orchestra's inaugural concert
1885	First Music Hall Promenade Concert, inaugurating the Boston Pops as a means to provide Boston Symphony Orchestra musicians with summer employment
1900	Mass immigration of Italians to United States, with thirty-one thousand in Boston by 1910
1908	Boston Opera Company established
1929	Arthur Fiedler starts the Esplanade Concerts, a summer series held on the east bank of the Charles River
1945	Berklee College of Music founded by Lee Eliot Berk

1948	Brandeis University founded
1954	Boston Camerata founded
1958	Sara Caldwell founds the Opera Company of Boston
	Joan Baez enrolls at Boston University
	Club 47 is founded as jazz venue
1969	Club 47 reconstituted as Club Passim
1973	Boston Baroque founded as first baroque orchestra in North America
1976	Boston Lyric Opera founded
	Voice of the Turtle founded
1979	Boston Village Gamelan (Javanese) founded
	Boston Early Music Festival and Exhibition founded
1990	World Music, a nonprofit Cambridge-based organization presenting world music concerts, founded
1993	Gamelan Galak Tika, Boston area's first Balinese gamelan, founded by Evan Ziporyn of M.I.T.

Much of Boston's musical life of record in the nineteenth and early twentieth century involved an elite in close contact with England and Europe. Major musical ensembles that are still prominent, such as the Boston Symphony Orchestra, were established during this time. Understanding the background of musical life in Boston is important not just to unraveling local musical culture, but also to appreciating Boston's nineteenth-century role in making Western European music and culture prestigious throughout the rest of the United States. We can regard Boston as an important springboard for the study of local musics in North America, because it exercised so much influence on national musical life at an early date.

Boston also provides a distinctive physical setting, which in many ways underpins its musical profile. Founded in the seventeenth century, the city is bounded by the Charles River and Boston Harbor. Boston's irregular, winding, narrow streets are similar to those of an English town. We will see the importance of Boston's setting to its cultural life.[2]

The old central area of Boston, known as Beacon Hill, sits alongside the distinctive, five-sided Boston Common and Public Garden that have been the city's public heart from earliest times. Beacon Hill still retains historic cobble-stone streets lit by gaslights and is located on the only one of Boston's hills to survive; the others were leveled in the nineteenth century to provide landfill in the Charles

LISTENING GUIDE 22

ON WEB SITE

You're Hearing Boston: Alexander's Feast

This short radio clip presents a performance on a cruise boat that sailed from Boston's Long Wharf; many such musical events take advantage of Boston's scenic harbor and Charles River during the spring, summer, and fall. This performance is by Alexander's Feast, one of many ensembles that over the years have presented historical musical traditions from Europe usually referred to as *early music*. Note the sounds of the waterfront in the background.

LISTEN TO this and the eleven other brief radio shows entitled "You're Hearing Boston," scattered throughout Chapter Four, for an overview of the remarkable diversity of musical traditions in the Boston metropolitan area. Written, produced, and narrated by Jim Metzner, these shows and hundreds of others were broadcast between 1976 and 1979 on Radio WEEI-FM, Boston. As you listen to the shows (found on the Web site), be conscious that the ear alone cannot capture the setting, action, and interactions of a soundscape.

River for the section of the city referred to as Back Bay. Other distinctive neighborhoods abound within the city limits, their names not reflecting their actual geographical locations in relation to the central Commons and Public Garden: for example the South End is not south of the city, nor is the North End north!

Along with their special locales, architectural features, and landmarks, many neighborhoods are also home to different socioeconomic and ethnic groups. The

This aerial shot gives you a bird's-eye view of how the banks of the Charles River—called the Esplanade—have been transformed into a performance space. At the center is the Hatch Shell, an open-air concert site that was restored and renovated for its fiftieth birthday in 1991. Free performances such as the annual July 4 celebration by the Boston Pops (shown here) are enjoyed by thousands, some listening from boats anchored on the river. The July 4 performance features patriotic choral works, rousing marches, and a rendition of Tchaikovsky's famous 1812 overture, enhanced by bells from nearby churches and firing of howitzers.

South End is a working-class neighborhood with an increasingly multicultural mixture of peoples from all over the world; Roxbury remains primarily African American, South Boston still has a heavily Irish population, and the colonial buildings of the North End still house longtime Italian residents. Moving out from Boston proper across the river to adjacent Cambridge, we find the main center for higher education in a metropolitan area that has more institutions of higher learning than any other North American city and more students enrolled than any other place of comparable size. We will return to this very important aspect of Boston

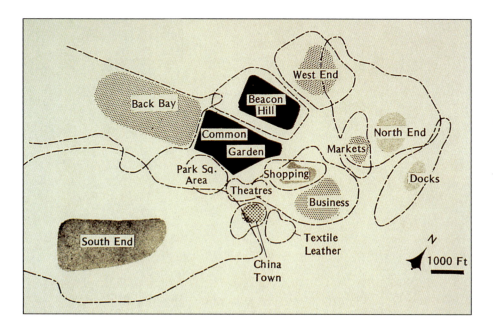

This map shows the location of the Boston Common relative to some famous Boston neighborhoods, as well as theater, shopping, and business areas.

life later. Other towns adjacent to Boston include Chelsea and Charlestown, as well as nearby Brookline and Newton, each of which has its own distinctive topography, architecture, and populations.

Boston can be divided according to political boundaries and to a lesser extent by economic and ethnic groups, but we can also map the city according to present and past locations of musical life. Some of these sites are actually inscribed on street signs; adjacent to Symphony Hall, the home of the Boston Symphony Orchestra, is Symphony Road, and nearby is Opera Place, which marks the former site of Boston's opera house.

But how can we map the musical life of the city not recorded on street signs? And how does music, in turn, map the city? In this chapter we will see how an investigation of local music can increase our understanding of what makes a particular urban landscape unique.

We can start by consulting listings of musical events and by mapping our encounters with musical performances. That will help us construct a picture of how musical life contributes to our total perception of the place in which we live. It's easy to start by raising and answering a series of questions about music in the city: what makes up musical life, where is music performed, when is music heard, who makes music, and why?

With its relatively compact size and many winding, narrow streets, Boston can best be experienced on foot, guided by this walking map with city topography included.

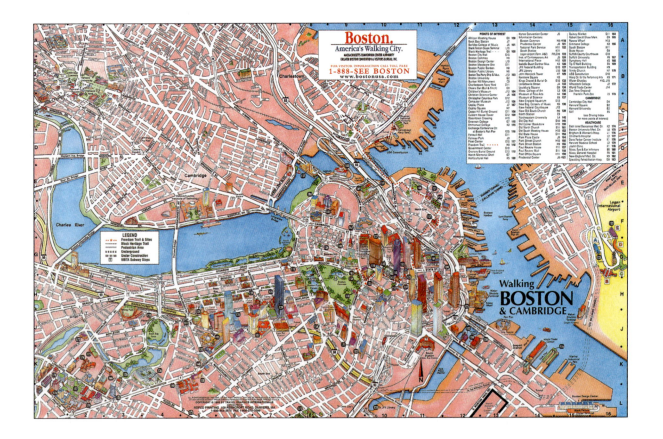

Musical Life in Boston

A select and very limited compendium, from the Boston Sunday *Globe*, 1995–1999, "Fall Arts Previews." Lists of this type almost never can be complete.

Folk, World, Country
Includes subdivision "Coffeehouses"

Jazz and Cabaret

Night Spots (by town)

Dance

Classical
Includes subdivisions "Orchestral," "Choral," "Opera," "Chamber Music and Recitals," "Performance Art and New Music," "Auditions," "Open Rehearsals"

Museums

Early Music

Churches and Organs

What Elements Make Up Boston's Musical Life?

We can get an initial overview of musical life in virtually any city, although often narrowly selective, through a quick look at listings in the weekly arts section of a major metropolitan newspaper. The *Boston Globe,* which has covered musical events since its founding in March 1872, is a good place to start in mapping present-day musical Boston. The main headings and some of their typical sublistings are summarized above. We need to look not just at what musical events are included, but at the manner in which they are organized and presented.

Note that events are classified not just according to conventional musical categories (*classical, folk/world/country*), but also by type of *ensembles* (large or small, voices, instruments, or both), mode of presentation (whether as a single event or as part of a series), and places of presentation (night spots, museums, and libraries). The listings are heavily weighted toward what would generally be termed "Western" musical styles, compressing folk/world/country music into a single category (see "Studying Music: Terms and Categories"). Reading about Boston's musical life in the *Globe,* we might conclude that Euro-American styles predominate. An alert reader unfamiliar with the city might raise an eyebrow at one special category of musical life in Boston we've already encountered in Listening

Guide 22 and to which we will shortly return: the complex soundscape of "early music."

For the student, newspaper listings provide only a limited map of Boston's active musical scene. Many of the events included are formally organized by

STUDYING MUSIC

Terms and Categories

Talking about music is a complicated matter, because many terms in common usage reveal problems on closer examination. Any one term—*folk music, vernacular music, traditional music*—gets its meaning mainly in relation to other terms. For example, we speak of folk versus classical, vernacular versus art, traditional versus popular and so on. Yet the boundaries that we construct with these terms are not always so strict in reality.

We can take the category of folk music as an example. In the American folk music revival and its soundscape cluster, the concept of *folk song* has a clear and unambiguous meaning with which everyone is familiar. But it can be very difficult to classify any given song as a folk song outside this context. Even *The M.T.A. Song* (discussed below), which emerged from a grass-roots effort to support a local candidate and which borrowed an older melody for these purposes, quickly moved from local oral tradition to national and international popularity through recordings and publicity in the mass media. As we will see, early music performers borrow pieces and performance styles from folk, classical, and even popular music.

Another longtime practice is to classify music according to its place of origin. However, this has also proven increasingly difficult in recent decades because individuals and groups move so frequently and because soundscapes within and between locales interact. Although we can often trace a given soundscape to a single place at a given time, most musical traditions arise from many sources and are constantly influenced over the course of their transmission and performance. Ultimately, the meaning that the musicians give to the music they make determines its category—as we have seen in the case study on "Vietnamese" music in Chapter 3.

For several decades, most ethnomusicologists (and record stores) have used the expression *world music* to refer to cross-cultural musical traditions. "World music" and the similar but more negative label "non-Western music" have mainly been used in opposition to "Western music" to refer to musical traditions that originated in different places around the globe. During the last decade or so, *world music* has taken on new layers of meaning and now includes cross-cultural popular music. Many people—from researchers to musicians—have begun to believe that calling something "world music" implies that it is something exotic, somehow not relevant to our everyday lives. In a 1999 article in the *New York Times*, the musician David Byrne wrote that he hates the term *world music* because "it groups everything that isn't 'us' into 'them'." *World music* has now become as ambiguous and problematic as any of the other terms.

    A closer look at just about any soundscape will likely turn up a range of characteristics that fly in the face of all of these conventional categories, as well as others we have not yet explored. Here we will try to minimize the use of misleading terms and the categories they imply. Instead, we will use the names of music styles— *khoomii, fado, gong kebyar, early music, folk music*—as people within the soundscapes themselves commonly use these names. We will try to work against the tyranny of old terms and categories by including the broadest range of musics, juxtaposing those not often treated together in the past.

LISTENING GUIDE 23

ON WEB SITE

You're Hearing Boston: Royal Dancers and Musicians of Bhutan

    Many of Boston's art museums host musical programs that are linked to their holdings and serve to attract visitors. This performance took place at the Museum of Fine Arts, which houses a fine collection of Asian art and artifacts and hosts musical events that are designed to bring the art "to life."

LISTEN TO an excerpt of music played to accompany Buddhist dances from Bhutan presented by a visiting troupe on their first American tour.

LISTENING GUIDE 24

ON WEB SITE

You're Hearing Boston: Boston Globe Jazz Festival

GEORGE SHEARING in performance and conversation

The annual *Boston Globe* Jazz and Blues Festival began in the 1960s and remains a highlight of Boston's musical life each summer.

LISTEN TO the jazz pianist George Shearing performing and commenting on Boston's similarities to his native London.

Robert Cray, recently nominated for his eleventh Grammy award, in performance with the Robert Cray Band as the closing act of the Boston Globe Jazz Festival in July 2000.

established ensembles or institutions that charge admission. Free and public events are not heavily represented, with the exception of major festivals, which tend to be highlighted. We therefore must search beyond newspaper listings to uncover the extraordinary range of music available on a regular basis in Boston. We need to ask where else we should look.

Where Is Music Performed?   Many soundscapes are rooted in and associated with particular places. For example, the Boston Symphony Orchestra performs at its majestic Symphony Hall, at the corner of Huntington Street and Massachusetts Avenue. Boston has many other well-known performance spaces, most of which serve not only their own resident ensembles—such as the New England Conservatory's Jordan Hall—but are also rented out regularly to a variety of other performance groups. Symphony Hall is host to a wide variety of musical events, particularly during the winter. Other large performance spaces, such as the Wang Center, which is the home of the Boston Ballet, also showcase major musical road shows and other traveling musical offerings.

Symphony Hall, the home of the Boston Symphony Orchestra, opened in 1900 and will celebrate its centennial during the 2000–2001 season. Note the organ pipes mounted on the wall behind the orchestra, with the organ console on the lower left-hand corner of the stage.

Boston churches sponsor a great deal of musical activity. Many Bostonians attend these services to hear, for example, the professional choir at the venerable Church of the Advent (established in 1844) and the renowned weekly performance of famous choral works by Johann Sebastian Bach (1685-1750), the Cantatas, at Emmanuel Church. Other houses of worship lend their facilities and sponsorship to appropriate musical ensembles outside the context of religious

LISTENING GUIDE 25

ON WEB SITE

You're Hearing Boston: **Russian Orthodox service**

Holy Trinity Russian Orthodox Church sustains a tradition of chant performed in old Church Slavonic and English.

LISTEN TO the blend of voices in close harmony singing a wedding song from the Republic of Georgia.

LISTENING GUIDE 26

ON
WEB
SITE

You're Hearing Boston: **Street Music**

Walk through almost any outdoor public area in Boston
during the warm-weather months and you will encounter
musicians. The sidewalks of Boston and neighboring towns
provide an energetic backdrop for a variety of performances
by street musicians (called by the old English term *buskers*).
These musicians perform around town, most by special
permit, attracting audiences and garnering donations from
passersby.

LISTEN TO this sampler of street musicians, including a brass
ensemble on Newbury Street, Jo-Jo the monkey at Quincy
Market, and a band in Harvard Square.

observances. For instance, the First Congregational Church in Cambridge hosts
the medieval music ensemble Tapestry in an ongoing residency.

Different soundscapes not only transform the interiors of buildings through
changing sounds and rearrangement of space; they transform city streets as well.

Among the places that always have performers, Harvard Square on Cambridge

*The presence of so many
musicians performing in
Harvard Square provides
rich material for humor!*

is one of the liveliest. There a wide variety of buskers ply their trade, including folk singers, accordion players, rock groups, Latin ensembles, and West African musicians, most of whom also sell recordings of their performances to onlookers.

City streets also provide a venue for special music events that are inevitably part of parades and festivals. The music offered by each event is similar to that found in any large American city, but a close look also gives insights into the musical preferences of Boston-area residents. At the annual Central Square World's Fair in Cambridge each June, Massachusetts Avenue and the side streets that cross it are closed down.

Underground transportation systems provide sheltered performance spaces for buskers, rain or shine. Here Felix (left) and Claudio Silva perform in the Harvard Square T station. Note the large panpipe mounted on a stand so that Claudio can play it and the guitar at the same time.

LISTENING GUIDE 27

CD 1
TRACK
25

Sikuri (traditional Peruvian melody)

PERFORMED BY Wayno (Nazca)

Various music groups from the South American Andes have also played in "the Square." Three brothers from Ecuador who make up the ensemble Yarina often appear. Since the late 1990s, the northern Peruvian group Wayno (also known as Nazca) has regularly stood outside the entrance to the Harvard Cooperative Society building (known as the "Harvard Coop").

LISTEN as the group of panpipes (*sikus*), flute, and drum (*bombas*) play a traditional melody with harmony.

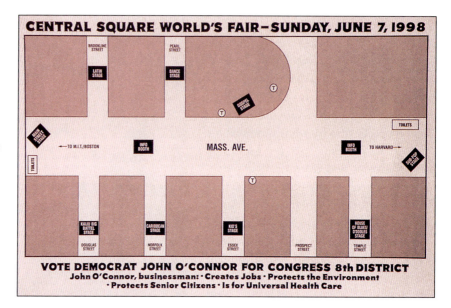

This "map" of the Central Square World's Fair was widely distributed as part of a program that provided performance schedules. Note the political advertisement at the bottom.

"Mass Ave," as it is known, accommodates booths with ethnic foods and souvenirs for sale. The main street stage houses jazz and rock performances, and on the side streets one finds a range of styles: a Latin stage (salsa, *punk mambo*, Cuban *son*), a gospel stage, a sub-pop stage (acoustic rock, country, ragtime), a Caribbean stage (reggae, soca, ska/reggae), a House of Blues stage, and a dance stage (German folk dance, ballet, modern dance, West African dance, tango).

Even the stately old Boston Common and Public Garden are transformed through musical performance on special occasions. Most noteworthy is the annual "First Night" celebration held every New Year's Eve since the early 1980s. Boston hosted the original First Night celebration in the United States, an event that has now spread to many other American cities. Boston's First Night features performances and exhibitions by over one thousand musical groups and artists. Throughout the day and evening, the open Common and the surrounding area are transformed into a variety of performance spaces. In the side-by-side performance of so many musical traditions and the transformation of the entire city center for the event, we encounter a common urban practice in which people reimagine local spaces, for a period of time, as landscapes of performance.

First Night features so many simultaneous events that participants must keep the multipage program close at hand.

LISTENING GUIDE 28

ON
WEB
SITE

You're Hearing Boston: First Night

PERFORMANCE BY The Pernucio Ensemble

In this example, we get an overview of the many musical dimensions of Boston's First Night. Here a musical/ cultural event has a social purpose: to weld Greater Boston into a "family" on New Year's Eve.

LISTEN TO sounds of the eighteenth century, featuring a harpsichord—an early keyboard instrument—and strings.

LISTENING GUIDE 29

ON
WEB
SITE

You're Hearing Boston: Christmas Tree Lighting

The annual lighting of the Christmas tree at Boston's Prudential Center is a beloved civic ritual and includes the singing of Christmas carols—such as "Deck the Halls"—and the sound of bagpipes.

Once again, LISTEN FOR the sounds of people and place that mix with the music.

When Does Music Making Take Place?   Just about any occasion can be—and usually is—celebrated by a musical event, each performance providing entry into a soundscape. Music often marks the beginning and end of civic ceremonial gatherings, highlighting the shared nature of the day.

Communal events link a special occasion to a familiar city space; music makes the occasion even more memorable. These local ceremonies, repeated with variations in many American cities at Christmastime, celebrate connections: here, between members of the larger Boston community and with the Nova Scotians who supplied the spruce tree for the occasion.

Girls from the Hellenic American School in Lowell, Massachusetts, perform a traditional dance in celebration of Greek Independence Day (in 1821, from the Ottoman empire) at Boston City Hall Plaza. Eighty-five thousand people attended the parade, including the mayors of Athens and several other Greek cities.

Who Makes the Music?   In multiethnic North America, almost any city or town has some measure of cultural diversity. Boston is home to a full range of ethnic communities. Some groups arrived in New England at early dates and have helped build the city into its present form. Others have come more recently.

The residents of any city must adapt to overlapping calendars that mark important occasions of different religious, national, and personal cycles. Boston, like most other metropolitan areas, must incorporate these events into the rhythm of city life. As the area's population has diversified, marking days important to different communities has become an increasingly important part of the shared civic calendar. These occasions often include musical events. Many take place at Boston's Government Center, a complex that includes Boston City Hall. Government Center was previously known as Scollay Square—the site of the famous Lighthouse Pub patronized by President John F. Kennedy during his student days, as well as other landmarks mentioned in the "M.T.A. Song," discussed below. The large and simple concrete plaza in front of City Hall was intended to be multifunctional and spacious enough to accommodate many kinds of ethnic celebrations.

ETHIOPIANS

One such event is the annual celebration of the Ethiopian new year, which occurs in September. In addition to special ceremonies in Ethiopian churches in the area, members of the Ethiopian community organize a gala party and feast at City Hall (**see "Snapshot: Ethiopian New Year at Boston City Hall"**).

Hagerei ("My Homeland"; Ethiopian song)

PERFORMED BY Ephrem Tamiru

Many immigrants use song to express memories of their native lands. *Hagerei* ("My Homeland"), popular among Ethiopian immigrants throughout North America, is sung here by Ephrem Tamiru, a favored Ethiopian singer now living in the United States. You will hear features of the Ethiopian highland vocal style: a rather nasal quality and many ornaments. This song is based on the traditional *tizita*, a pentatonic scale and melody that Ethiopians associate with songs of longing.

LISTEN TO the brief *vocalise*, a wordless introduction, by Ephrem at the beginning of the song. In addition to its Ethiopian heritage and subject matter, *Hagerei* reflects the influence of international popular music in its instrumental accompaniment and use of Western harmony. "Thirteen months of sunshine" includes a five-day thirteenth month in the Ethiopian calendar.

Ah . . .
From earth to heaven, how are you, my land?
All the surroundings and the neighborhood?
How are you, the country of my birth?
The land I miss all the time, from afar.
I will steal away and leave from far.
I cannot bear it, things of my land.
Time renews memories continuously.
I miss you, land of a people.

Ah . . .
Memories of my father,
The queen of the sea,
Land of thirteen months of sunshine,
I am unable to detach.
Natural beauty, graced by God,
A country of flowers, Ethiopia.

Across the sea, my country
Pain came with separation,
A wound to my tears.
I cannot come guided by a rainbow,
You are in my thought, year after year.

The aroma of herbs,
The trunk of the trees,
The comfort of the grass,
[words unclear]
In a foreign land is the sickness of man.

From earth to heaven . . . [*repeat 8 lines*]
                    —Translation by Meley Mulugetta

SNAPSHOT

Ethiopian New Year at City Hall

Boston City Hall at Government Center was open and brightly lit at 8:30 P.M. one Saturday evening in September 1997, for a celebration of the Ethiopian New Year. Hundreds of men and women, many festively attired in the traditional white Ethiopian *shamma*, crowded the massive, bilevel brick and stone atrium. To the left of the entry was a large bar area, where young men dispensed beer and soft drinks, and where cassette tapes and CDs of Ethiopian music were displayed for sale on the counter. Through adjacent double doors were tables filled with an array of covered dishes containing spicy Ethiopian stews, alongside trays piled high with *injera*, the flat, pancake-like Ethiopian bread.

Two large loudspeakers, standing at the bottom of the imposing staircase that led to the upper level of the atrium, were connected by cables to microphones placed on a spacious landing midway up the elevation. Shortly after 9:00 P.M., the singer Tsehay Yohannes climbed the stairs and joined a synthesizer player and bassist already in place. Dressed in an elegant *shamma* with a border of red, yellow, and green stripes (the colors of the Ethiopian flag), Tsehay began to sing arrangements of traditional folk songs in Amharic, the Ethiopian language. The pounding beat of the synthesizer's rhythm track encouraged people to dance, and all empty floor space was soon filled with couples performing both Western dance styles and the rousing Ethiopian shoulder dance, *esskesta*. The party continued until just before midnight, when, obeying a municipal ordinance, the building closed down, and people rushed off to catch the last evening buses and underground trains that took them to their homes throughout the metropolitan area.

IRISH

Irish immigrants began to arrive in New England during the eighteenth century, with their numbers increasing in the mid-nineteenth century because of hardships in Ireland, such as the great potato famine of the late 1840s. It is estimated that four million Irish arrived in the United States from 1820 to 1900 alone. Musical life in Boston reflects the Irish presence, in part, through the perpetuation of traditional Irish fiddling in pubs and the ubiquitous sound of bagpipes at many civic and cultural events.

You're Hearing Boston: St. Patrick's Ireland

Annual activities such as Boston College's Gaelic Roots summer festival (which teaches Irish music, song, and dance) have helped make Boston the "Irish capital of the United States." Home to one of the great concentrations of people of Irish descent, Boston is an important center for Irish-American cultural life, with major resources on Irish-American history, genealogy, and culture at the Boston Public Library and the Burns Library of Boston College.

LISTEN TO this excerpt from a musical program at Boston's World Affairs Council celebrating St. Patrick's day, featuring fiddling and drum.

Not surprisingly, Boston and its Irish inhabitants have also been the subject of songs composed and transmitted within the community. "The Ballad of Buddy McClean" (Listening Guide 32) is one such example in the tradition of the popular Irish ballad that commemorates important events and memorable individuals; it is also an anthem for Irish freedom. Many Irish ballads are openly political in their subject matter, providing a focal point for patriotic sentiments on important anniversaries of Irish history and longtime Irish resistance to English rule.

This sign in Gaelic ("Welcome to South Boston") is painted on a Dorchester Avenue building in South Boston.

The Ballad of Buddy McClean (Irish-American ballad)

COMPOSED BY John Hurley

PERFORMED BY Derek Warfield

The composer of this ballad, John Hurley, was a descendant of Irish immigrants to Boston. He composed the song to commemorate fellow longshoreman Buddy McClean, who was murdered after he resisted an effort by organized crime to take over the Boston dock workers' unions in the 1950s and 1960s. The text of the song links the resistance of Buddy McClean to compatriots in Ireland who fought for their own independence at various times in the past. This ballad is traditional in its strophic form, with a refrain recurring between verses.

LISTEN TO the vocal style and guitar accompaniment, which reflect the influence of the American folk music revival, a soundscape we will discuss later.

I'll sing you a song of the deeds that were done,
Of the struggles of conflict and tears,
Of men on the run who fought against guns,
That brought the community fear.
You never wanted the title of hero, sought fame or great power or acclaim.
You had no wealth or might but you knew wrong from right,
And your fight for justice was clear.

Refrain:
Sing away hills of Boston with the spirit of Buddy McClean.
The longshoremans' teamsters are talking of their hero now Buddy McClean.
What greater deed can a man do than to lay down his life for his friends?
Winter Hill tells the tale of a strong Irish gale who was loyal was pure and was true.

Those mobsters of crime said the good would be dying,
If you did not submit to their ways.
That the fit would be lame if you'd not play their game,
And your friends would know more happy days.
Men of liberty, freedom and courage believed that your stand it was true.
And the unions you saved for the homes of the brave and were joined by the faithful and few.
   Refrain: Sing away hills of Boston . . .

The Irish McCleans would kneel to no Queen.
They were proud of the old sod of green.
You were Buddy to all and you answered the call, on the waterfront you were the king.
Strong faith and hard work for a living for your wife and your family and home.
And you bowed to no one whether gangster or gun, and worked for the American dream.
   Refrain: Sing away hills of Boston . . .

You lived by the book and you hated them crooks, with their torture the neighborhood ruled.
And the truckers you saved and no riff raff you paid, and the gangsters were beaten and fooled.
You never lost at boxing or fighting, and when some didn't like it they ran.
Every town, every lane, the champion of fame was an Irish-American man.
   Refrain: Sing away hills of Boston . . .

With a hundred men dead, and the fear
And the dread went through every town, every hill.
Every action and tear though silent the cheer,
And your courage they talk of it still.
Men of all creeds and all countries, helped you see the battle right through.
Father Hogan your friend, was with you till the end, that justice depended on you.
   Refrain: Sing away hills of Boston . . .

Senior citizens from the Cape Verdean community perform traditional songs and dances as part of the ensemble Pilon Cola, named after the cola *(literally, "tail") dance that is performed around a pilon, the large wooden pestle shown here, which is used as both a corn grinder and drum. Many Cape Verdeans, who came from an archipelago off the West African coast (under Portuguese rule until it gained its independence in 1970), have lived in New England since the mid-nineteenth century.*

PORTUGUESE

The Portuguese are another community prominent in Boston. They were in fact among the earliest settlers in New England, although large numbers of Portuguese have also settled in New Bedford and Cambridge, Massachusetts, since the mid-twentieth century. These expatriate Portuguese communities consist mainly of immigrants from Portugal, the Cape Verde Islands, and the Azores.

A musical form popular among many Portuguese immigrants is the *fado*, a song closely associated with the Portuguese capital Lisbon and with the nightclubs where it was traditionally performed. *Fado*, which means "fate," gives voice to nostalgia for the country and the lovers left behind. (In its expression of longing for country, the *fado* is quite similar to the Ethiopian song *"Hagerei,"* despite its different origin and contrasting musical style.) The *fado* is said to have originated among Portuguese sailors who spent long periods of time away from home, but its most congenial modern setting has been in urban clubs and restaurants. Today Portuguese-Americans hear the *fado* largely through recordings imported from Portugal.

OTHER GROUPS

Immigrants from other places are more recent arrivals in Boston, drawn there by opportunities in business and education. With the arrival of a large Japanese community, Japanese shopping centers, bookstores, and restaurants have prolif-

The ensemble Kokoo performs an afternoon of shakuhachi *and* koto *music at Saint Paul's Church in Brookline in 1998, part of an annual concert series sponsored by the Consulate General of Japan in Boston and the Japanese Association of Greater Boston. The instruments, from left to right, include two* koto *(zithers with twenty strings and thirteen strings, respectively) and* shakuhachi, *bamboo flutes.*

LISTENING GUIDE 33

CD 1
TRACK
28

Fado Lisboeta (Portuguese ballad)

COMPOSED BY C. Dias and A. Do Vale

PERFORMED BY Amália Rodrigues, accompanied by Jaime Santos (guitar), Domingo Camarinha (guitar), and Santos Moreira (violin)

The late singer Amália Rodrigues was one of the foremost interpreters of the fado in twentieth-century Portugal. Born around 1920, she made her first recording in 1945. Her rendition of "Fado Lisboeta" is a classic that is widely distributed and played among Portuguese in the United States.

LISTEN TO how the song text sets a scene in urban Portugal.

Don't hold it against one who sings when a voice wells up in challenge, because his pain is not so great when confessed to a guitar. He who sings always retreats in the ashen hours of his suffering, and the cross he bears doesn't feel so heavy on the long road of misfortune.

Refrain:
I only feel *fado*, plaintive and sorrowful, while I sob quietly in the night. It touches my heart, so pained and as cold as the snow on the road, that weeps with longing or sings the yearning of one who has wept for love. They'll say that this is fateful, that it's only natural, but this is Lisbon, this is *fado*.

I hear the strumming of guitars and voices singing in the gloomy streets, as the lights go out announcing the break of day. Silently, I close the window, sounds of tenderness may be heard in the alleyway, the morning unfolds fresh and tranquil, only in my soul is it darkest night.

Refrain:
I only feel *fado*, plaintive and sorrowful, while I sob quietly in the night. It touches my heart, so pained and as cold as the snow on the road; that weeps with longing or sings the yearning of one who has wept for love. They'll say that this is fateful, that it's only natural, but this is Lisbon, this is *fado*.

—Translation by Nicola Trowbridge Cooney

LISTENING GUIDE 37

Taruna Jaya (composition for Balinese gamelan)

PERFORMED BY Gamelan Galak Tika

This recording of the Balinese gamelan based at the Massachusetts Institute of Technology presents a composition by the Balinese composer I Gde Manik titled *Taruna Jaya* ("Victorious Youth"). The music is a modern dance intended to convey the moods of youth on the verge of adulthood.

LISTEN TO the distinctive sound of *gamelan gong kebyar,* the Balinese gamelan most often heard in modern concerts. Particularly characteristic are the fast, interlocking parts (termed *kotekan*) played by two higher-pitched instruments. These two parts are played so quickly that they literally "interlock" and give the impression of being a single melody. The *kotekan* contrast with the somewhat slower melodies played below—and the deeper gong beats that mark off the regular rhythmic cycle.

SOUND SOURCES

The Balinese Gamelan

The gamelan, the main instrumental ensemble of Indonesia, includes instruments made mainly of bronze, wood, and bamboo. Most closely associated with the gamelan and the source of its distinctive sound quality are the large number of gongs and xylophone-type instruments made of bronze. Gamelan ensembles also include drums, flutes, and a bowed stringed instrument. There are two main Indonesian gamelan traditions, which arose on the islands of Java and Bali. They are closely related but are distinguished from each other by slightly different instruments, tunings, and playing techniques.

Although the metal-working technologies necessary for making musical instruments were established in Southeast Asia early in the first centuries of the common era, the history of the Balinese gamelan can be traced more clearly from the early sixteenth century, when members of the Javanese court and its musicians fled to Bali. Over the next several centuries, the Balinese gamelan developed and spread well beyond the court to Hindu temples and to villages across the island. Used in a variety of religious and secular ceremonies, as well as in musical theater, the Balinese gamelan became a pervasive presence in ceremonies and everyday life. In recent decades, the gamelan has been taught in music conservatories and has played an increasingly important role in the Balinese tourist industry as well.

Balinese gamelan music is organized according to rhythmic cycles, with the large gong sounding at a point that is simultaneously the end of one cycle and the beginning of the next. It has been suggested that this cyclic way of organizing musical time may reflect both the importance of reincarnation in Hindu belief and natural harvest cycles. Some instruments mark various parts of the rhythmic cycle, while others play a core melody or variations on it.[3] The complex, many-voiced texture that results from these layers of different rhythms and melodies is, as we have noted in Chapter Three, called polyphony.

Balinese gamelan music does not have a universal standard of pitch. However, the instruments of a gamelan are tuned to each other, lending each ensemble a distinctive sound quality. There are two main tuning systems, one utilizing seven tones and the other five tones, with the precise intervals between the tones varying slightly from one gamelan to the next. One of the most interesting and distinctive aspects of the Balinese gamelan is the use of the acoustical phenomenon called "beating tones," a type of shimmering sound that occurs when two of the same instruments are tuned not exactly in unison, but at slightly different frequencies.

Although apprenticeship with a master player remains the traditional way of learning the art of gamelan, professional instruction is now also available in Balinese music conservatories. Over the last thirty-five years or so the gamelan has built up a strong international presence, due in part to the support of universities in North America, Europe,

Members of Gamelan Galak Tika rehearsing on the steps of MIT's Kresge Auditorium, Cambridge, Massachusetts, 1995. Musicians include (left to right): Anne Rasmussen (back row), Jean Moncrieff, John Keith, Scott Davis, and Evan Ziporyn.

Australia, and East Asia. University programs worldwide now teach, perform, and promote the gamelan.

Today more than seventy-five Indonesian gamelan ensembles of various types are active in North America. Although the instruments in most of these ensembles have been imported directly from Indonesia, others have been manufactured or even reinvented and transformed in North America. Composers, too, have been attracted to the gamelan sound, some inspired by the experience of Colin McPhee, an American composer who lived in Bali in the years before World War II, and who wrote two books about the gamelan and his personal experience in Bali. More recently, composers such as Evan Ziporyn, founder and director of M.I.T.'s Galak Tika Balinese gamelan, have incorporated Western instruments such as electric guitars and keyboards into their compositions for gamelan. We will hear Ziporyn's work *Kekembangan* for gamelan and saxophones in Chapter 10.

Boston singer-songwriters and musicians perform songs that have been transmitted mainly by oral tradition, reflecting the concerns of everyday life. Drawing on—and transforming—an enormous stock of music from many ethnic communities, the American folk music revival had its artistic roots in the "beatnik" phenomenon of the 1950s, centered in the famous alternative lifestyles and artistic culture of New York City's Greenwich Village. With the increasing momentum of the civil rights movement in the 1950s, followed by the anti–Vietnam war initiative of the 1960s and the simultaneous flowering of the youth movement known as the counterculture, the folk-song revival became linked to broader political issues of that period. A watershed event was the civil rights march on Washington held on August 28, 1963, where Joan Baez, Bob Dylan, the group Peter, Paul and Mary and other folk singers performed, implanting songs such as "Blowin' in the Wind" and

In addition to staging concerts and running a cafe, the present Club Passim sponsors educational activities for children and has an archive project to document its own history. In this shot, we see (left to right) Rob Laurens, Lori McKenna, Mary Gauthier, and Jacinta Whitcome performing at Passim.

"If I Had a Hammer" into national and international consciousness. The independence movement in African colonies during these same years and the growing outcry against apartheid in South Africa brought new international musical sensitivities and influences.

With a healthy folk-music scene established even before Joan Baez entered Boston University in 1958 (see "**Individual Portrait: Joan Baez**"), by 1960

INDIVIDUAL PORTRAIT

Joan Baez

Joan Baez was born in Staten Island, New York on January 9, 1941 to a Scottish mother and a Mexican father, both pacifists who took their children with them to Quaker meetings. A minister, research physicist, and consultant to UNESCO, Baez's father eventually took the family to Boston. At fourteen, Baez began her musical career, accompanying herself on the ukulele (**see Chapter 10, "Sound Sources: The Ukulele"**) singing rhythm and blues songs such as *Earth Angel* and country and western songs such as *Your Cheatin' Heart*. One semester after entering Boston University in 1958, Baez took a job at Club 47—later named Club Passim—and played to standing-room-only crowds who came to hear her "crystal-voiced" renditions of old English and Irish ballads. Performing in coffeehouses and colleges along the East Coast, she soon became the "poster girl for folk," making her national debut at the Newport Jazz Festival in 1959. Her performance was released by Vanguard Records in 1960 on an album titled simply *Joan Baez*. The festival also saw the start of her long working relationship with folk singer/composer Bob Dylan, also then a newcomer. Baez asserts that it was Dylan who turned her into a political folk singer. At the August 28, 1963, March on Washington, Baez sang what was to become the theme song for the civil rights movement, *We Shall Overcome*. In 1965, she cofounded the Institute for the Study of Nonviolence in Carmel, California, and, in 1967, put her principles to the test: she was arrested for blocking the entrance to the Armed Forces Induction Center in Oakland, California. In December of the same year she spent time in jail for civil disobedience relating to protests against the Vietnam war.

On November 23, 1962, Joan Baez was featured on the cover of Time *magazine.*

Over thirty albums and countless performances later, Joan Baez is still waging her protest against violence. Her dedication to equality and human rights has been widely celebrated and she has received many honors, including the Legion of Honor from the French government.

LISTENING GUIDE 38

CD 2
TRACKS
2–3

Wimoweh (South African *mbube*)

PERFORMED BY Solomon Linda's Original Evening Birds

PERFORMED BY the Weavers

The music of South African migrant workers, called *mbube*, was widely distributed through recordings in the 1930s. American folk groups such as the Weavers heard these recordings and made new arrangements of these songs with English texts and guitar accompaniment.

LISTEN FOR *mbube's* prominent use of a high, male head voice called *falsetto* in cross-cultural terminology, as well as Western-style harmony borrowed from Western hymns and jazz. Compare the South African song with its American transformation.

Boston had become the country's number one folk scene. Today, an estimated two hundred or more places for live folk music performance remain in the metropolitan area. Among the historic sites for folk music performance is Club Passim, the successor to Club 47, which was originally located at 47 Palmer Street in the center of Harvard Square. New clubs are always coming on the scene, such as Irish pubs like Tir na Nog and the Burren, both of which accommodate newer kinds of contemporary and "roots" folk, which draws on a range of American styles from Appalachian fiddling to gospel. The annual Boston Folk Music Festival also provides important public exposure for hundreds of singer-songwriters.

The accessible sounds of folk music allow almost anyone to hear a song and sing along. Folk music performances almost always include the audience, which is invited to sing along on the well-known refrains of songs. With its straightforward styles and congenial settings, folk music was and is attached to a variety of political causes. Mary Travers of the group Peter, Paul and Mary recalled the social and

The Weavers, who attained international fame in the folk music movement, were caught up in the political turmoil of 1952 when they were among the many artists accused of being Communists and blacklisted. The group included (left to right): Pete Seeger, Fred Hellerman, Lee Hays, and Ronnie Gilbert.

political associations of folk music from her early days in New York City, where "folk music was a very integral part of the liberal Left experience. . . . It was writers, sculptors, painters, whatever, listening to Woody Guthrie, Pete Seeger, the Weavers. People sang in Washington Square Park [the "heart" of Greenwich Village] on Sundays, and you really did not have to have a lot of talent to sing folk music. You needed enthusiasm, which is all folk music asks. It asks that you care. . . . So for me it was a social mechanism. . . ."

The folk music movement also quickly put down roots in Boston, and the city itself is memorialized in one of the folk revival's most famous songs. The *M.T.A. Song*—referring to Boston's Metropolitan Transit Authority—was written for the political campaign of Walter A. O'Brien, Jr., a candidate in Boston's 1949 mayoral race. O'Brien did not win the election—indeed, he finished last—but his catchy campaign song was widely sung by folk musicians and eventually made famous through recordings, radio, and concerts.

The story behind the *M.T.A. Song* is worth recounting here. Candidate O'Brien had objected to a five-cent raise in the Boston M.T.A. fare. Beth Lomax Hawes and Jacqueline Steiner, the campaign workers credited with composing the *M.T.A. Song*, borrowed a well-known melody (taken from an earlier folk song titled *The Wreck of the '97*) and gave it new, campaign-related words. The process of composing a new song by borrowing an existing melody and providing it with new words is found worldwide, and is particularly common in oral traditions.

During O'Brien's campaign, the *M.T.A. Song* was broadcast by sound trucks that traveled through Boston neighborhoods to advertise the campaign. According to a reminiscence by Sam Berman, a musician active in the campaign, "In those

The M.T.A. Song (American folk song)

PERFORMED BY the Kingston Trio

LYRICS BY Jacqueline Steiner and Bess Lomax Hawes

In this song, which began in Boston election politics in the early 1950s, O'Brien's first name was changed from Walter to George to avoid any association with his Progressive party. Charlie, the luckless subway rider, paid his only dime to board the M.T.A. but, because he lacked another nickel due upon exiting, could not get off the train. The song was popularized through the national media.

LISTEN TO the catchy refrain and simple *strophic* form, which ensure that most people who hear the song once or twice can sing along.

Spoken:

These are the times that try men's souls. In the course of our nation's history, the people of Boston have rallied bravely whenever the rights of men have been threatened. Today, a new crisis has arisen. The Metropolitan Transit Authority, better known as the M.T.A., is attempting to levy a burdensome tax on the population in the form of a subway fare increase. Citizens, hear me out: this could happen to you.

Well, let me tell you a story of a man named Charlie
On a tragic and fateful day.
He put ten cents in his pocket, kissed his wife and
family,
Went to ride on the M.T.A.

Refrain:
Well, did he ever return?
No, he never returned,
And his fate is still unlearned.
He may ride forever 'neath the streets of Boston,
He's the man who never returned.

Charlie handed in his dime at the Kendall Square
station,
And he changed for Jamaica Plain.
When he got there, the conductor told him one more
nickel,
Charlie couldn't get off the train.
Refrain

Now all night long Charlie rides through the station,
Cryin', "What will become of me?
How can I afford to see my sister in Chelsea,
Or my cousin in Roxbury?"
Refrain

Charlie's wife goes down to the Scollay Square station
Every day at quarter past two;
And through the open window, she hands Charlie a
sandwich
As the train comes rumblin' through!
Refrain

Now, ye citizens of Boston! Don't you think it's a
scandal,
How the people have to pay and pay?
Fight the fare increase! Vote for George O'Brien!
Get poor Charlie off the M.T.A.!
Refrain

days, political campaigns culminated at a deli-
catessen in Dorchester, and different campaigns
used to try and drown each other out with their
sound trucks."

The words of the *M.T.A. Song* map Boston from
the perspective of the subway that runs beneath its
streets, describing areas of the city that no longer
exist. For instance, Scollay Square, mentioned
above, was razed in 1963 to accommodate Boston's
Government Center.

EARLY MUSIC

The third Boston soundscape cluster is the lively
world of early music activities and performance, a
movement in which musicians play repertoires of
the European past on reconstructed instruments,
striving to make their performances historically "au-
thentic." Well known for their activities on the Boston early music scene are, to
name just a few, the Boston Camerata, the Boston Baroque, the Handel and
Haydn Society, the Boston Museum Trio, Tapestry, and the King's Noyse. The
early music soundscape cluster also includes instrument makers, a biennial festival (the Boston Early Music Festival, which takes place every other June), and an
ongoing concert series that links up with other musical domains, including area
churches.

The early music movement draws on music of the historical past, but we have
only verbal descriptions of how it was performed at the time of its creation.
Therefore any performance of this music is subject to the players' research and
interpretation of the musical notation that survives. Yet the "otherness" of the
past both motivates and attracts
performers and audiences, who
revel in productions of works that
"you read about in history books
but never hear."[4] But however
carefully performers may reconstruct what early music sounded
like, inevitably their (and our)
twenty-first-century ideas and perceptions will influence any performance (see Listening Guide 40).

The roots of early music in
Boston go back to the turn of the
twentieth century, when individuals who undertook to reconstruct

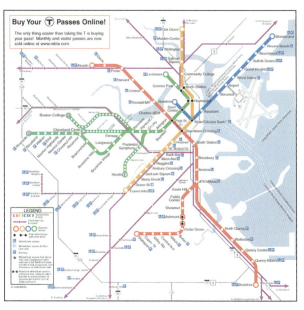

*Although the Massachu-
setts (Bay) Transportation
Authority operates buses
throughout the Boston
metropolitan area, the
underground trains run-
ning on four color-coded
lines (red, green, orange,
and blue) have been im-
mortalized in the MTA
Song.*

*The King's Noyse brings
together a consort of Re-
naissance stringed instruments with voice. The
members include (from
bottom, clockwise) David
Douglas, Robert Mealy,
Scott Metcalfe, Margriet
Tindemans, Emily Wal-
hout, and (center) Ellen
Hargis.*

LISTENING GUIDE 40

Barbara Allen (English ballad)

PERFORMED BY Ellen Hargis with the King's Noyse

This rendition of *Barbara Allen* from a recording made by the early music ensemble the King's Noyse, shows dramatically how early music and folk music soundscapes can converge. The ballad is sung by Ellen Hargis, accompanied by replicas of instruments dating to seventeenth-century England. Although it is unclear if such instruments were used to accompany ballads in England or Scotland at the time, the King's Noyse has created a version of this ballad that is pleasing to twenty-first-century listeners.

LISTEN TO differences in the text, stemming from the influence of written sources on this version of *Barbara Allen*. Compare the vocal style used here to those of the two singers we heard in Chapter 3.

In Scarlet Town where I was bound,
There was a fair maid dwelling,
Whom I had chosen for my own,
And her name was Barbara Allen.

All in the merry month of May,
When green leaves they was springing,
This young man on his death-bed lay,
For the love of Barbara Allen.

He sent his man unto her then,
To the town where she was dwelling,
"You must come to my master dear,
If your name be Barbara Allen.

"For death is printed in his face,
And sorrow's in him dwelling.
And you must come to my master dear,
If your name be Barbara Allen.

"If death be printed in his face,
And sorrow's in him dwelling,
Then little better shall he be
For bonny Barbara Allen."

So slowly, slowly she got up,
And slowly she came to him,
And all she said when she came there,
"Young man, I think you are a-dying."

He turn'd his face unto her then,
"If you be Barbara Allen,
My dear," said he, "come pity me,
As on my death-bed I am lying."

"If on your death-bed you be lying,
What's that to Barbara Allen?
I cannot keep you from your death,
So farewell," said Barbara Allen.

He turn'd his face unto the wall,
And Death came creeping to him;
"Then adieu, adieu and adieu to all,
And adieu to Barbara Allen."

As she was walking on a day,
She heard the bells a-ringing,
And they did seem to ring to her,
"Unworthy Barbara Allen!"

She turn'd herself around about,
And she spy'd the corps a-coming;
"Lay down, lay down the corps of clay,
That I may look upon him."

And all the while she look'd on,
So loudly she lay laughing;
While all her friends cry'd out amain,
"Unworthy Barbara Allen!"

When he was dead and laid in grave,
Then Death came creeping to she.
"O Mother! Mother! make my bed,
For his death hath undone me.

"A hard-hearted creature that I was
To slight one that lov'd me so dearly,
I wish I'd been more kind to him,
In time of life when he was near me."

So this maid she then did dye,
And desired to be buried by him,
And repented herself before she dy'd,
That e'er she did deny him.

As she was lying down to die,
A sad feud she fell in;
She said, "I pray take warning by
Hard-hearted Barbara Allen."

historical performance styles, such as Arnold Dolmetsch, settled in Boston. Boston provided a congenial location for professional musicians involved in early music, many of whom found homes at area educational institutions or with firms of instrument makers. Outstanding musicians who made Boston their home included the harpsichord virtuoso Ralph Kirkpatrick, the harpsichord builder Frank Hubbard, and the recorder maker Friedrich von Huene. These musicians sought to revive early instruments and to perform music composed in earlier eras. Many musicians gravitated to Boston after graduating from music schools elsewhere and studying in Europe; the concentration of musicians and variety of work opportunities in early music and classical ensembles proved to be powerful attractions.

Besides being the American center for the early music movement, Boston also has close ties to other places in the international early music network. In addition to its week-long international biennial gathering, the Boston Early Music Festival presents a year-round concert series that features visiting ensembles, many from abroad. "In-town" and "out-of-town" activity in the early music cluster are closely connected, with touring and recording activities bringing more prestige.

Early music life is well organized, in that many individual musicians and ensembles have ties to Boston institutions. Several area colleges, including the New England Conservatory, Boston University, Harvard and the Longy School of Music, have at different times offered degrees or certificates in early music, and early music groups are part of extracurricular musical life on many of the campuses.

On the surface, early music appears to be the quintessential Western musical experience, a living monument to the past of the Western art music tradition. Yet a closer look raises some questions. Many early music groups share music of different ethnic communities and professional folk singers. One example is the ballad *Barbara Allen.*

Many early music professionals are interested in other musical styles and incorporate them into their performances and, indeed their world view. For instance, the Boston Camerata has performed and recorded European Christian and Jewish repertories of the Middle Ages and Renaissance, Morroccan musics, and American Shaker music. The director of the Boston Camerata, Joel Cohen, notes, "I'm interested in other cultures besides European, but the only ones in which I'm personally happy is where I can feel like there's something that I share with the other culture."

One of the most interesting examples of the connection between early music and international musical styles can be found in the genesis and performance practice (that is, performing styles) of Voice of the Turtle, an early music ensemble with deep Boston roots. This quartet, formally established in 1978, began as part of Quadrivium, an eclectic early music performing group founded in Cambridge in 1967. Quadrivium's countercultural stance in its early years included all-night sessions featuring close listening coupled with techniques of yoga and meditation. The group's public performances were infused with ritual and were heavily choreographed. The initial repertories of Quadrivium and its offspring, Voice of the Tur-

The musicians of Voice of the Turtle, who all sing and play a panoply of instruments from around the world, include (left to right) Judith Wachs, Derek Burrows, Jay Rosenberg, and Lisle Kulbach.

tle, ranged from all types of medieval and Renaissance music to folk music of American and European origin. While working on songs of the Spanish Renaissance during 1973–74, one member of the group came across published versions of Spanish songs still being transmitted in the twentieth century—through oral tradition—by descendants of late–fifteenth-century Jewish exiles from Spain. These songs, with words in Judeo-Spanish dialects, later became Voice of the Turtle's central repertory.

Voice of the Turtle also emphasizes the historical Mediterranean roots of their Judeo-Spanish songs by accompanying them on guitar, the Middle Eastern 'ud, and a large array of Middle Eastern stringed and percussion instruments. The group further attempts to keep vocal and instrumental styles within a range they feel is consistent with those of the Mediterranean and Middle Eastern regions.

All three of our major Boston soundscape clusters—college music, folk music, and early music—are both local and international, with deep roots in Boston as well as in other places. All three are derived from European musical styles and institutions, yet incorporate the widest array of instruments from around the world, present and past.

Of the three soundscape clusters, the campus music scene is the most heterogeneous with every campus maintaining its own diverse and often multicultural world of music. At the same time, manifestations of both early music and folk music are incorporated into the broad and inclusive soundscapes of individual colleges.

Most unified in its sound and musical style is the folk music revival, with simple

LISTENING GUIDE 41

CD 2
TRACK
6

Durme, Durme ("Sleep, Sleep"; Judeo-Spanish lullaby)

PERFORMED BY Voice of the Turtle

Most of the Judeo-Spanish songs were transmitted by women, and the song included here is sung as a female solo. This traditional Judeo-Spanish lullaby is sung in a manner often heard in the early music movement, that is, without much vibrato. The guitar has been prominent for several centuries in Spain, but its use here was more likely influenced by the folk music movement.

LISTEN FOR the entry of the *'ud* (lute), which joins the guitar in the third verse, adding a Middle Eastern flavor. The voice, guitar, and lute, as played here, result in a texture that resembles the heterophony of Middle Eastern music, where all instruments and voices play nearly the same melody at the same time, without harmony.

Refrain:
Sleep my beautiful child;
Sleep without worry or pain.
Ooooh live, life, life.
[Close your radiant eyes
Sleep, sleep comfortably.]

From the cradle you will go
to enter school,
and there, my beloved son
you will begin to learn to read [Torah].
 Refrain: Sleep my beautiful child . . .

From school you will go,
take a beautiful bride
and then, my beloved son
you will have children.
 Refrain: Sleep my beautiful child . . .

strophic song forms, guitar accompaniments, and catchy melodies well suited to oral transmission and to the abilities of amateur singers. Many of the songs of the folk music revival are closely tied to the moment or place at which they were first sung. These songs have great meaning to many as the music of their youth, as a call to political action, and as a sonic symbol of human rights.

The special sound of instruments, vocal styles, and repertories from the past mark the early music movement. At the same time, the folk music and early music soundscape clusters share a countercultural edge. Folk music often displays its resistance in the texts of its songs. The early music movement differentiates itself from standard Western musical soundscapes by reviving older instruments, historical performance practices, and neglected musical styles.

It appears likely that Boston's status as a "university town par excellence" allowed it, over time, to become a congenial home for both the folk music movement and the early music scene. Boston therefore has a distinctive and somewhat paradoxical musical profile: It was *the* historic center and transmitter of European musical culture in North America, and over time it has provided a home for diverse, alternative, and often resistant musical cultures of the campus music, folk music, and early music worlds.

One way to sharpen and test our understanding of Boston's musical profile is to compare it with those of cities of different sizes, ages, and locations. Below are two brief profiles intended for a comparative mapping of the music of both a much larger city—Houston, Texas—and the much smaller town of Juneau, Alaska.

CASE STUDY: HOUSTON, TEXAS

When the Allen brothers bought land on Buffalo Bayou in the mid-nineteenth century and named it after General Sam Houston, they could not have envisioned the sprawling megalopolis that would be the fourth largest city in the United States little more than a century and a half later.

Twenty-first-century Houston is home to an increasingly heterogeneous population and diverse musical life. On one level, Houston has the musical institutions common to many other American cities. We find the Houston Symphony Orchestra in residence at Jones Hall, along with the Symphony North of Houston, the Houston Civic Symphony, and within an hour's drive, the Clear Lake and Galveston symphonies. The Houston Ballet has an active annual season (featuring, of course, the ubiquitous *Nutcracker* ballet during the weeks prior to Christmas), as does the Houston Grand Opera. A lively academic music

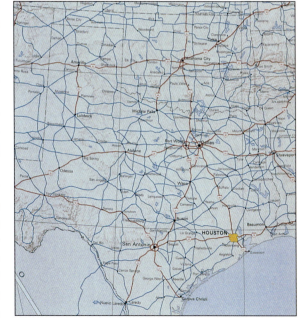

Houston, which sits fifty miles from the Texas coast, is the world's eighth-ranking port, thanks to an inland waterway that links the city to the Gulf of Mexico. Long a center for the exploration and production of oil and natural gas, Houston today has a diverse economy that includes medical research, high technology, and aerospace.

scene can be found on local campuses such as Rice University's Shepherd School of Music, the University of Houston, and the University of St. Thomas. With the help of the academic community, Houston is also seeing the beginning of an early-music community, including the founding of the Ars Lyrica Baroque music ensemble at the University of Houston.

Like most major metropolitan areas, Houston is the enthusiastic host to a wide array of artists and musical groups who annually tour North America—and the globe. The Compaq Center is the venue for many of these concerts, with thousands coming to hear stars such as Celine Dion and Alanis Morissette. Many rock concerts are mounted at the Woodlands Pavilion, with classic groups such as Aerosmith and newer names. Performers who came of age in the Houston area are warmly welcomed back. These include the singer-actor Lyle Lovett. In the 1970s and early 1980s he frequented the local Anderson Fair Folk Club, then returned to his home town in the late 1990s to celebrate his album *Step Inside This House*—a tribute to the Texas singer-songwriters who inspired his career.

Don't overlook the cowboy wearing a ten-gallon hat in the lower left-corner of this poster for the eleventh season of the Texas Music Festival at the University of Houston.

Truly international musical shows also make their appearance in Houston on a regular basis, such as "Tango Buenos Aires," presented along with other world music events by the Society for the Performing Arts in the Aerial Theatre at Bayou Place. Regular offerings include the Houston International Festival, which has focused on African themes in recent years, featuring such renowned musicians as Abdullah Ibrahim and Hugh Masekela. But the International Festival also incorporates musical traditions closer to home, reserving outdoor stages for American styles such as zydeco, blues, and soul, another for Caribbean styles including steel drums, and a special stage called the "Texas Zone."

And what might we find in the "Texas Zone"? So far, we have mapped musical institutions and trends that link Houston with other places in North America and the rest of the world. But what distinguishes Houston's musical profile? A quick glance at the events listed in the *Houston Chronicle* suggests some special categories: under "Live Music" we find a Tejano/Latin category along with a regular column about the Latin music scene. The annual Tejano Music Awards (TEMA) are presented by the Texas Talent Musicians Association. Many Mexican-American musical events are held in this city, which numbers a large community of Mexican Americans among its population. Diverse Mexican-American musical styles are represented, including bilingual Latino rap, performed by Carlos Coy, who uses the name "South Park Mexican." Many of these styles can be heard at popular Latino clubs in southwest Houston, such as Metropolis, Coco Loco, and Extasis, with Mexican and Chicano styles featured in the east and north sections at places like El Dorado.

Coy has released three albums through his own record company, Dope House Records, and can be found around town selling recordings and rapping; he also makes frequent appearances at local schools. Other popular Latino musical styles include those of El Salvador, Colombia, and Puerto Rico.

Nowhere is the growing nationwide interest in mariachi music livelier than in Houston, where small groups of mariachi musicians play old and new songs. Since 1992, an annual "Go Tejano Mariachi" competition has been held in Houston as part of a growing Tejano soundscape cluster. Although competitions place mariachi in the spotlight on special occasions, mariachi groups perform in a number of local restaurants most days of the week, including Mariachi Imperial, Mariachi Tenampa, and Mariachi Alma Latina.

Several Spanish-language FM radio stations play a wide range of Latin pop and Tejano musics. Spanish-language AM stations tend to play older styles from various Latin countries. Spanish-language newspapers—including *El Día*, *La Suvasa*, and *Viva México*—are widely distributed and include information on current musical events.

Houston is home to a large and long-established African American population as well. The African American impact on Texas musical life is pervasive and can be found in unexpected contexts.

For example, the song *The Yellow Rose of Texas* conveys information about an extraordinary chapter in Texas history, along with insight into the manner in which racial discrimination masked the heroism of a woman of color in the Texan war of independence from Mexico. The song was composed in commemoration of Emily Morgan, an indentured servant in Texas captured by the Mexican general Santa Anna. While a hostage of the general, Emily learned of his military plans and managed to warn General Sam Houston of an imminent attack by the Mexican forces. Her warning ensured that the Texans won the pivotal battle of San Jacinto on April 21, 1836.

The original text and melody of *The Yellow Rose of Texas* was first copyrighted on September 2, 1858 by the vaudeville singer Charles H. Brown, for whom the song had been composed and arranged by an anonymous composer known only by the initials "J. K." During the nineteenth century, the song was widely performed in North America and Europe by white minstrels wearing blackface makeup. The original text of the song described the "Yellow Rose," Emily, as a woman of color who was loved by the minstrel.[5]

A close look also shows that *zydeco*, a black creole music with deep Gulf Coast roots (our primary case study in Chapter 8), continues to be actively transmitted and performed in the Houston area. Recent years have seen the founding of a regional Zydecopalooza Festival in nearby Humble, Texas, and the emergence of

The Zydeco Dots, a quintet popular in Houston and the Gulf Coast region, has played at a variety of events ranging from the World Zydeco Festival in Plaisance, Louisiana to the Houston International Festival. The group seen here includes bass guitarist and vocalist Thurman Hurst, rub board/percussionist Mike Vee, drummer Joe Rossylon, guitarist Tom Potter, and accordionist and lead vocalist Leon Sam.

LISTENING GUIDE 42

CD 2
TRACK
7

The Yellow Rose of Texas (American song)

COMPOSED BY "J. K."

PERFORMED BY Richard Bales

During the Civil War, *The Yellow Rose of Texas* became a popular marching tune for Confederate soldiers. The Civil War version of the song substituted the word "soldier" for "darkey." However, the song text otherwise remained largely the same until additional variants were published by the Texas composer David W. Guion in 1936, to commemorate the Texas Centennial. Two pivotal changes were made in the text at that point: "The sweetest rose of color" became "the sweetest rose of Texas" and the word "darkey" was replaced by "fellow." Other smaller changes took place as the song entered into American popular culture and was widely performed across the United States, recorded by such stars as Mitch Miller.

Recent research[6] has clarified both the history of the song and the heroism of this Texas woman of color. In 1975, the state of Texas minted a special medallion to commemorate Emily Morgan's role in winning the independence of Texas. In 1976, the symbol of the yellow rose was placed beside the Texas Lone Star.

fresh, new zydeco talent such as J. Paul, Jr. and his Zydeco Newbreeds. A recent *Houston Chronicle* article noted that "zydeco has witnessed an explosion in popularity in the Houston area" and that its "distinctive accordion-and-rub-board flavor has even penetrated the play lists of mainstream R & B radio stations." Zydeco can also be heard all over town, from clubs to shopping malls to church dances to radio stations.

Music plays an intregal part in the many Houston festivals geared toward southwestern themes, most held in local parks and underwritten by local sponsors. The Bayou City Art Festival held in Memorial Park features arts, crafts, and music. The annual Texas Rodeo features a large menu of musical events presenting well-known local country and western performers as well as a range of Nashville's finest. Music is a regular and prominent part of the Houston Livestock Show and Rodeo at the city's Astrodome.

LISTEN TO this rendition with the original text. How does knowledge of the history of this famous song—and the changes in its text—reshape your understanding of its significance?

Refrain:
There's a yellow rose in Texas
that I am going to see,
No other darkey knows her,
no darkey only me;
She cried so when I left her,
it like to broke my heart,
and if I ever find her
we never more will part.

She's the sweetest rose of color,
This darkey ever knew,
Her eyes are bright as diamonds,
They sparkle like the dew.
You may talk about your dearest May,
And sing of Rosalee,
But the Yellow Rose of Texas
Beats the Belles of Tennessee!

Where the Rio Grande is flowing,
And starry skies are bright,
She walks along the river,
In the quiet summer night;
She think if I remember,
When we parted long ago,
I promised to return
And not to leave her so.

Oh, now I'm going to find her,
For my heart is full of woe,
We'll sing that song together,
We sang so long ago.
We'll play the banjo gaily,
We'll sing the songs of yore,
And the Yellow Rose of Texas
Shall be mine for ever more.

A great deal of local musical life can be found in area houses of worship. The growth and health of black churches in Houston have had a marked impact, including the rapidly expanding Brookhollow Baptist Church, which hosts a great deal of gospel music. The grass-roots interest in gospel has given rise to the Houston-based World Wide Gospel recording label, founded by Kerry and Fatiyah Douglas. Other religious denominations, such as Houston's active Jewish community, perpetuate musical events as part of their heritage and activities. Founded in 1854, Temple Beth Israel, the oldest synagogue in Texas, presents an annual music Sabbath and special cantorial concerts.

Bilingual street signs mark the presence of Saigon City Mall, just south of the skyscrapers of downtown Houston.

Many communities newer to Houston are quickly establishing an active musical life. Since 1993, several large record and video stores have sprung up in shopping centers near concentrations of Vietnamese residents. Along with ads for restaurants, grocery stores, bakeries, gift shops, and medical and legal services, the local Vietnamese-language newspapers carry ads for recordings and videos, as well as notices of upcoming concerts. Major musical events are supported by the Vietnamese community, including a Houston-based version of the international popular music event "Paris by Night," performed at the Houston Coliseum on March 31, 1996, and sold throughout the world on videotape.

In summary, musical life in Houston can be said to be distinctive in two main ways: it utilizes music to delineate and emphasize Houston's special regional identity as a modern, southwestern city rooted in the Gulf Coast landscape crossed by bayous; and music is also actively employed to celebrate and acknowledge the growing ethnic diversity of the metropolitan area. The increasing prominence of African American and Latin musical styles reinforces the longtime roots and growing political roles of communities of color in the American Southwest. It is not coincidental that events such as the four-year old annual Festival Cubano, an official celebration of Cuban culture, music, cuisine, and folklore, is mounted on the Houston City Hall Plaza. New communities, too, such as Houston's Vietnamese, give voice to their presence through an active musical life. Through music, Houstonians perform their pride in their distinctive locale and diverse cultural heritages, while opening a stage on which people of many backgrounds can begin to sing and dance together.

CASE STUDY: JUNEAU, ALASKA

Modern Juneau, nearby earlier settlements of the indigenous Tlingit people of the region, is a young town. Founded in the aftermath of the gold rush in the 1880s, in 1900 it was named capital of the Alaska territory, which subsequently became the forty-ninth state in 1959. Juneau's character is shaped by its history as a frontier town, but even more so by its geographic setting. Wedged between imposing mountains and ice fields on one side, and the Gastineau Channel separating it from Douglas Island on the other, Juneau is accessible only by sea and air—by "flying or floating," in local parlance. Its isolation has kept the town small, just over thirty thousand people, except for the hours each afternoon during the short summer season when the streets near the docks are crowded with tourists briefly disembarking from luxury liners sailing the scenic Inside Passage.

Yet despite its isolated locale and difficulty of access, Juneau has a vibrant musical life, sustained on a largely voluntary basis by people permanently living in the region. Many musical organizations have sprung up over time, founded by musicians who make their living mainly through regular jobs in a wide variety of professions and in the city, state, and federal government offices that play a prominent role in the local economy. In its musical complexity, Juneau provides an instructive example of the richness of musical life even in small and seemingly isolated places.

Music making is a regular item on the calendars of community organizations around town. Of course, music has always been a part of indigenous Tlingit life in southeastern Alaska, but the last fifteen to twenty years have witnessed a revival of the native musical heritage through the activities of organizations within native communities and with the financial support of the Sealaska Heritage Foundation. The Sealaska Celebration—a large, pantribal musical gathering held every two years and recorded on videotape—differs from the powwows of much of the rest of North America. It models itself on an indigenous ceremony involving gift exchange long practiced on the Northwest Coast.

In between the formal festivals, Tlingit musical traditions are main-

A view of Juneau as seen from the top of the adjacent Mount Roberts, with the Gastineau Channel and Douglas Island in the distance.

tained in Juneau through local institutions such as the Native Culture Center, which is the home of the Juneau Tlingit Dancers.

Juneau's large and active Filipino community had its beginnings when late-eighteenth-century Filipino seamen arrived with Spanish sailing expeditions and whaling expeditions. By the early twentieth century, Filipino men settled as workers in the Alaskan salmon cannery and mining industries, many marrying into Tlingit and other First Nation communities. The Filipino Community Center, an outgrowth of an organization started in 1929, was originally built so that Juneau Filipinos would have a place to host community events in the face of racial discrimination. Decades after the Juneau community integrated all facilities, the Filipino Community Center remains a center for community life, hosting Friday night as "family night," featuring *karaoke*, a type of amateur musical performance to pre-recorded music that we will encounter in Chapter 8. On other evenings, members of the local community as well as tourists used to visit the waterfront's City Cafe, which featured its own lively karaoke performances until it recently was torn down and replaced by a convenience store. All of Juneau looks forward to the colorfully costumed Filipino drummers who perform in the Fourth of July parade.

Music can also be heard regularly in local Juneau churches. The tiny blue and white Saint Nicholas Orthodox Church sits perched high on 5th Street, its cupola outlined against the mountain looming behind it. Since the church's construction in 1894 by Tlingit people and Russian immigrants, mass has been chanted on Sunday in English, Slavonic, and Tlingit amid colorful icons and the scent of incense.

Numerous local eateries provide venues for regular musical performance. The popular Fiddlehead Restaurant features local jazz ensembles on Friday and Saturday evenings. Folk musicians such as Betsy Sims and Buddy Tabor perform around town at places like the outdoor Salmon Bake and at historic saloons such as the Alaskan and the Red Dog. During the summer season, Concerts in the Park features an eclectic assortment of local music groups ranging from the Stroller White Pipes and Drums and Highland Dancers to Koinania to African Rain. During the warm weather, the Juneau Lyric Opera sponsors evening cruises leaving from the harbor, featuring performances of Gilbert and Sullivan operettas.

The influx of tourists has further encouraged presentations such as the Gold Nugget Revue. The most recent performance told the story of the founding of Juneau in a musical revue, complete with can-can dancers.

Other unexpected sites for musical performance include the State Office Building, where regular noontime organ concerts are performed on a Kimball theater pipe organ permanently installed in the atrium, and where listeners eat bag lunches while gazing out on the wooded slopes of Douglas Island to the accompaniment of nineteenth- and twentieth-century popular songs.

But music making in Juneau has also been institutionalized. The Juneau Symphony, founded more than thirty years ago, both provides a forum for local musicians to perform and offers educational programs. Individual players have founded smaller groups that play at events around town. Steve Tada's Fiery Gypsies, which

LISTENING GUIDE 43

Wanted, My Darling Papa (American song)

PERFORMED BY June Baldridge, with orchestra

Many songs recall the late-nineteenth-century Alaska gold rush, which brought settlers to the territory, including adventurers who rushed north from Minnesota in search of riches. This particular folk song has been sustained in the oral tradition by the singer, June Baldridge of Dodge Center, Minnesota, who was born in 1924 and recalls learning the song as a child. The composer is unknown, but the text is said to have come from a letter sent to the editor of the *Minneapolis Tribune* from a woman who wanted her father to come home from Alaska. This song is one of many that have been revived for the entertainment of tourists anxious to recapture the sounds of the gold rush. Because the discovery of gold in the adjacent Yukon region was the first and largest, many of the songs were written about the Yukon, but sung for the other Alaskan rushes as well.

LISTEN TO the story narrated in this song, which can be heard clearly in this solo, unaccompanied rendition.

includes the accordionist Dale Wygant, plays tango, klezmer music, brass quintet arrangements, and music for handbell choir.

Sally Schlichting, a Juneau Symphony flutist, comments that "in a small town you have to be creative with what you have. You have limited resources and always have to substitute." She offers as a prime example a chamber ensemble called Nimbus, of which she is a member and which takes its name from Robert Murray's free-form metal sculpture that now stands outside the Alaska State Museum. The ensemble, says Schlichting, "would be a string quartet" if a cellist had been available in Juneau. Instead of a cello, they have a *euphonium*, a brass instrument of about the same range. With first violinists also scarce, flutist Schlichting got the first violin part. Other than avoiding compositions that require specific violin tech-

The Fiery Gypsies perform at a Juneau wedding on July 15, 1999.

niques, Nimbus plays pretty much the standard quartet repertories, as well as early music and Beatles tunes. "It's an amazing sound," Schlichting reports. "Once you hear it, the blending is fabulous."

The Juneau community is closely linked in its economy and cultural life to neighboring communities of the Alexander Archipelago. Juneau has longtime ties to the nearby communities—Sitka, Skagway, Ketchikan, Petersburg, Haines— each a few hours away by ferry or a short flight. For many musicians raised in Juneau, this interactive musical environment brings a deep sense of regional community and collaboration. From their earliest years in schools, Juneau's children travel with their high school sports teams and musical groups to perform together in different southeast Alaskan communities. High school students, such as those currently in the Fireweed String Quartet, learn early on to contribute to local musical life.

Regional cooperation is at a height in the annual cycle of music festivals held in southeast Alaska. A small number of energetic musicians shoulder the responsibility for this aspect of local musical life—often sharing lives as well as musical pursuits. Since 1972, Sitka has hosted a classical music festival, including many musicians who are regular participants and who return each year for a summer residency as well as additional concerts in September and February. Paul Rosenthal, founder of the Sitka Festival, is married to Linda Rosenthal, who is both the founder and the coordinator of the Juneau Jazz and Classics Festival.

Since 1975, the Alaska Folk Festival has been held each April in Juneau's Centennial Hall. People come from all around the region, taking a welcome musical break near the end of winter when everyone is "fed up with the whole thing" and the folk festival provides "a little warmth."

During the rest of the year, regional folk groups such as the all-female Glacial Erratics continue to perform. Linda and Russ Hansen continue to teach country and western dancing in venues from bars to churches, the Pioneers home and the schools.[7]

The ties that bind this region—the unusual topography, a common lifestyle, and a deep background of Tlingit culture—ensure that many musicians will continue to participate in Juneau's musical life, despite careers that may take them far away. One recent example is the founding of the First Annual Southeast Alaska International Contemporary Music Festival—called CrossSound—in the summer of 1999, with two inaugural concerts held at Juneau's Northern Lights Church and the Chapel on the Lake. The Juneau native Jocelyn Clark—an ethnomusicologist and accomplished performer in the zither traditions of Korea, Japan, and China—returned to Juneau to found this innovative music festival with her husband, the German-born composer Stefan Hakenberg. With the support of the Juneau Arts and Humanities Council and the help of Clark's local family and friends, CrossSound revives and elaborates the vision of the "Alaska Music Trail," an international concert series that for twenty-five years annually visited eighteen Alaskan and Western Canadian towns, beginning in the 1940s. CrossSound restores the international vision of the earlier series but also encourages unexpected musical connections, commissioning and performing new works for instruments such as the Korean *changgo* drum and the Baroque cello. If Clark's Juneau roots have led her to renew an older tradition, Hakenberg's long experience in Europe with alternative cultural projects that mix professionals and amateurs in performing music also fits nicely into Southeast Alaska's musical milieu. As CrossSound develops, its founders hope that it will eventually be a winter festival, so that full-time Juneau residents can participate fully during the period of the year when they have the most free time. In Cross-Sound, old and new Juneau meet head on: a musical festival deeply rooted in Southeast Alaska traditions, emerging from local interests and experience, yet drawing on a full measure of outside creativity and stimulation from around the globe.

Dang, a Fairbanks band, plays swing music in the National Guard Armory Building for enthusiastic dancers during the Juneau Folk Festival.

Conclusion

As you think about the very different musical cityscapes of Boston, Houston, and Juneau, consider making some comparisons of your own. What are the major soundscapes of the city, town, or

place in which you live? Which soundscapes or combination of soundscapes provide a distinctive local musical profile?

You can begin to "map" your own city or campus musical life by following the processes suggested in Chapters Two and Four: Ask and answer a series of questions (what, who, where, when, why) about musics you encounter. To aid this process, begin a journal, listing and describing the soundscapes you encounter in the course of your daily life.

Approaching all the music of a given place and time can present a formidable challenge. An alternative is to study the most important social and individual processes in human life through the lens of musical expression. Of these, perhaps none is more prominent than the role of music in constituting and celebrating belief, our subject in Chapter 5.

IMPORTANT TERMS

ballad	"folk music"	qanun
beating tones	gamelan	rhythmic cycle
buskers	*gong kebyar*	soundscape cluster
early music	interlocking parts	*tizita*
fado	(*kotekan*)	*'ud*
falsetto	*mbube*	vocalise

CHAPTER

FIVE FIVE FIVE FIVE FIVE FIVE FIVE FIVE FIVE FIVE FIVE FIVE FIVE FIVE FIVE FIVE FIVE FIVE FIVE FIVE FIVE FIVE FIVE FIVE FIVE FIVE FIVE

Saint Yared (right) performs chant before the Ethiopian emperor
Gabra Masqal and is so transported by his own singing
and dancing that he does not notice the emperor's spear,
which has accidentally pierced his foot.

OVERVIEW

MAIN POINTS

Music serves in a wide range of worship settings to:

- shape and order the rituals that celebrate belief

- enact and convey ritual's symbolic power and meaning

- empower the ritual experience for participants

- sustain belief while incorporating change

Music of Worship
and Belief

Introduction

Throughout history, the public celebration of belief has provided important settings for musical performance. Indeed, it is scarcely possible to imagine rituals of worship without music, which has long shaped ritual form and marked off ritual time. Through song, instrumental music, and dance, rituals deeply impress our senses and help us communicate with deities.

We usually think of rituals in connection with religious practice, and that is the sense in which they are discussed in this chapter. But it must be understood that rituals extend well beyond the boundaries of religious belief. Many of their formal characteristics can also be found in secular circumstances such as parades, sporting events, concerts, and operas.

In popular usage, we find the words *ritual, sacred service, liturgy,* and *liturgical order* used interchangeably to refer to public acts of worship. All such terms refer to more or less formal events that are performed in specific contexts at particular times. The parts of rituals typically occur in a set order and serve to link the individual experience to that of a broader community.

Whatever their specific textual and musical content, rituals tend to share a common structure. Most rituals—especially those marking life-cycle events, such

155

Much of the power of rituals rests with our ability to bracket time in special ways, for example, by donning elaborate vestments or using substances such as wine or incense. Here, an Elvis Presley impersonator sings as part of a ceremony marking the renewal of a couple's marriage vows at Graceland Chapel, Las Vegas, Nevada.

as initiations and funerals—incorporate a symbolic process or an actual change of state that consists of three stages: separation, transition, and incorporation.[1] For example, a wedding ceremony is a rite of passage that separates the bride and groom from their single status, takes them through a brief transition, and finally incorporates them into the society of married couples.

Building on this view of ritual as a process, we see that a ritual guides a participant through time in special ways, bringing about a feeling of experience shared with others.[2] Not only can a ritual heighten emotions, its content and the objects associated with it can also have symbolic meanings embedded in the texts, music, and related bodily movements.

Although rituals are performed in a manner that emphasizes their separation from daily life, their content and significance are much more closely tied to secular concerns than we might think. We will take a close look at rituals that include prominent musical content and that are currently performed and transmitted in North America, delving into the different ways in which music has served both to sustain belief and to accommodate strong forces of change.

The Centrality of Chant

There is no better place to begin our discussion of music and belief than with the quintessential musical form associated with rituals of belief: *chant*. Chant, also called plainchant or plainsong, is often defined as simple song. In its purest form, chant is a type of vocal expression in which clarity and the precise articulation of the sacred words are of utmost importance. Some of the musical vocabulary that we have already encountered for songs grows out of the study of Western Christian chant, for example, the terms *syllabic* and *melismatic,* which describe the relationship of the words to the melody.

CASE STUDY: TIBETAN BUDDHIST CHANT

Chant can sound deceptively simple, but its musical surface can mask extraordinary depths of meaning. Tibetan Buddhist chant provides an example of such

In Nepal, Tibetan musicians play Tibetan trumpets and sound bells during a Cham ceremony (ritual dances for the New Year) near the Tibetan border.

complex significance, with the belief that performing chant is instrumental (quite literally!) in moving the singer through the ritual process to a transformed state. Once again we encounter, as we did with *khoomii* singing, a distinctive vocal style, generating a deep, fundamental pitch that produces audible harmonics. Indeed, it has been suggested that Tibetan monks may have learned this technique through contact with Inner Asian *khoomii* singers.

We will hear a chant sung by Buddhist monks of the Gyuto monastery, an institution that was founded in Tibet during the fifteenth century. The chant is a ritual meditation text (termed *sadhana*) that evokes the sacred and helps the monk visualize and unite with the deity. It is believed that the act of chanting—which includes recitation of a *mantra* (a ritual phrase or formula), prayers, and vocables—shapes this transcendent experience by connecting sound, breathing, and mind.

Although Buddhist chant was traditionally performed only in religious settings in its Tibetan homeland, since the 1959 exile of monks from Tibet to India, chant has occasionally been presented in public performance. In 1986, the monks of the Gyuto Tantric choir visited the United States for the first time, presented concerts, and released a recording authorized by the Dalai Lama. It is noteworthy that despite changing performance settings, the Gyuto monks continue to sing in a traditional vocal style. They also want the

Monks of the Gyuto Tantric University pose for a rare photograph by Mono Lake, California.

Ethiopia's location in the rugged plateau of the Horn of Africa protected it for most of its history from invaders and helped preserve its independence, except during a sixteenth-century invasion from the south and the Italian occupation of 1935–1941. The region along Ethiopia's Red Sea coast, Eritrea, became independent in 1992 following a long civil war.

emperor, Haile Selassie, during a revolution that began in 1974, and the subsequent years of civil unrest, drought, and famine, forced millions to leave modern Ethiopia and its surrounding regions.

The Ethiopian diaspora today includes thriving communities in far-flung locales, including Italy, Sweden, and Israel, but North America has emerged as the largest and fastest-growing home for Ethiopians abroad.

Ethiopian Christian chant, through its continued life in the diaspora, provides a rich case study of the surprisingly flexible relationship between music and belief. Of particular interest are the many changes that have taken place within the musical tradition since the chant's reestablishment in North America. Although Ethiopian chant continues to be closely associated with the rituals expressing Christian belief and is regarded by its practitioners as intrinsically meaningful, some centuries-old practices and associations have shifted under the pressures of a new environment. Changes were already under way in the Ethiopian homeland before the period of migration, as the flow of people to urban areas diminished the central role of the church in daily life. But changes aside, music of the Ethiopian-American diaspora still marks the ritual experience and provides continuity with the church's earlier traditions of worship.

Many of the changes in music and belief are shaped by events outside the religious domain, especially the tension between ritual practice and everyday life.[7] Rituals can provide a context in which old symbols are given new meaning and where new symbols can be incorporated. Such is clearly the case with Ethiopian Christian chant, which has brought longtime practices and values into the present while providing a creative setting for innovation and resistance.

A priest at a church in the Ethiopian countryside strikes the resonant stone slabs used for centuries to call the faithful to worship. Today, a metal bell usually serves the same function.

Ethiopian Christianity at Home in North America

The Ethiopian Christian Orthodox Church has established itself throughout North America, with many urban areas supporting several Ethiopian congregations. But virtually all lack their own meeting spaces and depend on the generosity of other American Christian denominations to provide room on Sundays and major holidays, following the regularly scheduled services. A striking exception is the Ethiopian church building in Seattle, Washington, which is wholly owned by the worshiping community.

Challenges confront Ethiopian Americans seeking to sustain their religious and musical practice in North America. The Ethiopian community, like that of the Vietnamese we encountered in Chapter 3, is a diaspora of recent origin, dating only from the mid-1970s. Many of its members were forced migrants who arrived in the United States only after periods of imprisonment or other hardships.

Priests and dabtaras *celebrate the final stages of construction of the new Ethiopian Orthodox church of Saint Gabriel in Seattle, Washington.*

The exodus from Ethiopia during the revolution established a sizable Ethiopian-American community. More than forty-six thousand immigrants born in Ethiopia entered the United States between 1971 and 1994; the community grew from around three thousand individuals prior to 1974 to a total in 1990 (including Eritreans) estimated at fifty thousand to seventy-five thousand people.

Ethiopian Americans have established both community organizations and social networks. Restaurants present the most public face of the Ethiopian community in large cities, but the widely circulated *Ethiopian Yellow Pages* shows a community with its own accountants, attorneys, and dentists, and a group that maintains culinary and cultural traditions by patronizing special groceries, restaurants, and stores. A large number of compact disc and video recordings, many recorded and distributed from studios in North America, are sold in these shops.

Although many diaspora Ethiopians have made a successful transition to new careers in academia, the professions, and industry, the majority are struggling,

Record stores selling music imported from Africa and recordings produced and distributed domestically are found in many American cities. This shop is located in the Adams Morgan area of Washington, D.C., a neighborhood where many thousands of immigrants from Ethiopia, Eritrea, and other African nations now live.

working-class people who hold low-paying service jobs in hotels, parking lots, taxi companies, and similar enterprises. These circumstances have made it difficult to gather the necessary funds to sustain even a modest Ethiopian Christian ritual cycle.

Beyond their economic needs, the Ethiopian churches in North America face a severe shortage of qualified clergy. There are no facilities for training Ethiopian priests or musicians in North America, and since the revolution in Ethiopia, few clergy have been trained there (see "**Individual Portrait: Berhanu Makonnen, Ethiopian Church Musician**"). The scarcity of clergy puts the church's musical traditions at particular risk in the diaspora, where a congregation is fortunate if it obtains the services of even a single priest, who then must officiate at the Mass and perform all other aspects of the liturgy as well. If a priest is not available, some congregations worship with the aid of cassette recordings imported from Ethiopia. Whenever possible, churches address this problem by importing musicians, at least for important holidays such as Christmas or Easter.

Ethiopian Chant in Its Historical Homeland

To understand musical changes in the Ethiopian diaspora, we must be familiar with the musical heritage from the Ethiopian Church's proud past. The creation of Ethiopian Christian chant, called *zema* (literally, "a pleasing sound," "a song," or "a melody"), is attributed in traditional Ethiopian sources to the divine inspiration of Saint Yared, a holy man said to have lived before the ninth century. Yared is credited with inventing the Ethiopian Christian musical system under divine inspiration, composing the chants and organizing them into service books. Although the texts of the Ethiopian liturgy were written down in the Ge'ez language in parchment manuscripts, performance of chant by church musicians was largely transmitted through oral tradition. In an effort to help the music survive in the wake of a devastating Muslim invasion in the sixteenth century, two musicians of the time, Gera and Ragu'el, invented a system of musical notation (see "**Studying Music: Systems of Music Writing**").

The Mass is the Christian ritual in Western church history with the most elaborate musical content, but in the Ethiopian tradition it was chanted simply, without accompaniment, by an ordained priest rather than a trained musician. The main setting for more elaborate chant performance in the Ethiopian church was the ritual called the Hymnary, performed before the Mass on Sundays and festivals. The musicians, traditionally all men, were obligated by church law to perform some of the nearly two dozen types of chants in the Ethiopian Christian Hymnary.

Ethiopian Chant in Its North American Diaspora

North American Ethiopians have tried to bring the Mass and the sacrament of communion closer to the practice of other American worship services in which these rituals are the main focus. Meanwhile, the Ethiopian Hymnary with its elaborate musical content is now performed mainly on special occasions such as annual holidays; even then, it is generally shortened. The regular Sunday Mass in most

INDIVIDUAL PORTRAIT

Berhanu Makonnen, Ethiopian Church Musician

The Ethiopian church musician, the *dabtara,* is one of the most highly trained musicians in the world. Years of study begin in early childhood in the Ethiopian liturgical language, Ge'ez, and in Christian liturgy. The following years are spent at a chant school (literally, a "*zema* house"), learning chant melodies, the notational system (*melekket*), and liturgical dance. Further schooling is specialized, in a specific chant book, in instrumental practice, or in liturgical dance. During their student years, *dabtaras* may work as merchants, particularly in the butter trade, to support themselves and their families.

Because of their reading and writing skills in a country where only a minority of the population is literate, some *dabtaras* write special scrolls that are commonly used by Ethiopians to heal illnesses. Only *dabtaras* can prepare and decorate these scrolls, which can be hung on the wall or rolled in leather cases and worn around the neck as amulets. The work of the *dabtara* as a healer extends beyond the Christian community to produce magical texts that are thought by

Alaqa Berhanu Makonnen (wearing cape) stands at the center of a group of dabtaras, *many of whom hold prayer staffs and liturgical umbrellas. In front of the group sits the* kebaro, *a church drum.*

peoples of different belief systems to defend against the spirits and devils that cause illness and misfortune. The *dabtara,* then, is musician, magician, singer, and healer, occupying a powerful role in traditional Ethiopian society.

In the past, several distinct styles of liturgical singing were associated with and named after important monasteries in northern Ethiopia where the musicians studied. Although three of these styles survive, that of the Bethlehem monastery predominated by the late twentieth century in urban Ethiopia. It is the style that is most often heard in diaspora churches.

In this chapter, we encounter a great Ethiopian musician who is both a *dabtara* and a priest: Alaqa (literally, a "learned man") Berhanu Makonnen, whom we hear singing *Yome fesseha kone* (see Listening Guide 46). Since the 1970s, Alaqa Berhanu has supervised the training of Ethiopian church musicians at the patriarch's office in Addis Ababa and has taught Ethiopian chant at the Theological College.

Alaqa Berhanu is as well known for his vocal prowess as he is for his encyclopedic knowledge of Ethiopian Christian traditions. During his training, which spanned thirty-one years, he earned diplomas in virtually every aspect of church liturgy and liturgical music. For twelve of those years, he studied at the famous Bethlehem monastery, where he later became the head teacher and was in turn succeeded by one of his own students.

While the Ethiopian dabtaras and the musical materials they transmit are critical to the perpetuation and performance of Ethiopian Christian rituals, events of the late twentieth century have led many *dabtaras* to work outside the church as well. With the loss of church land and revenues in 1975 because of land nationalizations during the Ethiopian revolution, a trend among *dabtaras* to accept employment outside the Church gained momentum. A leading *dabtara* declared that "Now they are ready to work everywhere the government asks."

An Ethiopian magic scroll (asmat) *is usually cut to the height of the person for whom it is made. Each scroll is decorated with motifs, drawings, and sections of prayers and incantations written in Ge'ez, the Ethiopian liturgical language. This detail from an early twentieth-century scroll shows checkered patterns and faces; the full faces usually represent the king of demons, whereas the seven pairs of half-hidden faces depict either demons or angels.*

Ethiopian American churches attracts a lively congregation, with a majority of the women and a few men wearing traditional Ethiopian dress. In most churches, the prayers are still sung in Ge'ez, but sermons are delivered in whatever Ethiopian language the congregation understands. The clergy use books imported from the Ethiopian capital, Addis Ababa. Few service books are to be seen among congregants, although photocopied texts are occasionally distributed.

Sound   The chants performed in the diaspora churches are sung in the traditional manner and adhere to the Ethiopian musical system. Ethiopian chants fall into three categories of melody (or *mode*) named Ge'ez, 'Ezl, and Araray. From the legend of Saint Yared come strong associations for each mode: Ge'ez is linked with God the Father, 'Ezl symbolizes the Son, and Araray represents the Holy Spirit.

Systems of Music Writing

We often use Western musical notation to write down, or "transcribe," the oral traditions we hear so we can study and analyze them. But many systems of music writing developed outside the West, including two that belong to soundscapes encountered in this chapter. The system for notating the Tibetan *dbyangs* is found in song books termed *dbyangs-yig* (literally, "written account of the song"), or *yang-yig* (see illustration below). Tibetan chant, written from left to right in two or three horizontal lines, indicates the name of the song,

The Tibetan notation shown here has been annotated to help readers. The numbers in circles indicate where each song begins and ends; dotted rings (or ellipses) are placed around meaningful Tibetan textual syllables to differentiate them from vocables, which simply extend the sound of the main syllable.

Ethiopian notation for the Christmas chant Yome fesseha kone, *discussed in Listening Guides 46 and 47. The manuscript reads from left to right, and the chant notation begins about two-thirds of the way toward the right margin on the top line. A small character that looks like eyeglasses marks where the chant text begins. The melekket (signs) are found between the lines of text. Above the third line in the manuscript, a double line of melekket begins, indicating that the words from there (at "He is Jesus" in the English translation) to the end should be repeated with a different melody. Even in Ethiopia, however, this repeat is not always taken and the singers in our recordings do not perform it.*

its author, the meaning of the song, and the use of introductory drum beats. Directions for performance style are sometimes indicated, instructing the singer, in one case, that a song should "be chanted like the sound of the wind." The text syllables are placed below the notational curves. Black and red ink are used to differentiate between textual syllables and instructions for their performance.

The notational system used in the Ethiopian church, developed in the late sixteenth century, contains several types of signs. The most important and largest number of signs are the *melekket,* some six hundred and fifty in all, each consisting of one or more characters from the Ge'ez alphabet, which is actually a syllabary, in which each symbol combines a consonant and a vowel. Placed between the lines of the prayer texts, each *melekket* is an abbreviation of the word or phrase that represents a specific short melody. The *melekket* are themselves divided into three categories, the most common of which we will meet in this chapter.

An additional dozen signs consist of dots, dashes, and curved lines that regulate aspects of pace and vocal style. Performing a chant from Ethiopian notation is possible only for a musician who already knows the music of the ritual as an oral tradition.

This transcription of the Ethiopian Christmas chant melody, performed in Listening Guides 46 and 47, "translates" the traditional Ethiopian notation into Western staff notation. Notational signs (melekket) placed above words in the Ethiopian manuscript are represented by alphanumeric formulas. For example, the number representing the first melekket, G259, indicates that it is the two hundred fifty-ninth sign in a comprehensive list of the known Ge'ez melekket.

The Ge'ez mode is used most often in chanting the Hymnary and is associated with no single occasion. The 'Ezl mode is used for the rituals for Holy Week and Easter, and the Araray mode is often used for daily morning services.

The Ethiopian Christmas chant in Listening Guide 46 is one of a group of chants named *engergari* ("excitement"). Called *Yome fesseha kone* after the opening words of its text, it is always sung as part of the ritual for Ethiopian Christmas and has remained central to the diaspora Christmas liturgy, probably because it directly refers to the joyous meaning of the day. This solo version, sung in a style called *qum zema* (literally, "plainchant"), was recorded during an interview with Berhanu Makonnen, the head musician of the Ethiopian church. Because the rhythm of the chant follows that of its text, the words may be clearly heard. At the phrase where the text describes the Wise Men bowing before the baby Jesus, the melody descends by the interval of an octave, perhaps symbolizing their deep bow.

This Ethiopian Christmas chant provides an opportunity for us to understand how differently music can be heard across cultural boundaries. As we have seen above, each Ethiopian notational sign (called a melekket) represents a short melody; these short melodies are linked together to constitute a chant. The

LISTENING GUIDE 46

CD 2
TRACK
11

Yome fesseha kone ("There Is Joy Today"; Ethiopian Christmas chant)

PERFORMED BY Berhanu Makonnen

The chant is set in the Ge'ez mode.

LISTEN FOR the frequent vocal slides (*rekrek*), which are heard only in the Ge'ez mode. Like most Ethiopian melodies, chants are also characterized by what is known in Ethiopian terminology as the "returning tone," a pitch that is repeated at phrase endings and cadences.

> There is joy today because of the birth of Christ from the Holy Virgin. He is Jesus the Christ before whom the Magi prostrated themselves [Matthew 2:11]. Truly, the glory of his birth is wonderful.
>
> —Translation by Getatchew Haile

Yome fesseha kone (Ethiopian Christmas chant)

PERFORMED BY *dabtaras* of the Bahta Church, Addis Ababa

Most performances of *Yome fesseha kone* during Christmas rituals are begun by singing "hallelujah."

LISTEN TO the manner in which two *dabtaras* alternate, the second singer echoing the musical phrase sung by the first. Compare this more elaborate performance style to the plainchant version you heard of *Yome fesseha kone* in Listening Guide 46.

melodies represented by the melekket are the smallest musical units perceived and named by Ethiopian church musicians. Although it is possible to transcribe Ethiopian chant in Western musical notation—indeed, as we have seen in the illustration on page 170—and to describe it in the same way we do Western melodies, Ethiopian dabtaras do not hear or conceive a chant as consisting of a series of individual pitches. Rather, an Ethiopian church musician hears and learns an entire chant as it is performed in rituals and then practices it by repeating the short phrases (each represented by a notational sign) in sequence after his teacher.

Ideally, a musician memorizes an entire chant, but should he forget, he can consult a notated manuscript. Therefore, Ethiopian chant is traditionally conceived, learned, performed, and heard by Ethiopian musicians in a manner very different from that of most outsiders. This subtle but significant difference in musical perception is fast disappearing in the Ethiopian diaspora. As complete rituals cease to be performed and taught in the traditional way, not only are fewer chants remembered, but the congregation may no longer hear the chants in the same way.

The Christmas chant continues to be performed in a traditional style in diaspora churches, usually with an alternation between two musicians in *antiphonal* style, referred to within Ethiopian practice as "singing on two sides."

The Impact of New Settings on Musical Performance   In traditional Ethiopian Christian musical practice, most holiday chants must be repeated at least five times in increasingly elaborate performance styles. We have

LISTENING GUIDE 48

Excerpt from an Ethiopian Christian ritual

PERFORMED BY *dabtaras* of the Bahta Church, Addis Ababa

LISTEN FOR the changing performance styles heard here as well as the growing sense of excitement they convey. This excerpt begins with a chant accompanied by sistra. At approximately 1:38, the drum (*kebaro*) first enters. At 2:19 you will hear the high vocal cry called ululation, softly sounded by women in the church expressing joy and thanksgiving. At 4:23, clapping and ululation accompany the music and dance.

already encountered two styles in our examples of the Christmas chant: as plainchant (Listening Guide 46) and in antiphonal style (Listening Guide 47). Additional chant repetitions are accompanied by waving prayer staffs in the air and pounding them on the floor; shaking sistra, hand-held metal rattles, in set rhythmic patterns; and accompanying the chant with dance, drumming, and vigorous clapping.

In the diaspora, these performance styles are maintained to the extent possible with only a few individuals to perform dance patterns intended for a dozen or more musicians. Only a few prayer staffs, a small number of sistra, and one or two drums (*kebaro*) are generally available to be brought out for annual holidays. Although attempts have been made to preserve ritual instrumental practice in the diaspora, the number of repetitions has been dramatically reduced.

In some instances, the Hymnary is no longer performed during church services at all but is presented at concerts for the Ethiopian

Ethiopian Christian musicians dancing during a performance of the Hymnary while pounding their prayer staffs (maqwamiya) *on the floor and playing sistra* (senasel). *Ethiopian liturgical dance is said to have been inspired by biblical accounts of King David and the people of Israel dancing around the Ark of the Covenant.*

community on holidays. These events can attract a sizable audience. One such Christmas gathering at an Ethiopian church in New York City transformed a sacred ritual into a concert with a banner decorating the stage announcing a performance of "Yared Music." Each chant was introduced and explained in English by a knowledgeable member of the community. In this case, a translator mediates between those in the congregation of a younger generation who no longer understand Ethiopian languages and the musicians, who are flown in from various Ethiopian diaspora communities around the world and who speak no English.

Sunday School Songs   As we have seen, Ethiopian church music changed among people of the diaspora. The regular performance of the Hymnary is mounted only on special occasions, while the Mass has gained emphasis. As a leader of one Ethiopian church in the United States noted: "It's easy to translate the Mass" and, in any event, "there is no one to do the music of the Hymnary."

Other noticeable changes have taken place as well. In prerevolutionary Ethiopia, women did not participate in Ethiopian Christian ritual performance other than to clap or to ululate at important points in the ritual. Indeed, women in Ethiopia traditionally stood in a separate area of the church, entirely apart from the male congregants, musicians, and priests.

The recent participation of women in Ethiopian Christian rituals and the presence of choirs singing hymns before and after Mass is a startling departure from traditional practice. At first glance, we might assume that these changes, like the new emphasis on the Mass, have been shaped by demands of the diaspora setting. Certainly, power has shifted from the clergy to the congregation, where women play increasingly important roles. New directions may also have been forged by the growing popularity among Ethiopian Americans of Pentacostalism, with its emphasis on lively strophic hymns, featuring congregational participation and clapping. While these factors have undoubtedly led to changes, the presence of choirs and the participation of women actually have another, unexpected source: they began not in diaspora innovations but in Ethiopia itself.

Members of the Ethiopian Youth Choir sing and drum at the Festival of the True Cross (Masqal) at River Park in Cambridge, Massachusetts, in September 1999. Note the prominence of the Ethiopian flag.

LISTENING GUIDE 49

CD 2
TRACK
14

Kasamay waradat ("He Descended from Heaven";
Ethiopian Sunday school song)

PERFORMED BY Women's Choir, St. Mary's Ethiopian Orthodox Tewahedo Church, Los Angeles, California

From Los Angeles to Boston to Washington, we can find
women participating regularly in Ethiopian Christian worship
and musical practice. Since the mid-1990s, young women
have stood alongside clergy during rituals, held prayer staffs
and sistra, and drummed the *kebaro*. Female choirs have been
founded in most churches—ranging from children to adult
women usually grouped by age—to sing newly composed
strophic hymns dedicated to the Virgin Mary.

LISTEN FOR the unison texture of this hymn, sung by a female choir accompanied by *kebaro*, clapping, and ululation.

kasamay waradat	He descended from Heaven,
kadengel mareyam tawaladat	Born from the Virgin Mary,
endihonan beza	So that he would be a Redeemer for us.
la'alam hullu	For the whole world,
labisu yamareyamin tsegga	What grace has Mary put on.

During the early years of the Ethiopian revolution, young city people sought
refuge in the church by attending Sunday school classes. Late-night church services
were hindered by urban violence, political surveillance, and restrictive curfews. The
Sunday schools could bring students together to study the Bible, church history, and
music of both the Hymnary and the Mass. As Sunday schools spread in the 1980s,
youths began to organize choirs. They also composed hymns—not in Ge'ez but in
the vernacular Amharic—and began to circulate their music on cassettes.

By the early 1990s, a new musical style had emerged. A young musician remembers that not only were the texts composed in Amharic, but "the sound had
changed." Today, in both Ethiopia and the American diaspora, these new hymns are
called "Sunday school songs." The new songs differ from chant, but congregants

Ethiopian women have brought their traditional music to a broader audience. Here, Aster Aweke, a leading Ethiopian-born singer now living in Washington, D.C., performs at the Charlotte (North Carolina) Jazz Festival. Aster fuses traditional Ethiopian songs and styles with American musical idioms, including rhythm and blues, jazz, and other repertories.

still consider them closely related to older musical traditions and feel that they honor the memory of Saint Yared.

The new Sunday schools opened a pathway for women to become active in Ethiopian Christian worship. Although women still cannot be ordained as priests or serve as *dabtaras*, they can now participate in liturgical performance and play the *kebaro*. The new hymns, most of which commemorate the Virgin Mary, have proved very popular. And though most are still imported from Ethiopia, transmitted by oral tradition and cassette, young Ethiopians in North America are now beginning to compose their own songs.

<u>Significances</u>   Changes in ritual orders, musical content, and performance styles—as well as in church administration—have brought additional shifts in meaning. The ritual music enables Ethiopians in North America to adjust to changing political and social conditions while expressing their belief in a familiar way. As the Ethiopian Christian church becomes an American ethnic church, it must be flexible enough to accommodate two very different streams of tradition—one based on long-standing practices, the other making room for innovation. At the center of this dilemma is the very American search to make liturgical content and practice relevant to everyday life.

Changes in Ethiopian worship cannot be attributed to new settings alone; new musical practices and the new genre of Sunday school songs emerged in part from political pressures in Ethiopia. All told, ritual and its musical content have been reshaped by the continuing interaction of homeland and diaspora.

Earlier we saw that a sixteenth-century invasion of Ethiopia spurred the development of a system for writing music. In the late twentieth century, revolution and political oppression gave rise to musical creativity. In the words of a young Ethiopian who lived through this revolutionary period and today teaches and sings the Sunday school songs, the new music "was the response of youths to the politics of the regime. The reaction was for youth to join churches. They became the backbone of the church. And women now play the drum."

Sacred music remains a vital part of the picture in the Ethiopian diaspora. Some of the musical traditions that embed and enact belief have been sustained there with great care and at great sacrifice, even as changes in sound and concept have been introduced. Familiar chants are retained but in shortened forms and new styles, performed by musicians new to their practice. Chant performance has also broadened from church ritual to ritualized concert, with secular performers adopting and adapting chants for purposes of entertainment. Strikingly, Ethiopian chant continues to influence music in the popular realm.

Conclusion

Clearly, it takes much care and significant sacrifice to preserve the musical traditions that sustain belief (see "Snapshot: The Pluralism Project"). Of particular

---

LISTENING GUIDE 50

CD 2
TRACK
15

Lent (EthioJazz)

PERFORMED BY Mulatu Astatke and ensemble

This song, adapted and arranged by Mulatu Astatke in the style called *EthioJazz* that he first developed in Ethiopia during the 1960s, alludes to the Ethiopian church music tradition through its title, its incorporation of psalm texts, and its use of vocal parts imitating Ethiopian Christian chant. The album that includes this song, *Assiyo Bellema*, takes its name and its title work from an Ethiopian song traditionally performed by young boys as a prelude to the new year, which falls at harvest time. The excerpt heard here is titled *Lent* in English.

LISTEN TO the blend of tradition and innovation as the instrumental ensemble, including saxophone, trumpet, trombone, drums, percussion, vibraphone (played by the composer Mulatu Astatke), keyboard, and bass guitar accompanies the singer Teodros Taddesse.

SNAPSHOT

The Pluralism Project*

In 1991, the Pluralism Project at Harvard set out to study multireligious America, beginning right here in Boston. Our research seminar visited the mosque in Quincy [Mass., like all the cities and towns named in this paragraph], built in the shadow of the great cranes of the shipyards by Lebanese immigrants who came early in the century, and we found that there were some 20 other mosques and Islamic centers that are part of the Islamic Council of New England—in Dorchester [a section of Boston], Wayland, Cambridge. We went to the spectacular new Sri Lakshmi temple in Ashland, a temple designed by Hindu ritual architects with tall towers decorated with the images of the gods and consecrated with the waters of the Ganges mingled with the waters of the Mississippi, the Colorado, and the Merrimack rivers. We visited half a dozen other Hindu communities in Boston, and two Sikh gurdwaras [places of worship] in Millis and Milford, and a Jain temple in Norwood, housed in a former Swedish Lutheran church. We found a dozen Buddhist meditation centers, with their respective Tibetan, Burmese, Korean, and Japanese lineages of instruction. And we visited the temples of the Cambodian Buddhists in Lowell and Lynn, the Vietnamese in Roslindale [another section of Boston] and Revere, the Chinese in Quincy and Lexington. Eventually, we published *World Religions in Boston,* a documentary guide to a city whose Asian population had doubled in 10 years, now a multireligious city.

It was clear that what was true of Boston might well be true of many other American cities. So the Pluralism Project sent a research team of students, multiethnic and multireligious, to study "hometown" America, fanning out across the United States every summer for three years. We were guided by three kinds of questions. First, who is here now in the 1990s? How many Hindu temples are there in Chicago? How many mosques in Oklahoma City? How many Buddhist temples in Houston? Second, how are these traditions changing as they take root in American soil? And third, how is America changing as Americans of many religions begin to appropriate this new multireligious reality and come to terms once again with our foundational commitment to religious freedom and, consequently, religious pluralism?

We found many remarkable developments. For example, Buddhist communities widely separated in Asia are now neighbors in Los Angeles, Seattle, and Chicago—Vietnamese, Cambodian, Thai, Chinese, Japanese, Korean, and Tibetan Buddhists. Here in America,

*Excerpted from Diana L. Eck, "Neighboring Faiths: How Will Americans Cope with Increasing Religious Diversity?" *Harvard Magazine,* September–October 1996, p. 41.

these Buddhist communities are just beginning to know one another and to meet the distinctive communities of "new Buddhists"—Americans of all races who have come to Buddhism through its meditation practices and its ethics. The Buddhist Sangha Council of Southern California, the Buddhist Council of the Midwest, the Texas Buddhist Association are evidence of the beginning of a new "ecumenical" Buddhism. There are American Buddhist newspapers and magazines, feminist Zen sitting groups, exemplary Buddhist AIDS hospice projects. Today Buddhism is an American religion.

The stupa *built on the roof of the Buddhist Church of San Francisco contains relics of the Buddha; it was presented in 1935 as a gift from Thailand to the Jodo Shinshu Buddhist Mission of America.*

~~~~~~~~~~~~~~~~~~~~~

What religious traditions are celebrated in your community? Try to attend the service of a religious tradition with which you are unfamiliar.

importance in keeping these traditions alive is the presence of an institutional structure in which musicians are trained and music can be regularly performed. In all three of these case studies—Tibetan chant, Santería, and Ethiopian church music—transplantation has not yet resulted in secure institutional settings. Thus, although Tibetans and Ethiopians in North America have sought to sustain ties with the past through ritual music, the meaning of that music is surprisingly vulnerable to change. Ties to the historical homeland, whether broken (as in the cases of Cuba and Tibet) or accessible (in the case of Ethiopia), remain important factors in diaspora religious and musical practice.

As the settings of rituals have shifted and the musical styles of chants have changed, so have their significance. The heirs of Saint Yared now include women as well as men, and the performance of Ethiopian ritual in the American diaspora has divided according to ethnic boundaries that have been intensely debated within Ethiopian political life. Santería, too, incorporates women in ritual chanting and drumming, domains once reserved exclusively for men.

One aspect of traditional ritual performance that has been sustained—with great enthusiasm—by these soundscapes is dance, perhaps the single area of traditional belief rituals in which all can participate, whatever their grasp of a given liturgical language or knowledge of its musical system. In the next chapter, we will delve into the remarkable capacity of dance, in deep union with music, to incorporate individuals into a larger community.

IMPORTANT TERMS

batá	liturgy	sistra (sing.
call and response	*melekket*	sistrum)
Changó	mode	Sunday school
chant, plainchant	*rekrek*	songs
dabtara	ritual	*toque*
dbyangs	*sadhana*	ululation
Ge'ez	Santería	*zema*
kebaro		

CHAPTER

SIX SIX SIX SIX SIX SIX SIX SIX SIX SIX SIX SIX SIX SIX SIX SIX SIX SIX SIX SIX SIX SIX SIX SIX SIX SIX SIX SIX SIX SIX SIX SIX SIX SIX SIX SIX SIX

*Delegates to the 1996 Democratic National Convention dance
the macarena in matching patriotic hats and sunglasses.*

OVERVIEW

MAIN POINTS

Dance:

• transforms a basic rhythm into a distinctive set of physical movements that are simultaneously heard through music

• invites anyone to participate who can master its basic movements, whatever their cultural background, social experience, or musical expertise

• incorporates the widest variety of meanings, from recreational to commercial

Music and Dance

Introduction

Like music, dance exists in time and space. Through physical motions, dance transforms that most basic physical unit—the pulse—into a complex rhythmic medium. Across communities, dance plays an important role as cultural display. Cultural values are created, expressed, and transmitted through this combination of music, movement, and dress (see "**Studying Music: The Study of Dance**").

One unique characteristic of dance is its availability to everyone, whether as spectators or participants. Dance's regular rhythms enable anyone who is motivated to join in without the ability to play a complicated instrument or sing an unfamiliar song text. Group dances are particularly welcoming to novices who must perform only a relatively fixed set of motions, anchored by a regular and recurring rhythmic pattern (see "**Snapshot: From Morris Dance to Macarena**").

At the same time, dance holds the possibility of rewarding those who master its intricacies, perform fluently, and add small variations to the basic motions. Dance is always open to the creative imprint of the individual who can express virtuosity while remaining within accepted boundaries. Dance is often a medium for intense competition, perhaps because of its ability to empower with such ease both individuals and groups of which they are part.

183

The Study of Dance

The study of dance for a long time was pursued mainly by a special group of scholars termed "dance ethnologists." Approaches to the dance have largely been divided between "choreological approaches," those emphasizing classification and description, and "contextual approaches," those stressing what dance tells us about society. Given the close relation between dance and music, and the presence of dance in so many of the soundscapes we have already discussed, it is vital that we study the dance and give attention to its special role in musical performance.

In order to preserve details of dance form and structure not accounted for or available from dancers themselves, dance ethnologists developed methods for the cross-cultural documentation of dance. One of the most important systems of dance notation is named after its creator, Rudolf Laban. Labanotation uses diagrams such as those shown in the illustration to describe dance motion in great detail. In recent years, film and videotape technology have been used to document dances.

Scholars of dance in recent decades have also become increasingly concerned with understanding dance's meaning. Drawing on the potential of visual and recording technologies, the ethnomusicologist Alan Lomax launched a project in 1962 to study the meaning of music and dance worldwide, reflecting the emerging anthropological interest in symbolic aspects of culture. Although Lomax's attempt to understand the relationship of song performance in its cultural context (termed "cantometrics," using a rating system that describes characteristics of recorded song performances so that they can be statistically compared and classified) is well known, he also developed a similar method for the comparative description of movement style. Termed "choreometrics," this rating system allows for

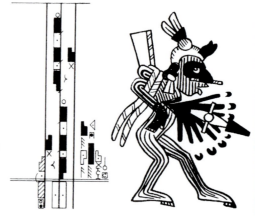

Notation can capture only a small part of dance's complexity. This brief example illustrates Labanotation, which uses symbols on either side of a vertical center line to represent dance movements. Symbols on the right side of the vertical line are for the right side of the body; those on the left, for the left side of the body. Each symbol indicates which part of the body moves in what direction and at what speed. The notation here indicates that the figure on the right, which is standing with a flexed back leg and retreating posture, should step backward with a double bounce on each foot.[1]

measurement of many categories of movement, including arm and leg motion, posture, dynamic qualities, use of space, movement flow, group organization, leadership roles, choreography, step style, and others. Lomax also compiled a preliminary "world history of the dance" and sought to link dance movements to those commonly found in other aspects of cultural life. Lomax has carried out his work on dance largely outside the mainstream of scholarship, which has been slow to recognize the importance of dance studies and to incorporate them within formal study programs.

SNAPSHOT

From Morris Dance to Macarena

According to South Asian belief, were the god Shiva to cease his eternal dance, the universe would descend into chaos. Although most present-day North Americans may not subscribe to this idea, the constant presence of dance during ceremonies, at celebrations, concerts, and at other moments of everyday life suggests that dance is indeed indispensable. Whether we prefer to waltz or salsa, or to simply watch the ballet, the body in motion—with music shaping its rhythms—captures our imaginations and makes us want to move.

   If you take a stroll through many American neighborhood parks or plazas early on May Day (May 1) or at dawn on the annual summer and winter solstices, you may encounter local Morris dancers costumed in white, with bells attached to pads strapped to their legs, dancing to the music of a fiddle, bagpipe, or penny whistle.

   The present-day Morris dance grew out of open-air, processional dances widely performed in late medieval England that possibly have even older roots in Druid traditions. First documented by folklorists in the late nineteenth century, Morris dancing was revived and spread

Morris dancers at Quoddy Head State Park, Maine.

internationally during the twentieth century, arriving in the United States around 1915 with the founding of the Country Dance and Song Society. Today, Morris dancing is widely performed by local clubs across North America for socializing and recreation, and to bring good luck on special occasions. The name *Morris dance* in fact is an overall term for several forms of English country dance, perhaps most frequently featuring six men or women carrying sticks or handkerchiefs. Dances are named after the tunes to which they are performed; local variations abound. (Check out one of the numerous Morris dance websites, which include histories, information on local clubs, and photographs.)

Some dances have deep historical roots and others mark present-day regional, ethnic, generational, and political identities, but most of the time people simply dance for fun. Occasionally, a style enters into popular consciousness, and it seems that everyone is dancing. The summer of 1996 brought such a dance craze—the macarena—to the top of the music charts and to virtually universal practice. The macarena fad started with a song of the same name, which had its roots in Spanish flamenco–influenced popular music. Released in a recording by the Seville singing duo Los del Río, the song soon topped the international charts. The macarena dance quickly followed and remains a staple of North American wedding celebrations, cutting across ethnic and religious boundaries.

Have you ever danced the macarena? If not, follow the motions sketched in the accompanying illustration.

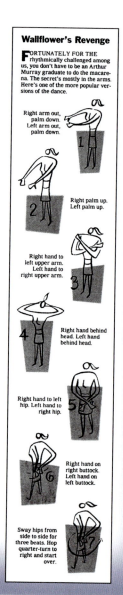

Wallflower's Revenge

FORTUNATELY FOR THE rhythmically challenged among us, you don't have to be an Arthur Murray graduate to do the macarena. The secret's mostly in the arms. Here's one of the more popular versions of the dance.

1. Right arm out, palm down. Left arm out, palm down.

2. Right palm up. Left palm up.

3. Right hand to left upper arm. Left hand to right upper arm.

4. Right hand behind head. Left hand behind head.

5. Right hand to left hip. Left hand to right hip.

6. Right hand on right buttock. Left hand on left buttock.

7. Sway hips from side to side for three beats. Hop quarter-turn to right and start over.

Hearing and Feeling the Dance

Most dances are performed to music with regular pulses, or *beats*. Dance musics often feature repeated groupings of beats, with the frequency of duple and quadruple rhythms no doubt stemming from the easy match of these musical patterns to human foot and leg motion. However, some dances—such as the waltz—are based on three-beat patterns. Whatever their grouping, the underlying beat structures of most dances remains fairly constant and can be sensed by the body.

CASE STUDY: MOVING THROUGH TIME AND SPACE WITH BHANGRA

Bhangra, a popular soundscape encountered within South Asian diaspora communities in North America and Great Britain, as well as on many U.S. college campuses, is an accessible dance style. Its strong rhythms and recurrent quadruple meter are clearly emphasized throughout by percussion instruments and vocal accents.

The movements of the competitive bhangra dance are tightly coordinated. Four to twelve dancers arranged in circles or pairs, sway from one leg to the other, with pronounced movements of their shoulders, occasionally waving their arms high overhead.

Usually, these motions are carefully choreographed to recorded bhangra music. Although the music and dance are inseparable, each supporting and feeding the energetic style of the other, the dance movements do not reflect or interpret the content of the song texts.

The sound and choreography of bhangra may seem

Jhummir, *a common* bhangra *motion, is performed with the arms raised and one leg lifted. The hands are raised upward, with index fingers straight and thumbs held touching the other fingers. The dancers jerk their shoulders on drum beats one and three; they jerk the raised leg on beats one, two, and three, and bring it to the ground on beat four.*

The 4 × 4 Bhangra Dancers perform the dance step chaal *at the Milk Cup Festival at Ballymoney, Northern Ireland, in July 2000. Shown, from left to right, are the dancers Billu Bains, Gurdish Sall, Sunny Sandher, and Marni Dhinsa, with Bill Sandher at the rear playing the* dhol.

LISTENING GUIDE 51

CD 2
TRACK
16

Aaoo Nachiye ("Come Let's Dance"; bhangra)

PERFORMED BY the Sangeet Group

This musical example is typical of present-day bhangra. The double-headed Indian drum (*dhol*) is just one ingredient in a stylistic fusion that draws on technologically enhanced musics ranging from disco and reggae, to techno and rap. Bhangra has its historical roots in South Asian Punjabi harvest festivals, where it was once danced in a circle and sung to the accompaniment only of drumming and hand-clapping. Present-day bhangra throughout the South Asian diaspora has added synthesizers, drum kits, and electronic manipulations.

LISTEN FOR the strong, regular pulse typical of bhangra. Following a brief drum introduction, a regular quadruple meter is established. Listen to the male voices crying out on the second and fourth beats of each grouping, producing an unanticipated shift in accent called *syncopation*.

Today my brother has come home after his wedding.
Sister-in-law looks gorgeous like the legendary Heer of the Siaal clan.
Her face beautiful like the full moon and her fragrance like flowers, she steps into the courtyard.
Come, let's dance in the giddha!
Let's dance, for brother has today come home after marrying his bride.

> In our courtyard the yarn is spun.
> The girl's from the UK and the guy's said to be from America
> And this couple went to a pub
> Yes, O folks, this couple went to a pub.
> This couple went to a pub.

straightforward on the surface, but both aspects provide entry into a soundscape of considerable complexity. For instance, the sound of bhangra music places it very much within the musical context of modern urban dance styles, while the text sheds light on conflicting currents of tradition and innovation within South Asian communities of Great Britain and North America.

All our wishes have been fulfilled today.
And today we'll dance to our heart's fill.
Dancing in rhythm and singing *bolis* we'll demonstrate what *giddha*'s like.
Come, let's dance in the *giddha!*
Let's dance, for brother has today come home after marrying his bride.

> In our courtyard the milk's churned.
> You're the king of my heart and I'm the queen of yours.
> I want you to stay mine forever.
> I want you to stay mine forever, o my *dhol* player.
> I want you to stay mine forever.

We're gonna dance so hard today
That it'll feel like an earthquake's hit the place.
This day of happiness won't be coming again
So let no anticipations of our hearts be left unexpressed.
Come, let's dance in the *giddha!*
Let's dance, for brother has today come home after marrying his bride.

I have taken the vows with you, darling.
I'll put all the comforts of the world in your lap
And what I say is true.
Yes, what I say is true, sweetheart.
What I say is true.

There's no day more joyous.
My love too knows no bounds.
Jind of village Ganday, the lyricist, will write a song about your wedding
if Rangroop plays the music.

Come, let's dance in the *giddha!*
Let's dance, for brother has today come home after marrying his bride.
Come, let's dance in the *giddha*
For today's a day of great joy.
Come, let's dance in the *giddha*
For brother has come home, now married.
Come, let's dance in the *giddha*
For today's a day of great joy.

— Translation by Rajwinder Singh

Traditional elements in the text include a reference to Heer, a fictional beauty in Punjabi culture, and mentions also the *bolis,* short solo phrases traditionally sung without accompaniment at the beginning of songs. The listener is invited to join the *giddha,* a dance still performed by Punjabi women as the equivalent to the all-male bhangra. The phrases translating "the yarn is spun" and "the milk is churned" were included strictly to enhance the rhyme within the original Punjabi text and have no other connection with the main theme of the song. Finally, the names of Jind and Rangroop, the song's lyricist and composer, respectively, are included in the last stanza according to traditional Punjabi practice.

Spreading from the Punjab to South Asian diaspora communities in Great Britain and North America, bhangra has become a traditional part of wedding celebrations. We should not be surprised, therefore, to find references added to a husband of Punjabi descent who "is from America" and a somewhat graphic metaphor—"oh my beloved *dhol* player"—used in reference to the groom. The line that says the "girl's from the UK" was altered from the original text "the bride's tall." Another striking textual change that links this rendition of *Aaoo Nachiye* to its diaspora setting is the use of vocables *yo, yo, yo* by the chorus at the beginning of the song, in addition to the much more common Punjabi expressions *oye, oye* and *hoye, hoye* heard throughout.

Modern bhangra retains traces of the music, text, and choreography of the harvest dance from which it derives, but its shifting settings have reshaped both its musical content and social meaning. By the 1980s, a range of bhangra styles, including bhangra beat, rock bhangra, and house bhangra emerged in Great Britain as a unifying musical symbol of the diverse British South Asian communities.

In the 1960s, bhangra allowed South Asian youths to affirm their identities in a positive way within a culturally hostile and exclusionary British environment. By the early 1990s, different bhangra styles emerged in Great Britain and bhangra began to cross over into the mainstream. Bhangra was featured on United Kingdom radio shows, and the songs of artists such as Apache Indian made a heavy impact on British society and musical culture.[2]

Bhangra has a continued life at home in North India. Here, a crowd of men wearing traditional clothes perform bhangra *at a festival.*

In North America, bhangra performance has spread to many American college campuses. Performances give young people of South Asian descent an opportunity both to come together to celebrate their shared heritage and to participate in increasingly popular competitions. Gender segregation into male and female teams performing bhangra and giddha respectively, is common, although some female teams will use male movements. The growing "team" aspect of North American bhangra performance both reflects and transforms aspects of this dance's complicated history. Many campuses now have bhangra clubs that participate in and host intercollegiate dance competitions, such as the 1998 "Bhangra Blowout" at George Washington University. The goals of this competition were to establish a South Asian scholarship and to "bring together the South Asian community in the hope of promoting unity and awareness of its vast and diverse culture."

Bhangra has also moved outside the college campus to enter the "Indipop" scene. Famous stars such as Daler Mehndi (the *badshah* or "emperor of bhangra") perform in countless concerts, movies, and television commercials. Since the late 1990s, bhangra has also been performed regularly at clubs in England and in urban North America, at places such as New York City's S.O.B. (Sounds of Brazil) and Basement Bhangra. One of the DJ-producers in part responsible for bhangra's high profile in England, Bally Sagoo, has said:

Bally Sagoo was born in New Delhi, India, and as an infant moved with his family to Birmingham, England. There he started as a deejay and a leading producer on the bhangra club dance scene. Sagoo's album Star Crazy *is popular worldwide.*

> You can't run away from the bhangra beat. It's an ethnic drum sound that makes you dance and incorporates a whole lot of ingredients. . . . It's progressed to where 50,000 screaming people are at Daler Mehndi shows—with more and more non-Asians.[3]

Dances both organize movements and interpret the rhythms, melodies, and texts with which they are associated. Therefore, they can have different meanings depending on the social setting of the performance. As we have already learned, bhangra originated as an outdoor harvest dance with few spatial constraints; wedding halls and staged competitions of today accommodate these unusually generous spatial needs inherited from the ancient festivals. Yet a further spatial dimension stems from the traditional separation of male and female dancers. We can compare the spatial separation of the sexes in bhangra with Western European couple dances such as the polka, in which couples actually embrace. Each dance configuration is a result of what its culture considers "proper" relationships between men and women; each idealizes or even caricatures those social relationships; and each reaffirms or asserts community.

In 1927, the polka was a part of everyday life on this farm in Getzville, New York.

CASE STUDY: THE POLKA

The polka originated in Central Europe among the Czech-speaking people of Bohemia. Over the course of one hundred fifty years, it has been played and appreciated internationally.

The polka is documented as having first appeared in Prague in 1837. The origin of its name is uncertain; it may be connected to a Czech word for "half" (a reference to its dance step) or, more likely, the name may derive from *polska,* the Czech term for a Polish girl. From its beginning, the polka was a dance style in duple time performed by couples and cultivated in urban ballrooms. Polka tunes, published in colorful collections, were either newly composed or adapted from other popular dance songs of the time. The polka step—a heel-and-toe half step—quickly became popular throughout Europe, then spread as far as Calcutta, India, where British colonials danced it in 1845 at a ball given in honor of Queen Victoria. By 1844, the polka was also known in the United States, where

Label from a 78-rpm recording of the Beer Barrel Polka *that was released by Victor in 1935.*

it was the source of jokes related to the name of the 1844 presidential candidate James K. Polk. The suggestive name of the dance, a well as its active perpetuation by Polish communities in the Midwest, resulted in the new and close association of the polka with Polish culture and identity by the 1920s.

The *Beer Barrel Polka,* one of the most famous early twentieth-century polkas, remains an active part of the polka repertory worldwide. Composed by Jaromir Vejvoda (b. 1902) under

SNAPSHOT

Dance's Indispensable Partner— Sound Recordings

Given the close ties between music and dance, by the first decades of the twentieth century sound recordings emerged as a major factor in the proliferation of the dance. Recordings expanded the settings of dance performance, enabling dance to be performed at virtually any time and place without the accompaniment of live musicians. In addition, recordings made it possible for anyone interested in a particular dance to learn and perform it even without expert musicians.

Perhaps most important, the spread of recorded dance music influenced the meanings people associated with dance. As dance music recordings crossed national boundaries and proliferated in public and private settings, dances easily crossed ethnic and cultural boundaries.

the title *Skoda Lasky* (and also known as the *Rosamunde Polka*), the *Beer Barrel Polka* was first recorded in Germany by Will Glahé's Musette Orchestra and was distributed in North America in 1935 or 1936 (**see "Snapshot: Dance's Indispensable Partner—Sound Recordings"**).

Although the origin of the polka predated the recording era by six decades, the polka achieved its greatest fame through recordings that introduced it to a wide cross-section of people and communities. Indeed, the polka soon became part of American popular culture with a best-selling recording of the *Beer Barrel Polka*— with English words—made by the Andrews Sisters in the late 1930s.

This song became popular largely through its ubiquitous appearance on juke boxes, machines that dispensed and played songs chosen from a list of well-known offerings of the time. Alvin Sajewski, son of the Polish immigrant who in 1897 founded the famous Sajewski Music Store in Chicago, traces the history of the song:

> And when the "Beer Barrel Polka" came out, things never stopped again until the war. It was the first thing like that ever came out. There were instrumentals before that, but not anything unusual, unless it was in the popular field. But "Beer Barrel Polka"

LISTENING GUIDE 52

Beer Barrel Polka

COMPOSED BY Jaromír Vejvoda

PERFORMED BY Valeria Longoria

The *Beer Barrel Polka* exemplifies the continued life and success of the polka outside of the Central European communities of its origin and beyond the boundaries of the European ballroom. The dance entered Mexican musical repertories along with other European dances and musics in the mid-nineteenth century. The interaction of Mexican and German immigrants in Texas also reinforced the popularity of the polka.

In this mid-1950s recording by Valeria Longoria, we hear the polka played by an instrumental group common along the Texas-Mexico border since the 1930s, *conjunto* (literally "united" or "connected," pronounced *con-hŏon-to*) ensemble, which features an accordion, along with a guitar, bass, and percussion (see **"Sound Sources: The Accordion"**). Born in 1924, Longoria, an accordionist, likely learned polkas during his Texas childhood and later while he was in the U.S. army in Germany during the 1940s. Longoria was well known for adapting a variety of musical styles and musical instruments to *conjunto* music.

LISTEN TO the basic, duple polka meter and the accented second beat of each measure, reflected in the short heel-and-toe half steps of the dance.

really started things going, and they never slowed down after that. It started the whole polka thing.

It was just as the juke boxes were coming out. The juke boxes were in the taverns. "Beer Barrel Polka" came out in the spring, so all the doors were open, and all the taverns with juke boxes put them right in the door and blasted away. That was a shot in the arm. People were getting jobs, and all of a sudden there was new life completely. You could get a big twenty-six-ounce stein of beer for a dime, and things were really rolling.[4]

In the early 1970s, some Roman Catholic churches began occasionally celebrating the Mass to the accompaniment of a live polka band. Melodies of familiar polkas are used to carry the words of traditional or newly composed hymns. Here, Father Wally Szcypula, an accordion embroidered on his vestments, celebrates a polka Mass in Rosemont, Illinois.

Walter "Li'l Wally" Jagiello, known as the "Polka King," has performed for the pope and the president. Here he plays the concertina, a type of button accordion, in his North Miami Beach studio.

The polka has had a long life, although its popularity has shifted over the years. Polkas continue to be widely performed at Polish weddings and have even been incorporated into the Mass.

In recent years, performance of the polka among people of German and Polish descent in Milwaukee, Wisconsin—once known as the "polka capital" of the United States—diminished and shifted to smaller towns in the Midwest, notably around Green Bay. Today, more polka festivals are held in northern and central Wisconsin, where the influence of country and western styles can be heard. In 1994, the polka was named Wisconsin's official state dance.

Dance Styles and Their Multiple Meanings

We sometimes assume that the nature of dance as physical movement limits verbal explanations and terminology. Indeed, the famous dancer Isadora Duncan is reputed to have remarked, "If I could tell you what I mean, there would be no point in dancing!" However, these nonverbal aspects of dance performance not

The Accordion

The accordion was first developed in early nineteenth-century Europe, with mass-produced push-button accordions joined later by those with treble (high-voiced) piano keyboards on one side and bass buttons on the other. The instrument spread quickly thanks to mass marketing in the 1830s, which, along with a grass-roots polka craze, insured that musicians throughout Europe became aware of the accordion's loud volume, portability, low cost, and full sound. European immigrants subsequently brought the instrument with them to the New World, resulting in the adoption of various types of accordions within a wide range of music and dance traditions. Instruments from the accordion family are prominent in the music of the polka and the tango.

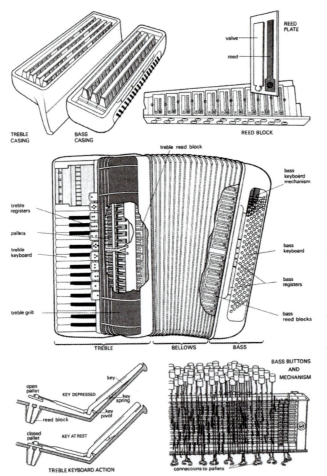

In this illustration, parts of the accordion that are normally hidden are made visible and labeled. The performer plays the melody on the treble (high-pitched) side of the instrument, which has either a piano keyboard, as seen here, or buttons. The bass (low-pitched) side, which always has buttons, is used to play supporting harmony.

The accordion consists of a bellows with a headboard on each side. Both headboards have multiple holes containing reeds of a type known as "free reeds," which sound in response to the entry or exit of air, which is controlled by the motion of the bellows. (The visible reeds used on a number of other wind instruments, such as oboes and clarinets, are termed "beating reeds," since they are set into motion and stopped by the mouth of the player.)

In addition to being able to sustain a high volume of sound over a long period of time, accomplished accordionists can achieve special effects. Perhaps most characteristic is "bellows shaking," which results in an intensified vibrato. The player controls the volume of the instrument by inflating the bellows quickly or slowly. The artistry entailed in inflating and deflating the bellows can be compared with the process of drawing a bow across a string on a violin, shaping the length of the musical phrases.

The button accordions, including the *bandoneón* used for the tango, have the bass buttons on the left and the melody buttons on the right. The piano accordion has the keyboard on the right side. The piano accordion has also been manufactured in two sizes, a regular "male" instrument, and a small "ladies" size, with keys closer together. Complex in their construction, accordions can also be elaborate in their artistic design, emerging as important artistic and visual symbols of cultural identity.

These dismantled accordion keyboards show how the treble keys and bass buttons work differently to open and close the reed blocks hidden within the cases on each side. The treble keys open and close pallets controlling each reed on the reed block; the bass buttons are attached to their pallets through rods and levers. Air pushed through from the bellows sounds the open reeds.

only encourage variations in choreography but also encourage multiple interpretations of dance's meaning. As we have seen with bhangra, dance's flexibility gives it meanings that shift at different times and in different places.

Although participation in a dance is the most direct route to understanding its form and meaning, performers have developed terms through which they can describe dance's qualities and explain them when teaching. Many dances have insider terminology to describe and cue motion as well as to define movements. A familiar example is the "do-si-do," a crossover between partners seen in square dances. Frequently, dance steps become known by the name of the dance with which they are most closely associated. For instance, the Morris dance, with roots in the British Isles and perpetuated today by dancing clubs throughout North America, reportedly incorporates the "polka step."

Although on one level we need to approach dance as structured motion shaped by and giving form to music, we must also consider the soundscapes of which dance is a part. We will take a close look at the rich tradition of the tango and the manner in which its sound, setting, and significance have been maintained and transformed over time (**see "Looking Back: The Tango"**).

CASE STUDY: THE TANGO

In the tango, we once again encounter a soundscape cluster, a group of closely related soundscapes that share many aspects of sound and meaning while retaining their different settings and historical frameworks. The sounds and movements of today's tango music and dance have their shared roots in the slums of late-nineteenth-century Buenos Aires, where rural Argentinean *gaucho* (cowboy) and long-time African influences joined with the creativity of European immigrants.

The early tango emerged in Argentina with the introduction of the *bandoneón,* a special type of accordion. Brought by German immigrants, the *bandoneón* slowly displaced the guitar in early tango. Its distinctive sound merged with the syncopated rhythms of traditional gaucho and African styles that gave the music and dance its distinctive rhythmic sense. Vivid descriptions of life's hardships in the slums of the *arrabal* (outskirts) of Buenos Aires pervade the poetic texts of tango songs. At the center of the tango's musical style and choreography, however, is the myth, affect, and exaggerated postures of the *compadrito,* (literally, "a man who has come to less") a type of urban gaucho who was at once Don Juan and pimp, dressed in a tight black suit and high-heeled shoes. The straight, unbending upper body of the tango dancer is said to be characteristic of the stance of the *compadrito;* the smooth pattern of the steps is thought to reflect patterns in knife duels; and the forward tilt of the man's body is attributed to his high-heeled shoes. Distinctive, too, is the interaction of the male and female tango dancers: the man moves forward in the dance, bent over the woman so that she is forced to retreat.

<u>Sound and Steps</u>   The tango's musical foundation is a quadruple meter, strongly emphasized in the bass. Other rhythms, particularly stress on the second half of the second beat, may be superimposed above and within the quadruple framework. Unlike most dances, which maintain a constant pace, the tango often slows down and speeds up for dramatic purposes. In contrast to the quadruple framework and rhythmic variations in the vocal melody or other instrumental parts, the physical motions of the tango dance usually stretch across two of these four-beat units, resulting in a pattern that is counted out as slow-slow-quick-quick-slow (2+2+1+1+2).

The tango is a circular dance, with steps that progress counterclockwise. Within the general parameters of this rhythmic pattern, the tango includes a number of standard motions, called "steps" or "figures." Many of these steps have become part of the tango (and broader "ballroom" dance) oral tradition. These include the basic starting stance called the "promenade position," and other common moves such as the "swivel," a type of sliding turn on one foot. Some steps, including the "fan," where the female partner is swung out to one side by the male, are also used in Latin dances such as the cha-cha and rhumba. It is important to realize that steps with the same names may be interpreted differently, depending on the dance and context, and can even vary within different tango styles. However, continuity of some movement names has been maintained over time through vintage dance manuals. The following passage from a 1914 manual describes a classic tango step sequence now called the "back corté":

A 1914 color lithograph by V. G. Barbier depicts a couple dancing the tango in the latest fashions of the day.

The man starts backward with his left foot and the lady forward with her right. The man steps and counts as follows: One, backward on the left; two, backward with the right and "brush" [a short, quick motion with the toe]; three, forward on the right; four, bend. Repeat four times. The reverse of the above for the lady. . . . After completing the Single Cortez as described above, take eight walking steps, the man backward and the lady forward.[5]

Needless to say, an accomplished tango dancer must have command of "floor craft" to avoid collisions with a partner or with other couples on the dance floor.

The classical tango song in Listening Guide 53 is one of the best-known examples of its genre, performed by the singer most responsible for the internationalization of the tango, Carlos Gardel (1887–1935). Gardel is himself part of the tango legend. The son of an immigrant Frenchwoman, Gardel grew up in

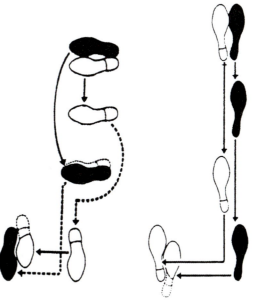

Two common tango steps: the swivel (left) and the back corté (right).

The Tango

1870	Influx of immigrants to the Rio del Plata region of Argentina
1880	Early musical development and invention of the tango as a result of the fusion of music traditions of Rio del Plata region with those of immigrants from Europe
1887	Carlos Gardel born, possibly in France
1890s	First true tangos composed in Buenos Aires
1900	Tango as a dance and early form of popular music establishes firm foothold in Buenos Aires. *Bandoneón* introduced into tango ensembles
1902	Earliest recordings of tango
1907–1908	Tango first introduced in Paris, where Camille de Rhynal, dancer and dance teacher, modifies abrupt tango movements considered too crude for ballroom dancing
1911	Columbia Records makes first tango recording
1912	Tango first introduced in London
1913–1915	Argentinean tango comes to Europe as a ballroom dance
1917	Gerardo Hernán Mastos Rodriguez composes *La Cumparsita* ("The Little Carnival Procession") as a march; Roberto Firpo changes it to a tango
	Samuel Castriota composes *Mi Noche Triste* ("My Sorrowful Night"); the lyrics by Pascual Contursi introduce a mood of pessimism, melancholy, and nostalgia into tango lyrics
	First film devoted entirely to tango—*El Tango de la Muerte* ("The Tango of Death") produced in Argentina
1921	Rudolph Valentino performs the first Hollywood tango in film *The Four Horsemen of the Apocalypse*
1924	Pascual Contursi and Enrique Pedro Maroni add lyrics to *La Cumparsita;* Carlos Gardel records the song
1920s–1940s	Golden Age of tango worldwide
1929	At height of political turmoil, Ministry of Navy in Argentina bans protest tangos (*tangos de protesta*) from Argentinean radio
Early 1930s	Great Depression reinforces acceptance of tango as misery, bitterness, and resentment expressed by dance are relevant to everyday life
1932	Addition of vibraphone, viola, cello, percussion, and harp to tango ensemble
1935	Carlos Gardel dies in a plane crash

1936	Wind instruments incorporated into tango ensembles
1950s–1960s	Tango of the 1920s and 1930s on the decline; new concert tangos develop
1980s	*Tango Argentino* opens on London's West End, New York's Broadway, and goes on world tour; the tango reenters popular culture

Buenos Aires and became a famous singer, the embodiment of all the dreams and aspirations of the lower class. After World War I, Gardel was a major force in popularizing the tango in Paris. His sudden death in a plane crash contributed to his legendary status in Argentina, where the dates of his birth and death are commemorated and his portrait—in tuxedo, bowtie, striped shirt, and hat—is widely displayed.

Carlos Gardel sings over the NBC radio system in 1934.

<u>Settings</u>   Whether the tango was sung or danced, its early home was the cafes and bordellos of Buenos Aires. The cafe setting is described in melancholy tango texts such as *Cafetín de Buenos Aires* by E. S. Discépolo.[6]

How could I forget you in this lament,
cafe of Buenos Aires,
if you are the only part of my life
which reminds me of my mother?
In your miraculous mixture
of know-it-alls and suicides,
I learned philosophy, dice, and gambling
and the cruel poetry
of no longer thinking of myself.

LISTENING GUIDE 53

La Cumparsita (tango song)

PERFORMED BY Carlos Gardel

In this recording, we hear the standard tango ensemble accompanying Gardel, with the *bandoneón* and violin prominent. The strong quadruple beat is often embellished with a long-short rhythmic pattern consisting of a long beat followed by one that is half its duration, usually referred to in Western terminology as a dotted rhythm (see Chapter 2). The singer occasionally slows down and speeds up to express the meaning of the words.

The form of *La Cumparsita* is fairly traditional, with an instrumental introduction, a simple statement of the main melody (A), a contrasting theme/verse (B), and return of the main melody as a refrain, dramatized and embellished (A'). Note that when the main theme returns, a solo violin plays a separate melody, termed a *countermelody*. The underlying rhythmic pulse, in typical tango fashion, emphasizes the second half of the second beat.

LISTEN TO the lyrics of the song, which express "views of love and life in highly pessimistic, fatalistic, and often pathologically dramatic terms."[7] The words here seem to contradict the strong, erotic dominance of the male dancer over his closely held female partner.

A	Si supieras, que aun dentro de mi alma	If you only knew that in my soul
	conservo aquel cariño	I still keep that affection
	que tuve para tí. . . .	that I had for you. . . .

Musicians called organ grinders (*organitos*) also played tangos throughout the barrio streets on small portable barrel organs, mechanical instruments turned by a handle that provides air to the pipes inside a wooden barrel. With these connections to the brothel and the barrio, the tango was associated in early twentieth-century Argentina with poverty, low social class, and even ill repute. Only the

Quien sabe si supieras
que nunca te he olvidado,
volviendo a tu pasado
te acordaras de mí. . . .

Who knows if you'll ever know
that I've never forgotten you;
if, returning to your past,
you'll remember me. . . .

B Los amigos ya no vienen
ni siquiera a visitarme,
nadie quiere consolarme
en mi aflicción. . . .

[My] friends don't come any more,
not even to visit me;
nobody wants to comfort me
in my grief. . . .

Desde el día que te fuiste
siento angustias en me pecho,
decí, percanta, ¿que has hecho
de mi pobre corazón?

From the day you left
I've felt anguish in my chest.
I said, grieving, "What have you done
to my poor heart?"

Al cotorro abandonado
ya ni el sol de la mañana
asoma por la ventana
como cuando estabas vos,
y aquel perrito compañero
que por tu ausencia no comía,
al verme solo el otro día
tambien me dejo.

To the abandoned bedroom
now not even the morning sun
shines through the window
as it did when you were there,
and that little dog, our partner
that because of your absence would not eat,
on seeing me alone the other day
also left me.

A' Si supieras, que aun dentro de mi alma.
conservo aquel cariño
que tuve para tí. . . .

If you only knew that in my soul
I still keep that affection
that I had for you. . . .

Quien sabe si supieras
que nunca te he olvidado,
volviendo a tu pasado,
to acordaras de mí. . . .

Who knows if you'll ever know
that I've never forgotten you;
returning to your past,
you'll remember me. . . .

—Translation by David Lyczkowski

migration of the tango to Europe—first to Paris, and then to other cities—insured its upward mobility in Argentina itself. Through the sponsorship of Argentine beef barons, the dance debuted in elite Paris circles. Through its simultaneous introduction by sailors to the French port city of Marseilles, it became rooted in European musical culture. Thus the history of the tango

Classic tango collections rereleased on CD include performances by (top row, left to right) Carlos Gardel; Ricardo Tanturi, Alberto Castillo, and Enrique Campos; and Troilo and Roberto Goyeneche; (bottom row) Juan D'Arienzo; Tita Morello; and Astor Piazzolla and Gary Burton.

resembles in part that of the polka, which had become popular in Paris in the mid-nineteenth century.

When the government closed Argentine brothels in 1919, the tango in Argentina slowly began to attract an elite audience, and Buenos Aires followed Paris's lead in welcoming the tango to upper-class cabarets and theatres. By the 1930s, with its acceptance into broader social circles at home and its growing popularity abroad, the tango became a symbol of Argentinean national pride. The

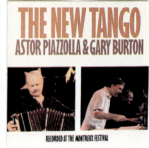

The worldwide spread of the tango extends to Japan, where the tango has long been popular in social and competitive circles.

tragic death of Carlos Gardel in 1935 solidified and institutionalized the tango as part of Argentinean culture, generating a type of public adoration for the musician and his music that has verged on religious veneration.[8]

As the tango increasingly assumed a role as Argentina's national music, musicians introduced innovations that demonstrated its versatility. Astor Piazzolla created a purely instrumental "new tango" (see "**Individual Portrait: Astor Piazzolla**"). Piazzolla's new tango retained the sound of the *bandoneón*-centered tango ensemble while expanding the rhythmic and harmonic complexity of the music. The "new

Astor Piazzolla

The life and career of the tango composer and *bandoneón* player Astor Piazzolla reflects the way that music and musicians have increasingly crossed boundaries. "My music is a popular chamber music that comes from the tango," he wrote. "If I do a fugue in the manner of Bach, it will always be 'tanguificated.'" Born of Italian descent in Argentina on March 11, 1921, Piazzolla moved to New York City with his parents in 1923. There he first heard the tango on old 78-rpm recordings. Piazzolla's father gave him a *bandoneón* for his ninth birthday. By age thirteen, Piazzola was already proficient enough on the instrument to play for the legendary tango singer Carlos Gardel, when Gardel visited New York.

In addition to his skill as a composer, Astor Piazzolla was a virtuoso bandoneón *player who had an active performing career with his ensemble* Quinteto Tango Nuevo.

In 1939, Piazzola returned to Argentina, giving up his accounting studies and devoting his life to music. While playing his *bandoneón* "in every cabaret in Buenos Aires" he maneuvered a meeting with the famed pianist Arthur Rubenstein, who in turn arranged for the ambitious young musician to study with the Argentinean composer Alberto Ginastera. By the early 1940s, Piazzola had learned to compose music in many classical styles. Piazzolla wrote prodigiously, eventually producing the 1953 piece (*Sinfonía*) that won him a scholarship from the French government to study in Paris with the legendary composition teacher Nadia Boulanger, who had already taught many famous composers. In an interview with the journalist Gonzalo Saavedra during Piazzolla's last visit to Spain in 1989, Piazzolla himself noted that Boulanger led him to realize that his distinctive voice as a composer rested not with the standard Western classical compositions, but with the tango. One day, after Piazzola finally admitted to Boulanger that he played the *bandoneón,* she asked him to perform one of his own tangos for her. After hearing some of his music, Boulanger "suddenly opened her eyes, took my hand and told me: "You idiot, *that's* Piazzolla!"

From that time on, Piazzolla composed in his own distinctive style, and in 1955 he returned to Argentina to found his own tango ensemble. In the years to follow, he developed his "new tango," a tango that experimented with rhythm, harmony, and form. At first his new tango was not well received, and Buenos Aires radio stations refused to play his music. By 1960, however, along with his Quinteto Nuevo Tango ensemble, Piazzolla became the leading performer and composer of this new type of tango. He received many honors in his native Buenos Aires, where he was named a Distinguished Citizen of the City, and he became famous throughout the world. Piazzola toured internationally and released many recordings before his death in 1992.

LISTENING GUIDE 54

CD 2
TRACK
19

Adiós Nonino (new tango)

COMPOSED AND PERFORMED BY Astor Piazzolla

One of Astor Piazzolla's most famous tangos is the beautiful *Adiós Nonino,* composed in 1959 in memory of his father, who died that year. This performance is by Piazzolla's Quinteto Tango Nuevo, which includes the *bandoneón,* violin, piano, guitar, and bass.

On first hearing, *Adiós Nonino* seems to be a substantial expansion of the traditional tango form, but with more repetitions of its themes than we heard in *La Cumparsita. Adiós Nonino* begins with an extended introduction for solo piano introducing the main theme (A). Next, the *bandoneón* and ensemble play a rousing rendition of a lively second theme (B), followed by a restatement of the first theme, played by the solo violin and ensemble. At this point, where a traditional tango would end, *Adiós Nonino* continues with a restatement of the first theme in the violin and then a restatement and development of the second theme performed by the entire ensemble. The piece concludes with a final rendition of the first theme, played once featuring the *bandoneón,* and then by the entire group.

Clearly, Piazzolla's tango is both longer and more complex than *La Cumparsita.* It reflects the influences of Western classical forms, most particularly the *sonata form* with its characteristic restatement and development of both themes, heard here beginning at 4:34. Piazzolla's

tango" was intended for performance in the concert hall, not for dancing. Thus, Piazzolla brought the tango across what had formerly been a divide between the popular and classical soundscapes.

By the 1950s, Piazzolla had popularized large orchestral tango arrangements, often expanding the ensemble to include several *bandoneóns,* strings, and percussion instruments, as well as piano.

Following World War I, well before Piazzola's "new tango," the tango had been incorporated into compositions by European classical composers such as Igor Stravinsky. However, Carlos Gardel transformed the tango into a truly popular form, and by the middle of the twentieth century it had spread beyond Europe through Asia to Japan, as well as to North America. It has been suggested that the orchestration is also quite complex, passing the melodies from piano to violin to *bandoneón* and back, and using unusual instrumental devices such as *glissandos* (a rapid scale produced by sliding the fingers on the piano keys or violin string). Piazzola's first and second themes contrast with and complement each other, with the first theme characterized by its songlike character and the second theme by its distinctive rhythm.

LISTEN TO the tango rhythms that can be heard in the background throughout the work, setting off the many colorful harmonies drawn from twentieth-century Western classical music and Latin jazz. The way *Adiós Nonino* uses two contrasting melodies as recurrent themes resembles that employed by composers of the classical symphony.

The following chart compares the forms of *La Cumparsita* and *Adiós Nonino*:

La Cumparsita	*Adiós Nonino*
0:00 Introduction (*bandoneón*)	0:00 (piano solo)
0:26 First theme (A) (voice)	1:37 (piano solo)
0:57 Second theme (B) (voice)	2:47 (*bandoneón* and ensemble)
2:09 Return of A (voice and violin)	3:33 (violin and ensemble)
	Extension:
	4:34 Restatement of A (violin and ensemble)
	5:15 Restatement/development of B
	(*bandoneón* and ensemble)
	6:19 Return of A (*bandoneón*)
	7:27 Restatement of A (ensemble)

worldwide financial depression of the 1930s and World War II rendered the tango's pessimistic and despairing themes relevant to the period.

During the second half of the century, the tango became part of the rapidly growing middle-class ballroom culture. Amateurs learned and practiced the dance to recordings. As the tango spread, different styles developed, including the Argentine style, the International Style, originally developed in France and Great Britain, and the American style. Riding several waves of ballroom revivals and increasing interest in a variety of Latin American musics and dances from the 1970s forward, the tango became an increasingly popular focus of dance clubs and competitions. In the 1990s, ballroom clubs proliferated in urban areas and on college campuses, many of them training teams to compete in different styles and competition

Cafe Tu Tu Tango of Atlanta, Georgia, is part of a restaurant chain that since 1993 has featured the tango along with other popular dance styles.

networks. Throughout the second half of the century, too, the tango appeared in Broadway musical songs like "Hernando's Hideaway," from *The Pajama Game* in the 1950s, in 1990s touring shows such as *Forever Tango,* and films.

Significance   The significance of the tango, given its roots in Buenos Aires barrio and its heavy sexual overtones, remains a source of dispute in Argentina itself. The lore of the tango has had a long life, and twenty-first-century students of the tango are still told tales of its roots as a dance of "lust and anger." These themes of open sexuality and male dominance are embedded in the choreography

The dancers Carolina Zokalski and Diego Di Falco star in Tango Magic, *aired in 1999 on public television stations.*

of the dance: the mannerisms and style of the Argentinean *compadrito* in late–nineteenth-century Buenos Aires, a skilled fighter, bully, dandy, and hero. The body language of the tango—especially the aggressive posture of male over his female partner—incorporates and perpetuates notions of masculine dominance.

As the tango spread from Argentina to Europe and beyond, it was considered to be "exotic" and fed what has been called "the economy of passion."[9] Others explain exoticism as a market-driven phenomenon by which Western culture appropriates other cultures, then profits from exploiting them. In Argentina, the tango has played a central role that moves beyond issues of gender and sexuality, developing from its origin as a comment on poverty and class resistance into a symbol of Argentinean national pride.

Conclusion

The tango draws together several themes we have explored in earlier chapters: it is the quintessential urban form, a music-dance tradition born as an indigenous musical style that adapted aspects of European music and instruments. Influenced by immigrants to Argentina, the history of the tango throughout the twentieth century has been one of continued movement and innovation. Over the course of this same period, the tango has moved from the Buenos Aires barrio into the lives of middle-class dance amateurs and professionals around the world.

The tango also embodies subjects and issues we have not addressed until now. The music, songs, and associated movements have strong sexual connotations; the dance re-enacts a particular set of gender relations. The body takes center stage as the main instrument in dance:

> People's experiences with the first form of power, their bodies, tap potent, dramatic, and easy-to-recall sources of images that influence their responses to dance as participant or observer. Using the signature key of sexuality, essential for survival and desirable for pleasure, dance resonates universal instincts and particular concerns. The medium is part of the dance message.[10]

Tango dancers have different identities in different places, from the Argentinean patriot to the ballroom competitor. Like other musical traditions, over the course of the last century the tango has been increasingly dependent on recording technology and part of the international entertainment economy.

This chapter has added the world of physical motion to our repertory. The tango's worldwide popularity must be due in part to the power of its rhythms as they become part of our "body memories." In the next chapter, we will continue to explore the subject of music and memory, investigating this important, reciprocal relationship.

What dances do you know? How did you learn them? Do you know any special terms associated with these dances?

Are you aware of any dances that have become popular recently?

Many communities have centers where dances from many traditions are taught. What dance resources can you locate in your community?

IMPORTANT TERMS

accordion	development	new tango
bandoneón	*dhol*	polka
bellows shaking	figures	polka-step
bhangra	*giddha*	sonata form
compadrito	glissando	syncopation
conjunto	juke box	tango
countermelody		

This painting copied from a photograph shows the Sakka family of Aleppo, Syria, gathered around their phonograph. Recordings were already an important part of Middle Eastern musical life in the first decade of the twentieth century.

OVERVIEW

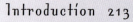

MAIN POINTS

We remember music through multiple encodings in the brain.

Music and its performance enable us to:

• preserve and reenact memories of people, places, and events

• commemorate people and events

• reconcile the past with the present

• express what cannot be expressed in any other way

Music and Memory

Introduction

Music, as we have seen, plays an important role in many facets of everyday life, among them the processes of memory. First, both song texts and melodies can remind us of people, places, and events, serving as access points to long-term storage of historical memories. Second, through repeated performances over time and in different settings, music draws on a partly subconscious bank of memories, sometimes triggering recollections—and emotions—long forgotten. Third, the physical processes involved in music making calls on "habit memory," the capability to dance or play a musical instrument without consciously thinking about every movement. Thus music, both through its content and through the physical act of performance, can bring our past into the present even when we seemingly have long forgotten the events.

Memories are stored in various sections of the brain, so in order to reconstruct a memory, we must retrieve parts of it from these different areas. Each half of the cerebral cortex, an outer layer of gray matter in the brain, is divided into four major lobes. The frontal lobes consist of distinct subregions that play important roles in such processes as encoding, retrieval, working memory, and recall of information. Specific regions within the other three lobes participate in the storage of long-term memories. These areas cooperate closely with structures in the inner sectors of the brain to allow us to remember what is happening right now.[1]

In light of this admittedly oversimplified description, we may conclude that the best time to retrieve a memory within music occurs at the moment when the piece

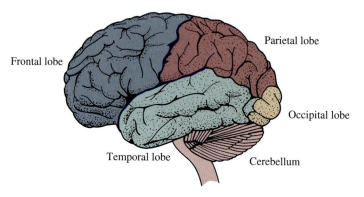

Frontal lobe

Parietal lobe

Occipital lobe

Temporal lobe

Cerebellum

This view shows the surface of one hemisphere of the brain. Deep inside the temporal lobe is the hippocampus, a small horseshoe-shaped structure that encodes new events and information.

is heard. When we play in or hear a musical performance, we experience the moment in which a memory is established. At the same time, observing a musical performance can provide us with information available nowhere else about the social and cultural factors that help shape the process of remembering. We already have evidence that everyday human behavior, such as singing folk songs and ballads, may give us insights into memory that we cannot get through formal psychological experiments. So, just as we can study how memories of music are physically stored and recalled through musical performance, we can also learn by listening to what people, especially musicians, tell us about music and memory.

What information have you learned by connecting it with music? For example, many English speakers learned and remembered the alphabet by singing it aloud to a simple melody. Do you remember the *Alphabet Song?* Note that the melody of the *Alphabet Song*, particularly memorable to the Western ear, is based on the children's song *Twinkle, Twinkle, Little Star.*

Music making also draws on both individual and shared memories, and the way in which music is conceived and transmitted makes that clear. A song is usually composed by an individual, but it is remembered only if it is learned and sung by others in a community. Quite simply, a song cannot survive in anyone's memory if it is not performed, though as we have seen, music notation and recording media do make possible the transmission and survival of music beyond the life span and physical location of its human carriers (see "Studying Music: Technologies of Transmission").

STUDYING MUSIC

Technologies of Transmission

Various forms of writing music have long served as memory aids in the transmission of older musical traditions. But remembering almost any music of the past century has been greatly helped by the presence of recording technology. The cylinder phonograph, with its recording and playback capabilities, was first marketed commercially in 1888, initiating a new age of musical experience mediated by technology.

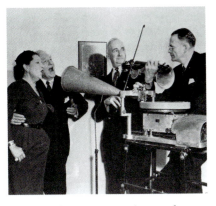

This staged reenactment of a recording session during the first decades of the twentieth century features an Edison disc recorder and a Stroh violin, fitted with a horn to amplify the sound. The artists include Zinka Milanov and Giovanni Martinelli.

Four major technological transitions provide a historical backdrop for understanding how recordings have transformed musical memory. The first period, from 1888 to 1940, can be termed the "phonograph era," since it was during this time that a series of different phonographs and gramophones were developed to record and play, respectively, wax cylinders and 78-rpm discs. Recording activities throughout Europe, Africa, and Asia fed what by the 1920s had become a thriving "ethnic record" market. Immigrants brought with them recordings of music from their former homelands and could order such recordings by mail. No longer were immigrants forced to rely solely on their own musical memories or on the live performance of others in their new homes. The emergence of radio in the 1920s provided yet another new technology for transmitting music and reinforcing it in memory.

After the disruption of World War II, the "LP era" began in 1948, followed a year later by the first commercial magnetic-tape machines. The new vinyl LPs (long-playing records) had improvements in both the fidelity and length of sound recordings, enabling people to listen to long musical works—thirty minutes or so of uninterrupted music—that previously had to be divided into five-minute segments, the most that would fit on one side of a 78. The increasing portability of tape recorders also helped the recording of music by people doing fieldwork, thereby feeding the growth of musical scholarship and paving the way for the publication and distribution of music from around the world.

Musical traditions once known only within a local community had the possibility of moving quickly into the international domain.

A third major transition took place in the late 1960s with the advent of the cassette tape recorder. Cassette technology allowed anyone anywhere to record and play back sound at very little expense. At the same time, the cassette made it easy for individuals and communities to share music, and it transformed musical pedagogy. The wide availability of the cassette—and eventually, the Walkman—for playback caused a further revolutionary shift from the public consumption of live music to private listening.

The introduction and proliferation of digital recording in the last decade of the twentieth century is a fourth technological innovation that has assisted musical memory and has even affected the very sounds of the music it encodes. Remastering sounds of earlier eras has also allowed us to hear music formerly obscured by the frailties of earlier technologies and to juxtapose separate traditions in new contexts.

The development of recording technology has enabled music of the past to live on into the indefinite future outside the workings of human memory, has allowed music to be separated from live performance settings, and has provided music with an afterlife in venues ranging from living rooms to sound archives. Recordings have served music as memory devices of tremendous power that can replace human memory and make a people's musical heritage almost impossible to forget.

In this unit, we will explore the union of music and memory in several different soundscapes. A number of song traditions sustain historical memories such as royal lineages or battles. The epic songs of West Africa, Southeast Asia, and the Balkans are well-known examples. Although these tend to be lengthy and are usually performed by musical specialists, shorter songs, such as ballads, also contain stories of great interest and importance. We encountered one such example in the ballad *Barbara Allen.* Here we will see how historical events have been conveyed in *corridos*, ballads composed and transmitted within communities of Mexican descent. The corrido has long preserved the memory of specific historical moments and documented the lives of important individuals in Mexican and Mexican-American history. We will see that the historical content of the corrido text depends heavily on the form of the melody itself.

Often, the corrido purposefully records a historical or political event and may over time commemorate all those involved. But there are other strong musical traditions for specifically commemorating an individual at the time of death. One very moving form is the New Orleans jazz funeral, although some of the music associated with this event is actively transmitted in other contexts. We will explore the jazz funeral later in this chapter.

Our major case study for this chapter will investigate the manner in which song can be a medium that binds together seemingly incompatible strands of cultural memory, reflecting, reshaping, and even transforming perspectives of the past. *Pizmonim* are songs sung by American Jews whose ancestors immigrated from Aleppo, Syria. These songs, with sacred Hebrew words set to popular Arab melodies, strikingly exemplify how musical performance can accommodate memories that may be difficult to express in other situations. These same songs also carry different streams of memory, sacred content in their texts and secular associations in their tunes, insuring music's persistence in different areas of long-term memory.

Remembering through Music

CASE STUDY: THE *CORRIDO*

The Mexican *corrido* (ballad) displays the ability of music to carry within it memories of particular places, people, and events. As noted previously, the ballad is a strophic song that tells a story, usually a historical narrative, whether set in real or mythical times. The *corrido* emerged as a particularly important medium for preserving historical memories during the first and second decades of the twentieth century, before and during the Mexican revolution. During this period, many Mexicans had resented North American hegemony in Mexico and were alarmed at the United States' treatment of its own Mexican-American citizens.

Hearing a strophic text set to a melody can make it easier for us to learn and recall the words. The melody helps us remember phrases, line lengths, stress patterns, and emphases, especially when the melody is simple, symmetrical, and repetitive. And indeed, most ballads have simple but catchy tunes and repetitive structures.

To summarize, music—and especially song—carries memories in its texts and its tunes. In the case of *Gregorio Cortez*, memories are carried primarily in the text, but the melody carries that text and helps the singer recall it during a performance. (Below we will see examples in which the melody itself sustains important historical memories.) The *corrido* recalls a particular series of events and records the actions of an important individual. Over time, this ballad has also come to commemorate Gregorio Cortez as a symbol of Mexican independence and power. Commemoration is a vital outcome of the relationship of music and memory, as we will see in the following section.

Gregorio Cortez in a photograph taken as a joke after his release from prison.

CD 2
TRACK
20

Gregorio Cortez (Mexican-American *corrido*)

PERFORMED BY Trovadores Regionales (Pedro Rocha and Lupe Martinez)

This famous *corrido* recounts the story of Gregorio Cortez, who, on June 12, 1901, shot and killed the Texas sheriff Brack Morris. The sheriff had just shot Cortez's brother while trying to arrest the men for a crime they had not committed. Gregorio Cortez fled, fearing—with justification—that he would be lynched. In the course of his flight on foot and horseback toward the Rio Grande and the safety of Mexico, Cortez eluded search parties trying to capture him. During this period he killed a second Texas sheriff named Glover and was also accused of murdering a constable.

Gregorio Cortez was finally captured near Laredo. The resulting trial galvanized the support of Mexican-Americans. Following a legal battle that lasted three years, Cortez was acquitted of murder in the deaths of Sheriff Morris and the constable, but was sentenced to life imprisonment for the death of Sheriff Glover. In 1913, Cortez was pardoned by Texas governor O. B. Colquitt. The *corrido Gregorio Cortez* records this dramatic story and marks in song what proved to be a milestone in Mexican-Americans' struggle for civil rights and social action.[2]

LISTEN TO the regular rhymes between the second and fourth lines of each verse and the mostly syllabic text setting. Note that the melody has a very narrow range with mainly conjunct (stepwise) motion. This performance, on one of the many "ethnic records" distributed on 78-rpm discs in the 1920s and 1930s, was recorded in San Antonio by singers performing in harmony, accompanied by two guitarists. Ballads such as *Gregorio Cortez* were transmitted by oral tradition.

En el condado del Carmen	In the country of the Carmen
miren lo que ha sucedido.	look what has happened
Murió el sherife mayor	The main sheriff died
quedando Román herido.	leaving Roman wounded.
Otro día por la mañana	The following morning
cuando la gente llegó	when the people arrived
Unos a los otros dicen	Some to the others said
no saben quien lo mató.	they don't know who killed him.
Se anduvieron informando	They were investigating
como tres horas después	and about three hours later

Supieron que el malhechor
era Gregorio Cortez.

Insortaron a Cortez
por toditito el estado.
Vivo o muerto que se aprenda
porque a varios ha matado

Decía Gregorio Cortez
con su pistola en la mano,
"No siento haberlo matado
al que siento es a mi hermano."

Decía Gregorio Cortez
con su alma muy encendida
"No siento haberlo matado
la defense es permitida."

Venían los americanos
que por el viento volaban,
porque se iban a ganar
tres mil pesos que les daban.

Siguió con rumbo a Gonzáles,
varios sherifes lo vieron,
no lo quisieron seguir
porque le tuvieron miedo.

Venían los perros jaundes
venían sobre la huella
Pero alcanzar a Cortez
era alcanzar a una estrella.

Decía Gregorio Cortez
"Pa' que se valen de planes,
si no pueden agarrarme
ni con eves perros jaundes."

Decían los americanos
"Si lo vemos que le haremos
si le entramos por derecho
muy poquitos volveremos."

En el redondel del rancho
lo alcanzaron a rodear,
Poquitos mas de trescientos
y allí les brincó el corral.

They found out that the wrongdoer
was Gregorio Cortez.

Cortez was wanted
throughout the state
Alive or dead may he be apprehended
for several he has killed.

Said Gregorio Cortez
with his pistol in his hand,
"I'm not sorry for having killed him
It's for my brother that I feel sorry."

Said Gregorio Cortez
with his soul aflame
"I'm not sorry for having killed him
self-defense is permitted."

The Americans came
like the wind they flew
Because they were going to win
the three thousand pesos reward.

They continued toward Gonzales
several sheriffs saw him
They did not want to continue
because they were afraid of him.

Came the hound dogs
they came on his trail
But to reach Cortez
was to reach a star.

Gregorio Cortez said
"What's the use of plans
If you can't catch me
Even with those hound dogs."

The Americans would say
"If we see him what shall we do to him,
if we face him head on
very few will return."

In the corral of the ranch
they managed to surround him.
A little more than 300 men
and there he gave them the slip.

(continued)

Allá por el Encinal a segun por lo que dicen Se agarraron a balazos y les mató otro sherife.	There around Encinal from all that they say They had a shoot-out and he killed another sheriff.
Decia Gregorio Cortez con su pistola en la mano, "No corran rinches cobardes con un solo mexicano."	Gregorio Cortez said with his pistol in his hand, "Don't run, you cowardly rangers from one lone Mexican."
Giró con rumbo a Laredo sin ninguna timidez, "¡Síganme rinches cobardes, yo soy Gregorio Cortez!"	He turned toward Laredo without a single fear, "Follow me, you cowardly rangers, I am Gregorio Cortez."
Gregorio le dice a Juan en el rancho del Ciprés, "Platícame que hay de nuevo, yo soy Gregorio Cortez."	Gregorio says to Juan at the ranch of the Cypress, "Tell me what's new I am Gregorio Cortez."
Gregorio le dice a Juan, "Muy pronto lo vas a ver, anda hablale a los sherifes que me vengan a aprender."	Gregorio says to Juan, "Very soon you will see him, go on talk to the sheriffs to come to arrest me."
Cuando llegan los sherifes Gregorio se presentó, "Por la buena si me llevan porque de otro modo no."	When the sheriffs arrive Gregorio presented himself, "You'll take me if I wish it, because there is no other way."
Ya agarraron a Cortez ya terminó la cuestion, la pobre de su familia la lleva en el corazón.	Now they caught Cortez now the case is closed, His poor family he carries in his heart.
Ya con esto me despido con la sombra de un ciprés Aquí se acaba cantando la tragedia de Cortez.	Now with this I take my leave in the shade of a cypress, Here we finish singing the tragedy of Cortez.

Commemorating through Music

CASE STUDY: THE JAZZ FUNERAL

Music is used in many cultures to commemorate individuals at the time of death. We have already seen two such examples in Chapter 2: mariachi music and bagpipe laments.

The jazz funeral, which is disappearing from practice and therefore from memory, marked the death of a musician or, occasionally, some other person of note (see **"Individual Portraits: Famous New Orleans Jazz Musicians"**). As the

INDIVIDUAL PORTRAITS

Famous New Orleans Jazz Musicians

When Louis "Satchmo" Armstrong died on July 6, 1971, he was given two funerals. One, without music, was held at the Corona Congregational Church near his New York City home. A second, two days later, was an old-fashioned jazz funeral in New Orleans, the city of his birth. These contrasting commemorations frame Armstrong's extraordinary career. The New York funeral included honorary pallbearers ranging from the mayor of the city, John Lindsay, to the entertainer Johnny Carson. Some twenty-five thousand people lined up to pay their last respects to Armstrong's coffin at the Seventh Regiment Armory on Park Avenue in Manhattan, before the church ceremony and burial in a Flushing, New York cemetery. In contrast, Armstrong's New Orleans jazz funeral included an immense parade of musicians and fans, with the Onward Brass Band playing traditional jazz tunes.

Louis Armstrong was one of the stars of the New Orleans jazz style in the early years following its genesis in the first decade of the twentieth century. A syncopated blend of ragtime and the blues, New Orleans jazz was played by small brass ensembles improvising both the melody and accompanying parts. **(See "Sound Sources: "The Jazz Band.")**

Other great musicians, too, were associated with the New Orleans jazz style. One was Ferdinand L. "Jelly

Louis Armstrong is carried in triumph in a traditional procession at Brazzaville's Beadouin Stadium after a 1960 concert in the Congo.

Roll" Morton (1890–1941), a pianist-composer who innovated in the rhythmic domain, expanding jazz's duple and quadruple rhythms by composing "jazz tangos." Morton was influenced not just by different African American musics from ragtime to blues, but also by Caribbean styles. Some have attributed this influence to connections through his Haitian ancestors. We have particularly detailed information about Jelly Roll Morton's life and experience thanks to a lengthy set of 1938 interviews with Morton by the ethnomusicologist Alan Lomax that are preserved today in the Folk Music Archive of the American Folklife Center at the Library of Congress.

Armstrong gained his early experience playing with another famous New Orleans jazz musician, Joseph "King" Oliver (1885–1938). King Oliver's well-traveled Creole Jazz Band and his "Dippermouth Blues" recording (1923) popularized the "wah-wah" sound of the cornet played with a mute. This recording launched Armstrong's career.

An instrumentalist, singer, and composer, Louis "Satchmo" Armstrong was particularly famous for borrowing and improvising on well-known popular melodies. Armstrong, especially in his "Hot Five" recordings, influenced jazz's musical style for decades to come. He was a major force in initiating the big band ensembles of the 1930s and in shaping the swing era of the 1940s.

As Armstrong became famous, he traveled widely and popularized jazz internationally. When Armstrong played an open-air concert in Accra, Ghana, on May 25, 1956, he drew one hundred thousand people. Particularly important were his tours sponsored by the United States State Department, which earned him the title "Ambassador Satch."[3] His 1960 trip to Africa provided inspiration to many there at a period when a number of African countries were gaining their independence from colonial powers. Reports of Armstrong's tours in newspapers and film footage on early television broadcasts also caught the attention of many at home in North America, bringing jazz a new, domestic audience.[4]

At the time of his death, Louis Armstrong was mourned internationally, by individuals ranging from heads of state to the members of his mass audience. It is not surprising that numerous memorial concerts have commemorated the centennial anniversary of his birth and the glorious career that led him away from his native New Orleans to perform on the world stage.

casket was driven slowly through the streets of New Orleans, it was followed on foot by a procession of friends and a jazz band performing solemn music (**see "Sound Sources: The New Orleans Jazz Band"**). On its return from the cemetery, the band struck up a joyous, lively jazz tune suitable for accompanying the departed to heaven. So rare is the jazz funeral today that when one such ritual was

The New Orleans Jazz Band

Brass, woodwind, stringed, and percussion instruments make up the jazz band. There are anywhere from five to fourteen instruments in the ensemble, including cornets or trumpets, trombones, violin and string bass, snare and bass drums, clarinets, and alto or tenor saxophones. In addition to funeral processions, the jazz band plays in many other settings. The style of the music often reflects the outdoor settings of its performances: loud volumes, penetrating quality, and wide vibrato all woven into a dense polyphony. The drums provide the beat while the trumpets, clarinets, violin and trombones take turns carrying the melody. A solo trumpeter often improvises at the final chorus of the piece. In general, bands with a maximum of three melody instruments will feature more improvised passages than those with four or more, which are likely to play arrangements.

Brass bands, such as this ensemble of German immigrants in an 1879 painting, were commonly heard in the streets of American cities during the last decades of the nineteenth century. Brass bands strongly influenced the development of the jazz band.

The birthplace of jazz was New Orleans at the turn of the twentieth century. During and after the American Civil War, marching or street bands, termed "tonk" bands, were particularly important in poorer districts of the city. Many seminal performers, such as Louis Armstrong and Jelly Roll Morton, got their start playing in these bands (**see "Individual Portraits: Famous New Orleans Jazz Musicians"**). At high-society events in the wealthier parts of town, another type of band, called the "society" band, drew on a repertory of waltzes and sentimental ballads. A third kind of band, the New Orleans dance band, performed for general dances, advertisements, and picnics. Early New Orleans dance bands included the Eagle Band, the Onward Brass Band, the Imperial Orchestra, and groups led by King Oliver and others. All of these bands—the tonk, society, and dance bands—served as models for the early jazz band.

Between 1900 and 1915, these bands evolved into the classic New Orleans jazz band. Driven by the social demand for jazzy dances, such as the foxtrot and the Charleston, occasional marches, hymns, and popular songs, the New Orleans jazz band played a diverse repertory in many different contexts. Within the first two decades of the century some bands toured the country, resettling on the West Coast and in New York and Chicago. Yet through its many transformations, the jazz band remained similar enough to nineteenth-century American brass bands that a 1917 poster described the Original Dixieland Jass Band as "a brass band gone crazy!"[5]

The Olympia Brass Band marches slowly through the streets of New Orleans on the way to a church or funeral home, its music establishing a solemn mood. The men at the front of the procession wear sashes to mark their status as marshals of the band's lodge or social club. The band, led by Harold Dejan and heard in Listening Guide 56, was founded around 1960.

performed in January 1999 to commemorate a colorful figure in the French Quarter of the city, newspapers carried descriptions of the event. The deceased, a practitioner of Vodoun, a religion of Afro-Caribbean origin, was known by the name "Chicken Man," because he performed a ritual that included the sacrifice of a chicken. The Chicken Man's jazz funeral included elements of Vodoun:

> The remains of the Chicken Man were borne off in a glass-cased hearse pulled by two white horses. . . . The cortège was accompanied by a mounted police escort and a jazz band and voodoo bongo drummers, including a figure in a long black dress. . . . Hundreds marched and danced in the "second line," which traditionally follows the mourners at jazz funerals, as the procession wound through the narrow streets where the Chicken Man once roamed.[6]

When the jazz funeral was performed more regularly, its repertory of songs remained fairly consistent. The hymn *Amazing Grace* was often performed at these ceremonies, during the subdued march to the cemetery, contributing additional layers of historical memory already embedded in the song itself.

The text of *Amazing Grace* was probably written by an eighteenth-century Eng-

"New Britain," from *The Southern Harmony*

1 Amazing grace! (how sweet the sound) That saved a wretch like me! I once was lost, but now am found, Was blind, but now I see

2 'Twas grace that taught my heart to fear, And grace my fears relieved: How precious did that grace appear, The hour I first believed!

3 Through many dangers, toils, and snares,
I have already come;
'Tis grace has brought me safe thus far,
And grace will lead me home.

4 The Lord has promised good to me,
His word my hope secures;
He will my shield and portion be,
As long as life endures.

5 Yes, when this flesh and heart shall fail,
And mortal life shall cease,
I shall possess, within the veil,
A life of joy and peace.

6 The earth shall soon dissolve like snow,
The sun forbear to shine;
But God, who call'd me here below,
Will be for ever mine.

Shape-note notation, also called fasola, is a system that uses different shapes to indicate the notes of the Western scale, which were also represented by the syllables do, re, mi, fa, sol, la, and ti.

LISTENING GUIDE 56

Amazing Grace (hymn)

PERFORMED BY DeJan's Olympia Brass Band

In this remastered recording of a traditional brass band playing *Amazing Grace* for a jazz funeral in the late 1960s, we hear DeJan's Olympia Brass Band, one of New Orleans's oldest brass bands.

Amazing Grace is technically classified as a hymn, or, loosely defined, a song praising God. Hymns are almost always strophic, with simple, easily remembered tunes that aid singers in learning and remembering multiple verses. In this performance, the trumpet plays the familiar opening phrase as an introduction, varying the melody in the first two verses before the saxophone takes over in the third. The trumpet then returns for the final chorus.

LISTEN TO the jazz band playing the hymn as a slow march, yet another example of a song crossing boundaries of genre.

lish evangelist and reformed slave trader John Newton. The tune to which Newton's text is sung today, known as *New Britain,* was transmitted through William Walker's *Southern Harmony* songbook, published in Tennessee in 1835 and still used today across racial boundaries in the southern United States. The hymns in Walker's songbook were printed in *shape-notes,* a system of notation that was devised to make hymn tunes easier to read. By the second half of the twentieth century, the hymn could be heard in a variety of North American settings. Its powerful theme of redemption struck a chord in the 1960s during the civil rights movement and the American folk music revival.

Amazing Grace, how sweet the sound
That saved a wretch like me.
I once was lost
But now I'm found
Was blind, but now I see.

By the turn of the twenty-first century, use of *Amazing Grace* for purposes of commemoration has cut across all boundaries, to the extent that—its Christian heritage notwithstanding—it was performed by a bagpiper at the funeral in 1999 of a Jewish police officer that was held at Temple Emanu-El in New York.

Reconciling the Incompatible through Music

CASE STUDY: THE SYRIAN JEWISH *PIZMON*

Sometimes music can sustain memories that conflict with present-day situations. Such is the case with the songs we will study next.

When Jews left Aleppo, Syria, in the early twentieth century and established new communities abroad, they brought the *pizmon* with them. The term *pizmon* (plural *pizmonim*) literally means "adoration" or "praise," and most of these hymns consist of Hebrew texts set to melodies borrowed from Middle Eastern Arab music.

Over the years, Syrian Jews have continued to sing these hymns and have also composed new *pizmonim*. The union of sacred Hebrew texts with melodies drawn from popular Arab music may seem ironic to outsiders, especially given the twentieth-century Arab-Israeli conflict. However, members of the Syrian Jewish community treasure these songs as part of their unique Arab-Jewish heritage. In the following case study, we find a colorful example of music not only conveying memories but also providing a setting in which memories incompatible in the present can be reconciled.

Syrian Jews perpetuate the culinary traditions of their historical homeland and patronize local grocery stores that stock Middle Eastern foods. The main Syrian Jewish shopping area in New York is in the borough of Brooklyn, near Ocean Parkway.

The Sound of the *Pizmon*   The *pizmon* tradition had its beginnings in the late Middle Ages, when Jews began to borrow melodies from the non-Jewish world around them to set new sacred Hebrew texts (see "Looking Back: The Long Syrian Jewish Past"). Creating a new song by borrowing an existing melody has a long and honorable history in many musical traditions. A work that results from this process is today termed *contrafactum* (pl. *contrafacta*). The use of a well-known, preexisting melody ensures, of course, that the new text will be remembered more easily. Indeed, it seems likely that *contrafacta* became so widespread precisely because the familiar melody helps us recall the new words.

The Long Syrian Jewish Past

c. 1000 B.C.E.	Jews said to have arrived in Syria during reign of King David
834 C.E.	Archaeological evidence of a Jewish community in Aleppo, Syria
c. 1500	Jews expelled from Spain (Sephardic Jews) arrive in Aleppo
1500s	First publications of Jewish hymns (*pizmonim*) with borrowed melodies and sacred Hebrew texts
1800s	General economic decline in Aleppo
1850	Revival of *pizmonim* in Aleppo by Rabbi Raphael Taboush
1869	Opening of Suez Canal decreases use of overland trade routes and speeds economic decline of Aleppo
1881–1914	Approximately 110,000 Arabic-speaking immigrants, including Syrian Jews, enter the United States
1888	Rabbi Raphael Taboush composes the *pizmon Attah El Kabbir*
1901	Syrian Jews found Great Synagogue Ades in Jerusalem
1903	Syrian Jewish community established in New York City
1911/1912	Syrian Jews in New York establish a synagogue on the top floor of a tenement building on the Lower East Side
1912	Cantor Moses Ashear leaves Aleppo and immigrates to New York
1914	Syrian immigration to the United States peaks at 9,023
1919–1920	First Syrian families move to Bensonhurst, Brooklyn
1920s	Syrian immigration to the United States declines as a result of the Immigration Quota Act of 1921 and the Immigration Act of 1924
1930s	Syrian Jews move to Flatbush, Brooklyn
1946	Muhammad ʿAbd al-Wahhab composes *The Wheat Song,* the Arab tune later borrowed for the *pizmon Ramah Everai*
1948	Israeli War of Independence; state of Israel founded
1956	Sinai War between Israel and Egypt
1973	Arab-Israeli "Yom Kippur" War
1977	Egyptian President Anwar L. Sadat visits Israel
1980s	Israeli cassette tapes reintroduce *Attah El Kabbir* to Syria
1982	Louis Massry composes the *pizmon Ramah Everai* for the bar mitzvah of Moses Tawil
Early 1990s	Most of the Jews remaining in Aleppo and Damascus immigrate to Brooklyn

LISTENING GUIDE 57

Attah El Kabbir ("You, God, Are Mighty"; Syrian Jewish *pizmon*)

COMPOSED BY Raphael Taboush

PERFORMED BY Moses Tawil and Ensemble

Although the text of the original Arab song is mostly lost, the *pizmon Attah El Kabbir* melody displays a well-known Arab form called a *muwashah*. A three-part form, the *muwashah* has a clearly recognizable melody at the beginning that returns after a contrasting middle section.

The *pizmon,* like the Arab song on which it was based, is in duple rhythm and proceeds at a spirited pace. It is performed by a soloist and chorus in unison, accompanied by an *'ud* (**see "Sound Sources: The *'Ud* and the *Qanun*" in Chapter 3**), resulting in a *heterophonic* texture—the voices and instrument play the same melody, here with slightly different ornaments. The text praises God, calling on the Creator to have mercy on his chosen people during their exile among strangers. An acrostic is embedded in the original Hebrew text: reading down, the first letter of each verse spells "I am Raphael," identifying the author of the text, Rabbi Raphael Taboush.

LISTEN TO the brief, improvised vocal introduction in *maqam nahawand* that begins this recording of the *pizmon Attah El Kabbir.* This type of introduction, called a *layali,* is frequently heard

Jewish religious tradition deems it acceptable to borrow melodies from non-Jewish sources. Setting these tunes with sacred Hebrew texts is thought to render them holy, to bring out a melody's "holy spark." Syrian Jews borrowed the music they most often heard, notably the Arab songs popular in their community. While living in Aleppo, where Jews and Arabs had regular contact and congenial relations, Syrian Jews acquired Arab tunes through oral tradition, hearing the songs in coffeehouses and concerts. Many *pizmonim* from the nineteenth century, set to Arab melodies popular at the time, are still sung today.

Most *pizmonim* borrow their tunes from Arab songs, and so are based within the Arab musical system, *maqam.* There are at least a dozen important categories of *maqamat* (pl.), each distinguished by its *pitch content* and the way in which those in Arab music to help establish the *maqam* of the subsequent song. Although it may sound as if the introduction is sung to vocables, its text is in fact derived from the Arabic words *la yahl* ("oh, night"), from which the introduction takes its name.

You, God, are mighty, your name is merciful,
Have pity on a chosen people,
For your compassion is abundant,
Without end and without limit.
> For your compassion is abundant,
> Without end and without limit.

My soul shall thank you, every moment and at all times
Accept my faithful praise!
With pity act upon me graciously.
> Accept my faithful praise!
> With pity act upon me graciously.

I shall not hold my peace, not in day or at night
My tongue shall utter your rightness
Desire my prayer as if it were a sacrifice
In place of sacred sacrifice or burnt offering.
> Desire my prayer as if it were a sacrifice
> In place of sacred sacrifice or burnt offering.

See, my rock, how long is the length of my exile
Strangers continue to lord it over me
Hurry now, please, the coming redemption.
> Strangers continue to lord it over me
> Hurry now, please, the coming redemption.

Give beauty and honor and strength
To the son of David, your anointed one
Who, every morning, gives forth hymns
With a voice of song and praise.
> Who, every morning, gives forth hymns
> With a voice of song and praise.

> My God, bless and strengthen this righteous people
> Bear them on eagles' wings
> Yet even higher.
> > Bear them on eagles' wings
> > Yet even higher.
> > —Translation by James Robinson

pitches are ornamented and developed within the song (see **"Snapshot: A Closer Look at *Maqam*"**). *Maqam nahawand,* which you will hear in a late-nineteenth-century *pizmon,* is still sung today by Syrian Jews around the world (see **"Snapshot: The Transnational Path of the *Pizmon Attah El Kabbir*"**).

Pizmonim were composed mainly to celebrate and commemorate joyous life cycle occasions such as the birth of a child, a *bar mitzvah* ceremony (held when a boy turns thirteen and officially becomes an adult in matters of religion), or a wedding. Usually, a song was commissioned by a family celebrating one of these occasions, and often the composer selected the melody of a favorite popular song at the request of the father of a newborn or the groom about to be married. The composer would also incorporate references to the occasion and the names of family

SNAPSHOT

A Closer Look at *Maqam*

Lying at the core of Arab music is the concept of *maqam,* described by a Syrian Jewish musician to be the "science behind Arab music" and the "bottom line of the entire culture we have absorbed and used." Each *maqam* (pl. *maqamat*), a term used in Arab music since at least the fourteenth century, is a category of melodies that share pitch content, range, and characteristic ornaments. The characteristics of a given tune determine its *maqam,* and the words of any given *pizmon* are composed only after the melody is selected.

The number of *maqamat* and their names have differed over time and across geographical areas in the Arab world. Even within the same locale, the total number of *maqamat* varies according to whether closely related *maqamat* are considered part of the same "family" or independent. Present-day Syrian Jews count eight *maqamat* as the most important.

Twentieth-century Arab music theory explains a *maqam* as a basic scale divided into two sections of four notes each. Musicians recognize a *maqam* by the intervals between the notes in the lower and upper sections. Syrian Jewish *maqam* theory emphasizes that the "nucleus of a *maqam*" can be found by identifying its final pitch and the two preceding. We might also recognize *maqamat* through practice and experience: musicians learn to listen to the end of a tune and match it to the *maqam* of a song they already know. This process works especially well with some *maqamat,* whose lower sections are quite distinctive.

In their Sabbath morning rituals, Syrian Jews prescribe one or another *maqam* to be emphasized each week. Selected *pizmonim* and important prayers are sung in the weekly *maqam.* The *pizmonim* we are studying in this unit are in *maqam ajam* and *maqam nahawand.*

members into the Hebrew text. The new *pizmon* would first be performed at the synagogue ritual at which the baby, young boy, or groom was blessed, and subsequently at various domestic rituals and parties (see "Snapshot: Syrian Musical Occasions—The *Sebet* and the *Haflah*").

SNAPSHOT

The Transnational Path of the *Pizmon* *Attah El Kabbir*

The blended sounds of the *'ud* (lute), violin, zither, and hourglass drum could be heard coming from the open folk arts stage in the Snug Harbor Cultural Center on Staten Island, New York, with each instrumentalist playing an improvisation on the melody of the *pizmon Attah El Kabbir.* How did this Syrian *pizmon,* composed in late-nineteenth-century Aleppo, come to be heard in a festival of Jewish arts on a Sunday in 1989? In fact, it took a full century of transnational wandering for the *pizmon* to arrive at Staten Island.

Attah El Kabbir was composed in Aleppo by Rabbi Raphael Taboush. The Hebrew text calls on God to have mercy on his chosen people, alluding to their exile among strangers. Its melody derives from a now-forgotten Arab song of the late nineteenth century. After its composition, the *pizmon* spread quickly, as Syrian Jews migrated to other locales. Thanks to a transcription made by an ethnomusicologist before 1910, we know that this song was sung in Jerusalem at that time.

Attah El Kabbir also spread, around 1912, to Syrian communities outside the Middle East, including one established in Mexico City by disciples of Raphael Taboush who immigrated there. At the same time, it was transmitted to New York City by Cantor Moses Ashear and other Taboush students. But in the decades after the death of Cantor Ashear in 1940, *Attah El Kabbir* fell out of use in New York. Some long-time residents who know many *pizmonim* remember learning the song, but only in the 1960s, when it was reintroduced by Israeli cantors who moved to New York. We can see, then, that despite its early introduction to New York, its presence there now stems back only some forty years. *Attah El Kabbir* was evidently forgotten in Syria as well and was reintroduced there through cassette tapes sent from Israel around 1980.

Today, *Attah El Kabbir* is very much alive in Israel, where it is sung in every Syrian Jewish synagogue in Jerusalem. It is also heard regularly in Mexico City and New York during prayer in the synagogue, at life-cycle events, at parties, and at concerts. Thus, the performance of *Attah El Kabbir* at the Staten Island festival can be seen as just another appearance of a *pizmon* that has traveled the world with Syrian Jews over the course of the last century.

Syrian Jewish Musical Occasions— The *Sebet* and the *Haflah*

The *pizmonim* play an important role in the Syrian Jewish liturgy and life cycle rituals. They also occupy a special place in the community's social life, where their frequent performances serve to embed them in memory. One important musical occasion is a Sabbath-afternoon songfest, the *sebet,* held among Syrian Jews in North America to celebrate special occasions:

> When a groom is going to get married, they give him the honor by calling him up to the reading of the scrolls. . . . and then they go home and they make a little party. They call that "Sebet." "Sebet" is in Arabic. . . . the Sabbath. They invite all their close friends. Sometimes they have over a hundred people. And they have very nice food prepared for them and they spend about two or three hours singing. . . . They have all types of songs. They sing, sometimes they dance. They do the same thing when they have an engagement, when they have a bar mitzvah, or when they have a new child, whether it be a boy or girl.[7]

It is said that Cantor Moses Ashear began this *sebet* tradition in early twentieth-century Brooklyn (**see "Individual Portrait: Cantor Moses Ashear"**); indeed, it is observed somewhat differently among Syrian Jews elsewhere. The Brooklyn *sebet* is a festive affair, with families clearing their public rooms of furniture and setting up long tables and folding chairs. Plates of food and bottles of cold drinks are set out on each table and replenished often while the men sing. The women in addition to serving, have traditionally gathered in the dining room, where the table is filled with buffet dishes and chairs line the walls. Recently, however, these traditions have begun to change, as many families now use professional caterers to serve and as young women, who have learned *pizmonim* in Jewish schools, start to participate in the singing. *Pizmonim* heard at the *sebet*—generally happy, upbeat, and celebratory—are sung unaccompanied because Jewish law prohibits playing instruments on the Sabbath.

The *sebet* has played a major role in Syrian life in Brooklyn, providing a regular time for

Any occasion can provide a setting for music making. Here musicians play qanun, 'ud, *violin, and drum* (darabukkah) *at a housewarming party in the Syrian Jewish community of Deal, New Jersey.*

music making in which the entire family can participate; as the elder Moses Tawil testified in 1984:

> It is a very necessary part of our, you might say, socializing. We can't use instruments, we don't use any other electrified type of music. So what do you do really in a social affair? Outside of talking, talking, talking, talking to someone? We sing! And you come, we put the very nice table, we put the drinks, and we start singing the *pizmonim*. So we want. . . . our younger people to grow into it, to be familiar with it, so that they do not feel estranged and feel "What kind of oddball would do it?" And they have grown into it. So this is the way we train them? . . . And they still go for this in a big way. They like it very much. This is the way.[8]

The *sebet* contrasts with another social event that features music, the party known by the Arabic word *haflah*. Held any evening except the Sabbath in a party hall or club, the *haflah* celebrates special occasions such as anniversaries. For these parties, it is customary to hire a singer and professional instrumentalists playing synthesizer, violin, zither, *'ud* (see Chapter 3), flute, and drum. Rather than singing *pizmonin* with Hebrew texts, musicians at a *haflah* perform only the original songs from which the *pizmonim* have been taken, complete with their Arabic language texts. Thus, the *haflah* features songs in Arabic with instrumental accompaniment, whereas the *sebet* includes only unaccompanied *pizmonim* sung in Hebrew.

The Legacy of Arab Music in the *Pizmon*

The wide availability of sound recordings and the spread of Western musical notation have helped standardize many of the *maqamat* across the Middle East and have brought Arab music increased international attention. Recordings have also brought Middle Eastern musicians into direct contact with other musical traditions, as we saw in our encounter with Fairuz's song *Ya Ana* in Chapter 3. Syrian Jews owned phonographs before they left Aleppo, and they continued their habit of listening to recorded music after they resettled abroad. It is clear that some *maqamat* became more popular because they were widely circulated on recordings; *maqam nahawand* was additionally attractive in cross-cultural settings because it sounds similar to the minor scale of Western music.

The Influence of American Musical Traditions

Most Syrian Jews who came to North America entered through New York City, and most settled, for at least a time, in the Lower East Side section of Manhattan. The

Mi Zot ("Who Is She"; Syrian Jewish *pizmon*)

COMPOSED BY Moses Ashear

PERFORMED BY Hyman Kaire, Brooklyn, New York, March 14, 1985

One memorable example of the interaction between the music of Syrian Jews and that of other immigrants to New York is the *pizmon Mi Zot,* which borrows a melody taken from a well-known Italian song.

Composed by Teodoro Cottrau, a Neapolitan who was a colleague of Bellini and other Italian opera composers of the nineteenth century, the song, called *Santa Lucia,* was sung by Italian immigrants who settled in Lower Manhattan's Little Italy. Cantor Ashear, the story goes, heard *Santa Lucia* from his apartment window played by an Italian organ grinder and decided on the spot to use the tune for a *pizmon* he was composing in honor of a newborn baby girl. The new text began with a paraphrase of words from the biblical Song of Songs 6:10, an appropriate choice for the occasion.

This *pizmon* is classified as *maqam ajam,* a *maqam* that parallels the Western major scale of *Santa Lucia.* In Syrian tradition, Western melodies are classified as *maqam ajam* if they are in a *major* key like *Mi Zot,* and *maqam nahawand* if they are in a *minor* key.

LISTEN TO the recording. Do you recognize the melody?

Notice that midway through his rendition, the singer forgets what comes next, pauses, and then haltingly resumes, suggesting that *Mi Zot* is not often sung today. In this recording, too, you can hear a listener's amused reaction on recognizing the *Santa Lucia* melody, a typical response when a familiar tune is heard in an unexpected setting.

Who is she that shines through like the dawn, tired. She is radiant and beautiful, the pleasing
    daughter of Zion.
Your king and your God will surely rejoice over you. And all of your sons will raise the banner flag.
Your glory and your redeemer will add to your redemption and will complete your work, the
    Hevrat Kadimah.
Your delightfulness, your peacefulness, Jerusalem, your hope. There will she carry your song, in it
    the happiness of rejoicing.
I will raise my music, my song, my righteousness that I loved, I lay out, as the apple of my eye
    and in complete adoration, in honor of the Hevrat Kadimah.
The permanent destiny for Israel is to return to the city, the lovely gift of God. The shadow of His
    kindness will hasten to those who hope for God, from time eternal.

—Translation by Joshua Levisohn

LISTENING GUIDE 59

Mifalot Elohim ("The Works of God"; *pizmon*)

COMPOSED BY Moses Ashear

PERFORMED BY Hyman Kaire, Brooklyn, New York, March 14, 1985

Sometimes melodies from other soundscapes were incorporated without full knowl-edge of their origins. The *pizmon Mifalot Elohim* was commissioned during the 1920s in New York on the occasion of a Syrian wedding. At the request of the groom, Cantor Ashear borrowed the melody of the groom's high school song for his wedding *pizmon*. Neither groom nor cantor realized that the high school had itself borrowed the melody from the famous Christmas carol *O Tannenbaum.*

   O Tannenbaum was written more than a century before *Mifalot Elohim,* although it had apparently failed to cross ethnic boundaries in New York City when the *pizmon* was composed. Because the melody is now so closely associated with Christmas, *Mi-falot Elohim* is rarely heard in Syrian Jewish circles.

LISTEN TO the melody, which, like the previous example, is classified as *maqam ajam.*

Gaze upon the works of God, pay attention and speak aloud.
Sing to him in choirs, in the happiness of brides and grooms. To Him alone are the adulations, they suit Him, they suit.
Rock of the world, raise the lofty house of Aaron, the donners of the Urim and Thumin [breast-plate worn by the high priest of the biblical temple], they serve you in holiness.
Be strong for He comes hither to raise the destiny of the right hand as in the day of Mordechai the Benjamite—with a good heart, drink your wine.
God, remember the sons of Rachel, for the sake of Isaac, the close friend of God, and the House of Jacob—the tribes of God, their eyes turned toward you.
My King, guard them like the apple of your eye. And bequeath to them with love a world that is entirely Sabbath, day and night will they rest.

                                                        —Translation by Joshua Levisohn

An organ grinder like this one (left), with a dancing monkey, photographed on a New York City street in the early 1900s, played Santa Lucia *outside Cantor Moses Ashear's window. Joe Bush (Boscio), seen here (right) with his monkey, George, is one of a handful of organ grinders still active in the United States today. Joe wears turn-of-the-twentieth-century dress and uses an antique organ made in 1904 to play music of that period. Joe and George have appeared in films, theater productions, and commercials. Because of George, Joe's performances are monitored by the New Jersey Wildlife and Game Commission.*

pizmon composers of this era, such as Cantor Moses Ashear (**see "Individual Portrait: Cantor Moses Ashear"**), drew directly on recordings of Arab music imported from the Middle East, but they also soon began to draw on the soundscapes they encountered in their new home.

> Almost all of us have sung new words to a familiar melody at one time or other. What *contrafacta* do you know and sing? Have you ever composed one yourself?

A *Pizmon* and Its Arab Model   Composers of *pizmonim* have borrowed from a wide array of soundscapes throughout history, but they continue to depend most heavily on the Arab musical tradition for their inspiration despite the passage of nearly a century since the departure of Syrian Jews from the Middle East.

We will now investigate the relation of one *pizmon* composed in the late twentieth century to the Arab song from which its melody was borrowed. At the same time, we will see how the text and tune of the *pizmon* sustain two different but complementary channels of memory.

INDIVIDUAL PORTRAIT

Cantor Moses Ashear

Moses Ashear, born in Aleppo, Syria, in 1877, was a cantor—a singer of Jewish prayers and *pizmonim*—there until his immigration to New York City in 1912. On his arrival, he sent for his wife and children to join him. Overjoyed at their arrival, the Ashears named their newborn son Amerik ("America"). Amerik (Albert) Ashear, who shared his memories of his father's life and music in an interview before his own death in the early 1990s, used to say proudly that he himself was "the seed of Aleppo and the fruit of America."

After his immigration to New York City, Cantor Moses Ashear learned new Arab melodies for pizmonim *from recordings imported from the Middle East.*

An expert in Hebrew poetry as well as a lover of Arab music—which he listened to for hours on 78-rpm recordings—Moses Ashear soon began to serve as cantor for a small Syrian congregation that met in a New York tenement on the Lower East Side. Later, he moved with the Syrian community to Bensonhurst, Brooklyn, where he became cantor at Magen David Synagogue, a post he held for the rest of his life. Despite his cantorial duties, Ashear also worked long hours as a bookkeeper in order to support his family.

Moses Ashear had learned the *pizmonim* from his teacher in Aleppo, the revered Rabbi Raphael Taboush. He then insured that the songs were sung and transmitted in North America by training many students. He also composed many new *pizmonim,* songs that were particularly beloved because their texts contained the names of people in the community to whom the *pizmonim* were dedicated.

Albert Ashear recounted that his father Moses died while recalling the melody of an Arab song that had been made into a *pizmon*. The older Ashear is remembered by Syrian Jews for having composed *pizmonim* that honor others, but he himself is also memorialized in a *pizmon, Melekh Rahaman* ("Merciful King"), composed in Aleppo by Rabbi Taboush to celebrate Moses Ashear's wedding in the 1890s. Over the course of the last century, Moses Ashear's wedding *pizmon* spread throughout the Syrian diaspora, where it is universally remembered and still sung today.

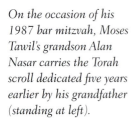

On the occasion of his 1987 bar mitzvah, Moses Tawil's grandson Alan Nasar carries the Torah scroll dedicated five years earlier by his grandfather (standing at left).

SETTING

The *pizmon Ramah Evarai* was composed for the bar mitzvah of Moses Tawil, which took place on May 23, 1982. The song was first sung as the youth was called forward to read from the Torah, the five books of Moses. This *pizmon* also celebrated a second event that took place on the same day: the dedication of a newly copied Torah scroll that had been donated to the synagogue by the youth's grandfather, the senior Moses Tawil. *Ramah Everai* commemorates both a young boy's coming of age and the philanthropy of his grandfather, a respected community leader, but this *pizmon* was even more of a family affair than most: the composer was Louis Massry, the senior Moses' brother-in-law, a businessman who is both a scholar of Hebrew and a player of the *'ud*. The text of the *pizmon* embeds memories important to the Tawil family as well as memories of the religious community as a whole, while the melody conveys a connection with Arab popular culture.

SOUND OF THE ARAB MODEL

The melody chosen for the *pizmon Ramah Evarai* was borrowed from the *Wheat Song,* written in 1946 by the famous Egyptian composer Muhammad 'Abd al-Wahhab (1910?–1991). The long lag between the initial circulation of the original Arab song and the composition of the *pizmon,* some thirty-six years, is unusual.

Louis Massry displays his 'ud, handsomely decorated with mother-of-pearl inlay.

LISTENING GUIDE 60

CD 3
TRACK
4

The Wheat Song (Egyptian film song)

COMPOSED BY Muhammad 'Abd al-Wahhab

PERFORMED BY Muhammad 'Abd al-Wahhab and ensemble

The Wheat Song was composed for a scene in an Egyptian film, *Lastu Malakan* ("I am not an angel"), in which Egyptian peasants are harvesting wheat. The song is light and short by Arab standards: it has a strophic form with a refrain. The original text is a poem in colloquial Arabic celebrating the harvest.

Muhammad 'Abd al-Wahhab was known for his striking innovations in Arab musical style, particularly in his film songs, where he used a large instrumental ensemble that combined traditional Egyptian and Western instruments. The original 78-rpm recording of *The Wheat Song,* transferred to audio cassette, is heard here with 'Abd al-Wahhab himself as soloist.[9]

The Wheat Song begins with an eight-beat rhythm played three times by the drums at a moderate pace. When the rhythm is repeated again, a solo piccolo enters playing a melody based on the flute theme from the second act of Tchaikovsky's *Nutcracker* ballet. 'Abd al-Wahhab was known for frequently "quoting" from a wide variety of Western classical compositions he learned from recordings.

Next, the instruments establish the pulse underpinning the song proper, a duple rhythm with an accent on the second beat. The song is set in *maqam 'ajam,* but here again 'Abd al-Wahhab looks west and strongly implies a Western major scale. The nod to Western music is further enhanced by the presence of Western harmony instead of the traditional Middle Eastern heterophonic texture, and by the entrance of European singers, borrowed from the Cairo Opera Company, performing a high countermelody.

LISTEN FOR the distinctive sound of the *'ud* (lute) and *qanun* (zither), as well as Egyptian percussion instruments (three large frame drums), six violins, a cello, bass, accordion, piano, piccolo, and women's choir.

Ramah Evarai ("Let My Whole Being Testify"; *pizmon*)

COMPOSED BY Louis Massry

PERFORMED BY Moses Tawil and ensemble

Let us turn now to *Ramah Evarai,* the *pizmon* based on *The Wheat Song.* Many Syrian Jews knew and loved *The Wheat Song* although most were unaware that it was originally composed for a film. The *pizmon's* composer, Louis Massry, used the melody of *The Wheat Song* for *Ramah Evarai* because it was a "catchy tune, not a deep song, but a light, catchy song a lot of people could sing." His concern that the melody be "catchy" is an aesthetic value echoed by others in his community. As a second person put it, "The poem depends on the music that he's putting words to. It's the music that controls the words that are being said." A third community member insists that *The Wheat Song* is often played at parties because of its "excellent tempo," which is "beautiful for dancing."

LISTEN TO this well-known, catchy tune that helped many Syrian Jews learn *Ramah Evarai* and retain it in memory as a very popular *pizmon.*
   Ramah Evarai is a *contrafactum* that follows precisely the form, melody, and rhythm of the original *Wheat Song.* However, listen to how it substitutes a new instrumental introduction for 'Abd al-Wahhab's original and eliminates the women's chorus. Although we might at first be surprised that *Ramah Evarai* omits the original introduction to the *Wheat Song,* which includes the Tchaikovsky *Nutcracker* ballet melody, the omission makes sense given the limited instrumental resources available and given that the borrowed Tchaikovsky melody would not be recognized by most of the *pizmon's* listeners.

Let my whole being testify that there is none other besides him who dwells the
    heaven above,
Bless and send him the blessing of Abraham, and Moses the son of Amram, yes bless
    and send him.
In honor of the bar mitzvah, let them sing the song in the glorious city of Zion, and
    the city of Hannah.
Bind the words of the Shema on your hand, ah ah ah ah, and let it be for you a sign,
    ah ah ah ah,
To Moses his servant, the secrets of the Torah he revealed to him,
Yes, bless and send him.
Gladden the hearts of your parents and honor them, and observe the commandments
    of your Maker, and this precept will lengthen your days.
Father, place upon me, ah ah ah ah, the *tefillin* between my eyes, ah ah.
I will meditate on the Torah and keep its commandments, and rejoice in all its words.
Zion will be rebuilt for ever, and whose presence was even in the burning bush, lead
    them in love and compassion.
Give of your food to the hungry, to the poor and needy, and the Lord shall spread His
    bounty of goodness on you.
Let them be heard in Judah, singing and rejoicing, songs and praise to him who
    dwells on high.
God bless our congregation, ah ah ah ah, And send the redeemer speedily, ah ah
    ah ah.
And to Moses, his servant, the secrets of the Torah he revealed.
Who dwells in the heavens above, bless and send him the blessing of Abraham and
    Moses the son of Amram.
Exalted God, bless and send him.

—Translation by Louis Massry

But the composer, Louis Massry, explained that like many in the Syrian community, he knew the song from recordings: "I have every record and tape of 'Abd al-Wahhab; as soon as a new one came out, I would buy it."

Although the melody of *Ramah Evarai* is well known to Syrian Jews as borrowed from *The Wheat Song*—thereby carrying memories of Middle Eastern life and other works of the beloved composer 'Abd al-Wahhab—the Hebrew text of this *pizmon* establishes an entirely Jewish framework, with references at its core to Jewish law and custom.

This *pizmon* text, like most others of its kind, is filled with hidden meanings. For example, the Hebrew letters of the first word, *ramah,* when read as numbers, add up to 248, symbolizing both the number of parts in the human body, according to Jewish tradition, and the number of positive commandments ("thou shalt"s) enumerated in the Torah. The metaphorical meaning of these equivalents is that the young man's entire body should be devoted to the service of God. The text contains numerous other references to liturgical custom. For example, it mentions the *tefillin*—scriptural passages enclosed in two black leather boxes that are strapped on one arm and the forehead during weekday morning prayer services.

The reference in the song text to Moses' encounter with the Burning Bush is particularly meaningful, given the name of the boy and his grandfather. Finally, the "secrets of the Torah" revealed to Moses allude both to Jewish mysticism and to the Torah scroll dedicated that day by the senior Moses Tawil.

Along with numerous references to Jewish ritual, literature, and folklore, the

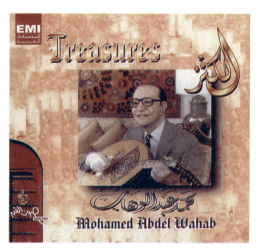

The music of Muhammad 'Abd al-Wahhab (1910?–1991), who made innumerable recordings during his long career, was popular across ethnic and religious boundaries throughout the Middle East.

Following the traditions mentioned in the text of pizmon Ramah Evarai, Alan Nasar dons tefillin (phylacteries) for the first time, for prayers during the week before his bar mitzvah.

names Abraham and Moses, representing four generations of Tawil men, are encoded in the *Ramah Evarai* text. That Abraham and Moses were also prominent biblical figures brings additional honor to the family and meaning to the song. (The name "Hannah" found in the text does not refer to a Tawil family matriarch, but rather to the city of Hannah, mentioned in Joshua 19:14.)

SIGNIFICANCE

The melody of a *pizmon* such as *Ramah Evarai* carries memories of popular musical trends that Syrian Jews share with the broader Middle Eastern community around the world. Simultaneously, the *pizmon* text incorporates reminders of historical Jewish prayers and psalms, weaving in the names of family members taking part in a meaningful life-cycle event. The content of this Syrian *pizmon,* then, combines the residue of a dual Jewish and Arab identity. We should recall that prior to the twentieth century, when political conflicts in the Middle East divided Jews and Arabs, these peoples shared for centuries both a musical tradition and a way of life. The *pizmon* incorporates this hybrid identity and continues to sustain it as part of a remarkable Jewish-Arab heritage, decades after Syrian Jews left their homeland.

If *pizmon* texts and tunes purposefully construct memory on multiple levels, their union also arouses the emotions. Songs are not only heard, they reverberate in our other senses (**see "Studying Music: Music and the Senses"**). Strains of a familiar *pizmon* can transport listeners back to important moments in their own lives. Songs can also elicit powerful memories of a deceased relative or some other experience of loss. That songs continue to be sung in situations similar to those in which they were first performed and heard sets in motion and reinforces the highly charged process of reminiscence. For the performer as well as the listener, *pizmonim* both arouse and recreate earlier events and emotions.

Conclusion

Embedding an idea or visual image in our long-term memory requires the use of different brain networks, a process termed "elaborative encoding." Musical performance—which involves the senses of sight, sound, smell, taste, and touch, as well as movement—necessarily draws on materials that have been encoded in many ways and in different areas of the brain. As we learned earlier, bonding a text to a melody establishes a durable memory that can more easily be recalled—just think of our ability to sing complete songs with texts many years after we first heard them. In part because music, and especially song, embeds itself so readily in memory, songs can and have been used intentionally to help people remember. For this reason, too, music is used to commemorate events and memorialize individuals.

STUDYING MUSIC

Music and the Senses

We have already learned that we perceive music not just in the ear but throughout the body. Some individuals, when hearing music, actually experience sound as a color, taste, or smell, a phenomenon known as "synesthesia." Many musical traditions draw on images that cross sensory boundaries. In the Syrian *pizmon* (and, as we will see, in other musics), we come on an unexpected network of connections—between music and food.

Some of the associations between music and food arise situationally, because so many of the occasions at which *pizmonim* are sung—life-cycle events in the home, parties—involve the consumption of special foods. Food carries extensive symbolic meaning in Syrian Jewish life, and publications such as the *Syrian Festival of Holidays Recipe Book* prescribe in detail the foods to be used in celebrating the important Jewish holidays. For instance, at the Jewish New Year (Rosh Hashanah), special foods are eaten as the blessings for the day are sung. These foods include swiss chard or spinach used to protect against enemies;

This page from the Syrian Festival of Holidays Recipe Book presents the menu of traditional foods for the Jewish New Year (Rosh Hashanah) within a neo–Middle Eastern frame. The preliminary blessings (berachot) are accompanied by fruits, vegetables, meat, and fish. The main course includes ground meatballs (kibbe geraz), vegetarian meatballs (kibbe naya), stuffed grape leaves (yebra), and stuffed Swiss chard (yebra sileet).

a special candy called *hilu,* made from squash, syrup, and nuts, to insure that God will guard the community with prayer; and a combination of black-eyed peas and lubiah fish to help the community "propagate and multiply like the fish in the sea and the abundance of peas."

In the Arab musical tradition shared by Syrian Jews, food metaphors are liberally applied to music. Each *maqam* is said to have its own "flavor," which can be "sweetened" by ornamentation and improvisation. Syrian Jews further extend this aesthetic by prescribing that both the *pizmonim* and the food should be "sweet, not sour." A book containing Syrian *pizmonim* is dedicated to the memory of "the sweet singer of Israel" (Moses Ashear) and to the holy songs, "which are sweeter even than the honey and the honeycomb." In this way, the memory of song is reinforced and strengthened by invoking a food with which it shares both settings and associations. The following comment from a Syrian woman shows how completely the two are intertwined:

> Everybody knows everything, what they do on holidays, they have certain foods on different holidays. On Purim, we make kibbeh—meatballs—with mushrooms. We always have that, they are best on Purim. And we used to sing, get drunk. Oh there's a lot of songs. I used to know them all. . . . For Rosh Hashanah we used to make rice and sweet sauce, you can't make a sour sauce. Everything sweet, you know. And different songs. Every holiday has a song. . . . And the funny part is, on Saturday, when they sing the songs, they bring in the melody that goes in with the time.[10]

Although the *pizmonim* are almost all composed by men for men and their performance was historically limited to males, food in the Syrian community has long been the domain of the women. Women prepare and serve the traditional foods at home rituals while the men sing at these events. If men's domain is song, women's is a complementary one of cooking and food. Similarly, just as the men passed on *pizmonim* by oral tradition and through written collections featuring blank pages to accommodate newly composed songs, the women have transmitted recipes in the same way, publishing cookbooks with blank pages at the end of each section so that "everyone can add her own recipes."

In this chapter, we have encountered several examples of musical performance linked to memory. The *corrido* and hymns such as *Amazing Grace* are preserved in memory largely through the support of a repetitive melody. The *pizmon* tradition of borrowing preexisting melodies for reuse in situations where their original identity is also remembered exemplifies a compositional device used to sustain memory across cultures. The widespread use of *contrafacta* over time and across cultural boundaries suggests that deep-seated cognitive factors may in fact be at work.

The growing knowledge about how the brain forms memories will, no doubt, expand what we know about musical composition, transmission, and performance. In the next chapter, we will explore how these musical processes express individual and collective identities.

Try an experiment. Play a recording of your favorite song and write down the memories it evokes. Can you recall the first time you heard the song? Describe the setting in as much detail as you can. What emotions does the song arouse?

IMPORTANT TERMS

bar mitzvah	hymn	*muwashah*
conjunct motion	jazz funeral	*pizmon*
contrafactum	*layali*	shape-note/fasola
corrido	*maqam*	*'ud*

Ida Guillory became known as "Queen Ida" after she won a crown at a Mardi Gras celebration in the San Francisco Bay area in 1970. Her music making has always been a family affair, whether she is performing with her brothers Al Rapone and Willie Lewis, or her sons Ronald and Myrick "Freeze" Guillory.

OVERVIEW

MAIN POINTS

• Music embodies diverse identities, including those associated with nationality, region, ethnicity, race, class, religion, and gender.

• Music conveys the identities of individuals and groups.

• Text, melody, body motion, instrumentation, and vocal
style all transmit multiple meanings within the same musical event.

• Music can establish clear boundaries of identity and
provide a site for the transformation of identity.

Music and Identity

Introduction

Identities are complex formations that rarely stay static. Each of us is a mix of competing and interacting identities. Depending on the situation, we may choose to emphasize or play down one or more of these aspects of identity.

Among the many elements that constitute our identity are ethnic background, race, class, gender, and religious orientation, to name just a few. National or regional heritage, language group, political affiliation, and occupation also contribute to our identity. Needless to say, both the meaning and boundaries of each can vary greatly. Although identity is expressed differently by each individual, it is almost always constructed against the background of a group: we either seek to be part of it or to distinguish ourselves from it. The identities we are slowest to recognize and name are those that make up a seemingly uniform group, often a majority. Yet whatever identity we give preference to at a given moment, it is often expressed or reinforced through music. Whether we sing *pizmonim*, listen to jazz recordings, or attend orchestra concerts, our musical choices can serve as a guide to who we think we are and who we wish to be.

With the exception of gender, most other aspects of identity—including race, class, religious orientation, and descent—often fall under the broad umbrella of ethnicity. An ethnic group is composed of people within a larger society who have (or believe they have) common ancestry, memories of a shared historical past, and elements in common, such as kinship patterns, physical continuity, religious affiliation, language, or some combination of these.[1]

Music is often transmitted actively to children within ethnic communities, who may begin acquiring instrumental skills at an early age. Here, three-year-old Louis Ancelet, the son of the Cajun folklorist and radio show host Barry Ancelet, demonstrates what he has learned about the accordion from the many musicians around him.

This definition implies that although many aspects of ethnic identity are indeed shaped by descent, others are determined by consent and consciously chosen through affiliations. We find a similarly mixed picture when we try to define musical identity. Many musical traditions are transmitted through biological families and communities linked by descent; our case study of the Syrian *pizmon* provides an excellent example. However, many musical traditions (such as the bagpipe or Santería traditions examined earlier) have been popular with individuals who choose as adults to participate in the performance and transmission of these musics.

In some cases the musical styles that symbolize identity maintain strong links with the past or with an original homeland. In other instances, newly invented musical styles convey equally important meanings. The phrase "invention of tradition" concisely describes the way in which identities are created without reference to actual historical realities.[2] Most often, we find a fluid situation in which inherited traditions are continually enriched and transformed through new experiences and exposures.

We have already encountered invented traditions; among the most colorful of these is the bagpipe, which became a marker of Scottish identity, along with the kilt, only in the late seventeenth century. The kilt and the bagpipe were adopted both as symbols of protest against the Union with England and as a "distinguishing badge" of highland society.[3] The bagpipe case study (see Chapter 2) also demonstrated how traditions are often "reinvented" in North America, where the instrument has had a new, rich life in cities and in competitions.

In this chapter we will explore not only how people express their identities through music, but also the way music communicates aspects of identity that are difficult to express otherwise. We will hear the voice of individual identity in the flute concerto of Reza Vali, a composer of Persian descent living in the United States. We will also unlock the surprisingly deep national and cultural associations of *karaoke* music—music that has roots in Japanese society but has distinctive forms elsewhere in Asia and in popular culture worldwide.

A twenty-first-century challenge in charting identity and its expression through music is the increasing separation of identity from place. Music scholars have long assumed that people and their (musical) traditions are "grounded" to a specific geographic locale. One of the most striking aspects of music is that it often retains traditions of a particular place, despite the movement of people and their music well beyond these geographic boundaries. An excellent example is seen in this chapter's major case study of Cajun and Creole musics, which both have origins in southern Louisiana, where many French-speaking people resettled after long periods of displacement. As these Cajun and Creole styles moved out of southern Louisiana and interacted with other musics—most notably African American traditions—they gave rise in the second half of the twentieth century to a new Creole style called *zydeco* music.

Today, Cajun and Creole musics are performed not just at the Festival Internationale de Lousiane, but also at events such as the annual Rhythm and Roots Festival in Rhode Island. Cajun and zydeco musicians tour the world and their recordings are distributed internationally. For this reason, Cajun and zydeco traditions provide a rich case study of music and identity: the celebration of deep historical and geographic roots and new-found affinity through both old and new musical traditions.

Expressing Individual and Group Identities through Music

At its most basic level, music becomes a symbol of identity through its sound and settings. The multiple channels of text, tune, dance, instrumental practice, and performance style sustain further layers of meaning. An expression of individual identity can be heard in the flute concerto of Reza Vali, a composer who lives in Pittsburgh, Pennsylvania.

CASE STUDY: THE MUSIC OF A PERSIAN COMPOSER

Reza Vali was born in Iran in 1952, but as a child he was not educated in the techniques of Persian music (**see "Individual Portrait: Reza Vali"**). Rather, he grew up in the Western classical music tradition. His exposure to that tradition was not unusual in Iran. From the nineteenth century until the Iranian Revolution in the late 1970s, Iranian rulers supported Western musical involvement. Thus, Vali's knowledge of Western musical instruments and styles was acquired at home in West Asia and further developed in Europe, well before the composer settled in the United States. Although his interest in indigenous Persian music also began when he was a teenager in Iran, his early involvement in it focused on ethnomusicological work rather than writing original compositions.

Here we will explore Vali's flute *concerto* (a work for orchestra and soloist) in which multiple elements from the composer's background and musical experience come together. The Concerto for Flute and Orchestra was commissioned by the Boston Modern Orchestra Project and was first performed on February 13, 1998. At first glance, the instruments used in the piece appear to fit squarely within the Western orchestral framework (**see "Sound Sources: The Western Orchestra"**), although Vali employs a scaled-down ensemble called a chamber orchestra, rather

INDIVIDUAL PORTRAIT

Reza Vali

Born in Ghazvin, Iran, Reza Vali attended the Conservatory of Music in Tehran, where he studied trumpet and trombone. Following additional musical studies at the Academy of Music in Vienna, he came to the United States, where he earned a Ph.D. in music theory and composition from the University of Pittsburgh in 1985.

Vali became interested in Persian music when, as a teenager in Iran, he learned that the composer Béla Bartók had listened to, recorded, and transcribed folk music in his native Hungary. Vali began to do the same, collecting and transcribing Persian music. When he began to study Persian classical music, which he describes as "unbelievably rich and extremely complex," he programmed a computer to recreate the melodic system, called *dastgah,* that is unique to Persian music.

Reza Vali, whose compositions combining Persian and Western classical elements have been commissioned and premiered by well-known ensembles such as the Kronos Quartet.

In 1989, Reza Vali returned for a long visit to Iran, further exploring music as well as the famous architecture in the cities of Shiraz and Isfahan. This added exposure to the sights and sounds of his homeland, which he had largely missed during his formative years because of Iran's policy at the time of westernization, led Vali to incorporate more Persian elements into his recent compositions.

Today, Vali is a member of the music faculty at Carnegie Mellon University in Pittsburgh. He has composed for orchestra, string quartet, piano and voice, electronic and computer media, and chamber ensembles. Reza Vali's works have been performed internationally and can be heard on numerous recordings.

than a full-sized orchestra. In addition to the soloist, a second flutist also plays the alto flute and piccolo; an oboe player doubles on the English horn; a clarinetist plays different sizes of clarinets; a bassoonist also plays contrabassoon; two horns; one trumpet; one trombone; one tuba; one harp; a battery of percussion instruments; and a full array of violins, violas, cellos, and basses.

SOUND SOURCES

The Western Orchestra

Although the term *orchestra* is used to describe a wide variety of large instrumental ensembles, in the Euro-American tradition it refers to an organized body of bowed stringed instruments (chordophones) with more than one player to a part, to which may be added any number of wind and brass instruments (aerophones), along with percussion (idiophones and membranophones). The word *orchestra* comes from the Greek, literally meaning "a dancing place," referring to the semicircular space where the Greek stage chorus sang and danced. The Western orchestra originated with small groups (termed *consorts*) of instruments formed for ceremonial and entertainment purposes in English, French, Italian, and German courts of the sixteenth century. Consorts grouped sets of like instruments—such as strings or winds—in different sizes and ranges, but over the course of time these consorts combined and intermingled, leading to the typical Western orchestra constituted of brass, woodwinds, strings, and percussion.

By the 1720s, new instruments had been added, such as the double bass, which was incorporated into Parisian court and opera orchestras. Over the course of the eighteenth century, stringed instruments grew in importance and eventually became the backbone of the ensemble. As a result of the Industrial Revolution, technical improvements, especially to brass and woodwinds, allowed increases in volume and distinctive sound quality.

By the end of the eighteenth century, a standard orchestra had strings divided into five parts (first violins; second violins; violas; cellos; and basses) and included two each of the

The Minnesota Symphony Orchestra, showing the standard orchestral seating arrangement, with stringed instruments deployed in a semicircle fanning out from the conductor; woodwind, brass, and percussion instruments at center and back.

following: flutes, oboes, clarinets, bassoons, trumpets, horns (sometimes there were four); and timpani.

In the nineteenth century, this basic configuration varied according to function and location. For example, small chamber ensembles were hired for events in private homes, while larger groups served the concert halls. Nineteenth-century composers enlarged the orchestra's sound by introducing instruments that had not traditionally been used in the orchestra, such as various types of clarinet. The orchestra also expanded in size during the nineteenth century, so that composers such as Bruckner, Mahler, and Strauss required one hundred players or more for some pieces.

The most notable developments in the twentieth-century Western orchestra have occurred in both its size and composition. Economic constraints imposed by the two world wars resulted in the growth and popularity of smaller ensembles such as chamber orchestras and modified orchestras for new works. In addition, the orchestral sound of the twentieth century has been enriched by an enormous increase in the number and variety of percussion instruments, many of which are borrowed from outside the West. The use of new and innovative performance techniques on traditional orchestral instruments has been another outcome. In this way, Reza Vali's Concerto for Flute and Orchestra reflects recent trends in both musical composition and playing techniques of the modern orchestra.

A closer look reveals evidence of Iranian influence as well. The flute soloist is instructed to "hum" while playing to produce a breathy quality, resembling the sound of the traditional Persian flute, the *ney.* Although Vali uses Western instruments playing within the Western harmonic system, he adds "Persian" color through these unusual flute and percussion effects. Also, the percussion instruments include the *darabukkah,* an hourglass-shaped drum common across the Middle East.

Not only does the Vali flute concerto draw on different soundscapes in the composer's background, it also prompts associations within the listener's musical experience. If, for instance, we are familiar with the classical concerto, we might perceive this composition within the broader Western orchestral soundscape, grouping it with "exotic" or "experimental" late-twentieth-century compositions. However, a listener familiar with Persian folk and classical music would recognize the specifically Persian sounds and rhythms. For Persians who migrated from Iran and settled in North American cities, the Vali concerto has the power to evoke

Behzad Faruhari plays the Persian ney *during a concert by the Iranian Ava Ensemble at the Asia Society in New York City, September 1998.*

In the flute part to his concerto, Reza Vali instructs the player to sing and play simultaneously in order to mimic the sound of the Persian ney.

memories of musical life in prerevolutionary Iran, where Western symphonies existed alongside Persian traditional music. Indeed, Vali's music describes a new, hybrid soundscape that grows out of the interaction between Persian and Western musics and reflects a Persian-American identity.

Concerto for Flute and Orchestra

COMPOSED BY Reza Vali

PERFORMED BY Alberto Almarza, flute, and the Boston Modern Orchestra Project, conducted by Gil Rose

The main influences in the two movements of this work are Persian classical and folk music. The unusual flute technique brings out additional overtones, altering the sound quality of the instrument. The first movement is written for flute, strings, harp, and percussion. However, the composer conceives of these instruments as divided into three ensembles playing together. The first is a "quasi gamelan" ensemble consisting of two chimes, the harp, and vibraphones. The second group is a "chorus" of strings, featuring four solo violins along with the first chairs (that is, the leading players) of the viola, cello, and bass sections. The third incorporates all the rest of the strings playing parts that interlock "like strands in a Persian carpet." The form of the movement is intended to replicate a multihued carpet or the mosaic patterns decorating a mosque, where a variety of details give rise to an overall design. The composer calls this technique "mosaic elaboration," producing a more static effect than the usual Western classical techniques of elaboration or development, which are more linear with strong climactic moments.

LISTEN TO the way multiple melodies interweave in this movement, with no single melody dominating.

An excerpt from the lively second movement is heard next, using rhythms that resemble cycles in medieval Persian music.

CASE STUDY: THE MULTIPLE MEANINGS OF KARAOKE

Although some soundscapes, such as the Vali concerto, are personal musical statements that have potential significance for broader communities, other soundscapes appear at first to belong to the group as a whole, but these are also shaped and molded by individuals. One such sound-scape cluster—the tradition known as *karaoke*—carries a range of both ethnic and national associations.

Karaoke—which in Japanese literally means "empty" (*kara*) "orchestra" (*oke*)—originated in 1972 at a snack bar in Kobe, Japan.[4] It spread throughout Japan, from there to the rest of East Asia, and then became popular internationally. Karaoke machines include playback equipment that amplifies a live performance of a song's main vocal part and mixes this with the song's often familiar instrumental tracks. Typically, a video screen that can be read easily by the singer and the spectators displays the lyrics of the song.

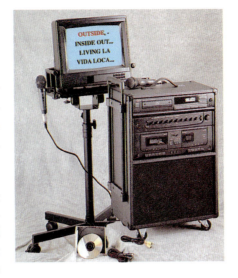

Standard karaoke equipment includes a playback machine with amplifiers, a microphone, and a monitor to display the text. The equipment shown here is portable.

Although a casual observer might dismiss karaoke as a simple or homogeneous form of popular entertainment, actually it encompasses many different styles, is performed in varied social contexts, and carries substantial meaning for many of its performers. For instance, although Japanese karaoke is performed in public restaurants and in private homes, Korean karaoke, termed *no rae pang*, is performed most often by groups of friends in private rooms at North American restaurants. Similarly, Chinese-Americans have adapted karaoke to a variety of settings, including concerts, life-cycle occasions, and home performances. In addition to its role as a transnational form of popular entertainment, karaoke can express identity within many different settings of social life.

A ten-year-old boy sings karaoke with his family at home in Tokyo.

Karaoke albums displayed in a Vietnamese-owned media store near downtown Houston, Texas.

One of the precedents for karaoke was a long tradition in Japan of communal, public singing in which the act of participation was considered to be more important than the quality of the performance. Karaoke draws on the Japanese aesthetic principle of *kata* ("patterned form"), which pervades a range of Japanese arts, including the tea ceremony, flower arranging, dance, and the martial arts. All of these expressive forms are composed of precise, named patterns. Form is considered to be more important than content, and deviations from the established pattern are discouraged. In learning to replicate songs, dances, or tea ceremonies, the individual becomes part of a historical continuum linked together through rituals of repetition.[5]

Karaoke originated in male-dominated nightclubs, where conviviality was expressed through participatory activities such as singing. Whereas speech was thought to be variable and unpredictable, song was valued for its structure and pattern. Revelations of self were thought to occur within such highly patterned forms, their very repetitiveness engendering trust, empathy, and intimacy.

Hibari Misora's meteoric career as an enka *singer is memorialized through recordings and by a museum dedicated to her in Kyoto, Japan.*

One Japanese popular song genre, called *enka*, is performed as karaoke. This nostalgic style is well known and meaningful to the generation of Japanese who came of age in the period immediately following World War II. Some Japanese musicians compare *enka* music to the tango, in that both have melodramatic themes of love and the capacity to bring their listeners to tears.

Although karaoke has deep roots in traditional Japanese values, its broad-based popularity in Japan is supported by an active "karaoke culture." Monthly magazines list the most popular songs—

LISTENING GUIDE 63

CD 3
TRACK
8

Ringo Oiwake ("Apple Blossoms"; *enka* song)

MUSIC BY Masao Yoneyama; lyrics by Fuiko Ozawa

PERFORMED BY Hibari Misora

This *enka* song is performed by Hibari Misora, the singer known as "the Queen of Enka" and "the Lark." Misora, whose music is revered in Japan, was often compared during her lifetime to the famous tango singer Carlos Gardel, who was known as "the Thrush." The Japanese tango singer Abo Ikuo even composed a tango titled "The Thrush and the Lark," which seeks to convey the affinity between the songs performed by these singers, who in fact never met. The similarity of the *enka* and tango repertories in both style and subject matter may account for the popularity of both genres in Japan and among Japanese Americans.[6]

This *enka* song is the poignant reminiscence of a girl from the north part of Japan (Tsugaru) who has become a packhorse driver in the years after World War II. The song's nostalgic text, typical of the genre, is a meditation on the transience of natural beauty. These thoughts conjure memories of the girl's mother, who died in Tokyo.

LISTEN FOR the rhythm mimicking the horse's gait.

Sung:
Apple blossoms falling in the wind,
Quietly on a moonlit night, moonlit night. . . .

A Tsugari girl cried for the hard farewell.
Apple blossoms falling in the wind,
Ah . . .

Spoken narration:
When over the top of Mount Oiwaki,
A cloud like cotton slowly floats and
Peach blossoms, cherry blossoms,
And then, early apple blossoms.
It has been our favorite season.

But as it rains and the white petals fall,
I remember my mother who died in Tokyo, and
I, I. . . .

Sung:
A Tsugari girl cried for the hard farewell.
Apple blossoms falling in the wind.
Ah . . .

—Translated by Takashi Koto

the texts of which are available in booklets for purchase—and a Japanese television series airs karaoke singing lessons. Individuals often join karaoke clubs or circles, and compete in contests where participants attempt to emulate the moves and mannerisms of famous singers. Although transmitted by millions across different national and cultural boundaries, karaoke performance derives its significance from these intimate settings, which allow individual performance within a given group.

The karaoke singer must not only reproduce the song's words and music, but also must imitate the original singer's style. Thus, the performer inevitably has a model in mind, mimicking the soloist whose voice is absent in the karaoke version which contains only an empty orchestra. For this reason, the karaoke song repertory tends to be accessible to amateur performers, predictable in style, and centered around popular singers.

As we have seen in this chapter, music can appeal to different and rapidly transforming identities. The Vali flute concerto illustrated how a musical composition can simultaneously be part of several soundscapes, depending on the background and perceptions of its listeners. Other soundscapes, such as karaoke, grow and diversify into soundscape clusters over time, proving flexible enough to incorporate new styles and settings. Next, we will take a close look at the multiple identities evident in the soundscapes that originated in the Gulf Coast regions of Louisiana and Texas.

CASE STUDY: MULTIPLE IDENTITIES IN CAJUN AND ZYDECO MUSIC

The closely related Cajun and zydeco soundscapes present myriad issues that relate to identity in the twenty-first century by incorporating place, ethnicity, class, race, and gender. The two musical styles share the same geographical base and spring from common historical roots that continue to be celebrated through music. Cajun and zydeco musics are defined by their similarities, as well as through their differences.

The French Heritages of Creoles and Cajuns
The Creoles and the Cajuns share the same language—French—and the same geographical space—Southwest Louisiana. But although their cultures and musics developed side by side and display many common features, present-day Creoles, in particular, go to great lengths to point out the distinctions between the two.

Some Creole and Cajun traditions can be traced back to the French-speaking people of Louisiana in the sixteenth and seventeenth centuries (**see** "**Looking Back: Creole and Cajun Histories**"). Others, such as French folk songs and lullabies, came directly from France. The Creoles—of mixed French, Spanish, and African or Afro-Caribbean descent—arrived somewhat later. Although many

LOOKING BACK

Creole and Cajun Histories

1600s	Term *Creole* first used to describe people of African, French, Spanish, or Portuguese descent living in West Indies and what is present-day southern United States
1604	Samuel de Champlain founds Acadia, populated by French-speaking settlers from coastal France
1620	England extends claims to include Acadia
1670	France regains Acadia
1713	Treaty of Utrecht cedes Acadia back to Britain, which turns most of Acadia into British colony
1718	New Orleans (la Nouvelle-Orléans) founded by Jean-Baptiste le Moyne on behalf of John Lewis Company of the West
1719	Wholesale importation of slaves from Africa to Louisiana begins
1724	Promulgation of *code noir* ("black code"), a three-tier social system with a free black class that enjoys legal rights and privileges but not social status of whites
1745	British threaten to expel Acadians unless they take an oath of allegiance to King of England; Acadians refuse
1755	The beginning of the forced migration of French people from Acadia known as La Grand Derengement or the Expulsion of 1755; most migrate to south Louisiana
1763–1776	About two thousand four hundred Acadians arrive in Louisiana from North American colonies, West Indies, Nova Scotia, and St. Pierre and Miquelon islands
1779	Term *Creole* first used in Louisiana documents in reference to persons of color
1780s	Louisiana encourages merchants to import African and Creole slaves from West Indies
1785	Second group of Acadians come to Louisiana through combined efforts of French and Spanish governments
1791–1809	Insurrection in Santa Domingo adds over ten thousand French-speaking people to Louisiana—whites, free blacks, and black slaves
Late 1803	United States takes control of Louisiana from Napoleon through Louisiana Purchase
1803	Many Haitian refugees in Cuba come to New Orleans

1809	Six thousand French refugees fleeing West Indies political turmoil arrive in Louisiana
1870s	Accordion introduced to Louisiana by German settlers
1928	First Cajun record, *Allons á Lafayette,* made by Joe Falcon and his wife, Cleoma Breaux Falcon
1929	Creole accordionist Amédé Ardoin and Cajun fiddler Dennis McGee record *Eunice Two-Step,* a landmark bringing the music of Cajuns and Creoles together
1930s	The accordion becomes the instrument of choice for early zydeco musicians
1950s–1960s	Surge of Cajun pride as music begins to gain national attention and acceptance from mainstream America
1965	Clifton Chenier records *Zydeco Sont Pas Salé* in Houston, Texas
Early 1970s	Cajun renaissance movement
1980s	Shift toward English lyrics in zydeco accelerates as younger generation cannot speak French
1982	First annual Southwest Louisiana Zydeco Festival in Plaisance, Louisiana
1986	Accordionist Boozo Chauvis establishes new zydeco aesthetic of minimalist lyrics in song *Dog Hill*
1987	A watershed year for popularization of zydeco music: the movie *The Big Easy* boasts a Louisiana sound track, and Paul Simon's *Graceland* album includes tribute to Clifton Chenier
1990s	New zydeco groups formed outside of Creole circles across the United States and around the world

Creole people preceded the Cajun migration into the region, the present-day musical style most closely associated with Creole identity—the zydeco tradition—emerged only in the mid-twentieth century. For this reason, we will begin our discussion with the Cajun soundscape, which predates the zydeco tradition, and then return to the present-day Creole musical tradition.

<u>Musics of Place</u>   In 1755, French refugees in Acadia, the region off the eastern coast of Canada later to be called Nova Scotia, were expelled by British troops and forced to migrate once again. Some settled in the northeastern United

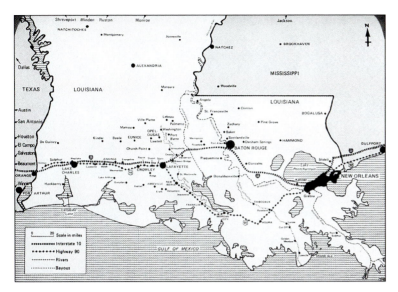

The map locates south Louisiana Cajun towns such as Eunice, Mamou, Basile, Gueydon, and, of course, Lafayette.

States, but the majority migrated south to the French territory of Louisiana. The name "Cajun" derives from the adjective *acadien,* meaning a person from Acadia.[7]

Shortly after the Cajuns settled in Louisiana, the area was transferred to Spain. Unwelcome in New Orleans, many Cajuns moved to the tidal flats and lived alongside the bayous (inland channels with thick vegetation) of what is now southwest Louisiana. There, they sustained French traditions and language and came into contact with a number of other peoples, including Spanish, Native Americans, Euro Americans and African Americans. The mix gave rise to a rich, distinctive culture—and musical style—that came to be known, along with the people themselves, by the once-pejorative term *Cajun.*

Evidence suggests that long before the late-twentieth-century popularization of their music, the Cajuns contributed to other well-known American musical styles. Alan Lomax, who with his father, John, made musical recordings among Cajuns from the 1930s onward, noted that Cajun cowboys sang a song with the French-

Bayous are found throughout much of the state of Louisiana and range from small, slow-flowing creeks to swampy inlets along the Gulf Coast.

The famous Cajun accordionist Joe Falcon performed both with his first wife, Cleoma, a guitarist (pictured here), and with his second wife, Theresa, a drummer. The importance of Cajun music to familial and ethnic identity is underscored by the presence of young Lulubelle Falcon, standing between her parents.

derived refrain "Hip and Tiyo," (Taïaut) which may have inspired the cowboy song "hipiyaye, tipiyayo." The Cajuns had a very active horse culture in Louisiana, and it appears that songs sung by their cowboys later spread to Texas and the West. Whatever its origin and possible range of influence, the refrain *Hip and Tiyo* was in wide circulation among Cajun singers. For instance, in a song recorded in 1934, the Cajun musician Joe Falcon sings of two dogs named Hip and Taïaut who stole a sled.

Joe Falcon's 1928 version of *Allons à Lafayette,* in which he was accompanied by his wife Cleoma Breaux, is generally considered to be the first recording of a Cajun song. This recording initiated an active ethnic record business within the Cajun community (see "**Studying Music: Ethnic Recordings in North America**").

The text of the song pays homage to Lafayette, an important Cajun center and one of many South Louisiana towns memorialized in Cajun music. As with many songs transmitted through oral tradition, the text exists in multiple versions, three of which are reproduced here. You will notice that there is a derogatory reference in the second version to Italians, who immigrated to Louisiana in the late nineteenth century and became the targets of considerable discrimination.

Although we might wonder at the widespread popularity of a song with such thin and variable textual content, there is little question that the emphasis here and in many other Cajun songs is on the *sound* of the words. Cajun French has declined dramatically: until the late twentieth century, the language could not be taught officially, or even legally, in Louisiana schools. Young people were discouraged from learning or speaking Cajun so that they might better fit into mainstream society. For these reasons, Cajun song was one of the few means of preserving the special Cajun French dialect. Cajun music, therefore, has recently been at the center of efforts to revive Cajun culture by a generation that has lost the ability to speak the language. The emphasis on language as sound, which has been termed

Ethnic Recordings in North America

"Ethnic recordings," targeted toward a group united by shared national, linguistic, racial, or religious background, were distributed on 78-rpm discs between 1900 and 1950. Because of the large immigrant population in its cities, the United States became the center for these ethnic recordings, and a new, distinctively American genre of recordings was born.[8] Between 1900 and 1940, the major record companies (Victor, Columbia, Edison) even sent out teams to "discover" new musics. One particularly colorful story relates the genesis of the first Cajun record, made by Joe Falcon in the late 1920s:

> George Burrow, a jewelry store owner in Rayne, persuaded Falcon to go to New Orleans with him to make some records to be sold in Burrow's Rayne store. "We went over there," Falcon recalled. "They looked at us—we was but two, just myself and my wife Cleoma Breaux, she played the guitar—but they were used to recording with orchestras. 'That's not enough music to make a record,' they said. So George had 250 records paid for before I even went to make them. So George started talking: 'We got to run it through because that man there,' he said, pointing to me, 'is popular in Rayne; the people are crazy about his music and they want the records.' But they said, 'We don't know if it's going to sell.' They then turned around and asked him, 'How much would you buy?' He told them he wanted 500 copies as the first order. 'Ah,' they said, '500! When are you gonna get through selling that?' 'That's my worry,' he said, 'I want 500.' And he made out a check for 500 records. They started looking at each other. 'Well,' they said, 'you go ahead and play us a tune just for us to hear.'[9]

Thus, the first Cajun record, *Allons à Lafayette,* was made in 1928. Evidently, in those days ethnic recordings did not have to sell by the thousands to satisfy the companies. In the same interview, Joe Falcon recalls that Cajun people were impressed and proud that one of their own had cut a record: "Even some of the poorest country fellows, they buy as high as two records. They ain't got no Victrola, but they buy and go to their neighbor's and play it!"

In general, ethnic recordings were characterized by their small runs of perhaps one thousand copies. They cannot be defined by their musical content (traditional, folk, classical), because the music overlaps a variety of styles, including spoken-language. A popular category of ethnic recordings of the 1920s and 1930s, known as "race records," consisted of musics performed by and for African Americans. Many of the early jazz recordings appeared in this context.

The ethnic recording industry began to decline in the depression of the 1930s and was seriously constrained during World War II. By the 1950s, independent companies had taken over the recording of various identity musics (on LPs), paving the way for the growing world-music record market, which proliferated in the last two decades of the twentieth century.

LISTENING GUIDE 64

Allons à Lafayette ("Let's Go to Lafayette"; Cajun song)

PERFORMED BY Joe Falcon

This recording is not the 1928 original—it was recorded live at the Triangle Club in Scott, Louisiana, in 1963 and released after Falcon's death. Joe Falcon plays accordion and sings; his vocal style and dialect French are distinctive, as are the instruments used. In addition to the accordion, the ensemble consists of fiddle, guitar, triangle, and drums, the latter played by Falcon's second wife, Theresa Falcon. (Women tended to perform Cajun music publicly only when in the company of their husbands.) The fiddle undoubtedly traveled with the Acadians when they were forced to migrate south from what became Canada. The accordion, introduced into Cajun music by German immigrants during the second half of the nineteenth century, came to dominate Cajun music during much of the twentieth. In the late 1900s, electric guitar and drum sets were incorporated into Cajun bands.

The button accordion is at the heart of the Cajun sound, making songs longer by what Cajuns refer to as "turning the verses," repeating the tune between verses.[10]

LISTEN CAREFULLY TO the Cajun French lyrics of *Allons à Lafayette,* which are pronounced in a slightly slurred manner. Unlike other ballads we have examined (such as *Barbara Allen*) the words in *Allons à Lafayette* do not recount any kind of sustained narrative or story, though two versions refer to a marriage. Rather, the only consistent theme of the song is the journey to Lafayette, retold at the beginning of each verse.

"cajunization," evokes a certain nostalgia, since, through music, one can in a very real sense still "speak Cajun." This perspective comes through in a description of the important Cajun fiddler Dennis McGee, who is said to have used words for their rhythm and sound, not simply to tell a story.[11]

In addition to Cajun music's important role in reviving and perpetuating a language rarely spoken, the music was also performed in settings that insured its close association with Cajun family and social life. Community dances continue to play an important part in keeping Cajun music alive. A variety of dances are

Version 1
Allons à Lafayette c'est pour changer ton nom.
On va t'appeler madame, Madame Canaille Comeaux.
Trop petite et trop mignonne pour faire ta criminelle.
Qui sait que ton petit coeur pour faire sans mon petit coeur?

Let's go to Lafayette for to change your name.
They're going to call you Madame, Madame Canaille Comeaux.
Too small and too cute to be guilty.
Who knows what your little heart can do without my little heart?

Version 2
Allons à Lafayette secourir les petits Dagos
Parce qu'ils sont tous malades, couchés sur le parterre.
Rien pour leur faire du bien, du "gin" our les soulager.
Doudoun a juste un oeil, petit frère a la patte cassée.

Let's go to Lafayette to help the little Dagos
Because they are all sick, lying on the floor.
Nothing for to do them good, some gin for to comfort them.
Dadoun has just one eye, little brother has a broken limb.

Version 3
Allons à Lafayette, c'est pour changer ton nom,
Pour t'appeler ma femme, minir nos jours ensemble.
Jeunes gens de la campagne, prenez exemple sur moi,
Mariez vous autres jamais, la farine ça coûte trop cher.

Let's go to Lafayette for to change your name.
For to call you my wife, to finish our days together.
Young country folk, take me as an example,
Never marry another, flour is too expensive.

—Translated by Patricia Tang

performed to Cajun music, ranging from country square dances to waltzes and polkas. Although a single fiddler or accordionist might suffice for a small private dance in a home, the grand ball of Cajun society, called the *fais-dodo*, requires a full band. The name *fais-dodo*, (literally, "go to sleep") which was given both to the ball itself and to the building in which it was held, comes from the old custom of bringing along small children who would be lulled to sleep by the music.

By the middle of the twentieth century, too, with the advent of the radio and the phonograph, new influences shaped Cajun music. Through recordings, touring musicians, and festivals, the music began to spread outside the immediate community in which it had existed for centuries in oral tradition. Among the outside influences on Cajun music were country and western tunes, which many Cajun musicians borrowed to supplement the repertory of traditional Cajun songs. This modeling on more "American" musical styles likely reflects the Cajun culture's gradual move into broader American society. At the same time, these borrowed tunes were "cajunized" by blurring the clear declamation of their words and instead emphasizing the "feeling of loss and longing" through the sound of the text.[12] New instruments, such as the pedal steel guitar, and techniques, such as new fiddle styles, entered Cajun music as well, occasioned by the revolutions in music technology since the 1950s (**see "Sound Sources: The Ukulele and Steel Guitar," Chapter 10**).

Throughout its history, Cajun music has benefited from musical cross-fertilization, but of all the influences that shaped it, it was the Creole peoples that have had the greatest impact on both Cajun music and emerging styles, such as the zydeco tradition.

Singing Ethnicity, Race, and Class
As noted in the introduction to this chapter, people do not define their identities in a vacuum, but necessarily establish them in relationship to the identities of others. For the French-speaking peoples of Louisiana and the Gulf Coast, music became a reflection of the distinct identities of two groups—Cajuns and Creoles—who shared the same language and economic hardship, but who were of different racial backgrounds.

The division between Cajuns and Creoles extends to their names for the very places they jointly inhabit. Many Creoles take exception to the Louisiana state

This chart summarizes the complex interchange between Cajun and Creole traditions over time. Some styles, such as swamp pop, which first emerged in the late 1950s, blend Creole and Cajun musics with other soundscapes, such as rhythm and blues.

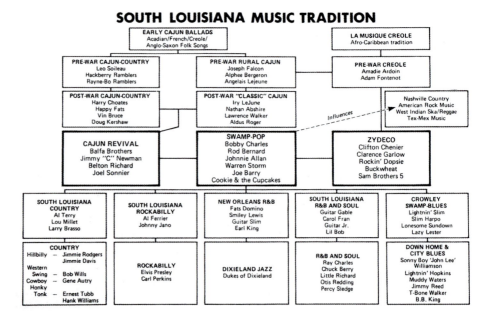

SOUTH LOUISIANA MUSIC TRADITION

EARLY CAJUN BALLADS
Acadian/French/Creole/
Anglo-Saxon Folk Songs

LA MUSIQUE CREOLE
Afro-Caribbean tradition

PRE-WAR CAJUN-COUNTRY
Leo Soileau
Hackberry Ramblers
Rayne-Bo Ramblers

PRE-WAR RURAL CAJUN
Joseph Falcon
Alphee Bergeron
Angelais Lejeune

PRE-WAR CREOLE
Amadie Ardoin
Adam Fontenot

POST-WAR CAJUN-COUNTRY
Harry Choates
Happy Fats
Vin Bruce
Doug Kershaw

POST-WAR "CLASSIC" CAJUN
Iry LeJune
Nathan Abshire
Lawrence Walker
Aldus Roger

Nashville Country
American Rock Music
West Indian Ska/Reggae
Tex-Mex Music

Influences

CAJUN REVIVAL
Balfa Brothers
Jimmy "C" Newman
Belton Richard
Joel Sonnier

SWAMP-POP
Bobby Charles
Rod Bernard
Johnnie Allan
Warren Storm
Joe Barry
Cookie & the Cupcakes

ZYDECO
Clifton Chenier
Clarence Garlow
Rockin' Dopsie
Buckwheat
Sam Brothers 5

SOUTH LOUISIANA COUNTRY
Al Terry
Lou Millet
Larry Brasso

SOUTH LOUISIANA ROCKABILLY
Al Ferrier
Johnny Jano

NEW ORLEANS R&B
Fats Domino
Smiley Lewis
Guitar Slim
Earl King

SOUTH LOUISIANA R&B AND SOUL
Guitar Gable
Carol Fran
Guitar Jr.
Lil Bob

CROWLEY SWAMP-BLUES
Lightnin' Slim
Slim Harpo
Lonesome Sundown
Lazy Lester

COUNTRY
Hillbilly — Jimmie Rodgers
            Jimmie Davis
Western
Swing — Bob Wills
Cowboy — Gene Autry
Honky
Tonk — Ernest Tubb
       Hank Williams

ROCKABILLY
Elvis Presley
Carl Perkins

DIXIELAND JAZZ
Dukes of Dixieland

R&B AND SOUL
Ray Charles
Chuck Berry
Little Richard
Otis Redding
Percy Sledge

DOWN HOME & CITY BLUES
Sonny Boy 'John Lee' Williamson
Lightnin' Hopkins
Muddy Waters
Jimmy Reed
T-Bone Walker
B.B. King

"Rendez Vous des Cajuns" is a radio show broadcast every Saturday evening from the Liberty Theatre in Eunice, Louisiana. The audience includes local fans and visitors from out of state, as entire families come to celebrate their Cajun heritage. Because the show is completely in French, visitors often turn to local people sitting near them to ask questions, thereby establishing a context through which they learn about Cajun music and culture and through which the insiders validate their own cultural heritage. Here Ally Young and the Basile Cajun Band (including bass player Claudia Wood, accordionist Ally Young, guitarist Erroll Guilbeau, drummer Eston Bellow, and fiddler Lee Manuel) plays as audience members dance. Longtime host Barry Ancelet can be seen sitting on the stool at the far left of the stage.

legislature's decision to label the region Acadiana and refer to it as Southwest Louisiana. "The Cajuns have done a good job of promoting their culture," according to one musician, "but I'm not a Cajun. I'm Afro-American Creole, black Creole—whatever you want to call me other than a Cajun."[13]

The relationship between Cajuns and Creoles has been complicated and remains so, perhaps because Cajun and Creole cultures have had much in common. Scorned by urban whites, poor Creole blacks and Cajun whites worked side by side in the same fields. This prolonged period of cultural exchange resulted in culinary and linguistic blending. The spicy Creole *gumbos* (stews) combined French, African, and American ingredients, while the Cajun dialect of French took on distinctive local features. At times Cajun and Creole musicians even played together, as in the famous duets in the 1920s and 1930s of the Cajun fiddler Dennis McGee and the Creole accordionist Amédé Ardoin.

Yet it is also widely remembered that Ardoin received a brutal beating after playing for a (white) Cajun dance, from which he never recovered. Racial tensions pervaded the history of these two communities. One story has it that a black Creole accordionist playing for a dance was forced by the lighter-skinned Creole dancers to don white gloves, stand outside a window, and reach into the room so that only the gloves and his instrument were visible from inside.[14]

Out of these complicated musical and cultural interactions emerged, after World War II, a distinctively Creole music that came to be called *zydeco*. Much more than Cajun music, zydeco has borrowed from other African American and

Caribbean traditions, including the blues, rhythm and blues, and reggae, adopting the bass guitar, percussion, and even, on occasion, the saxophone. Although zydeco was influenced by Cajun music at first, the tables turned in the second half of the twentieth century, and zydeco began to influence Cajun musicians.

Zydeco uses the same core ensemble as Cajun music: voice, fiddle, accordion, electric guitar, and sometimes piano. Zydeco musicians, led by Clifton Chenier, also began using the piano-key accordion instead of the old button accordions popular for years (although button accordions were revived by some in the 1980s; see "Snapshot: More Accordions").

SNAPSHOT

More Accordions

Women of Brazzaville in the Congo adopted the accordion from Europeans who colonized their county in the late nineteenth century.

The accordion, a byproduct of the European Industrial Revolution, revolutionized music internationally. By the late nineteenth century, the instrument had spread around the world, giving rise to numerous accordion soundscapes in unexpected places; the European colonial presence, for example, spread the instrument to Africa. Throughout the twentieth century, the instrument continued to travel, establishing itself in many places including Japan and Cape Dorset in Nunavut, Canada. Although the piano is generally considered to be the instrument that spread Western music to much of the world outside Europe, the accordion, in both its button and keyboard varieties, deserves considerable credit as well. In fact, it was the top-selling instrument in the United States in the 1940s.

The accordion has fed the imagination of many. It has even been the subject of literature, as in E. Annie Proulx's 1996 novel *Accordion Crimes*, in which Proulx recounts a century of American immigration by tracing the path of a small green accordion through its various owners, who are of different national and ethnic origins. In one episode, nearly a century after the accordion arrived, the instrument is bought by the zydeco musician Octave, who plays it at the Blue Moon Dance Heaven in Houston:

> He started hot and hard, held the accordion over his head for a triplet bellows shake, rotating the corners of the bellows in a semicircular twist, rolled out like a plane flying acrobatics into diatonic clusters using every inch of the long bellows and shifting its

action skillfully, swooping and diving into a rocking palm section that had the dance floor jammed tight in three minutes. He knew what to do. He screamed, "ah, ha, ha! You gonna burn! You burnin yet?" Then it was *J'ai trois femmes* slap-staccato bundles of notes hitting the dancers, the drum knocking their hearts, the rub board hissing and rattling like a snake, *hincha ketch a ketch a hinch*. Bright drops of sweat flew. Etherine shouted, "you sweat and stomp, you hot, you *will* be back!" Octave was

During the second half of the twentieth century, the accordion became popular in Japan, where ensembles such as Takaharu Onoe, seen here in 1981, play in concert.

bending at the knees now to drive the intense nervous energy up into his hands. His fingers raced and hit, trills and violent tremulo, the notes vibrating with the force of his upward lunges, a left-hand trill going on and on and the heel of his right hand knocking hard and quick against a mass of buttons, a jam of close notes, discord that pulled yells from the dancers and then a sudden stop leaving everybody panting and laughing, and then—it's a trick folks—right back into it again, wringing and twisting out modal harmonies.[15]

Over time, the accordion, nicknamed "squeeze box," moved into mass culture, becoming a regular fixture on Lawrence Welk's TV show in the 1950s and 1960s. Frank Yankovic, crowned "the Polka King" in 1948, was active until his death in 1998 in bringing the accordion and its polka repertory to a nationwide audience. He won a Grammy award, played for Hollywood movies, and accompanied popular-music singers such as Doris Day.

That the accordion has been the butt of many jokes seems only to have enhanced the reputation of the instrument and encouraged its players to have a sense of humor and enjoy the music for its own sake. Even accordion manufacturers have joined in the fun, making display instruments in a full range of sizes.

A miniature accordion, only a bit larger than a small box of matches.

This giant accordion, a novelty item manufactured for museum display in 1938, can be played by six people at once.

However, the venerable squeeze box may indeed have the last wheeze. According to the National Association of Music Merchants, accordion sales were up 30 percent in the mid-1990s, and accordion schools are reporting increased enrollments. Musicians as diverse as Madonna, Barenaked Ladies, Sinead O'Connor, and Luciano Pavarotti have used the accordion as accompaniment. From zydeco to Tex-Mex to polka, an accordion revival is under way. According to Carl Finch, an accordionist for Brave Combo, an alternative polka band from Texas, "we look at the accordion as just another cool instrument."

Accordions have crossed musical boundaries and have been used by groups such as They Might Be Giants.

John Delafose and the Eunice Playboys features John Delafose playing accordion, Germaine Jack on rub board, and Gino Delafose on drums. Note the construction of the rub board.

Zydeco's distinctive sound, however, came in large part from a "found" instrument: a steel washboard or rub board (*froit-toir*), usually used for washing clothes, against which is rubbed a bottle opener, spoon, or other implement. Clifton Chenier is credited with inventing the usual form of the instrument seen today: a corrugated steel plate, extending from a collar draped over the player's shoulders, that covers the chest. (Chenier is said to have found using an old washboard tied by a string around the neck awkward and asked a friend at the Gulf Oil Refinery near Houston to make a new design.) The close fit of the rub board allows the player not only to keep the rhythm, but also to move around and lead the dancing that inevitably accompanies zydeco music performance.

In Black Creole society, as in Cajun circles, music long flourished in *bals de maison* ("house dances"). For these parties, young people would "borrow" the home of an elder and clear away the furniture. At the party, they would eat *gumbo,*

Zydeco Sont Pas Salé ("The Beans Are Not Salty"; zydeco song)

PERFORMED BY Clifton Chenier

The name *zydeco* is said to derive from a French expression, *les haricots* (literally, "the beans"), alluding to a metaphor popular among Creole peoples of color that "the beans are not salty," that is, they are unflavored by salted meat that is too expensive to buy during hard times. The phrase was first recorded in a musical setting by the Lomaxes in 1934 as part of the lyrics to an old French song at a Church in Port Arthur, Louisiana. It was only in 1965, when accordionist Clifton Chenier recorded a piece called *Zydeco Sont Pas Salé,* that the term became permanently attached to a black Creole musical style.

LISTEN TO the fast, syncopated rhythm with accordion chords stressing the second beat of each pair. Listen, too, for the distinctive scratching sound of the rub board providing yet another layer of rhythmic accompaniment.

O Mama! Quoi elle va faire avec le nègre?
    Zydeco est pas salé, zydeco est pas salé.
T'as volé mon traîneau, t'as volé mon traîneau.
    Regarde Hip et Taïaut, regarde Hip et Taïaut.

Oh, Mama! What's she going to do with the man?
    The beans aren't salty, the beans aren't salty.
You stole my sled, you stole my sled.
    Look at Hip and Taïaut, look at Hip and Taïaut.[16]

drink, and—most important—dance. Music at these *bals* was a catalyst for social interaction, as it was at a Cajun *fais-dodo.* With the development of zydeco and its spread through the record industry, zydeco became a regular part of concert life and dance clubs throughout North America and elsewhere.

"King" Clifton Chenier plays a keyboard accordion at the Cajun Music Festival in Lafayette, Louisiana, in the mid-1970s.

ZYDECO'S KINGS AND QUEENS

The use of the titles "king" and "queen" by famous zydeco musicians derives, according to Cajun lore, from Joe Falcon, who called himself the "Famous Columbia Record King" early in his recording career. But without doubt, the first "king of zydeco" was Clifton Chenier. Although there are conflicting stories about where Chenier got his crown—some suggest it was just a publicity gimmick—Chenier claimed in an interview that he became the king of zydeco in 1971 by winning an accordion contest in Europe:

> They had a lot of accordion players, but they couldn't capture my style. But I could play their style, so that's how I walk out with that crown.[17]

Whatever the source of Chenier's crown, the image of zydeco kings became a standard part of zydeco mythology. When Chenier died in 1987, his crown was buried with him.

RAISING VOICES TOGETHER: UNITING CAJUN AND ZYDECO

After a long period of racial tension extending from after the Civil War through the twentieth-century civil rights movement, interaction between Cajuns and Creoles is once again beginning to emerge. New bands are now bridging the racial and musical gap. One such band is Filé, which incorporates elements of Cajun and zydeco and includes musicians of both traditions. Filé draws on both traditional Cajun repertory and newer zydeco songs, keeping traditional instruments such as accordion, fiddle, and guitar, while adding a keyboard and harmony to the vocal parts.

The group Filè, which now tours internationally, includes (left to right) David Egan (piano and vocals), D'Jalma Garnier (fiddle, guitar, banjo, vocals), Peter Stevens (drums), Kevin Shearin (bass), and Ward Lormand (accordion, rub board, triangle, vocals).

LISTENING GUIDE 66

C'est Moi (It's Me"; zydeco music)

PERFORMED BY Queen Ida Guillory

Zydeco kings ruled this male-dominated tradition, and only a very few women were able to make a career as zydeco musicians. Ida Guillory, however, is a marked exception among zydeco musicians (**see "Individual Portrait: Queen Ida Guillory"**). Queen Ida's zydeco embodies all the hallmarks of zydeco musical style while showcasing her own virtuosity as an accordion player. Many of her songs comment on aspects of her identity as a zydeco musician with roots in south Louisiana (*Zydeco, Home to New Orleans*), her unusual status as a woman in the largely male world of zydeco musicians (*Hard-Headed Woman*), and issues of race (*Hey Negress*).

Queen Ida's *C'est Moi* is a song in English and French comparing her personal background in south Louisiana with the reality of her life as a female musician "on the road." Guillory's song has a strophic form, with a verse and refrain typical of zydeco music.

LISTEN TO the rub board rhythm and backup vocals characteristic of zydeco. In this song, Queen Ida plays a three-row button accordion in a straight-out zydeco style, with little reference to Latin or rock-and-roll influences heard in much of zydeco music and in other songs of hers.

Listen to my story, I come from Louisian'.
I play my music on an old accordion.
Oo la la, je suis comme ça. (Oo la la, that's the way
    I am.)
Hotel rooms, I've seen all before.
My favorite room is the dance hall floor.
Oo la la, je suis comme ça.
C'est moi, c'est moi, oh, je suis comme ça. (*twice*)

Oh there was a time I had myself a man.
He didn't realize, he didn't understand.
Oo la la, je suis comme ça.
That's the way I am, it's everything I know.
Playing with the band and singing zydeco.
Oo la la, je suis comme ça.
C'est moi, c'est moi, oh je suis comme ça. (*twice*)

You have to put it down, everybody say.
This won't last, so then you walk away.
Oo la la, je suis comme ça.
That's the way I am, going to work at nine.
Three in the morning is about my suppertime.
Oo la la, je suis comme ça.
C'est moi, c'est moi, oh je suis comme ça. (*three times*)

INDIVIDUAL PORTRAIT

Queen Ida Guillory

Ida Guillory was born in 1930, to rice-farming parents in Lake Charles, Louisiana. She spoke only French until she was seven, learning English when she went to school. In 1940, her family moved to Beaumont, Texas and seven years later to San Francisco. Following her marriage to Ray Guillory, Ida raised three children and drove a school bus. Her mother, an accordionist, passed on the instrument to her daughter. Ida played the accordion on her own for recreation, until one day in 1975 when she sat in with her brother's band, which needed an accordionist for a Mardi Gras fundraising festival. Ida had never played in public before, since "it wasn't feminine for a girl to play any instrument unless it was a piano or violin."

Newspapers picked up word of this performance, and soon Queen Ida and the Bons Temps Band were playing regularly. Within a year, she had a record contract. She quit her job as a bus driver in 1977 to perform full time and in 1982 won a Grammy for the best ethnic/folk recording.

An interesting aspect of Queen Ida's career—and the zydeco tradition as a whole—is the close connection between music and food. Queen Ida published a cookbook in 1990 with the same name as her album, *Cookin' with Queen Ida.* The cookbook features Creole recipes such as gumbo, jambalaya, boudin, and shrimp creole that she had brought from Louisiana to California. According to Queen Ida, "there's little difference between creole and Cajun cuisines. . . . Like zydeco, Creole cooking is just a bit spicier."

Queen Ida's ensemble incorporates other members of her family, including her brother, Wilbert Lewis, who plays rub board, and her son, Myrick "Freeze" Guillory, who plays accordion and does vocals. On occasions when her brother can't play, Queen Ida drafts her daughter.

When Queen Ida and her family are not touring, they reside in a San Francisco suburb, where they participate in the active zydeco music and dance scene in the Bay area. Among the travels she deems particularly memorable were her visits to five former French colonies in Africa. "For me it was like going back to Louisiana, where the people speak French, or going to France or Switzerland," Ida explains. "It gave me a chance to speak my *patois* with the people there. They understood me better than I understood them."[18]

Conclusion

All of the musicians discussed in this chapter express multiple aspects of their identities—ethnic, national, regional, race, class, gender—through their music. In every case, the sound itself contains distinctive markers of identity, providing entry into a soundscape rich in meaning. Sound conveys a sense of place and past through unique instruments such as zydeco's rub board; through rhythms imitating the steady clip-clop of the packhorse's gait in an *enka* song; or through special flute-playing techniques in a concerto. In those examples with lyrics, words play a central role as an integral part of sound that preserves speech dialects. The words also refer to places that evoke nostalgia, such as the Louisiana cities and bayous named in Cajun lyrics or the happier seasons recalled in the *enka* song.

As important as sound is, the setting of each of the musical styles discussed in this chapter also contributes immeasurably to meaning of the sound. Whether performed in a concert hall, restaurant, dance club, or home, all of these musics come to life when linked to people, places, and the broader stream of tradition. To step into a musical setting—whether a *fais-dodo, bal de maison,* or karaoke bar—is to be surrounded by associations emerging from both the music making and the social interaction. In the case of Cajun and zydeco musics, the inseparability of the dance from the music gives rise to soundscapes that are not just sounded, but embodied.

Individual musicians are linked to a group through live performance and to an immense public through recordings. Today the sounds of karaoke and zydeco have moved from the private and local realms to public and increasingly international contexts, transmitted by mass media well beyond boundaries of a single community or place. Thus, country singer Hank Williams can have a hit titled *Jambalaya*

Beau Jacques and the Zydeco High Rollers perform at the Southwest Louisiana Zydeco Music Festival in September 1992.

LISTENING GUIDE 67

CD 3
TRACK
12

One Foot in the Bayou (Cajun/zydeco song)

PERFORMED BY Filé

The song text, with its mention of a "down home" girl, signals that it draws on an old style of southern ("down home") country blues. Many traditional blues songs have a standard form—called the *twelve-bar blues* form—in which each verse consists of three textual lines. The second line usually repeats the first, and the third serves as a kind of "punch line." Each line is generally set to four measures (bars) of music, and the twelve-bar verses are accompanied by the same sequence of harmonies.

"One Foot in the Bayou" draws on, expands, and varies the traditional blues form just described, expanding it to sixteen bars. Let's look at the first verse and its music in detail. The four-bar musical setting of the first line (marked "a") is repeated for the new words of the second line (marked "a′"). The third line (marked "b") carries the expected melodic and harmonic contrast to the first lines, followed by a fourth line that ends the verse and recurs as a refrain in subsequent verses. Note that the texts of the third and fourth lines do not fill out the full four measures, which are rounded out by the instruments. The verse form of "One Foot in the Bayou" can therefore be represented as a-a′-b-refrain, totaling sixteen measures.

("On the Bayou"), and major films such as *The Big Easy* can feature scenes of both Cajun and zydeco music and dance. In these contexts, local details are changed to make the songs more accessible to a mass audience.

Although many people have deplored the impact of mass media on the traditional identities such as those of the Cajun and Creole communities, in some instances a broader audience has reinforced musicians' commitment to their roots. The impact of commercialism can at times be positive, as in the case of Dewey Balfa, a beloved Cajun fiddler. Mr. Balfa was invited as a last-minute replacement to perform in the 1964 folk music festival at Newport, Rhode Island. Learning of

LISTEN CLOSELY following verse 2, where the instruments alone play the complete sixteen-measure form without the words and you can more easily hear the changes of harmony. Following the instrumental section, the blues form is varied even more, with two contrasting lines (marked "c" and "c'," respectively) followed by a return of "b" and the refrain, both repeated to constitute a full verse.

In an innovative move, the cymbals of the drum set replace the traditional zydeco rub board. At the same time, this song maintains traditional Cajun and zydeco references, naming places on the Gulf Coast, alluding to "bayou culture," and drawing on food metaphors such as candied yams and turnip greens. The ensemble Filé's name derives from food, in this case, an herb mixture containing sassafras and other ingredients.

a	Diamond rings, limousines, down home girl, uptown dreams.
a'	Penthouse suites, Broadway shows, just don't move her like the zydeco.
b	She done gone up to the city, now she don't know what to do.
refrain	She got one foot in New York City and one foot in the bayou.

a	Taxi cabs, traffic jams, sure do miss her candied yams.
a'	She packed her bags, you should a seen, the big suitcase full of turnip greens.
b	She done gone up to the city, still got mud on her shoes.
refrain	She got one foot in New York City and one foot in the bayou.

c	Well, if she's gone, I wish her well, she might come home, you just can't tell.
c'	But if she runs out of luck, I'll drive right up and get her in my truck.
b	'Cause she done gone up to the city, now she don't know what to do.
b'	Born and raised in Morgan City, still got mud on her shoes.
refrain	She got one foot in New York City and one foot in the bayou. (*twice*)

the invitation, his local newspaper wrote an article characterizing his decision to play Cajun music in this public context as "an embarrassment, especially to those trying to put their country roots behind them." His daughter Christine remembers that her father "had never seen more than 200 people together at one time before. And 17,000 people gave him a standing ovation after the first song. And that changed his life. He became a strong advocate for Cajun culture."[19]

Because music conveys so many aspects of identity, it can emerge as a powerful element when the struggle for identity becomes a basis for political action. The union of music and politics will be our topic in Chapter 9.

IMPORTANT TERMS

accordion
Cajun/Acadian
chamber orchestra
concerto
Creole
darabukkah
enka

fais-dodo
fiddle
flute
karaoke
kata
ney

Persian (Iranian)
  music
rubboard
triangle
Western orchestra/
  concerto
zydeco

CHAPTER

NINE NINE NINE NINE NINE NINE NINE NINE NINE NINE NINE NINE NINE NINE NINE NINE NINE NINE NINE NINE

Cover art and advertising copy for the 1986 CBS reggae anthology Rhythm Come Forward *puts the focus on the power of rhythm.*

OVERVIEW

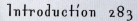

MAIN POINTS

- Music is frequently used for symbolic communication in political contexts.

- Music conveys official ideologies, as in national anthems.

- Music conveys what cannot be spoken publicly, giving voice to resistance.

- Music can shift or accrue additional meanings in different political contexts.

Music and Politics

Introduction

The subject of music and politics is not a new one in *Soundscapes*. We have already encountered many examples of music's link to political events, from the historical role of bagpipes as instruments of war to songs that recall the pain of forced migrations. In these and other instances, musical styles and their performance settings provide a mode of expression for individual and collective political action.

On the level of national and corporate politics, music is consistently invoked in overt and purposeful ways. Music has always been an integral part of formal displays of political power, conveying both national identity and official ideologies through symbolic acts, such as the singing of a national anthem. Here we must recognize the difference between open and coded political messages. Musical displays of official power, or *public transcripts,* openly affirm and perpetuate an existing power structure. *Hidden transcripts,* on the other hand, are musical performances and repertories that embed messages through metaphorical or coded terms. Although hidden transcripts are most often used to oppose the dominant culture or political establishment, the powerful also have hidden transcripts representing the aspects of their rule that cannot be openly acknowledged.[1] As we see from these two categories, music is crucial in helping us to understand and interpret how power is enforced as well as how it is challenged. In this chapter, we will take a close look at the genesis and significance of the new national anthem of

A Farm Aid Concert in Champaign, Illinois, September 25, 1985. Mass concerts such as this one, mounted to raise money for important social causes, became increasingly common in the late twentieth century.

South Africa, which combines both public and hidden musical transcripts from the past that have been further transformed to symbolize a new political order.

Musics of Power and Resistance

An individual song can incorporate many layers of different meanings, partly because music has the power to convey what cannot be spoken or what might not be heard in everyday speech. We have already seen that music can express different channels of memory through melody, rhythm, and textual content. Because of its ability to code and represent, music has historically been a way both to assert power and to give voice to overlooked or actively suppressed issues. Frequently, re-

Open transcripts of resistance were conveyed through the rap music of groups such as N.W.A. (Niggaz Wit' Attitude), which gained a following in the late 1980s with the gangsta rap style. The Los Angeles group's song lyrics and album cover art graphically depicted urban violence. Their albums, such as Straight Outta Compton, *raised intense national controversies. However, N.W.A. argued that the brutality of text and image in their albums was not sensationalist; it simply reflected the world they lived in as ghetto teens.[2] Pictured here in the late-1980s inner-city setting that gave rise to their music are N.W.A. members (left to right) DJ Yella (born Antoine Carraby), MC Ren (b. Lorenzo Petterson), the late Easy-E (b. Eric Wright), and Dr. Dre (b. Andre Young).*

sistance is couched in language and musical styles fully accessible only to insiders who know the correct social context and linguistic code.

Musical styles are extraordinarily flexible: they can begin within a particular soundscape as an emblem of resistance, then move to broader audiences as vehicles of popular entertainment. African American rap music provides an example of this flexibility, since it has its roots as a hidden transcript of urban black resistance to oppressive institutions.[3] Rap has remained an important medium of political expression, while moving to a broader audience and deeply influencing the styles of other musics. A similar process can be seen in the history of reggae music, which we will trace from its inception as a music of resistance through its move into the popular mainstream.

Some soundscapes contain aspects of both resistance and incorporation. We will explore these seemingly contradictory tendencies in the music of the Shoshone powwow. The powwow provides a musical transcript that is at once public and hidden, both celebrating and resisting the historical and present-day situations of Native Americans.

CASE STUDY: THE BIRTH OF A NATIONAL ANTHEM

Through music, the history of shifting power relations can be confronted, redressed and affirmed. One such example is the South African song *Nkosi Sikelel' iAfrika* (*Lord, Bless Africa*). The song originated little more than a century ago as a Christian hymn, was quickly transformed into a musical emblem of political resistance, and in the 1990s became a respected national anthem. Over time, this song has inspired resistance against apartheid in South Africa, becoming in the end an international symbol of victory in the fight for racial equality.

The story of *Nkosi Sikelel' iAfrika* begins with Enoch Mankayi Sontonga (1873–1905), a choirmaster of Xhosa descent who was a teacher at a Methodist mission school near Johannesburg, South Africa. In 1897, Sontonga composed *Nkosi Sikelel' iAfrika* as a hymn, and it was first performed at the ordination of a minister in 1899. Sontonga composed only the melody, first verse, and chorus of *Nkosi Sikelel' iAfrika*. An additional seven verses were added later by the South African poet S. E. K. Mqhayi and the full English text was published in 1927. However, the text is sung in several different South African languages and is varied by singers during performances (see "Sound Sources: Vocal Ensembles").

The choirmaster Enoch Mankayi Sontonga both composed Nkosi Sikelel' iAfrika *and conducted public performances of the song with his choir until his premature death in 1905. On September 24, 1996, Sontonga's grave in Johannesburg, South Africa, was declared a national monument, and a memorial was unveiled on the site by President Nelson Mandela.*

Vocal Ensembles

The human voice is the first of all musical instruments.

Members of the ensemble Ladysmith Black Mambazo sing and perform the side kick.

As we have seen throughout *Soundscapes,* the voice is used as an expressive instrument in a wide range of cultures. Like any instrument, the voice can be used alone or combined with other voices. In Chapter 1, we explored the manner in which a given vocal style incorporates different articulations, methods of vibrato, and distinctive ornaments. In the same way that we learn about a culture through the development of its vocal style, so we can also gain insights into many important aspects of social life and politics by examining how voices are combined.

Many of our musical examples were performed by amateurs. For instance, the recording of *Nkosi Sikelel' iAfrika* as hymn is a field recording made in a South African church, while the song as new national anthem was recorded at a university ceremony honoring Nelson Mandela in 1998 (see Listening Guides 68 and 69).

However, this song was spread internationally by an amateur group that entered professional circles—the all-male South African choral group Ladysmith Black Mambazo. We encountered a singing style similar to that of Ladysmith Black Mambazo in Chapter 4, when we heard the first example of South African *mbube* recorded in 1939, which became the model for the folk song *Wimoweh.* Ladysmith Black Mambazo maintains this vocal tradition, which combines traditional and contemporary Zulu music and dance with Western musical practices.

Mbube developed as an all-male competitive choral tradition in urban South Africa in the 1930s, although its origins have been traced back to the late 1800s. Mission-educated black South Africans founded traveling choral groups in the 1890s, combining Western four-part hymns, ragtime, minstrel music, and Zulu dance and wedding songs.[4] By the late 1930s, *mbube* groups had developed individual identities through distinctive names, repertories, and dress: the Durban Evening Birds, for example, donned striped suits, signifying urban sophistication, as their uniform. Members of a given group were usually linked by kinship, by occupation, or hometown. The men of Ladysmith Black Mambazo share the same hometown, as their leader Joseph Shabalala recounts in an oral autobiography:

The name Black Mambazo is a name that I had been using at home, because where I come from, it is a place of music and musicians are called oxen. I'm sure you know that oxen on a white man's farm are called span, sixteen of them. Now singers in our district are called oxen. Now coming to the word *black,* it is like this: a span of black oxen, among other spans which are black, red, white, and colored, being three types of spans—the black span was very strong. This is why I decided to call my span Black. Then I called the group Black Mambazo. Now coming to the word *Mambazo.* The word *Mambazo* in fact depicts an *imbazo,* an axe, because when we went home from Durban at Christmas in 1964, people were shocked. We started to axe them, axing them on their head, meaning chopping all groups we came across and winning all competitions. Then I said to people, 'That's because I have an axe, a black axe.' That's how the name Black Mambazo came into being.[5]

From the beginning, many *mbube* ensembles sang as a form of political protest, performing at the Durban Workers' Club and intentionally using English-derived terms in their musical vocabulary. The parts in Western harmony, for example, are described as *bes* (bass), *thena* (tenor), *altha* (alto), and *fas pathi* (first part, or soprano). Falsetto, call-and-response sections, strong bass lines, repetitive harmonic progressions and dances involving intricate footwork are all elements of the *mbube* style.

Although dozens of ensembles have been important in the history of *mbube,* Ladysmith Black Mambazo's collaboration with the American musician Paul Simon and frequent concert tours sparked publicity and further support for the antiapartheid movement.

By 1912, *Nkosi Sikelel' iAfrika* was sung at meetings of the organization that would later become African National Congress. The ANC, whose leader for much of the second half of the twentieth century was the imprisoned Nelson Mandela, led the fight against apartheid. Over the years, the song *Nkosi Sikelel' iAfrika,* like the liberation movement it symbolized, became a focus of controversy and a target of repression, banned by the South African government as subversive.

Following the official end of apartheid in the early 1990s and the 1994 election of Nelson Mandela as South Africa's first black president, the nation needed a new anthem. Since 1957, an Afrikaaner song, *Die Stem van Suid Afrika (The Call of South Africa),* had served as the South African national anthem. After Mandela assumed the presidency, *The Call of South Africa* and *Nkosi Sikelel' iAfrika* were, for a period of time, designated as dual national anthems. The use of the two songs was a first step toward reconciliation after a deeply divided history. Indeed, in an official publication on the national symbols of the Republic of South Africa,

LISTENING GUIDE 68

CD 3
TRACK
13

Nkosi Sikelel' iAfrika (South African hymn)

COMPOSED BY Enoch Mankayi Sontonga

PERFORMED BY Congregation, St. Paul's Church, Soweto

The melody of *Nkoski Sikelel' iAfrika* in this field recording (**see "Sound Sources: Vocal Ensembles"**) and the hymn's harmonic texture reflect the influence of Western hymns introduced to South Africa by Christian missionaries.

LISTEN FOR the internal repetition within the melody and rhythm of the five phrases of the song's refrain. This repetition reflects the structure of indigenous South African melodies. And despite its strophic structure, the hymn is sung in a style emphasizing the "call and response" performance practice common in Africa.[6]

Nkosi, sikelel' iAfrika,
Maluphalkanyisw' uphondo Iwayo;
Yizwa imithandazo yethu
Nkosi sikelela,
Thina lusapho Iwayo.

Lord, bless Africa,
May her spirit rise high up;
Hear thou our prayers
Lord, bless us,
Your family.

Refrain:
Woza Moya
Woza Moya
Woza Moya, Oyingowele.
Nkosi sikelela,
Thina lusapho Iwayo.

Refrain:
Descend, O Spirit,
Descend, O Spirit,
Descend, O Holy Spirit,
Lord, bless us,
Your family.

Morena bokoka setjhaba sa heso,
O fedise dintwa la matshwenyeho.
O se boloke setjhaba sa heso,
Sethaba sa heso.

Lord protect our nation,
And end the wars and tribulations.
Protect us, our entire nation,
Our nation.

Makube njalo,
Kuze kube nguna phakade.

Let it be so,
Forever and ever.

LISTENING GUIDE 69

CD 3
TRACK
14

The New South African National Anthem

PERFORMED BY The Kuumba Singers

By 1998, the use of two separate anthems had become increasingly awkward for South Africa, and with reconciliation between the races moving forward, the two songs were shortened and combined to form a single, composite national anthem. The new South African national anthem consists of four verses in four different languages: Zulu and Lethoso (two versions of the chorus from *Nkosi Sikelel' iAfrika),* and Afrikaans, and English (from *The Call of South Africa).*

LISTEN FOR the changes of language within the song.

Nkosi sikelel' iAfrika
Maluphakanyisw' uphondo lwayo;
Yizwa imithandazo yethu,
Nkosi sikelela, thina lusapho lwayo.

Lord, bless Africa,
May her spirit rise high up;
Hear thou our prayers,
Lord, bless us, your family.

Morena boloka setjhaba sa heso,
O fedise dintwa la matshwenyeho,
O se boloke, O se boloke setjhaba sa heso,
Sethaba sa South Afrika—South Afrika.

Lord, protect our nation
And end the wars and tribulations.
Protect us, protect us, our entire nation,
Our nation, South Africa—South Africa.

Uit die blou van onse hemel,
Uit die diepte van ons see,
Oor ons ewige gebergtes,
Waar die kranse antwoord gee,

Ringing out from our blue heavens,
From our deep seas breaking round,
Over everlasting mountains,
where the echoing crags resound.

Sounds the call to come together,
And united we shall stand,
Let us live and strive for freedom,
In South Africa our land.

Sounds the call . . .

The South African president Nelson Mandela dances with a choir after the signing of a new South African constitution in Sharpeville on December 10, 1996.

Mandela described the validation of two national anthems as "a manifestation of the desire to achieve a national consensus."[7] During this period, *Nkosi Sikelel' iAfrika* continued to be transmitted as an anthem of freedom and independence throughout Africa, also becoming the official anthem of countries such as Tanzania and Zambia.

Over the years, *Nkosi Sikelel' iAfrika* has carried increasing layers of meaning—as a Christian hymn, as a song of resistance, and finally, as an integral part of a new national anthem. Beyond the importance of this song within South Africa's new political order, the song has had a second life as a worldwide anthem of human rights.

> What national anthems do you know?
> Sing one and listen closely to its text and melody.
> What agendas does it set forth?

CASE STUDY: REGGAE

The fight against apartheid dominated North American concerns about African politics in the last decades of the twentieth century. Songs such as *Nkosi Sikelel' iAfrika* became familiar to an international audience in part through concerts mounted to free Nelson Mandela. During the first half of the twentieth century, however, a different African leader captured the imagination of people of color in North America and the Caribbean—Ethiopia's Ras Tafari, who became regent in 1916 and assumed the throne as Emperor Haile Selassie in 1930. Ethiopia's his-

toric, successful fight for independence from
colonial powers, and the subsequent courage of
its emperor when its autonomy was challenged
in 1935, provided a symbol for the political/
religious movement that became closely associated with the musical style known as reggae.

Rastafarian movement has its philosophical
roots in the 1920s, when Marcus Garvey
founded the "Back to Africa" movement, seeking to reclaim black pride through a return to
Africa. In 1927, Garvey was deported from the
United States and returned to his homeland, Jamaica. There he and others predicted that the
crowning of a black king in Africa would

*Bob Marley performs in
front of a backdrop em-
blazoned with the image
of the Ethiopian emperor
Haile Selassie.*

presage deliverance for all black people, pointing to passages in the book of Revelations that forecast the rise of the Lion of Judah. The coronation of Ethiopian Regent Ras Tafari as Haile Selassie I, the Lion of Judah, was greeted by many as a
fulfillment of these prophecies. In the West Indies, an outcome of these events
was the formation of groups—some called Ethiopians, others called Rastafarians—who supported the new Ethiopian emperor.[8] The accession of Ras Tafari to
the Ethiopian throne was thought to herald the downfall of "Babylon" (white colonial powers) and the subsequent deliverance of oppressed blacks.[9]

The genesis of Rastafarianism provided fertile ground for the development of a
rich array of associated rituals and symbols. These new traditions, constructed and
established within a "brief and datable" time provide another example of the "invention of tradition." As we have seen in Chapter 8, invented traditions are characterized by the fast pace at which they are conceived and adopted, and by their
association with a network of symbols.

The symbols of Rastafarianism include the green, yellow, and red colors of the
Ethiopian flag, "dreadlock" hairstyles, and mind-altering substances. At first, no

*Symbols of Rasta life and culture printed on
T-shirts include the green, yellow, and red colors
of the Ethiopian flag overlaid with images of the
reggae performer Bob Marley, marijuana, and the
Lion of Judah.*

The singer-songwriter Peter Tosh performing in an undated photograph. Born in Jamaica in 1944, by age twenty-two Tosh was a rising musician in the world of ska, famous for his performances and recordings with Bob Marley and the Wailers. After leaving the group in 1973, Tosh released a number of solo albums before being murdered in 1987 at his home in Kingston, Jamaica. The first Grammy Award for best reggae album was awarded to him posthumously in March 1988.

single musical style was associated with Rastafarianism. Rather, several Jamaican musics, including the drumming of the Afro-Jamaican Burru and Kumina cults, as well as rural *mento* music (a local tradition related to calypso) influenced the newer styles that emerged in Jamaican urban areas in the 1950s and 1960s. Musical influences from outside Jamaica, including jazz as well as rhythm and blues, also fed into the mix that eventually produced reggae.

By 1964, groups such as Toots and the Maytals were playing a predecessor of reggae called ska, which was quickly followed by rock steady. In 1968, *reggae* entered the scene, taking its name from a song by Toots and the Maytals entitled *Do the Reggay*.[10] Many musicians were important in developing reggae's musical and political profile, the most controversial being Peter Tosh (Winston Hubert McIntosh, 1944–1987). Throughout his short life, Tosh was always on the front lines to protest inequality, whether through political action or through his performances. His most famous protest music, in addition to the song *Get Up, Stand Up* (see Listening Guide 70), included the albums *Legalize It* (1977) and *No Nuclear War* (1987).

Rhythm is essential to the Rastafarian reggae tradition, laying a foundation for metaphors of resistance in a song's text. The reggae term *ridim* is derived from the English word "rhythm"; however, its meaning extends beyond the main beat—and beyond the emphasis on the second and fourth "off" beats—to include the pace, the relationship between the bass and rhythm instruments, and the repeating patterns they form. In contrast to most Western music, where the rhythmic framework is a steady pulse, the ever-changing, syncopated rhythms of reggae—and many other African-derived musics in the New World—are highly symbolic. Much of the subversiveness of the Rasta subculture and its associated soundscape has been coded into its rhythms. We find both public and hidden transcripts in reggae's sound: public in its rhythmic properties and dance associations, but veiled in its implicit resistance to Western musical styles. The subversive power of reggae rhythms, and the soundscape of which they are a part, is captured by the advertisement for a reggae recording seen in the illustration at the beginning of this chapter.

LISTENING GUIDE 70

CD 3
TRACK
15

Get Up, Stand Up (reggae)

COMPOSED BY Peter Tosh

PERFORMED BY Peter Tosh

In *Get Up, Stand Up,* we hear the rhythmic characteristics that are typical of reggae: a strong, regular pulse of twos and fours, crosscut by syncopated counter-rhythms.

LISTEN FOR the way Rastafarian beliefs expressed in the text address the political situation.

Refrain:
Get up, stand up,
Stand up for your rights.
Get up, stand up,
Don't give up the fight.
(twice)

You, preacher man, don't tell me,
Heaven is under the earth.
You are doubting and you don't know,
What life is really worth.

It's not all that glitter is gold,
And half the story has never been told.
So now we see the light,
We gonna stand up for our rights.

Come on
Refrain (twice)

'Cause you know most people think,
A Great God will come from the skies.
And take away everything,
And left everybody dry.

But if you know what life is worth,
You would look for yours right here on earth.
And now we see the light,
We gonna stand up for our rights.

Refrain (twice)

We're sick and tired of this game of technology,
Humbly asking Jesus for his mercy.
We know, we know, and we understand,
Almight Jah is a living man.

You fool some people sometimes,
But you can't fool all the people all the time.
And now we see the light,
We gonna stand up for our rights.

Refrain (twice)

As we have heard in *Get Up, Stand Up,* many reggae song texts emphasize the connection between music, dance, and resistance. The song *Chant Down Babylon,* on Bob Marley's album *Confrontation,* invokes music and its performance as a device through which people of color can triumph over oppression:

> With music, we chant down Babylon
> Music, you're the key, Talk to who, please talk to me.
> Bring the voice of the Rastaman,
> Communicating to everyone.

Throughout their careers, many reggae musicians have taken strong political stands through their music. Burning Spear (Winston Rodney), for instance, released songs such as *Marcus Garvey, Slavery Days,* and *Red Gold and Green.*[11] However, it was Tosh's partner in the Wailers, Bob Marley, who, since his death in 1981, has come to be the musician most widely associated with reggae and other Jamaican musics internationally. As a musical style, reggae has had a continued life after its early period, moving on to "roots reggae," and from 1983, to "dance-hall," also known as "ragga" or "dub" outside Jamaica.

Bob Marley, who was born in 1945 in Jamaica and died when he was only thirty-six, came to public attention in the Caribbean when his first single, *Judge Not,* was released in Jamaica in 1962. He gained an international following with the release of the historic 1975 album *Natty Dread,* its title referring to the dread-lock hairstyles worn by Rastafarians.

As reggae entered mass culture through recordings, it led an increasingly dual life as both a cult and commercial music, much like Santería (see Chapter 5).

The reggae singer Bob Marley has been idolized since his death, becoming what has been termed a "brand name" in popular music. He is even memorialized in household shrines.

Reggae has also continued to accrue new musical influences through its interaction with other soundscapes such as rap.

Since the 1980s, reggae has joined with other styles to produce hybrid forms. West Indian and South Asian immigrant communities in Great Britain incorporated reggae, and the resulting new styles have been applied to new political contexts. For example, the singer Apache Indian (Steve Kapur) has merged reggae, rap, and Anglo-American pop with bhangra into a style called "bhangramuffin." Apache Indian has transformed reggae music and Rastafarian beliefs and traditions into a public transcript challenging older notions of singular and distinct British, Asian, and black identities.[12] Apache Indian's recordings have also resonated among young Indian Canadians, who interpret his music as "a sign of respect for Indian traditions."[13]

Buju Benton, who burst onto the reggae scene in the 1990s with his band Shiloh, performs a wide variety of reggae styles conveying socially conscious messages.

CASE STUDY: THE SHOSHONE POWWOW

All of the soundscapes we have explored so far originated abroad before becoming well established in North America. The Native American musical tradition, in contrast, is indigenous to North America. We will take a close look at the music of the Native American powwow as it is sustained by Shoshone people of the Wind River Reservation in Wyoming, and the powerful role this music plays in Shoshone political life.

Both voluntary and forced movements within North America have indelibly marked Shoshone history. The Shoshone were originally a people from the Great Basin, a desert region of the western United States lying mostly in Nevada but extending into California, Oregon, Idaho, and Utah. One group migrated out on to the Plains in the 1500s, where it subsequently split in two. Those remaining on the northern Plains were known as the Eastern or Wind River Shoshone, and those moving on to the southern Plains were known as the Comanche. (We encountered a Comanche lullaby in Chapter 2.)

A group of Northern Shoshone settled in Idaho, while the Western Shoshone remained in their ancestral homeland of the Great Basin. The Eastern Shoshone today live on the Wind River Reservation in central Wyoming on lands formally deeded to them by the American government in 1868.

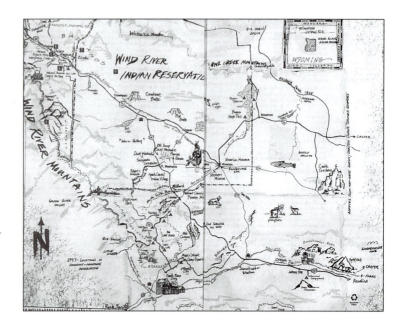

Sites of local importance on the Shoshone
Wind River Reservation in central Wyoming.

Although the Shoshone have been classified as a Great Basin people, present-day Shoshone have been more influenced by the Plains Indian horse and buffalo culture of which they were a part for centuries. By the early twentieth century, all of the Plains peoples, including the Shoshone, were forced to abandon their traditional patterns of hunting and warfare in the face of pressures from United States expansion and urbanization (see "**Looking Back: Native American History**").

The Shoshone chief Washakie, who negotiated the 1868 treaty with the American government, is shown with his tribal council. Said to have been born in Montana in 1798 of a Flathead father and a Shoshone mother, Washakie is remembered as a wise leader. He chose a region known to the Shoshone as Eu-ar-eye, which means "warm valley," to establish a reservation. Oral tradition also credits the chief with discovering the local oil fields while on a buffalo hunt.[14]

LOOKING BACK

Native American History

30,000 years ago	Paleo-Indians migrate to North America from Asia
By early 1500s C.E.	Ancestors of Wind River Shoshone migrate eastward crossing the Rocky Mountains on to the Plains
Early 1700s	Eastern Shoshones split; one group moves south and becomes known as the Comanche
1827	*Pawwaw* recorded as a word meaning religious practitioner among Northeastern Algonquian tribes
1828	Forced removal of Native Americans peaks during Andrew Jackson administration
1830–1838	Trail of Tears: United States government forces thousands of Native Americans from various southeastern tribes to migrate west on foot
1847	Mormons move to Salt Lake region among Shoshone
1848	Treaty of Guadeloupe Hidalgo ends the Mexican war; Mexico cedes territory to the United States, including the Great Basin, where the Shoshone live
1850s	Gold rush brings many settlers to Great Basin
1851	Fort Laramie Treaty initiates settling western tribes on reservations
1868	Treaty of Fort Bridger establishes Wind River Reservation
1869	Nevada Indian initiates a first Ghost Dance religion

This painting of the Trail of Tears by Robert Lindreau captures the trauma of the removal and forced march of tens of thousands of Cherokee peoples from the eastern United States to what is now Oklahoma in December 1838. Troops under orders from President Andrew Jackson patrolled the march, during which thousands died.

1878	United States government forces the Northern Arapahoes, traditional enemies of Shoshone, to resettle on Wind River Reservation
1879	Bureau of Ethnology (later changed to Bureau of American Ethnology) is established within Smithsonian Institution to coordinate and conduct American Indian studies
1880s	Theodore Baker conducts first musical study of and transcribes Native American music
1886	Wind River boarding school founded by United States government
1887	Dawes Severalty Act relocates parcels of land to individual ownership, thereby overturning tribal practices of land collectively held through the maternal line
1889	Jesse Walter Fewkes makes first sound recordings of Native American music
1889	A second Ghost Dance religion, originating with Wovoka, a Northern Paiute prophet, spreads to the Plains Indians
Late 1800s	First Native American powwow held
1890s	Composers become interested in Native American music, resulting in compositions based on Native American themes
1890	Wounded Knee massacre of Ghost Dancers on Pine Ridge Reservation in South Dakota
1890	Blending of peyotism, a Native American religion, and Christianity begins
1890–1924	United States government bans many Native American religious practices
1891	United States outlaws Ghost Dance
1893	Alice C. Fletcher's study of Omaha Indian music is first description of Plains Indian music
1896	United States Bureau of Ethnology publishes James Mooney's 1892–1893 study of Ghost Dance religion
1900	Beginning of war-dance competitions on Southern Plains
1914–1918	World War I; rejuvenation of war songs, as Native American men become warriors once again
1918	Native American Church founded; the church is banned in 1940 by Navaho Tribal Council and then reinstated in 1967 when the council relents
1920s	Modern powwow is developed in Oklahoma as a symbol of "Indianness"

1924	Cayuga chief Deskaheh presents official proclamation from Iroquois confederacy to League of Nations in Geneva documenting Native American independence and sovereignty as recognized in treaties with Dutch, British, and Americans
1924	Citizen Act of 1924 grants citizenship to all Indians who had not previously received it; the act is viewed as a first step toward taxation and loss of political and territorial sovereignty
1926	Frances Densmore publishes *American Indians and Their Music*
1926	Indian Defense League of America is formed to "obtain justice for Indian people"
1930s–1960s	Bureau of Indian Affairs relocation project in effect
1934	Indian Reorganization Act allows American Indians to participate in aspects of their culture and religion once more
1945 on	Intertribal powwow develops
1950s	Dances begin to be performed as competitions at powwows
1955	Beginning of war-dance competitions on Northern Plains
1957	First Wind River Shoshone powwow is held; called "Indian Days"
1968	Indian Bill of Rights, passed as part of Civil Rights Act of 1968, extends Bill of Rights to Native Americans living under tribal self-government
1990	Supreme Court rules that Bill of Rights "free exercise of religion" clause in First Amendment does not extend to Native American Church
1994	President Bill Clinton signs American Indian Religious Freedom Act Amendments of 1994

For Shoshone living on the reservation, life was increasingly strained by discrimination and poverty, the latter only partially mitigated by income from the mineral and gas deposits found on their lands.

Many changes have also taken place in Shoshone social roles. Women, in particular, developed new roles during the twentieth century, some of which are manifested in the musical practices we will explore below (see "**Individual Portrait: Writing about Native American Musicians**"). The traditionally dominant male roles have changed in many complex ways as well. One of the most striking of

Writing about Native American Musicians

Throughout *Soundscapes,* we have read about the lives and experience of musicians. Here we will look briefly at the career and writings of Judith Vander, an ethnomusicologist, musician, and composer whose prize-winning book *Songprints* provides insights into Shoshone musical life. Although Native American musics have been frequently studied, the role of women in Native American musical life has for the most part been overlooked. Judith Vander's work, a striking exception, also delves into the history and politics of writing about music.

Judith Vander follows in the wake of more than a century of women who have studied Native American music, among them Alice C. Fletcher (1838–1923), Natalie B. Curtis (1875–1921), and Frances Densmore (1867–1957). While studying ceremonial music at the Wind River Reservation in 1977 and 1978, Vander noticed that women, including Helene Furlong, were participating in the powwow and began to inquire about the involvement of Shoshone women in music making.

On the basis of her observations, Vander made contact with other women, resulting in *Songprints,* which charts the life and musical experience of five generations of Shoshone women.

Judith Vander, dressed in traditional regalia, participated actively in inter-tribal dances during the Wind River Shoshone Indian Days.

Through Vander's work, we hear the voice and read the words of Helene Furlong, the first Shoshone woman to drum at the Eastern Shoshone Indian Days. As a young adult, Helene also performed the fancy war dance in male regalia. As she matured, Helene backed away from these innovations, but they left a mark on the Shoshone community, where her influence helped pave the way for the fancy shawl dance.

Judith Vander's many years of research among the Wind River Shoshone have resulted in two other books about Shoshone women and their roles as carriers of musical traditions, *Ghost Dance Songs and Religion of a Wind River Shoshone Woman* (1986) and *Shoshone Ghost Dance Religion: Poetry, Song and Great Basin Context* (1997). Her collaboration with Shoshone women has also inspired her to compose music based on her years of exposure to their music, including her piece *Powwow Time for Organ and Flute.*

these changes has been the substitution of American military service in place of traditional warrior roles. The manner in which Native American musical performance mediates between the worlds of the warrior and soldier will be examined in our discussion of the Shoshone powwow.

The Setting of Shoshone Indian Days

The first Native American powwow was held in the late nineteenth century. A little more than a century later, the number of North American powwows is estimated at more than two thousand per year.[15] Today, powwows are mounted in all regions of North America, mainly during the summer

A poster advertising Eastern Shoshone Indian Days, 1998.

months when weather permits outdoor gatherings (see **"Studying Music: How to Be Courteous at Powwows"**).

The Algonquian word *pawwaw,* first recorded in 1827, referred to "religious practitioners" and evidently to healing ceremonies as well. By 1900, the word was applied to any type of gathering and along with other Algonquian words—such as *tomahawk, wampum,* and *wigwam*—*powwow* made its way into American English.

The modern intertribal powwow has its origins in Oklahoma in the 1920s where it was first begun as a symbol of "Indianness." The Wind River Shoshone mounted their first powwow in 1957, calling it "Indian Days," following a model popular among many Native Americans since World War II. The large, intertribal powwow became increasingly widespread over the years, with participants from a variety of tribes and regions traveling great distances to attend.

Like most annual Indian Day celebrations, the Eastern Shoshone festival is held on a warm summer weekend, part of the increasingly well-established "powwow circuit" that boasts participants from the region and beyond. Indian Days celebrations follow similar patterns: people camp out in the vicinity of the powwow grounds, socializing during the days and participating in organized, competitive activities such as foot races, tugs of war, tepee-raising contests, and hand games. The families or attendants of young girls who have been crowned "powwow queens" plan giveaways, celebrating their good fortune by presenting gifts to others attending the powwow. This important ceremony, which has its own special song and dance, emphasizes deep-seated cultural values of generosity and public honoring.

How to Be Courteous at Powwows

How should you behave at a musical event of a tradition with which you are unfamiliar?

This is one of the trickiest questions facing anyone studying music, a challenge growing increasingly important as performances of different musical traditions proliferate. Ethnomusicologists do a great deal of background research before attending an event they wish to study; they check descriptions of past performances, often consulting a knowledgeable insider for advice on everything from dress to etiquette. What they cannot learn in advance, they try to ascertain on the spot by carefully observing the behavior of those who appear to be regular participants.

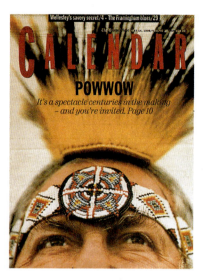

Newspapers carry regular notices of intertribal powwows in both urban and rural locations throughout North America.

As these musical events are more regularly opened to outsiders, the sponsors or performers of an event often make written guidelines available. Such is the case in Wyoming, where frequent powwows attract many outsiders who have never before attended a powwow and who are therefore unfamiliar with expectations for their behavior.

The following guidelines for how to behave at a powwow appeared in a local Wyoming newspaper, *The Ranger,* on May 21, 1998, before the beginning of powwow season:

It is important to be aware of the ways to behave at a pow wow.

Pow wows are celebrations, social gatherings and friendly dance competitions, but there are sacred traditions which are part of this coming together.

Many dances are done in a circle which represents the circle of unity, the circle of life. Dancers often follow the clockwise path of the sun. Some of the regalia and ornaments signify special events in a person's life, religious tradition or legends from the past.

While most pow wows welcome both members of other tribes and non-Indians, it is important to be aware of the ways to behave at a pow wow. For instance, when the eagle staff is brought in during the grand entry, everyone should stand, and those wearing hats should remove them.

If an eagle feather falls during the dancing, everything stops until the feather has been properly returned.

The use of cameras varies from pow wow to pow wow. Flash cameras should not be used during the dance contests.

Videotaping is often discouraged. Permission should always be asked before taking an individual's photograph outside the dance.

It is improper to bother the performers or those preparing to sing and dance.

Do not touch the regalia or the ornaments. Many of these are delicate heirlooms, and many are handmade and highly valuable.

If the master of ceremonies issues the invitation, feel free to join in intertribal dances.

Honor the drug-free, alcohol-free policy of the pow wow.

In trying to judge the appropriate behavior for an unfamiliar event, we must always be alert to subtle differences in dress and manners.

The evenings of Indian Days are given over to the powwow ceremonies; here, "intertribal dances" open to any and all visitors (including non-Indians) are interspersed with dance competitions restricted to contestants from any tribe in tribal regalia displaying official, numbered badges. Competition plays an important role—the youngest dancers compete for cash prizes during the early evening hours, with older dancers moving to center stage as the evening goes on. The

Colorful regalia are worn during dances at an intertribal powwow in Cashmere, Washington.

dance and music competitions are critical to the powwow's success, and prizes can be quite substantial. Some powwows, such as the huge event mounted by the Mashantucket Pequot Tribal Nation (which owns the Foxwoods casino in Mashantucket, Connecticut) lasts several days, includes more than two thousand dancers, and offers more than $850,000 in prize money.[16] Generally, it is the Fancy War Dance—a more recent development than the traditional War Dance—that carries the largest cash prize.

During the powwow, a moderator announces the various events and offers commentary on everything from the performances of drum groups to current political issues. Shoshone Indian Days include speeches by dignitaries on inspirational and political subjects, openly discussing past injustices and calling for equal rights and opportunities for Native Americans (see "**Snapshot: The Shoshone Powwow 1998**").

In other aspects of the powwow, the political message is less overt and is coded in musical performance and dance. Below we will consider two frameworks for

SNAPSHOT

The Shoshone Powwow 1998

The Wind River Reservation of the Eastern Shoshone sits in a fertile valley ringed by the foothills of the Wind River Mountains, whose snow-covered peaks can be glimpsed in the distance.

Today, Shoshone tribal life is centered in the town of Fort Washakie, named after the nineteenth-century chief whose skillful leadership ensured the founding of the reservation. Fort Washakie is a small, dusty town, with neighborhoods of modest homes, a

The Wind River Shoshone Arbor is a wooden structure that shelters spectators and drumming groups from the sun and rain during the long hours of dancing and competition at powwows.

historic cemetery, a medical clinic, and a Shoshone Cultural Center. The official buildings, overshadowed by the imposing Shoshone-Arapaho Tribal Center, are flanked by the acres of open fields surrounding the "arbor" that houses the powwow.

The circular, wooden arbor is the focus of powwow activities. Spectators sit under the shelter of the arbor, either on permanent wooden bleachers or on folding chairs. The large space in the arbor's center, planted with grass, is reserved for dancers. In the middle stands a large pole that proves to be without ritual significance: it supports speakers that broadcast the narration by the master of ceremonies and the music of various drum groups that accompany the dancing.

Around the periphery of the arbor are various refreshment stands and small shops selling T-shirts, clothing, jewelry, cassettes, and other goods. In the fields beyond, tepees and campers accommodate individuals who plan to remain at the grounds for the three-day duration of the games. Several acres are filled with cars in the evening hours as the powwow dance competitions increase in intensity. A major powwow such as the Eastern Shoshone Indian Days draws participants from throughout the West, including Wyoming, Montana, Colorado, and Idaho.

The modern intertribal powwow features multiple drum groups that take turns accompanying the dancers. Each group sets up its bass drum under a different section of the arbor, and four to six drummers gather around the large drum in a circle. A microphone is circulated to each group in turn so that their performance can be amplified throughout the arbor and surrounding area. Most drum groups at the Eastern Shoshone Indian Days come from other reservations in the region, but a few travel from area institutions, including universities. Most have Native American leaders and participants, but many contain players of other ethnic backgrounds. Although drummers are still predominantly male, female drummers participate on occasion and several all-female drum groups do exist.

The brightly colored regalia worn by participants reflects the changing fashions of the powwow. The traditional male war dance, with its small feathered bustles, and the traditional shawl dance, performed by dignified women with embroidered shawls draped over their arms, have lost some of their popularity as younger people are attracted to the more athletic fancy war and fancy shawl dances. New dance and costume styles have also entered the powwow recently, such as the grass dance with its fringed attire and the jingle dance, in which young girls sport costumes covered with jingles made from the tops of chewing-tobacco tins.

communicating both public and hidden political messages—the flag ceremony and the war dance.

The Flag Song's Sound and Significance

Every powwow begins with a "grand entry"—a formal procession of all the costumed contestants, who dance single file into and around the perimeter of the dance area. This display is followed by the formal presentation of the colors. Veterans carry in the American flag, the state flag, and banners of the Veterans of Foreign Wars and move straight across the arena. This flag presentation is accompanied by a special song, called a flag song, signaled by a regular, slow drum rhythm. The flag song is performed with great solemnity, filling a sonic space that in other American contexts, would be occupied by the national anthem. Participants and spectators remove their hats and stand during the performance.

The wide range of the song's melody is described by Shoshone in terminology that is both visual and linear. Songs have curves and dips that can be straightened, smoothed out, made more curvy, and zigzagged.[17] A high, tense vocal quality provides the stamina male singers need to sing clearly for long hours during a powwow. Indeed, in the past it was conventional to "stretch" (lengthen) a song, a practice that has fallen off in recent years. It has also been traditional to repeat whole songs. The English term *push-ups* indicates the number of times a song is repeated. The term *push-ups* has been traced to the Sioux, who used the word *pawankiye,* meaning "to push the voice upward."[18] In its original Sioux use, the term referred to the repetition of the opening call of a song. Today Shoshone and other powwow singers use the broader meaning of the term.

A concession trailer at the Shoshone Indian Days flies a U.S. flag with a Native American face superimposed on it. The adjacent campground, with tents and teepees, can be seen in the background.

LISTENING GUIDE 71

Flag Song (Shoshone song)

PERFORMED BY Helene Furlong and Wayland Bonatsie

This flag song was recorded during the Wind River Shoshone Indian Days in 1977. The singers, Helene Furlong and her brother Wayland Bonatsie, learned and adapted this Shoshone song from a Cheyenne flag song they heard in Lame Deer, Montana, at the Northern Cheyenne Reservation. The slow, deliberate tempo is punctuated by the drum on every other beat, and a sliding drum and voice flourish can be heard at the end, followed by ululation.

LISTEN FOR Helene, who sings in a high register an octave above her brother Wayland. The text consists of vocables which are mainly set in a syllabic style. According to Helene, some individuals use slightly different vocables, although patterns are widely shared.

The Shoshone repertory contains many flag songs that are consistently sung during the presentation of the Colors. The flag songs convey several different political messages; most important, they honor particular people and events, or offer formal respect for the flag, country, and veterans.

However, the Native American flag ceremony replaces the American national anthem (*The Star-Spangled Banner*), with a Native American flag song. The flag song has great significance especially for Native American veterans of the United States armed services, who have composed new flag songs to commemorate the different conflicts in which they have fought.

LISTENING GUIDE 72

CD 3
TRACK
17

Flag Song for Desert Storm (Blackfoot song)

PERFORMED BY the Black Lodge Singers, of White Swan, Washington

The flag song for Desert Storm is one of many composed by Native American veterans of the 1992 conflict. This Blackfoot song, intended to be sung during the Grand Entry, was recorded at an event where a man who served in the gulf war entered carrying a green Saudi Arabian flag to honor Indian tribe members just back from the military conflict. Unlike the Cheyenne example we heard earlier, this song has a fast tempo, which may reflect generational differences.

Song text: Our Indian boys have returned from Desert Storm.

Native Americans have made important contributions to the American military, including the ingenious use of their languages during World War II as a basis for constructing codes. On June 6, 1994, Native American veterans participated in a commemoration of the D-Day landing at Omaha Beach in Normandy, France, fifty years earlier.

Honoring Warriors in Song: The War Dance Yet another integration of past with present is evident in the motions of the war dance. Twentieth-century wars—World Wars I and II, Korea, Vietnam—have reinforced traditional Native American cultural practices, such as the war dance, that otherwise would have atrophied. Songs and dances have publicly celebrated the heroic actions of Native American soldiers, thereby preserving these cultural forms and encouraging tribal pride.

Like flag songs, war songs make an

overt political statement, especially since they were once performed for armed conflict. In the twentieth century, however, the warrior-fighter has given way to the warrior-dancer and present-day war dances mimic traditional military movements.[19] Some of the motions sustain the war dance's historical connections to the wolf dance, in which the dancer mimics a wolf stalking its prey.[20]

The war dance is also connected to nature by Helene Furlong through the sound of the powwow drum, as she explains in the following quotation:

HAVE A GREAT **Pow Wow SEASON**

We're proud to have served with our Native American neighbors.

VFW BINGO
Wednesdays - 7:00 p.m.
Sundays - 1:30 p.m.

VFW Post 3628 & Auxiliary
Riverton, WY

A local Veterans of Foreign Wars post in Riverton, Wyoming, salutes powwow season.

"And I think the style of dancing is adopted from nature—the sage chicken. Have you ever seen a sage chicken dance? It's beautiful. There's one type of War Dancing—I forget what they call it now—it's one beat at a time, almost like a stomp, and it's a slow kind of War Dance. I guess it's similar to a Chicken Dance of today. That's the reason why it's called that because of the sage chickens. And if you happen to be around a place where the sage chickens are, like in March, and then before the sun is just beginning to come up, that's when you notice these. If you creep up on 'em, you see these sage chickens dancing. Every once in a while you'll hear 'mphhh' and then 'boom.' Just like a regular Indian drum, you know, going 'boomph, boomph.' And that's their whole chest bag. It comes out and then it hits and then the back end of their feathers spread out just like a bustle. Beautiful! And then when part of their feathers

Helene Furlong, seen here singing and playing the drum with her brother, Wayland Bonatsie, has lived most of her life in Crowheart, a small community forty miles north of Fort Washakie. A Head Start teacher educated both on and off the reservation, Helene learned Shoshone songs from her father and grandfather and was one of the first women to participate in the war dance. Her family drum group, which is no longer active, was known as the Big Wind Singers.

LISTENING GUIDE 73

War-dance Song No. 9 (Shoshone song)

PERFORMED BY Helene Furlong and Wayland Bonatsie

Wayland Bonatsie and Helene Furlong learned this war-dance song from powwow singers in the Blackfoot tribe. Midway through the song, Helene Furlong picks up a set of the large bells that war dancers traditionally secure around their knees and begins to shake them in time to the song. At the end of the song is a short additional section called a *nduah* (literally, "son" or as often referred to by other Plains' singers, the "tail.")

ONCE AGAIN, LISTEN TO the female singer's part. Women traditionally enter after the opening call and response section and then sing all the way through to the end. The pulsation in the male vocal style alternates pulses of loud/soft intensity on an unbroken tone. Finally, as in most war dances, the song ends with a decisive final drumbeat.

touch the ground it makes that noise, just beautiful noise. . . . It just really makes you feel good to see it. I know a lot of these dances have been adopted from nature."[21]

The war dance song is the centerpiece of the powwow, sung and drummed during both the traditional war dances and the more recent "fancy" war dances. The war song repertory changes quickly and songs enter and fall out of use from year to year.

What makes a good war song? According to Wayland Bonatsie, "It depends on how many get up and dance to that song."[22]

As we have seen in both the flag dance and the war dance, Shoshone singers often borrow songs from other groups, including the Cheyenne and the Blackfoot. Indeed, the intertribal powwow seems to encourage borrowing. Some songs even borrow from non–Native American sources, although these are not so common and require replacing the original text with vocables, as heard in the following example.

LISTENING GUIDE 74

War-dance Song No. 7 (Shoshone song)

PERFORMED BY Helene Furlong and Wayland Bonatsie

This war-dance song borrows the melody of the hymn *Amazing Grace,* and replaces its text with vocables. Although the song originated in Albuquerque, New Mexico, Helene Furlong learned it from a friend's tape in the mid-1970s. Helene is aware that this is "a white man's song," but thinks that only certain singers in the white man's world "make it beautiful."[23] (She thinks a song is beautiful when it is sung "high.") As a war-dance song, this tune has not been popular and is not widely sung, although the manner in which it was transmitted—by personal contact or tape recording across regional boundaries outside the setting of the powwow—is quite common.

LISTEN FOR the faster pace of the third verse. Consider, too, the use of *Amazing Grace* for a war dance—within other American circles this song conveys meanings of revelation and commemoration.

The Changing Settings of Powwow Music

The music of the powwow has also shifted to other settings, from special performances at rodeos and football half-time shows, to lecture-demonstrations on college campuses. In addition, the powwow and its songs have also begun to reach out to new audiences through various forms of mass media.

Groups such as the American Indian Dance Theatre, which includes members from nearly a dozen Native American communities, perform widely at dance festivals. They present traditional dances, such as the shawl and hoop dances, as well as new choreography. References to other musical traditions and other political agendas are also incorporated. For example, a recent performance of a modern

A young dancer performs a war dance during intermission at an athletic competition, 1998.

fancy dance by the American Indian Dance Theatre featured a dancer wearing black gym clothes in a subtle reference to the gumboot dance, a dance of resistance performed by South African miners.

The powwow is a remarkable example of an event with many meanings. Not only does the powwow provide an opportunity for socializing and expressing Native American identity, it also reaffirms the vitality and political strength of the community and its institutions. The powwow transmits and affirms Native American power both inside and outside the immediate community. The dual nature of the event is represented by the clear division between intertribal and contest dances, as well as the narration of the moderator who alternately speaks to insiders and "translates" for visitors.

Conclusion

The powwow provides an opportunity for making a variety of political statements, some public, others hidden. It explores the relationship of Native Americans to mainstream white society, while simultaneously celebrating the Indian Nation it-

As we can see in this CD cover art, Native American musicians such as Brulé have adapted their own traditional music for wider audiences.

A powwow parade, featuring horseback riders, decorated floats, and costumed walkers in a procession across the powwow grounds, occurs at the beginning and end of the multiday event. At intertribal powwows, the parade features the powwow queen and members of her court, all of whom have been chosen competitively and are dressed festively to celebrate this honor.

self. In contrast, the song *Nkosi Sikelel' iAfrika* and the reggae music of Jamaica are more open markers of—and rallying points against—social, racial, and economic inequities.

A counterpoint to mainstream culture is evident in the restriction of contest dances to Native American participants; this is reinforced by the use of the flag song instead of the national anthem. Other strong statements include the display of colorful traditional regalia and the maintenance of clear ritual orders.

However, the powwow thrives today, in part, because its boundaries are porous. Even the borrowing of songs from the outside world, such as *Amazing Grace,* can be seen as a transformation that enhances the beauty of the hymn. Musical commemoration and reenactment of historic battles through war dances pay tribute to past courage as well as to the modern Indian veteran of American wars. In the case of reggae, this versatile music style has served both Rastafarians and a much broader audience around the world. Likewise, the song *Nkosi Sikelel' iAfrika* has signified the struggle for equality both as the national hymn in the fight against South African apartheid and, more recently, as an international call for human rights.

The music of all three case studies in this chapter combines elements that both define and defy past and present political realities. Like so many of the soundscapes we have encountered throughout our study, all have been touched by real world events and concerns. And so it is to music in the real world that we turn in our concluding chapter.

IMPORTANT TERMS

fancy shawl dance	*nduah*/"tail"	ridim
fancy war dance	powwow	shawl dance
flag song	"push-ups"	war dance
national anthem	reggae	

This American advertisement dating from about 1900 for Hohner, a popular manufacturer of harmonicas, seeks to attract a multicultural clientele for the instrument.

OVERVIEW

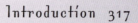

MAIN POINTS

• Real-world issues surround and shape the presentation and performance of music.

• Music is an important signifier of place and, therefore, a major factor in travel and tourism.

• New technologies and commodification have merged with musical creativity to give rise to new musical vocabularies and hybrid musical styles.

Music in the Real World

Introduction

Throughout *Soundscapes,* we have approached music as an integral part of all aspects of daily life. In this chapter, we will examine the real world elements and material social practices that influence and give meaning to our musical experiences.

Because of the deep-seated Western concept of the arts as aesthetic objects that transcend the material world, casual observers run the risk of overlooking the economic factors and political conditions that influence musical performance and transmission. In Chapter 1, we noted that our understandings of music are inevitably shaped by translation processes that operate as we encounter music in performance. In addition, the very factors that shape musical production simultaneously color our perceptions and interpretations of a musical event. These factors range from corporate decisions shaping the content of a concert or recording to the marketing of music and musicians.

The diverse settings for music's presentation are critical to its public reception today. Many performance settings have their roots in the "exhibition culture" that emerged in Europe and the United States in the mid-nineteenth century. The first American Exposition in 1853 displayed live Native American people for profit, entertainment, and public edification. Later exhibitions

Many advertisements represent "exotic"—that is, unfamiliar or foreign—cultures as links to an ancient past that is depicted as a "primitive" stage of cultural development. These advertisements, which are intended to validate such musics, are in fact based on popular misconceptions of social evolution.

reproduced whole native villages and scenes from daily life, including musical performances. The World's Columbian Exposition (Chicago, 1893), which featured musical performances by Kwakiutl Indians of the Northwest Coast and others, has been termed "an early form of touristic consumption."[1] Many of these displays presented so-called exotic traditions in "panoramic" exhibitions in which the observer entered and interacted. Others adopted a more "panoptic" or

Members of the brass band of Claflin University, a historically African American university in Orangeburg, South Carolina, photographed resting on a stairway with their instruments. This image was part of an exhibit on African American life at the Paris Exposition of 1900.

The 1939 Golden Gate Exposition in San Francisco, where the opening ceremony featured dozens of bands, included a Chinese drum and bugle corps (center).

"all-seeing", approach, with the viewer watching from a distance, commanding a supreme vantage point.[2] Holdovers from these early panoramic and panoptic exhibitions are still detectable in present-day musical performance, whether at festivals or in concert halls, raising many thorny issues for those who mount, perform, attend, or study these musical performances (**see "Snapshot: 'Presenting' Music and Musicians"**).

Who presents concerts of different soundscapes in your community? What arts organizations, institutions, or promoters are involved? How are the events marketed, and to whom?

With the proliferation of recordings and the international spread of once primarily local soundscapes, economic issues begin to intrude on our reception of music. When music becomes a commodity that can be bought or sold, we tend to lose sight of the fact that it carries valuable clues about the culture that created it. We must keep this in mind when studying how soundscapes move through various channels from the musician to performance venues and record shops. An awareness of the economics of music also raises a set of challenging ethical issues for scholars (**see "Studying Music: Ethical Concerns"**).

The soundscapes around us are influenced by both historical factors and present-day circumstances. In addition, the quick rate of change in modern technologies is a powerful factor in the transformation of musical sound itself, as well as in the

'Presenting' Music and Musicians

"Think Globally, Listen Locally" advised the February 4, 2000, headline of a *New York Times* article celebrating the fifteenth anniversary of the World Music Institute, a major presenter of global music in New York City. Indeed, as we have seen throughout *Soundscapes,* today it is possible for most of us to travel only a few minutes from our own living rooms to attend concerts of musics from around the world.

Great changes have taken place over the last century and a half in the presentation of music. Following the period of the great exhibitions that first brought global styles to local settings, the presentation of public concerts was dominated throughout much of the twentieth century by individual impresarios (organizers) who managed—and sometimes mismanaged—individual careers.

During the second half of the twentieth century, an increasing number of not-for-profit organizations began to contract with musicians for performances. The World Music Institute is only one of a number of relatively recent major institutions that now organize musical tours. Many universities,

With the Capitol building in the background, His Holiness the Dalai Lama waves to the crowd at the Smithsonian Folklife Festival on the Mall in Washington, D.C., on July 2, 2000. Approximately forty thousand people came to witness the Nobel Peace Prize winner preside over a Great Prayer Ritual led by Tibetan monks. The 2000 Smithsonian Festival featured a celebration of traditional Tibetan culture, including the performance of ritual dances; the creation of traditional Tibetan Buddhist sand mandalas and butter sculptures; the construction on the site of a twenty-eight-foot Buddhist monument ringed by thirty prayer wheels; and the celebration of a secular Tibetan festival including Tibetan opera performances.

museums, and cultural organizations regularly present live performances. And as we saw in Chapter 4, many cities and towns sponsor festivals that feature both local and imported musical talent. Presentation is even done on the national level: each summer in Washington, D.C., the Smithsonian Institution sponsors a National Folklife Festival, bringing together musicians from many sectors of American and international musical life.

Most musical performances by artists from soundscapes without mass audiences are sponsored by not-for-profit organizations that underwrite expenses through a precarious combination of ticket sales, private donations, and grants from agencies such as the

National Endowment for the Arts, with occasional corporate support. But the world of musical presentation is changing radically. In particular, major new developments in corporate involvement are transforming the promotion, production, and presentation of live musical events.

A new corporation, SFX Entertainment, has become a major force in presenting music, theater, and dance events in North America—and increasingly, worldwide. SFX has also created a network of companies that span the entertainment industry and produce and promote musicians as diverse as Britney Spears and TLC. What distinguishes SFX from earlier presenters, such as record companies that have long sponsored their artists in national and international tours, is that SFX both contracts with artists and operates the largest network of performance facilities in the United States. As of the spring of 2000, SFX operated 110 venues, including forty of the forty-six amphitheaters in the country. This includes the major performing sites we discussed in Chapter 4 such as Houston's Compaq Center and Aerial Theater at Bayou Place, and Boston's Wang Center. According to SFX's own figures, 60 million people attended 23,000 SFX events during 1999, including music concerts, theatrical shows, family entertainment, and motorsports shows. Although SFX's shows tend to focus on the most marketable musicians, they also mount "second stages" at many of their events to bring less well-known musicians to new audiences.

SFX has also raised deep concerns in many sectors. Not-for-profit presentation organizations with the goal of supporting musical diversity cannot compete with SFX's resources and scope. Many musicians and listeners have also voiced concern about corporate control over performance and the impact of this control on existing traditions, as well as on new artistic directions in the name of "marketability."

Although we have touched on many important issues relative to music's role in the real world throughout *Soundscapes,* the new and powerful corporate presence in musical presentation is just the type of change that demands thoughtful and informed discussion.

exposure of soundscapes to each other and to new audiences (**see "Looking Back: Changing Sound Technologies"**).

Some scholars have begun to tackle this complex situation and have proposed frameworks for better examining the forces that shape musical production, performance, and reception. One approach has been to study "micromusics," which are "small musical units within big music-cultures." This approach includes three interacting and overlapping levels that can be referred to as subculture, superculture, and interculture.[3]

Ethical Concerns

The real world influences the way ethnomusicologists study and document music. Professional ethics have long been a major consideration for music scholars, but each year brings new realizations and new concerns.

Many of the early recordings of Native American musical traditions have been repatriated to the tribes from which they came. This photograph shows a recording session at the Smithsonian Institution in 1913.

Ethnomusicology, like the closely related field of anthropology, emerged as a discipline during the late nineteenth century, when European colonization of Africa and Asia was at its height. Many early ethnomusicologists were able to enter the field abroad precisely because of the residual power and resources of postcolonial institutions such as universities and government agencies. Unlike music scholars from Eastern Europe and South Asia, who primarily worked within their own national boundaries, North American ethnomusicologists did not begin serious work at home in North America—except for early research among Native Americans—until the last three decades of the twentieth century. These American scholars found that conducting local research aids regular contact and ongoing relationships with research associates. Yet fieldwork at home does not resolve all the economic, political, and personal issues that continue to provide challenges.

One vexing issue concerns how the ethnomusicologist should mediate between musicians and a broader public, whether in the classroom or in other public contexts, when setting up performances. In what ways does the ethnomusicologist unwittingly join in the politics of exhibition and display when he or she "presents" a musician to an audience of outsiders? How does this lead to turning the music into a commodity and contribute new variables to already fast-changing sounds, settings, and significances? A common, related dilemma facing ethnomusicologists who have published recordings as part of their scholarly research is how to guarantee economic equity for the musicians. Some have solved this problem by assigning royalties to the musicians with whom they worked.

Beyond economic issues, most ethnomusicologists feel an obligation to work for the welfare of the musicians whose musics they study. More and more, scholars are seeking to collaborate, building resources within communities to ensure that traditions are conserved and represented in manners consistent with the desires of the people who transmit them.

Scholars are gratified by their potential to help document musical traditions that might otherwise be lost beyond the lifespans of the musicians who perform them. In some cases, musical research has led to important new understandings about social relations or provided new insights about the history of a community. Most ethnomusicologists seek both to memorialize the musicians who share their traditions and to ensure continued access to the materials they transmit.

LOOKING BACK

Changing Sound Technologies

1877–1878	Thomas Edison invents and patents cylinder phonograph
1888	First commercial phonograph
1890	Introduction of 6-inch-long wax cylinder
1894	Introduction of spring-driven phonograph
1895	Emile Berliner introduces prerecorded 78-rpm twelve-inch discs
1896	Edison produces crank-wound phonograph with prerecorded wax cylinders
1898	Valdemar Poulsen invents wire recorder
1902	First recording of the tenor Enrico Caruso
1910–1912	Pathé and Columbia cease to manufacture wax cylinders
1913	Edison stops manufacturing home cylinder phonographs but continues to produce prerecorded cylinders
1920	First regular radio broadcast in the United States
1924	Microphone and electrical amplifier first used in sound recording
1925	Electrical recording introduced with increased fidelity
Late 1920s	Custom-built portable disc recording equipment created
1932	Electrically driven portable disc recording machine invented
1945	45-rpm seven-inch vinyl disk first appears
1948	33-1/3 rpm vinyl long-playing disk (the "LP") appears

1948	First commercial, magnetic tape recorders are manufactured
1955	Stereophonic recording
1958	First stereo LPs and first stereo tape recorders
1963	Cassette tape created
1982–1983	Compact disc (CD) developed
1986	Commercial marketing of compact disc (CD)
1992	Philips Digital Compact Cassette
1992	Entry of MiniDisc, which uses computer instead of laser technology
1993	Central Research Laboratories' Sensaura Audio Reality for live music recordings, with five-channel surround sound on only two speakers
1995	Enhanced CDs
1998	MP3 players compress audio files into digital format that takes up one-tenth the computer memory of previous technologies
1998	Rio introduces Walkman-like music player that carries an hour's worth of CD-quality MP3 music on a computer chip
Spring 1999	Sony-Philips puts out Super Audio CD in Japan; can be played on both CD and DVD players Entry of DVD Audio, which requires a DVD player

A representative of World Music Radio publicizes his station at a musical event in San Diego, California.

Throughout this book, we have worked mostly at situating music within its subculture. The subculture includes local, personal, familial, occupational, and community networks. It is within the subculture of an individual soundscape that most of the musical traditions we have explored—from the *fado* (Chapter 4) to the *pizmon* (Chapter 7)—have been generated and sustained even if they are now widely available to outsiders through recordings.

The second sphere of interaction is the interculture. On this level, subcultures influence each other through economic or commercial connections, proximity, or affinity. A fine example of intercultural interaction is the remarkable dispersion of the accordion. The accordion (Chapters 6 and 8) was spread by migration to many musical subcultures and was incorporated into diverse musical styles.

The third, overarching sphere of musical interaction is the superculture, which consists of the power of the state and the international economy. In our study we have encountered several musical practices that had very local beginnings and were nourished through intercultural exchange. They were then transformed through the influence of the superculture. The tango (Chapter 6), karaoke (Chapter 8), and reggae (Chapter 9) are notable examples.

Another way of looking at how formerly local musical traditions—such as reggae or zydeco—are subject to complex societal forces can be seen reproduced in the chart below. This approach sets forth in more detail the complexity of the superculture. It takes into account the impact of national policy, the music industry, the media, and international economic forces.

This chart by Roger Wallis and Krister Malm traces the interaction of international factors, organizations, and activities with national and local organizations, industries, government agencies, and performers, mapping the complex real world of musical life.

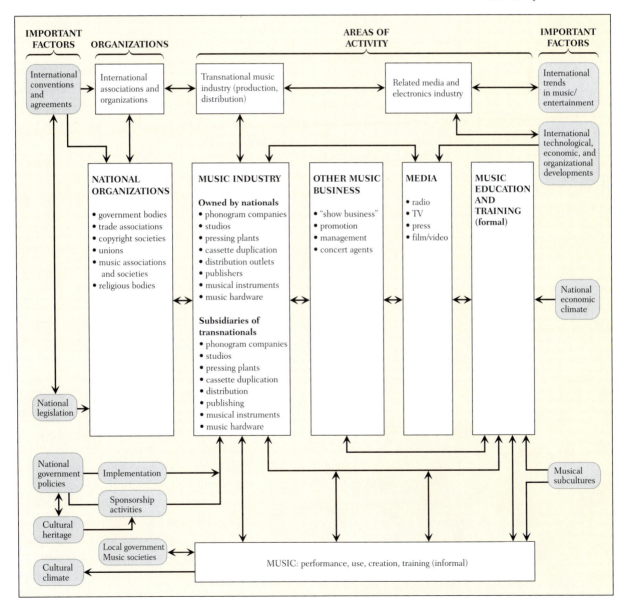

The case studies in this chapter explore several important forces shaping sound-scapes in the real world. We will look first at the impact of travel and tourism on the Hawaiian steel-guitar tradition. Next, we move to a soundscape we have al-ready encountered—the tango—reexamining it in light of the musical creativity made possible through new technologies. Finally, we will hear new compositions for both Balinese gamelan and harmonic singing that illustrate the power of music cultures to inspire new musical styles.

Travel and Tourism

CASE STUDY: THE HAWAIIAN SOUND

In considering the exhibition and presentation of music, it is necessary to arrive at music shaped by the travel and tourism industries. Musical events are important attractions in most locations and are actively marketed to visitors. We need only think of the lure of the Grand Ole Opry in Nashville, jazz clubs on the South Side of Chicago, and Broadway musicals in New York City.

As new technologies made travel easier and more affordable in the twentieth century, the exhibition and sale of soundscapes became a lucrative industry. In Hawaii, the distinctive sounds of the steel guitar and ukulele became inseparable from the burgeoning Pacific tourist trade. Now they signify "Hawaii" whenever and wherever we hear them (**see "Sound Sources: Steel Guitar and Ukulele"**).

The foremost performers of Hawaiian music were not native to the islands and spent virtually all of their adult lives abroad. The members of the Moe family per-formed Hawaiian music for over a half-century. The four Moe brothers, who were born in Samoa, moved to Hawaii at an early age and married there. With their wives and other musicians, they became known as the Royal Samoan Dancers and in 1928 left Hawaii for a tour of the Far East.[4]

Eventually, the brothers split up into separate ensembles. Tau Moe continued to perform with his family, establishing his headquarters in Brussels. Over the years, Pulu Moe and his wife, Louisa, joined with a third musician to constitute the Pulu Moe Trio; Louisa sang, danced, and played the ukulele while Pulu played a steel guitar and also performed a Samoan knife dance. After spending a few years in London, they were signed in 1941 by the impresario Felix Mendelssohn (not the

The Pulu Moe Trio, including (left to right) Kaili Sugondo (guitar), Louisa Moe (ukelele), and Pulu Moe (steel guitar), performing in Copenhagen in May 1951.

Steel Guitar and Ukulele

Several lively oral traditions exist regarding the development of the steel guitar. Some say the Hawaiians adopted the instrument from Mexican herders who arrived on the island around 1830.[5] Others credit Joseph Kekuku with the invention of the steel guitar after he experimented with pulling a comb or pen knife across the strings of an ordinary Spanish guitar.[6] Yet a third account credits a young stowaway from India with applying playing techniques used on Indian zithers to the guitar while en route to Hawaii in 1884.

The Hawaiian music expert Bob Brozman plays the steel guitar.

The player produces the characteristic sounds of the steel guitar—a pronounced vibrato and slides up or down to a pitch—by using the left hand to slide a steel bar across a string on the neck of the guitar or, on more recent models of the instrument, by using a pedal. Picks—called plectra—on the thumb and first two fingers of the right hand pluck the strings or can be drawn across all the strings to produce a glissando. Vibrato on individual pitches is produced by vibrating the hand holding the steel bar. The steel guitar is played like a zither, held flat on the lap.

It is easy to produce harmonics on the steel guitar by flattening strings with the palm of the hand; the resulting overtones are called "palm harmonics" or "chimes." Formal characteristics of steel guitar music are named by insiders. The repeated final phrase at the end of a verse, for instance, is called the "turnaround."

A second chordophone closely associated with Hawaii is the ukulele. Resembling a small guitar with four strings, the ukulele is a descendant of the Portuguese *braguinha* that was likely brought to Hawaii in the late 1870s by immigrants from the island of Madeira. The name *ukulele* means "leaping flea" in Hawaiian, and according to local legend this strange name could refer to either the diminutive and lively English ukulele player Edward Purvis, or the movements of a skilled player's fingers.

Vintage ukuleles are collector's items today. Beginning in the 1920s and 1930s, some instrument makers decorated their ukuleles with everything from Hawaiian scenes, as here, to pineapples.

Soon after its introduction to Hawaii, the ukulele gained popularity due to the efforts of its early makers as well as to royal patronage. Augusto Dias, Manuel Nunes, and José do Espirito Santo, who set up ukulele instrument-making and repair shops in the 1880s, were active promoters of the instrument. The ukulele was also King David Kalakaua's favorite instrument, so it had a prominent role in many cultural events within the royal palace.

By the beginning of the twentieth century, the ukulele had become a media symbol for the Hawaiian Islands' fledgling tourism industry. The 1915 Panama-Pacific International Exposition in San Francisco introduced the instrument to the American mainland. Its portability, simple playing technique, and low cost made it instantly popular nationwide. Even Hollywood movies capitalized on the ukulele's associations with idyllic island life, featuring grass-skirted beauties strumming ukuleles on moonlit beaches. Celebrities including Elvis Presley and Tiny Tim played the instrument, and it was used to sell products ranging from Listerine to Dole pineapples.

Ukulele culture is a living tradition, as we can see from the range of activities announced on the Web site of the Ukulele Hall of Fame.

The ukulele is traditionally made of koa wood, a tree of the acacia family that grows in Hawaii. Ukuleles come in a variety of sizes and shapes and can be decorated with elaborate inlaid mother-of-pearl designs or paintings. Although the instrument is relatively easy to learn, it takes a virtuoso to master the ukulele. A recent revival of interest in Hawaiian culture has led to an increased demand for ukulele instruments and lessons, and has produced an annual ukulele festival in Honolulu's Kapiolani Park.

famous German composer, who lived in the first half of the nineteenth century), for whom they made their first recording. As a result of that recording, the group became quite well known in Europe and Asia. Both the Pulu Moe and Tau Moe ensembles at times played with other bands under Mendelssohn's management and kept busy with broadcasting and recording. Mendelssohn himself managed the Pulu Moe ensemble, arranging the details of its shows, costumes, and publi-

LISTENING GUIDE 75

Ellis March (Hawaiian steel guitar march)

PERFORMED BY Tau Moe with Mme. Rifiere's Hawaiians

The characteristic sound of the steel guitar is produced by vibrato, slides up and down to pitches, and audible overtones. The distinctive "slide" often covers a great number of pitches, a technique we earlier encountered in accordion music, termed a *glissando*. Exaggerated vibrato, slides, and glissandos are so frequent in Hawaiian steel guitar music that one ethnomusicologist suggested that these ornaments alone signify Hawaiian music to listeners outside of Hawaii.[7] The *Ellis March* contains classic steel guitar playing.

LISTEN FOR the descending glissandos. Even on this re-mastered recording, originally made decades ago, we hear the multiple harmonics produced by the steel guitar.

---

city. Mendelssohn promoted the Pulu Moe ensemble vigorously, riding a wave of European fascination with "foreign" and "exotic" traditions.

Following the devastation of World War II, however, Mendelssohn fell on hard times and eventually declared bankruptcy in the late 1940s. After Mendelssohn's death in 1952, the Moe Trio disbanded. Pulu Moe worked in a factory in London until he returned to Hawaii in 1962. The Tau Moe family, however, continued to tour and lived in Brussels until their return to Hawaii when they were in their eighties.[8]

Both the acoustic properties and the playing style of the steel guitar and ukulele came to be strongly associated with Hawaii shortly after the turn of the twentieth century. The popularity of the instruments also spread during the "ukulele craze" of the 1920s and 1930s, and then revived through recordings in the 1950s. Early television shows such as that of Arthur Godfrey, who played the ukulele, contributed to the international popularization of Hawaiian music as well.

Music as Art and Commodity

The commercialization of soundscapes raises important issues involving creativity and copyright. Copyright, the legal protection of intellectual property, is more difficult to apply to musical sound than to a literary text, especially if the music is transmitted as an oral tradition. Western intellectual property laws also become problematic when standard Western expectations of individual composition are applied to the music of other traditions. For example, when music is considered to have sacred origins, to have been inspired through revelation, or to be the intrinsic property of a specific group, the issues at stake are both ethical and economic. Complex situations arise, such as when Native American songs are, without permission, borrowed, transformed, and marketed by individuals from outside a particular First Nation (Native American) community.

A brighter side of the commercial music industry is that recording technology has helped to preserve the quickly changing styles of oral traditions. We can reconstruct early steel-guitar techniques largely because of the survival (and technologically enhanced mastering) of commercial sound recordings of the Moes and others (see "Studying Music: Preserving Musical Ephemera"). Recording technology has also been widely used within soundscapes, as when performers at Native American powwows learn and transmit the latest flag songs and war dances. At a powwow, drummers listen attentively to recordings played on their portable cassette players as they mentally rehearse and learn new songs while awaiting their turn to perform. Recordings make it possible to preserve and pass along songs

Advertisements can bring local musical traditions to wider audiences.

STUDYING MUSIC

Preserving Musical Ephemera

In the real world, the sound archive plays a vital role in saving recordings from oblivion. Sound archives initially began as repositories for recordings made by collectors in the field. From the beginning, they have been a valuable resource for scholars seeking to study and analyze music, much of it unavailable in their home locales.

The first sound archive of early research recordings was founded in 1900 in Berlin for the collection and storage of wax cylinders. Today, sound archives containing field recordings are scattered across North America, including the important national collection now housed at the American Folklife Center of the Library of Congress. This collection dates from the 1920s and contains field tapes and early recordings from government-supported projects such as the Federal Cylinder Project.

The pioneer ethnomusicologist Frances Densmore (1867–1957) used a wax-cylinder phonograph to record the language and music of the Blackfoot Indians in 1916. Many of her recordings are preserved in the American Folklife Center's Archive of Folk Culture at the Library of Congress.

Recordings made by individuals "in the field" have long been placed in archives as a matter of course so that these musical records can be physically preserved beyond the normal life of their technologies, their performers, and their collectors. However, we have been slower to acknowledge that the cassette or compact disc on the shelf of a record shop is already well into its life span and needs preservation as well. When a commercial recording has steady sales, it will stay on the shelf. If it does not "move," it will inevitably be returned to a distributor and eventually discarded as "out of print." The short and fragile life of a commercial sound recording is a matter of increasing concern to ethnomusicologists, since once a recording becomes unavailable, its sounds are condemned to silence.

Commercial sound recordings are fast becoming important sources for research purposes. Most musicians and groups—whatever their size or professional status—now produce and market their own recordings for sale. These recordings serve as indispensable resources for charting the history of individual soundscapes and their musical styles, presented in a manner deemed appropriate by the musicians who made them.

Commercial recordings carry most of the sonic history of twentieth-century musical trends. In the case of jazz, both commercial recordings and discarded outtakes in record company archives remain the primary sources for access to the genesis and development of this important American musical tradition.

Though the term *ephemera* is most often applied to print materials of fleeting significance, it seems a useful term to apply to recordings. They, too, are ephemera, and the sounds they convey can be sustained and heard only if they are preserved in archives.

that have fallen out of use. Indeed, many communities are beginning to systematically record and archive their own music so that it can be handed down to future generations.

There is no doubt that the proliferation of recording technologies has also helped to spread musical styles across ethnic and national boundaries, promoting new forms of musical transmission that move through technological channels. And as we see in the next case study, recordings can also provide remarkable technological opportunities to revisit older musical styles in new contexts (see **"Sound Sources: The World of Electro-Acoustic Instruments"**).

SOUND SOURCES

The World of Electro-Acoustic Instruments

Electro-acoustic instruments have become increasingly prominent in the musical world today. The rapid rate of technological advancement—including the advent of the computer—has allowed the sounds of even most traditional instruments to be simulated in electro-acoustic terms.

The synthesizer, first used as a compositional tool in electronic music studios, has also become common as a performance instrument, especially in popular music. The generic performance synthesizer is an "electrophone" that produces and manipulates sound. Its

The electrical engineer Max Mathews, cocreator of the first music synthesizer, is seen here composing in a recording studio at Bell Laboratories in 1981.

central features are its ability to create, alter, and combine sounds electronically, and its programmability.[9]

The first instrument that could both generate and shape sound with electricity was probably Thaddeus Cahill's "Telharmonium." Completed in 1900, it featured two velocity-sensitive keyboards and produced multiple sound qualities. Its high cost, unwieldy size, and high consumption of energy prevented its commercial success, however. Experiments in the field led to the invention of new instruments (for example, the theremin and the Hammond organ). In the mid-1960s, the computer began to play an important role in the further development of electronic instruments.

The standard features of a self-contained synthesizer are a performance interface, programming controls, and a sound engine. The performance interface lets the performer manipulate the sound through pitch selectors (for example, a keyboard) and ancillary controllers (for example, a joystick or foot pedal). Controls allow the synthesizer to be programmed and for those programs to be recalled in performance. The editing controls enable the performer to choose the types, tones, and dynamics of any given sound. The engine generates sounds, either by synthesis or sampling (using digitally prerecorded sounds as the basis for sound production). All the components described above share a number of practical features: an operating system, internal memory, an external storage data device, a display, program selection controls, audio connections and controls and MIDI (Musical Instrument Digital Interface) connections.

A typical performance synthesizer in the early twenty-first century is digital and programmable, and uses both synthesized and sampled sound sources. It has a built-in audio-effects unit, a computer editor, and a keyboard. Its versatility has made it an almost indispensable instrument on the popular music scene today, as we have seen in our study of Duy Cuong's arrangement of his father's song cycle, *The National Road*, in Chapter 3.

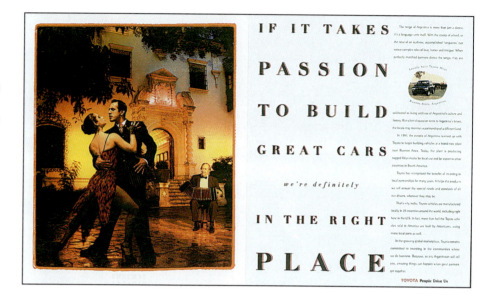

Toyota compares its collaboration with Argentina on the construction of a new auto plant in Buenos Aires to the partnership and passion needed to dance the tango.

CASE STUDY: A RETURN TO THE TANGO

A striking example of the reinvention of older musical styles through new technologies is a recent recording by the accomplished American cellist Yo-Yo Ma (**see "Individual Portrait: Yo-Yo Ma"**). In notes accompanying his compact disc *Soul of the Tango,* Ma writes:

> Unlike other tangos, Piazzolla's tangos you listen to. One of my great regrets is never having met Piazzolla. But coming to Buenos Aires and working with his fellow musicians has brought me closer. Now, through the miracle of modern technology, Piazzolla and I have gotten even closer: Using some outtakes of Piazzolla playing the bandoneón, Jorge Calandrelli composed music for me, so that in the piece called "Tango Remembrances" we *are* playing together. Now, I feel I have a real sense of how Piazzolla breathed. And all that is in this recording.

INDIVIDUAL PORTRAIT

Yo-Yo Ma

Yo-Yo Ma provides a model of the twenty-first-century musician who performs in a growing range of musical styles, crossing frequently and intentionally between soundscapes. Born in Paris in 1955, Ma moved to New York City when he was seven. He studied at several schools, including the Professional Children's School and Juilliard,

Yo-Yo Ma, the violinist Mark O'Connor, and the bassist Edgar Meyer kick off their Appalachian Journey Tour at the Grand Ole Opry House in Nashville, Tennessee, on March 30, 2000. Their collaborations, which explore the common ground between American classical and folk musics, have been recorded on audio and video.

where he was taught by Leonard Rose. After graduating from Harvard University in 1976, Ma quickly distinguished himself in competitions.

Throughout his career, Yo-Yo Ma has collaborated with the classical pianist Emmanuel Ax. In the early 1990s, Ma began to collaborate with musicians well established in other soundscapes. In 1992, his album *Hush,* with the versatile singer Bobby McFerrin, was listed as a "Top Classical Crossover Album" in *Billboard* magazine. He won one of his thirteen Grammy awards for *Soul of the Tango.* Although he has continued to record Western classical music and to produce an innovative series of recordings and films of Johann Sebastian Bach's unaccompanied cello suites, Ma has reached out again and again to new musical styles ranging from American folk music to early music to music of the Kalahari Desert in southern Africa. Since 1998, Ma has been working on a new cross-cultural project, finding and performing works from soundscapes along the ancient Silk Road in Asia and commissioning music from composers of adjacent regions.

Yo-Yo Ma exemplifies the extraordinary versatility of top musicians today, many of whom continually explore new musical challenges and reach new audiences. A virtuoso in Euro-American classical music, he has extended his range beyond the standard Western cello repertory to explore the relationship between music and dance, and to include new soundscapes. Ma describes his efforts as "pushing the envelope . . . I'm seeking to join, to connect things, that were not precisely joined together: from Bach to the Kalahari to music along the Silk Road, to country fiddling and the tango." [10]

LISTENING GUIDE 76

CD 3
TRACK
21

Tango Remembrances

PERFORMED BY Yo-Yo Ma, cello (April 1997) and Astor Piazzolla, *bandoneón* (August 1987)

As we have seen in Chapter 6, the "new tango" of Astor Piazzolla captured the imagination of musicians well beyond his native Argentina, establishing a new domain within the already international tango soundscape cluster.

LISTEN AS Yo-Yo Ma performs a duet with the late Piazzolla, a collaboration that was produced in a studio and that exists only on compact disc. This recording is an example of an attempt to reach a "crossover" audience, one that cuts across taste boundaries through the combination of musical styles. *Tango Remembrances* crosses through time to unite different styles, instruments, and eras.

Inventing New Musics at Home

CASE STUDY: NEW MUSIC FOR BALINESE GAMELAN

Many North American composers have drawn on sound recordings and live performances of other musical styles for inspiration. The Indonesian gamelan, in particular, has influenced many American composers such as Lou Harrison, who have drawn on the Javanese gamelan, building their own newly designed American gamelans and writing compositions for them.

In Chapter 2, we encountered a Balinese gamelan in residence at the Massachusetts Institute of Technology in Cambridge, Massachusetts. The long-time director of that ensemble, Evan Ziporyn, is also active as a composer and a performer within avante-garde musical circles. Ziporyn has incorporated a deep knowledge of Balinese gamelan techniques and trends into his own compositions.

Gamelan Son of Lion, based in downtown New York City, was founded by the ethnomusicologist Barbara Benary in 1976. The ensemble, which plays new compositions by American composers, uses instruments made in Javanese village style out of materials readily available in the United States. The locally made instruments have steel keys and cans for resonators. The ensemble most recently toured Java in 1996, participating in gamelan festivals.

LISTENING GUIDE 77

CD 3
TRACK
22

Kekembangan

COMPOSED BY Evan Ziporyn

PERFORMED BY Gamelan Sekar Jaya

Ziporyn's composition *Kekembangan* (1990) draws on the Balinese composer Nyoman Windha's piece *Kembang Pencak*. In addition to the musical dialogue with Nyoman Windha, *Kekembangan* offers a musical commentary on differences between Balinese and American musical systems and ways of hearing.

LISTEN TO how Ziporyn—building on Windha's composition for gamelan, male dancers, and singers—substitutes a saxophone quartet for singers, intentionally blurring the boundaries between sound sources and musical styles. According to Ziporyn, the saxophones sometimes blend with the gamelan parts, prompting the Western listener to hear the Balinese phrases in a more Western framework.

The text accompanying this CD presents traditional musical instruments and concepts within the framework of new age ideas, describing music as a powerful source for relaxation, meditation, and healing. It also conveys a sense of universalism, suggesting that music is a "natural" phenomenon that can successfully cross all cultural boundaries.

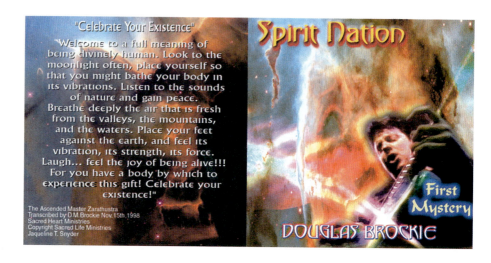

"Celebrate Your Existence"

"Welcome to a full meaning of being divinely human. Look to the moonlight often, place yourself so that you might bathe your body in its vibrations. Listen to the sounds of nature and gain peace. Breathe deeply the air that is fresh from the valleys, the mountains, and the waters. Place your feet against the earth, and feel its vibration, its strength, its force. Laugh... feel the joy of being alive!!! For you have a body by which to experience this gift! Celebrate your existence!"

The Ascended Master Zarathustra
Transcribed by D.M. Brockie Nov. 15th, 1998
Sacred Heart Ministries
Copyright Sacred Life Ministries
Jacqueline T. Snyder

Spirit Nation

First Mystery

DOUGLAS BROCKIE

CASE STUDY: TOWARD A NEW ART OF HARMONIC CHANT

Although the collaborative pieces we have just heard cut across musical styles, neither example tries to establish a new music culture. There are, however, a number of soundscapes emerging from newly invented, hybrid musical styles that seek to establish broader cultural frameworks.

This case study, an exploration of harmonic chant styles created by David Hykes, provides a vantage point from which we can see certain soundscapes—in this case Mongolian *khoomii* singing and Tibetan chant—as sources of inspiration for new musics. Throughout his career as a musician, Hykes has sought to move beyond musical sound to innovate, perform, and transmit what he terms "a new, global sacred music" through his experiments with the acoustic universals of the overtone series (see Chapter 1).

David Hykes performs "harmonic chant" at a November 1998 concert in Brussels, Belgium.

A chance encounter with a recording of Mongolian *khoomii* singing inspired David Hykes to teach himself the *khoomii* vocal style. In 1975 he founded the Harmonic Choir, which combined *khoomii* techniques with those of Tibetan overtone singing. After a decade in New York City, Hykes moved to France in 1987. There he continues to work both with the choir and as a soloist. Hykes's compositions have been subsequently influenced by other musical traditions, including vocal styles derived from North Indian classical singing and new rhythmic elaborations drawn from the Persian hourglass drum, the *zarb*.

Hykes devotes considerable energy to the spiritual aspects of music making, drawing on a range of Central Asian and Sufi philosophies, as well as the universalist ideas shared by many New Age musicians. He describes his spiritual experience in the notes distributed at his concerts:

> I found myself listening in a new way. There seemed to be a knowledge and sense of purpose in these ancient forms which we had lost. I felt called by a special quality of these musics. I knew it wasn't just technique, but there was plenty to learn about that, too. I set to work.

Hykes exemplifies a new trend, moving beyond composition and performance to the creation of a new soundscape with its own special combination of sounds, settings, and significances. Of his sound world, Hykes has written:

> It's a way to create a world of music. We are working with the very elements of sounds, the pure waveforms which in their infinite variety of composition give rise to all the musical sounds we hear. Of course, electronic and computer composers deal with these elements all the time. But I feel the living voice can always make sounds come to life more vividly.[11]

Hykes's music, although partially precomposed, incorporates improvisation during live performance. At the center of Hykes's intention was a desire to produce a "myth of creation," a search for spiritual enlightenment. Hykes creates a unique spiritual atmosphere in his attempt to formulate a "new traditional or sacred art." Many of his performances over the years have been held in resonant church naves lit by candlelight. Sometimes Hykes and his musicians sit on Turkish pillows, wear nomad-style clothing, and accompany themselves on Middle Eastern drums.

David Hykes and his harmonic chant provide an appropriate conclusion to *Soundscapes* as they lead us back to where we began in Chapter 1, with the sound of biphonic singing. Hykes's music also serves as a beginning—an example of a germinal soundscape, as well as an example of the kind of unique combinations you will encounter as you continue to observe the musical world around you.

Any telephone pole can serve as a bulletin board for posting musical items, like this advertisement for Latin dance lessons.

Conclusion

The real world continually shapes our access to and perceptions of music. Very practical issues surround the presentation and performance of music, ranging from the construction of instruments to the nature of recordings to the availability of concert tickets. Music has always been important in signifying place and is an increasingly major factor in travel and tourism. Music pervades every aspect of our

LISTENING GUIDE 78

CD 3
TRACK
23

Windhorse Riders

COMPOSED BY David Hykes

PERFORMED BY David Hykes, voice, and Djamchid Chemirani, *zarb*

Windhorse Riders is the title track of David Hykes's solo album. Hykes says that the title evokes a Tibetan concept of the sacred art of breathing. According to Hykes's comments in the CD liner notes, he was inspired by traditional harmonic chant "as found in Mongolia—and the Mongolia I know best—New Mexico." (Hykes was born in Taos, New Mexico in 1953.)

LISTEN TO how Hykes's *khoomii* vocal style produces a range of harmonics above an unchanging fundamental.

lives, resounding within us as we move through our days and nights, carrying our beliefs, giving expression to our fears, needs, and dreams. Through music, we can reimagine ourselves and everything around us, allowing ourselves to perceive new ways of hearing and understanding the world.

IMPORTANT TERMS

bimusicality	palm harmonics,	slide
copyright	chimes	steel guitar
harmonic chant	saxophone	ukulele
impresario		

Epilogue

In *Soundscapes,* we have followed an itinerary that has taken us through more than thirty musical traditions. All of these soundscapes are currently sustained in North America, and many are reaching increasingly wider audiences, through individuals and groups or the mass media. Most of the musics we have encountered have roots in different regions of the globe. Today these traditions continue to move, interact, and change within North American society.

In addition, we have seen that each soundscape has the potential to convey a complex collection of sounds with a rich variety of significances. At the same time, a soundscape interacts with others to transform these sounds and significances, as is the case of the bagpipes, which can signify an ethnic identity, a time of mourning, or a school affiliation. In all cases, soundscapes are the outcome of individual or collaborative creativity as people orchestrate their musical lives in new settings.

Soundscapes can reinforce or blur the boundaries of belief, identity, or imagination. Twenty-first-century North America is rich in musical diversity, through which a record of its past and the conflicts of its present are loudly sung, played, and danced. Musical traditions maintain their individual complexities of sound, setting, and significance, while moving across boundaries that would have been impossible to traverse in another age. They create a new musical pluralism, a musical environment defined more by its multiple styles than by any single dominant tradition.

The larger musical memory charted by *Soundscapes* is, in large part, constructed of shared sounds and meanings. We find shared sound sources such as the accordion sustaining repertories as different as tango and zydeco. This instrument, with its roots

in the European Industrial Revolution, accommodates a variety of soundscape-crossing styles. At the same time, the accordion and other instruments, such as the piano, force the music they play into the Western tonal system.

In North America, many soundscapes share settings and are juxtaposed at civic events and festivals. This has led to new musical communities born of affinity, with individuals hearing and participating in previously unfamiliar musical traditions. Many songs have moved across soundscapes. *Amazing Grace* is an example. We have heard this eighteenth-century hymn sung and played in settings as diverse as bagpipe performances, jazz funerals, American folk scenes, and Native American powwows. Although the settings and style of the hymn vary, inevitably it marks solemnity, loss, and commemoration.

We have seen that music is entwined with a sense of movement—of immigration, forced migration, displacement, and travel. All music moves, and transplantation is a theme cutting across virtually every soundscape we have encountered. Whether celebrating travel or mourning displacement, music's motion through time and space affirms the present in relation to both the past and future. Transplantation, this constant theme of texts and tunes, forces musical traditions into new settings and compels people to transcend these settings. Through music, too, individuals can travel instantly to places in their past, such as a home left behind in China or to times past—a moment retained in the mind and ear through a lullaby.

Musicians in each soundscape may combine sounds to innovate or delight. Hearing *khoomii* or Ethiopian chant in North America challenges the ear and forces the listener to grapple with both inadvertent and intentional change.

Through repeated acts of performance, sounds become closely associated with particular settings, accruing great significance over time. Syrian *pizmonim* gain meanings as they are sung at life-cycle events, generation after generation. Shoshone war-dance songs may change over the years, but always reinforce the powwow. Their constant transformations are vital to a tradition that emphasizes boundaries between insiders and outsiders. Sound and its performance settings can remind us of whether we are Cajun or Creole in southern Louisiana, or just an enthusiast delighting in the beat.

Hybrid sounds often intentionally blur constructed boundaries, encouraging us to sing and dance across barriers of class, region, race, or gender. At times multiple styles merge into new creations, weaving such remarkable conflations as the Vietnamese karaoke tango in Listening Guide 79. The Vietnamese musical memory

Smithsonian Folkways, founded in 1987 at the Smithsonian Institution within the Center for Folklife and Cultural Heritage, issues sound and visual recordings of a wide array of American and international music traditions. Smithsonian Folkways also serves as an archive for musical preservation and research. (Please note that the telephone number for catalog requests given at the foot of the advertisement has been changed to 202.275.1143 and the E-mail address is now folkways@aol.com.)

Bai Tango Cho Em ("A Tango for You"; Vietnamese karaoke song)

PERFORMED BY: Elvis Phuong and Ai Van

Bai Tango Cho Em ("A Tango for You") is sung in Vietnamese and exists in different karaoke versions: one constructs a visual narrative of life in the old Vietnam of memory, while another follows a teenage couple in suburban Long Beach, California.[1]

LISTEN TO the classic tango rhythm underpinning a story of travel—of both departure and return.

Woman:	Since you came back to me, My house is filled with moonlight Love was absent from my heart for a long time And now it overflows like a rushing stream.
Man:	I loved you the first moment I saw you move in sadness With sadness quickly clouding your eyes. Could this meeting last forever?
Woman:	The sound of music, harmonious and soft, As you move ever more gracefully, The sad melancholy tune hovers in the air, Our two souls are lost in their own world.
Man:	Hold me tightly as we dance, So I can feel the burning of your passionate heart.
Duet:	Why regret anything when the sky is limitless. Why harden ourselves with any cares, for they will remain with us all our lives.
Woman:	Now that we're together,
Man:	Your laughter makes life beautiful,
Duet:	We'll journey a thousand miles and cross a deep ocean And hand in hand we'll enter our new home. We'll build a wall of everlasting love. We'll overcome all obstacles. We're thankful to be together, We'll engrave the memory of our first meeting on our hearts, With this tango dedicated to you.

—Translated by Mai Elliot

retains the tango, a legacy of the French colonial era. The worldwide dispersion of karaoke has entered into the rhythms of everyday Vietnamese life as well, and has been adjusted in ways distinctive to Vietnamese social life and identity. The resulting song, "Bai Tango Cho Em," brings together these three streams of tradition.

This song is indeed engraved in memory through its uncanny ability to transcend time and space, to cause the voice to sing, the body to dance, to allow the spirit to soar—the quintessential qualities of any soundscape.

Appendix: Classifying Musical Instruments

As European museums expanded their collections in the late nineteenth century to include musical instruments from around the world, the need arose for categorizing and comparing instruments across cultural boundaries. In 1914, Curt Sachs and Erich M. von Hornbostel published a classification system based on the methods by which sound is produced. Their system, recently expanded to include instruments that generate sound electrically, comprises five categories—each subdivided according to different principles—that accommodate most musical instruments in existence.[1]

I. IDIOPHONES

Idiophones (from the Greek for "self" and "sounds") are instruments made of naturally sonorous materials. The instruments in this category do not require any additional attachments, such as strings or drumskins, to produce sound. Idiophones are set into vibration by the action of the player.

   A. Concussion idiophones are struck together or against another surface. Instruments in this category sometimes exist in pairs, such as clapping hands and stamping feet; cymbals, such as those used for Tibetan Buddhist ceremonies; and castanets accompanying the Spanish flamenco.

   B. Struck idiophones consist of individual pieces of wood, metal, stone, bamboo, or glass that are struck with a stick or mallet. Examples are xylophones, gongs, bells, and many of the instruments in a gamelan (most of which are termed *metallophones* because the material struck is bronze).

C.   Stamped idiophones (rare) are pits covered by boards on which people stamp their feet to elicit sounds.

D.   Stamping idiophones include instruments, such as the Ethiopian prayer staff, that a musician pounds on the ground in a vertical motion.

E.   Shaken idiophones are rattles of various sorts, such as a gourd or hollow tube containing seeds or other materials that make noise when shaken. Some shaken idiophones, such as the sistrum, have their rattling parts strung on rods.

F.   Scraped idiophones are notched objects, such as shells or bones, that are scraped with a stick or some other rigid item; for example, a stick passing over the notched surface of a zydeco rub board, makes a loud, grating noise.

G.   Plucked idiophones have flexible metal or bamboo strips attached to a frame, which are then plucked by the fingers or another implement. Examples include the African *mbira,* a small wooden box to which metal tongues are attached, and the European music box, in which the carefully tuned "teeth" of a steel comb are plucked by studs on a revolving cylinder.

H.   Rubbed or friction idiophones produce vibrations through the friction arising between two rough surfaces, such as sandpaper (usually held by wooden blocks). Rubbing the rims of wineglasses with moistened fingers is a method of producing sound that dates from at least the seventeenth century and that gave rise to the most famous friction idiophone, the glass harmonica, invented by Benjamin Franklin in 1761.

II.   AEROPHONES

Aerophones, often called "wind instruments," feature a tube enclosing a column of vibrating air. What sets the air into vibration can be the compressed lips of the player (as in the trumpet), the movement of an open reed (oboe) or an enclosed reed (accordion, bagpipe, organ), or the edge of a mouthpiece (flute). Aerophones are arbitrarily subdivided into three main categories.

A.   Trumpets and horns are usually grouped together because over time they have combined and intermingled despite separate histories. Trumpets were originally made from hollowed-out tree branches or tubes of bamboo. The player blows into the mouthpiece with vibrating lips, usually producing a brilliant sound. Horns were originally just that—curved animal horns. They have a wider passage for air and a more mellow tone. The mouthpiece on trumpets and horns may be at the upper end of the tube (end blown) or pierced into the side of the instrument (side blown). If the lower end expands, it is called a bell. Western trumpets and horns of various types, such as the trombone and the cornet, are commonly termed "brass instruments" because most are made of brass.

B. Plain pipes and reed pipes are also grouped together. Like trumpets and horns, they are hollow tubes into which the player blows, but without vibrating the lips.

    1. Plain pipes, called flutes, are most often tubular with finger holes that the player covers or uncovers to determine the pitch. Flutes can be either open or closed at the lower end. Less common are globular flutes, molded from clay or fashioned by cutting holes in a dried fruit shell or gourd. End-blown flutes are classified as "vertical," side-blown flutes as "transverse." Panpipes are sets of small flutes—each pipe producing one pitch—that are tied together in bundles.

    2. Reed pipes use one or more reeds to produce sound. The reed may be set in motion directly by the lips—as in the clarinet, which has a single beating reed, or the oboe, which has double reeds—or indirectly, as in the bagpipe, which has an enclosed reed, also called a free reed.

C. Free aerophones do not enclose a column of air, but act directly on surrounding air. The Australian bullroarer, for example, is a thin board that the player whirls overhead by an attached cord, producing a roaring or wailing sound. Mouth organs and accordions are free aerophones that have a single reed for each pitch.

III. MEMBRANOPHONES

Membranophones, or drums, produce sound when a vibrating membrane stretched over an opening is set in motion. Drums can be played singly, in pairs, or in sets, like the *batá* drums (see Chapter 5). In the Sachs-Hornbostel system, drums are not classified; rather, they are described, using the following characteristics:

A. Materials (wood, coconut, gourd, bamboo, clay, and metal, among others)

B. Shape

    1. Tubular drums
        a. Cylindrical (straight tube)
        b. Barrel (bulging tube)
        c. Conical (tapered tube)
        d. Hourglass (cup-shaped ends with a narrower waist in between)
        e. Footed (large and stationary, with one end shaped to form a foot)
        f. Goblet (footed but small and portable)
        g. Handle (having one or more loop handles)

    2. Kettledrums, which have a vessel-shaped body, are termed hemispheric if the largest diameter is at the top, as in the timpani, or egg-shaped, if the largest diameter is below the top, as in the *kebaro* (see Chapter 5).

    3. Frame drums have a frame instead of a solid body.

C. Number of membranes (also called skins or heads): A drum with one membrane is referred to as single-headed, one with two membranes as double-headed.

D. How the membrane is fastened to the body: It may be glued, nailed, buttoned, neck-laced (tied with a circular cord near the head), or braced (also called "laced"). Braced fastenings are laced either directly through holes in the edge of the membrane, or indirectly through hoops that can be either open or concealed.

E. The drum's playing position: It may be positioned on the ground or on a stand, or the player can hold it in place by the hand, arm, or legs; a drum may also be suspended from the ceiling, from a stand, or from the player's body.

F. How the drum is played (either by striking or rubbing) and what it is struck or rubbed with (bare hands, sticks, mallets, among other objects). A drum can have a friction chord or stick that passes through a center hole in the membrane.

IV.   CHORDOPHONES

Chordophones are instruments whose sound is produced by vibrating strings. The strings may be made of fiber, gut, horsehair, silk, metal, or other material, and can be strung singly, in pairs (double strung), or in threes (triple strung). Some stringed instruments, such as in some North Indian instruments, have additional, thinner strings called "sympathetic strings" attached below or behind the main strings to add extra reverberation and resonance. The strings may be plucked with bare fingers, fingernails, or a plectrum (a guitar pick, for example); bowed with a bow of horsehair or other material; or struck with sticks.

The main structural sound box, or resonator, for the instrument is called the body. The flat or curved front of the body, which receives and reflects vibrations from the strings, is usually made of wood or skin and is called the soundboard. The wooden crosspiece that holds the strings away from the soundboard is called the bridge. Sound holes are sometimes cut into the soundboard to improve the acoustics and to decorate the instrument. The fingerboard against which strings are pressed (or "stopped") by the player's fingers is called the neck, or handle. Some instruments have small ridges, called frets, along the fingerboard to mark off pitches of the scale. Players tune stringed instruments by turning dowels at the top of the neck called tuning pegs.

Chordophones are classified by shape and by the relationship of the strings to the body of the instrument.

A. In this system, lutes comprise all stringed instruments with a neck that allows the strings to be stretched beyond the top of the body. Lutes may be plucked or bowed. This category includes the Western violin family, the Middle Eastern 'ud, the guitar, and many other familiar instruments.

B. Zithers are instruments in which the strings are stretched between opposite ends of the body, which also serves as a resonator.
    a. Stick zithers have sticks in place of bodies and have an additional resonator attached, as in the Vietnamese dan bau.
    b. Tube zithers have a tube as a resonating body to which strings are attached lengthwise.
    c. Board zithers have strings stretched over a soundboard and glued into a box. Examples include the piano, qanun, dulcimer, and harpsichord.
    d. Long, narrow zithers, such as the Japanese koto, fall between tube and board zithers.

C.   The harp is the only chordophone in which the strings are stretched at an angle away from the soundboard. Most harps have numerous strings, which are plucked. The bodies of most harps are angular (that is, with the body and neck at an angle to each other), but there are examples of arched harps, in which the body is elongated at one end into an arched neck.

D.   Lyres are similar to lutes but are differently constructed: in place of a neck, they have a yoke with symmetrical or asymmetrical arms, the upper ends of which are connected by a crossbar. The strings are attached to the front of the body and run up to the crossbar, to which they are fastened. Most lyres are plucked.

V.   ELECTROPHONES

A.   Electromechanical instruments, such as the Hawaiian steel guitar, produce vibrations mechanically and then transform them into electric oscillations, which are amplified and reproduced by electric speakers.

B.   Radioelectric instruments are those in which the oscillations of electric circuits are transformed into audible vibrations by electric speakers. They are often referred to as "analog electric instruments" because the electric oscillations are analogous to the acoustic vibrations created by the speaker. A common example is the analog synthesizer.

C.   Digital electronic instruments, such as the digital synthesizer, are those in which a specialized computer emulates acoustic patterns. These digital simulations are converted into electric oscillations, which are then amplified and transformed into audible vibrations by electric speakers.

Although the Sachs-Hornbostel system of classifying musical instruments is not without its inconsistencies and flaws, and other methods of instrument classification have been proposed intermittently during the later twentieth century, most museums and writings about instruments continue to use the framework set forth above.

Notes

CHAPTER 1

1. Levin 1997.

CHAPTER 2

1. Radano 1989.
2. Tanenbaum 1995.
3. Trehub, Unyk, and Trainor 1993.
4. Neher 1962.
5. Rouget 1980.
6. Fabbri 1981.
7. Sheehy 1997.
8. Collinson 1975, 39–60.
9. Moloney 1985.
10. Collinson 1975, 140.
11. See Collinson 1975, 98.
12. See Collinson 1975, 141–54.
13. Shepherd 1992.
14. Shepherd 1992.
15. Hobsbawm and Ranger 1983

CHAPTER 3

1. Seeger 1966.
2. Su Zheng 1992/1993.
3. Naff 1985.
4. Faison 1998.
5. Kartomi 1990.
6. Sowell 1996.
7. Epstein 1997, 323.
8. Radano 1996.

9. Oliver 1980.
10. Reyes 1999.
11. Gibbs 1977.
12. Nguyen and Campbell 1990, 67.
13. Pham Duy 1975, 23–42.
14. Wong 1998.
15. Reyes Schramm 1986.

CHAPTER 4

1. Block 1998, 105.
2. The following description of Boston draws on Downs and Stea 1977.
3. Tenzer 1991.
4. Tomasini 1997.
5. Turner 1976.
6. Turner 1976.
7. Juneau *Empire,* July 9, 1999.

CHAPTER 5

1. Van Gennep 1960.
2. Turner 1977.
3. Smith, Stevens, and Tomlinson 1967.
4. Vélez 1994.
5. As quoted by Vélez 1994, 293.
6. Amira and Cornelius 1992.
7. Comaroff and Comaroff 1993.

CHAPTER 6

1. Hanna 1979/1992, 321.

2. Sharma 1996, 39; Huq 1996, 78–79.
3. Bessman 1999, 100.
4. Spottswood 1982, 150.
5. Walker 1914, 62.
6. Taylor 1976, 277.
7. Béhague 1980, 563.
8. Taylor 1976, 287.
9. Savigliano 1995.
10. Hanna 1992, 323.

CHAPTER 7

1. After Schacter 1996, 54.
2. Paredes 1976, 30–31.
3. Collier 1998, 29.
4. Bergreen 1997, 494.
5. Schafer 1977, 56.
6. Wilkie, January 31, 1999.
7. Catton.
8. Tawil.
9. Azzam 1990, 114, 123, 129.
10. Cohen.

CHAPTER 8

1. Definition after Reyes Schramm 1983, 15.
2. Hobsbawm 1983.
3. Trevor-Roper 1983, 15.
4. Yano 1996, 4.
5. Yano 1996.
6. Savigliano 1995, 188–89.

7. Post 1997, 23.
8. Gronow 1982.
9. Strachwitz 1970, 15.
10. Post 1977, 31.
11. Emoff 1998.
12. Emoff 1998, 292.
13. Tisserand 1998, 3; quoting Wilbert Guillory, founding director of the Southwest Louisiana Zydeco Fesitval.
14. Tisserand 1998, 3.
15. Proulx 1996, 259–60.
16. Tisserand 1998, 13–14.
17. Tisserand 1998, 222.
18. Hildebrand 1990, 39.
19. Jennings 1998, 38.

CHAPTER 9

1. Scott 1990.
2. Costello and Foster Wallace 1990, 112.
3. Rose 1994, 101.
4. Erlmann 1996, 46–77.
5. Shabalala in Erlmann 1996, 289.

6. Erlmann 1996, 54–57.
7. Brownell 1995, 2.
8. Singer 1998, 27–28.
9. Hebdige 1998, 34.
10. O'Brien Chang and Chen 1998, 41, 95.
11. O'Brien Chang and Chen 1998, 54.
12. Kaur and Kalra 1996, 226.
13. Lipsitz 1994, 15.
14. Costello and Foster Wallace 1990, 112.
15. Goldberg 1997, 4.
16. Goldberg 1999.
17. Vander 1998, 194.
18. Powers 1980.
19. Powers 1980, 219.
20. Vander 1988, 46.
21. Vander 1988, 143.
22. Vander 1988, 144.
23. Vander 1988, 156.

CHAPTER 10

1. Hinsley 1991, 363.
2. Kirshenblatt-Gimblett 1991, 413.

3. Slobin 1993.
4. Kanahele 1979, 241–49.
5. Davies 1989, 207.
6. Hood 1983, 144.
7. Hood 1983, 141.
8. Clifford 1977, 26.
9. Pressing 1992, 12.
10. Tassel 2000, 45.
11. Hykes, March 20, 1981.

EPILOGUE

1. Wong 1994, 161–62.

APPENDIX

1. The new system is based on Curt Sachs, "Terminology," in *The History of Musical Instruments* (New York: W. W. Norton, 1940).

Glossary

Terms in *italics* refer to other definitions in the Glossary.

A 440 The *sound* produced when a string or air column vibrates at 440 cycles per second, assigned the *pitch* value A. Western *orchestras* tune to A 440.

accent Emphasis on a *pitch* by any of several means, such as increased *intensity*, altered *range*, or lengthened *duration*.

accompaniment *Instrumental* support for a foreground *melody* or *solo* instrument.

accordion A *free aerophone* with *reeds* that are hidden within two rectangular headboards that are connected by a folding bellows, with keys or buttons to play a *melody* and *chords*.

acoustics The science that deals with *sound*.

acrostic A word spelled by reading down the first letters of the lines of a poem.

aerophones Instruments that sound by means of vibrating air; one of the five main classes of instruments in the *Sachs-Hornbostel system*, subdivided into *trumpets* and horns, pipes (*flutes* and *reeds*), and *free aerophones*.

air In Scottish *bagpipe* music, a long, slow, main theme, also known as a tune or ground. See also *allrd urlar*.

air and variations A musical form in which a main theme is repeated with a series of alterations to its *melody*, *harmony*, *rhythm*, and so on.

allrd urlar A *Gaelic* term for the *ground* or *melody* that is used as the *theme* in a *pibroch*.

antiphony A *performance practice* that features alternation between two or more groups of singers or players who may be separated from each other spatially.

arbor The circular structure surrounding the courtyard where a *powwow* is held.

articulation The way a note is begun or finished. See also *slides*.

bagpipe An *aerophone* with one or more *drones* and a *chanter*, all attached to an air reservoir, or bag, allowing for uninterrupted sound production.

ballad A song *genre* commemorating important events and memorable individuals, usually in *strophic form*.

ballroom dance Partnered, structured dances for recreation or competition.

bandoneón A "button *accordion*" associated with the *tango*.

banjo A plucked *lute* with a long neck, predominately metal strings, and a shallow, single-headed *membranophone* as its body.

bar mitzvah The religious ceremony that marks the formal passage of Jewish boys to adulthood at age thirteen.

barrel organ A small, portable organ with a rotating barrel fitted with pins that trigger individual pipes to sound. The player is typically called an *organ grinder*.

barrio A Spanish term for an urban district or suburb.

batá Double-headed *membranophones* usually played in sets of three (the *iyá*, the *itótole*, and the *okonkolo*) in *Santería* ceremonies.

beat An individual *pulse*.

beating tones *Acoustical* phenomenon perceived as a shimmering *quality* when two slightly different *pitches* are played at the same time.

bellows shaking An *accordion* technique that results in an intensified *tremolo* or *vibrato*.

Bembé A traditional *Santería* religious feast.

bhangra A tightly choreographed men's group dance, originally from the Punjab region of north India and Pakistan, with pronounced leg and shoulder movements and occasional waving of arms high overhead; bhangra has become a popular competitive dance in the Asian *diaspora*.

bhangramuffin An amalgam of *bhangra*, *reggae*, *hip-hop*, and Anglo-American pop.

bimusicality Proficiency in two different musical traditions.

biphonic singing A singing technique of Inner Asian origin in which two tones, the *fundamental* and an emphasized *overtone*, are made audible simultaneously by a single singer; also known as harmonic singing.

birl A quick *ornamental* figure of two adjacent *pitches* in *bagpipe* music.

blowpipe The pipe through which a *bagpiper* blows to fill the air reservoir, or bag.

bolis A short solo phrase that is traditionally sung without *accompaniment* at the beginning of a Punjabi song.

bombo Peruvian *membranophone*.

break dancing A dance form that emerged from the *hip-hop* movement.

broadside English or American narrative poem of the sixteenth to nineteenth centuries, printed on one side of a page, that generally addressed contemporary events and personalities.

busker Public street performer who collects donations from passersby.

button accordion See *bandoneón*.

ca hue Vietnamese *chamber music*.

cadence A melodic or harmonic figure, typically at the end of a phrase or piece, that creates a sense of repose or resolution.

Cajun A corruption of the term "Acadian," a French-speaking people in Louisiana; their style of music; their cultural life.

call and response A *performance practice* in which a leader makes a musical statement and another performer (or group of performers) responds with a musical answer.

cancionero A Spanish term for a collection of lyric poems, sometimes including music.

canntaireachd See *mouth music*.

ceilidh A social or musical event dating back to the eighteenth century and associated with Celtic traditions.

chain migration A process of migration in which immigrants follow a network of extended personal and familial networks to a particular community.

chamber music Music written for small ensembles, often played in more intimate performance venues than concert halls.

changgo A Korean double-headed hourglass *membranophone*.

chant A musical setting of a sacred text, or a repertoire of such works.

chanter A pipe, with fingerholes, on which a *bagpiper* plays the melody.

charro Mexican cowboy whose fancy dress is closely associated with the *mariachi* identity, consisting of a sombrero (wide-brimmed hat), a short jacket, a large bow tie, and tight trousers with rows of botonaduras (shiny buttons).

chicken dance *Shoshone* war dance that imitates the behavior of the sage chicken.

chord A set of three or more pitches sounding simultaneously.

chordophones Instruments with strings that can be plucked or bowed, one of the five main classes of instruments in the *Sachs-Hornbostel system*, in which they are subdivided into *zithers*, *lutes*, *lyres*, and *harps*.

chorus (1) A large *ensemble* of singers performing together, sometimes under the guidance of a conductor. (2) *Refrain*.

classical (1) A cultivated or esoteric musical tradition. (2) *Western classical music*.

commodity A product that is bought and sold.

compadrito A type of urban *gaucho* reputed to be both Don Juan and pimp.

concerto Music written for *orchestra* and a solo instrument.

concussion idiophones A subclass of *idiophones* consisting of instruments that are struck, often in pairs.

conjunct motion Stepwise melodic movement using small intervals, as opposed to *disjunct motion*.

conjunto A distinctive style of *accordion* music, popular among Mexican-Americans, whose ensemble includes an *accordion*, a guitar, bass, and percussion.

contour The shape of a *phrase* or section of music, generally as understood through the way its *pitches* move; the pitches of an ascending contour go up, those of a descending contour go down.

contrafactum A song in which new text is set to a borrowed or preexisting melody.

conventional signs A category of Ethiopian *notational* signs that do not derive from the Ge'ez syllabary.

copyright The legal protection of intellectual property.

corrido A type of *ballad*, usually *strophic*, that commemorates important events and memorable individuals in Mexican and Mexican-American history.

countermelody A *melody* that contrasts with a main *melody*, or tune, and played at the same time.

cross-cultural Of more than one *culture*.

culture The collection of beliefs, concepts, arts, crafts, skills, ideas, customs, and practices held jointly by a group of people during a particular period of time.

cutting The insertion of *grace notes* between two notes of the same *pitch* in *bagpipe melodies*.

dan bau A *Vietnamese zither* with a pitch-bending bar.

dan ken A *Vietnamese double-reed aerophone*.

dan nguyet A moon-shaped, long-necked *Vietnamese lute* with two strings.

dan nhi A Vietnamese two-stringed *lute*.

dan tranh A Vietnamese sixteen-stringed *zither*.

dabtara Ethiopian church musicians who are also scribes and healers.

darabukkah A Middle Eastern *membranophone* with an hourglass shape.

dbyang A type of *biphonic* Tibetan chant characterized by sustained notes in a low *register* and audible *harmonics*.

dbyangs-yig A song book of Tibetan *dbyang*, literally "written account of the song."

development (1) The process of elaborating or varying a *theme*. (2) The middle, contrasting section of Western music *sonata form*.

dhol A double-headed South Asian *membranophone* associated with *bhangra*.

diaspora A people living outside their historic homeland who maintain memories of, and attachments to, their place of origin.

digital electronic instrument An *electrophone*, such as the digital *synthesizer*, in which a specialized computer emulates acoustic patterns.

disjunct motion Melodic motion by leaps of large intervals, as opposed to *conjunct motion*.

dotted rhythm The pairing of a long and short rhythm, as in iambic meter, so named because a dot represents the rhythm in Western notation.

double reed A *reed* made of two thin strips of cane bound together so that they vibrate against each other.

drones A pipe on a *bagpipe* that produces a steady single tone.

duple meter A grouping, or *measure*, of two *beats*.

duration The way *music* organizes time; can be described in terms of *rhythm*, *pulse*, and *meter*.

dynamics The *intensity* of a musical event.

early music Music of the European past or its twentieth-century revival.

electromechanical instruments *Electrophones*, such as the *Hawaiian steel guitar*, whose vibrations are produced mechanically and transformed into electric oscillations that are amplified and reproduced by electric speakers.

electrophones Instruments that produce sound using electricity, one of the five main classes of instruments in the *Sachs-Hornbostel system*, subdivided into *electromechanical instruments*, *radioelectric instruments*, and *digital electronic instruments*.

engergari A group of celebratory *Ethiopian Christian chants*.

English ballad A *ballad* that commemorates important events and memorable individuals in British history; often based on the text of a *broadside*.

enka A *genre* of popular song with melodramatic themes of love, used in Japanese *karaoke*.

ensemble A group of instruments or musicians who perform together.

Ethiopian Christian chant The music of the Ethiopian Christian *liturgy*. See also *chant* (*zema*).

ethnic recordings 78-rpm discs issued approximately from 1900 to 1950, that are targeted for a particular subgroup united by shared national, linguistic, racial, and/or religious background.

ethnomusicology A field of study that joins the concerns and methods of anthropology with the study of music.

ezengileer Literally "stirrup," a type of *khoomii* that features a *rhythmic* pulsing, said to imitate singing while riding a horse.

fado Literally "fate," a song *genre* closely associated with Lisbon and popular within Portuguese expatriate communities.

fais-dodo A *Cajun* term meaning dance music; the dance halls where such music is performed.

falsetto The process of singing by men in a high *register* above the normal male singing *range*.

fancy shawl dance A virtuosic *shawl dance* performed by Native American women.

fancy war dance A virtuosic *war dance* performed by Native American men.

fasola See *shape-note*.

fiddle (1) A name used for the *violin* in the context of a wide range of Euro-American *folk* and vernacular musics. (2) Any bowed instrument of the *lute* family but commonly understood to mean *violin*.

fieldwork Research conducted while living among the people whose culture one is studying.

figure A stereotyped motion that is part of a given dance, such as the dos-a-dos in square dancing.

fixed form A musical *form* in which aspects of its content are predetermined.

fixed tuning The singing or playing of music at a pitch level determined in reference to a standard, fixed *frequency*, such as A 440 for *Western orchestra* tuning. Contrasts with *relative tuning*.

flag song A Native American song performed during a *pow-wow* flag ceremony to honor the American flag.

flute An *aerophone*, such as the *ney*, that is generally tubular and whose air column is set into vibration by the player's blowing against a sharp edge.

folk music A category conventionally applied to styles of music transmitted by *oral tradition*, maintained in collective memory by a group of people, generally associated with nonprofessionals, and often regarded as the cultural property of a group of people bounded by national, social, or ethnic identity, often called "traditional music" or *vernacular music*.

form The structure of a musical piece as established by its *qualities*, *pitches*, *durations*, and *intensities*, typically consisting of distinct sections that are either repeated or are used to provide contrast with other sections.

frame drum A *membranophone* with a skin stretched over a round frame, such as the tambourine or Tibetan *rnga*.

free aerophones *Aerophones* that act directly on the surrounding air, such as the Australian bullroarer.

free rhythm *Rhythm* that is not organized around a regular *pulse*.

frequency The number of vibrations per second of a vibrating string or column of air, usually measured either in cycles per second (cps) or in hertz (Hz) and kilohertz (kHz). Perception of frequency determines *pitch*.

friction idiophone An *idiophone* whose sound is produced by an object rubbing its surface.

fundamental The lowest tone in a *harmonic* series, also referred to as the "first harmonic" or "first partial," which determines the perceived pitch of a sound.

Gaelic The language associated with Celtic culture, including Irish Gaelic, Manx, and Scots Gaelic.

gamelan A large Indonesian ensemble consisting mainly of *metallophones*.

gaucho The Argentinian equivalent of a cowboy.

ge'ez The most important of three categories of *mode* in Ethiopian Christian ritual music.

Ge'ez The Ethiopian Christian liturgical language.

genre A type, or kind (of music).

Ghost Dance religion Indigenous Native American religion with associated ceremonial dances.

giddha A dance performed by Punjabi women that is equivalent to the all-male *bhangra*.

glide See *slide*.

glissando A musical gesture that entails sliding from one pitch to another.

gong kebyar A type of Balinese *gamelan*, known particularly for its shimmering sound and interlocking parts (*kotekan*).

grace notes The addition of one or more notes in slight anticipation of a *pitch*.

gracings The practice of inserting *grace notes* into *bagpipe* melodies.

grass dance A women's dance at a *powwow*, named after the fringed regalia worn in performance.

great highland bagpipe The large Scottish outdoor *bagpipe* with a nine-note *chanter*, three *drones*, and a bag filled by mouth through a *blowpipe*.

grip A quick *ornamental* figure of two non-adjacent *pitches* that serves as a set of *grace notes* in *bagpipe* music.

ground An English term for the slow-moving *air* or *melody*, almost always a bass line, that is used as the *theme* for a set of variations in Scottish *bagpipe* music.

guitar A plucked *lute* that has a hollow resonating body with waisted sides, such as the *guitarrón*, *Hawaiian steel guitar*, *ukulele*, and *vihuela*.

guitarrón A large, plucked, four- or five-string bass *lute* with an expanded belly, that serves as a key instrument in a *mariachi ensemble*.

haflah A party, held among Syrian Jews to celebrate a special occasion such as an anniversary, that usually features a professional *vocalist* who sings popular Arabic songs with *accompaniment*.

harmonic series See *harmonics*.

harmonic singing See *biphonic singing*.

harmonic texture See *harmony*.

harmonics The series of simple vibrations that combine to create a complex pitched sound, also called the harmonic series. The lowest, or first, harmonic, called the *fundamental*, determines the basic **pitch** of the sound. The remaining harmonics, called *overtones* or *partials*, influence the sound's perceived *quality*. They are inherently present in the sounding of any string or air column.

harmony The collective sound of a series of *chords*, serving as a support to a *melody*. The term also refers to an intricate set of rules that govern the progression of *sound* in *Western classical music*.

harp *Chordophone* whose strings run at an angle away from the soundboard, subcategorized by shape, playing position, and *tunings*.

Hawaiian steel guitar An *electromechanical instrument* derived from the guitar, usually placed flat when played, whose characteristic sounds include a pronounced *vibrato*, *slides*, and "palm *harmonics*" or "chimes."

Hebrew The Semitic language used in Jewish prayers and spoken in modern Israel.

heterophony A musical *texture* in which two or more *parts* sound almost the same melody at almost the same time; often with the *parts ornamented* differently.

hip-hop The cultural movement associated with African American urban life in the 1970s that emerged at once in the graphic arts (graffiti), dance (break dancing), and music (rap).

ho A Vietnamese work song.

homophony A musical *texture*, as in the Western *hymn*, where the parts perform different *pitches* but move in the same *rhythm*, as opposed to *polyphony*.

hymn A *strophic*, sacred *vocal genre* sung *homophonically* during worship ceremonies.

Hymnary The most elaborate musical *ritual* of the Ethiopian church performed before the *Mass* on Sundays and festivals.

idiophones Instruments that produce sound by being vibrated. One of the five main classes of instruments in the *Sachs-Hornbostel system*, idiophones are further classified by the way they are caused to vibrate: *concussion*, *struck*, *stamped*, *stamping*, *shaken*, *scraped*, *plucked*, or *rubbed*.

impresario A manager of performers or a director of a concert series.

improvisation The process of composing music as it is performed, while drawing on conventions of preexisting patterns and styles. Examples include *cadenzas*, jazz riffs, and *layali*.

Indian Days Annual Native American gatherings that feature social and competitive events during the days and *powwow* ceremonies in the evenings.

instrumental Music produced on instruments, whether by one person or many.

intensity The perceived loudness or softness of a *sound*.

interculture The sphere of interaction between musical *subcultures*. Contrast with *subculture* and *superculture*.

interlocking parts *Instrumental* or *vocal* parts in which silences in one part occur simultaneously with sound in another, creating the sense of a single musical line.

intertribal Refers to an event or dance in Native American tradition that incorporates people of different tribal backgrounds.

interval The distance between two *pitches*.

Irish ballad A *ballad* that commemorates important events and memorable individuals from the Irish past while referring to contemporary political subjects.

itótole The middle-sized double-headed *membranophone* in the *batá ensemble*.

iyá The largest and deepest of the double-headed *membranophones* in the *batá ensemble*.

jazz funeral See *New Orleans jazz funeral*.

Jew's harp A *plucked idiophone* held in the mouth that consists of a metal tongue attached to a frame. The tongue of the instrument is plucked while the mouth provides a resonating chamber that can be shaped to emphasize particular *harmonics*.

jig A lively dance tune popular in Ireland and among Irish-Americans; some jigs date back to the sixteenth century.

jingle dance Women's dance in present-day *powwows*, named after the metal "jingles" that cover festive dresses.

Judeo-Spanish songs Songs in a Judeo-Spanish dialect transmitted through *oral tradition* by descendants of late-sixteenth-century Jewish exiles from Spain (Sephardic Jews).

juke box A machine that dispenses and plays recorded songs chosen from a list of current offerings.

karaoke Literally "empty orchestra"; live singing, usually into a microphone, with a recorded accompaniment, performed in restaurants, clubs, or private homes.

kata Japanese aesthetic principle, literally "patterned form."

kebaro Ethiopian double-headed conical *membranophone*.

key The relationship between *pitches* in *Western classical music* as defined by a central *pitch* and related *harmonies*.

keyboard accordion An *accordion* with a keyboard on the melodic headboard.

khoomii *Biphonic* Tuvan throat singing, originally from rural *Inner Asia* and now heard in concert halls worldwide. Types of khoomii include *sygyt*, *kargyraa*, and *ezengileer*.

kotekan An Indonesian term for the *interlocking parts* heard in Balinese *gamelan* music.

kyrgyraa A style of *khoomii* characterized by text sung in a low *register*.

Labanotation Rudolf Laban's system of dance notation, which uses ideograms to represent dance motion in great detail.

lahan (1) A tune, in Arab music theory; (2) the *melody* to which a *pizmon* is sung.

lament A song of mourning.

layali In Arab *vocal* music, an *improvisation* that introduces a song and establishes the *maqam* used in the rest of the piece.

liturgical order The order in which sacred *rites* are performed.

liturgy The context of a religious *ritual*.

lute *Chordophone* whose strings are stretched along a neck and body, such as the 'ud, *ukulele*, and *guitar*.

lyre *Chordophone* whose strings are stretched over a soundboard and attached to a crossbar which spans the top of a yoke.

macarena A mid-1990s dance.

major mode A particular set of eight *notes* in *Western classical music*. See *major scale*.

major scale The *scale* of *pitches* in the *major mode* possessing the following *interval* relationships, from lowest to highest: two *whole tones*, one *semitone*, three *whole tones* and one *semitone*.

maqam (pl. maqamat) The system governing *pitch* and *melody* in Arab music.

maqam ajam A *maqam* that resembles the Western *major mode*.

maqam nahawand A *maqam* that resembles the Western *minor mode*.

march A piece in *duple meter*, usually with a quick pace, suitable for accompanying and coordinating a group of people marching.

mariachi A Mexican *instrumental ensemble* that includes the *guitarrón*, *vihuela*, *violin*, and *trumpets*; the musicians in the group.

Mass A Christian *ritual* that includes the sacrament of Communion.

mbube A South African *vocal genre* popularized in recordings and spread internationally, featuring *falsetto* singing and Western-style *harmony*.

measure The unit of time in *Western music* and musical *notation* in which one cycle of the *meter* takes place.

melekket The *notational* symbols in *Ethiopian Christian chant*, derived from Ge'ez language characters, each representing a short melodic fragment.

melismatic text setting *Vocal* music in which each syllable of the text is sung to two or, usually more, *pitches*.

melody A sequence of *pitches*, also called a "tune," heard in the foreground of music.

membranophones Instruments whose sound is produced by a membrane stretched over an opening. One of the five main classes of instruments in the *Sachs-Hornbostel system*, membranophones are distinguished by their material, shape, number of skins (or heads), how the skins are fastened, playing position, and manner of playing.

metallophone *Struck idiophone* made of metal.

meter A term describing the regular *pulse* of much of *Western classical music* and its divisions into regular groupings of two, three, four, or six *beats*.

minor mode A *mode* of eight *notes* in *Western classical music*. See *minor scale*.

minor scale The *scale* of *pitches* in the *minor mode* possessing the following *interval* relationships from lowest to highest: one *whole tone*, one *semitone*, two *whole tones*, one *semitone* and two *whole tones*.

mode A flexible term that can refer, depending on the context, to a musical system or a particular *scale* of *pitches*. Examples of modes are *ge'ez*, *major mode*, *minor mode*, and *tizita*.

modulation The process by which music moves from one *key* or *scale* type to another.

Morris dancers English country dancers costumed in white, with bells strapped to their legs, who dance to the music of a *fiddle*, *bagpipe*, or pennywhistle.

mouth music *Vocal* music ("canntaireachd") that imitates the sound of the *bagpipe*.

movement A large section of a musical composition typically separated from other such sections by a pause.

muk'yu A *genre* of traditional Chinese *vocal* music whose texts deal with the concerns of everyday life, performed by men or women in public or private.

music The purposeful organization of the *quality*, *pitch*, *duration*, and *intensity* of *sound*.

musical ethnography The process of identifying a musical scene and studying the *soundscape* of which it is a part. See also *participant observation* and *fieldwork*.

muwashah A *classical* Arab *vocal form* marked by a regular *rhythm* and rhyme scheme and a three-part *form*.

Muzak Programmed, recorded music designed to create sonic background environments in public spaces such as elevators, shopping malls, and restaurants.

Native American Church A religion that blends indigenous Native American beliefs with Christian elements.

nduah Literally "tail," a Blackfoot Indian term that refers to a short section added to the end of a song.

New Orleans jazz funeral A ritual marking the death of a musician that includes a procession with a jazz band.

"new tango" A *tango* composed expressly for listening.

ney An end-blown Middle Eastern *flute* whose sound has a breathy *quality*.

no rae pang (1) Literally "song room," a Korean style of *karaoke* performed with a small group of friends in a private rented room; (2) the room where the *karaoke* takes place.

non-Western Outside the *Western classical music* arena; an increasingly problematic term in an increasingly transnational world.

notation The representation of musical sound in written form.

note A single *pitch*, or the representation of a single *pitch* in musical *notation*.

octave (1) The eight consecutive notes that make up a major or minor *scale*; (2) the interval spanning the first through the eighth notes of any such scale. The *pitch* of the highest *note* of an octave has a *frequency* exactly twice that of the lowest *note*.

okonkolo The smallest of the double-headed *membranophones* in the *batá ensemble*.

oral tradition Tradition preserved in people's minds through singing or speech, in contrast to written tradition, which is recorded through writing or *notation*.

orchestra A large Western *instrumental ensemble*. See *Western orchestra*.

organ grinder Itinerant street musician who plays a small portable *barrel organ*; called *organito* in Spanish-speaking communities.

organito Spanish for *organ grinder*.

orisha Saint, in the *Santería* tradition.

ornaments Melodic, rhythmic, and timbral elaborations or decorations such as *gracings*, *rekrek*, and *grace notes*.

ostinato A short musical pattern that is continually repeated.

outdoor style A *vocal* or *instrumental* style with substantial *volume* or penetrating tone quality, originally meant to be performed out of doors.

overtones The *harmonics* above the *fundamental*.

pìob mhór Literally "great pipes," the *Gaelic* name for the *great highland bagpipes*.

panoptic mode View of an event or performance from a distance, from a detached vantage point. Contrast with *panoramic mode*.

panoramic mode View of an event or performance from within a setting in which the spectator enters. Contrast with *panoptic mode*.

parallel motion Occurs when different *parts* move in the same direction at the same time; a type of *homophony*.

part The *melodic* line of a particular voice or instrument.

partials Another term for *harmonics*.

participant observer What a researcher becomes when studying a living tradition during *fieldwork*.

pawwaw See *powwow*.

pentatonic scale A *scale* that contains five *pitches*, or the music that is based on such scales.

performance practice The manner in which music is interpreted and performed.

phrase A brief section of music, analogous to a phrase of spoken language, that sounds somewhat complete in itself, while not self-sufficient. One phrase may be separated from the next by a brief pause, as if to allow the singer or player a moment in which to breathe.

pibroch, piobaireachd A *genre* of *solo bagpipe* music which consists of a set of elaborate *variations* on a theme, called the *allrd urlar*.

pipe band A military-style marching and performing *ensemble* consisting of *great highland bagpipes* and drums.

pitch The highness or lowness of a *sound*.

pizmon (*pl.* pizmonim) Hymns, sung by Middle Eastern Jews, featuring sacred Hebrew texts and popular Arab melodies.

plainchant See *chant*.

plainsong See *chant*.

plectrum (*pl.* plectra) A small piece of hard material, such as horn, shell, or plastic, used to pluck a stringed instrument.

plucked idiophones *Idiophones*, such as the *Jew's harp*, that have plucked metal tongues.

polka A fast dance in *duple meter* that has become identified with Polish peoples, although it originated in Bohemia.

polka step The *polka* dance step, usually described as a heel-and-toe half step.

polyphony A musical *texture* in which the parts move in contrasting directions, as opposed to *homophony*.

powwow Native American social gatherings that feature ceremonies, celebrations, and dance competitions; formerly "pawwaw" in the Algonquian language.

prayer staff A pole on which *dabtaras* lean when performing the *Ethiopian liturgy* and which is used as an *idiophone* that is pounded on the floor during dance.

pulse The short, regular element of time that underlies *beat* and *rhythm*.

push-button accordion See *bandoneón*.

push-ups Insider term used by the *Shoshone* and other Native Americans to indicate the number of times a song is repeated.

qanun Middle Eastern trapezoidal *zither* with twenty-six sets of three-strings, played polyphonically with *plectra* attached to the index fingers of both hands.

quadruple meter Rhythmic organization based on groupings, or *measures*, of four *beats*.

quality The color of a *sound*, arising from acoustical properties of the *harmonic* series.

quinceañera A traditional Latino celebration marking the passage of fifteen-year-old girls into adulthood.

radioelectric instruments *Electrophones*, such as the analog *synthesizer*, in which the oscillations of electric circuits are amplified and transformed into audible vibrations by electric speakers.

rag-dung Tibetan *trumpet*.

range The distance between the highest and lowest *pitches* that can be sung or played by a voice or instrument.

rap The genre of musical expression that arose out of the *hip-hop* movement, featuring words recited rhythmically.

Rastafarianism A religious movement from Jamaica whose adherents venerate the Ethiopian emperor Haile Selassie ("Ras Tafari").

reed A thin strip of wood, metal, or plastic, that is fixed at one end and free at the other and that produces sound when set into vibration by moving air.

reel A *genre* of Scottish and Irish dance music, typically played on a *bagpipe*. See also *strathspey*.

refrain A fixed stanza of text and music that recurs between *verses* of a *strophic* song.

reggae A style of urban Jamaican popular music that originated among the *Rastafarians* of Jamaica in the 1960s.

register A subset of the *range* of a voice or instrument.

rekrek The *vocal slides* characteristic of the *ge'ez mode* in Ethiopian Christian chant.

relative tuning Singing or playing at a pitch level determined by what is comfortable for the performer, as opposed to *fixed tuning*.

revival The reintroduction or reinvention of an earlier tradition.

rhythm The temporal relationships within *music*.

rhythmic cycle A long, repeating *rhythmic* sequence that may be subdivided in complex and constantly changing ways.

ridim Insider term for the various marked rhythmic properties of reggae that convey, in coded form, the subversiveness of the *Rastafarian subculture* and its associated *soundscape*.

rite A religiously prescribed or customary act or observance.

ritual An established set of *rites*, or the observance of such a set of *rites*.

rnga Tibetan *frame drum*.

rol-mo Tibetan cymbals (*concussion idiophones*).

ru A Vietnamese lullaby.

rub board A *scraped idiophone* made of metal, used in the *Zydeco* tradition.

Sachs-Hornbostel system A classification of musical instruments, named after the scholars who developed the system.

sacred service The performance of *liturgy*.

sadhana A Tibetan Buddhist *ritual* meditation text.

Santería An Afro-Cuban religious and musical practice.

saxophone A Western European *single-reed aerophone* made of metal.

scale A series of *pitches* set forth in ascending or descending order.

scraped idiophones *Idiophones*, such as the *rub board*, that vibrate by being scraped with a hand-held tool.

Sebet A Sabbath-afternoon songfest of unaccompanied *pizmonim* held among Syrian Jews in North America to celebrate a special occasion.

seconds Singing an octave or two above another singer in the *Shoshone* tradition.

semitone, half-step The smallest *interval* in *Western classical music*. There are twelve semitones (also called "half steps") in the Western *octave*.

Sephardim Descendants of Spanish Jews who were forced into exile in 1492.

setting The context of a musical performance, such as the structure of the performing space or behavior of those present.

shaken idiophones *Idiophones*, such as the Ethiopian *sistrum*, with sounding parts that strike together when the instrument is shaken.

shape-note Also called "fasola," a system of musical *notation* for American *hymns* in which the shape of the note indicates the *pitch*.

shawl dance A dignified, traditional dance performed by Native American women with shawls draped over their arms. See also *fancy shawl dance*.

Shoshone A Great Basin people who migrated to the Plains, some settling on the Wind River Reservation in Wyoming.

significance The range of meanings conveyed to musicians and listeners by musical *sound* and its *setting*.

siku Andean panpipe.

single reed A *reed* constructed from a single thin, vibrating strip. Examples of single reed instruments include *aerophones* such as the *accordion*, *saxophone* and *clarinet*.

sistrum (senasel) *Ethiopian* Christian *shaken idiophone*.

slide Smooth linking of *pitches*, characteristic of the *Hawaiian steel guitar*.

smallpipes *Bagpipes*, such as the *Irish uilleann pipes*, with a low sound intensity, usually played indoors; the bag is generally filled by a bellows rather than by mouth.

sojourner A person who migrates with the intent to stay for a time and then return home.

solo Literally "alone," in Italian, refers to musical sound that is produced by only one singer or instrumentalist, either individually or with the *accompaniment* of a larger *ensemble*.

sonata form A *Western classical form* that generally consists of an exposition, in which one group of *themes* is presented in a "home" *key* and a second in a "foreign" *key*; a "development" section, in which the *themes* are elaborated on; and a recapitulation, in which both groups return, in the "home" *key*.

song cycle A group of songs that are composed as a set, sometimes because they have texts by the same poet or are connected in some other way.

sound Vibrations with *frequencies* in the audible spectrum (from 20 Hz to 20 kHz). Musical vibrations can be produced by voices, instruments, or electronic resources. A sound can be described in terms of its *quality*, *pitch*, *duration*, and *intensity*.

soundscape The distinctive *settings*, *sounds*, and *significances* of a musical *culture*.

soundscape cluster A group of closely related *soundscapes* that share *sounds*, *settings*, and *significances*.

spiritual A genre of songs, usually with *verses* and a *refrain*, that emerged from the musical expression of slaves converted to New World Christianity.

stamped idiophones *Idiophones* that are stamped on, such as boards, pots, beams, mortars, or slit drums.

stamping idiophones *Idiophones* that are hit on the ground in a vertical motion, such as sticks, tubes, or gourds.

steel guitar See *Hawaiian steel guitar*.

strathspey A kind of *reel* with a slower *tempo* and more elaborate *melody* and *ornamentation* than a simple *reel*.

strophic form A form in which all *verses* of text are set to the same melody. Strophic form can include a *refrain* that is sung between *verses*.

struck idiophones *Idiophones*, such as the *triangle*, that are struck by a hand-held tool, such as a stick.

subculture A group of people who share a common identity and related practices, whether based on ethnicity, religion, language, or generation, that are perceived as distinct from the predominant *culture* in a given society. Contrast with *interculture* and *superculture*.

Sunday School songs A repertory of Ethiopian Christian hymns that emerged in the early 1990s with texts primarily in Amharic instead of *Ge'ez*.

superculture The sphere of musical interaction that involves the power of the state and international industries, and the assumptions and expectations they generate. Contrast with *subculture* and *interculture*.

sygyt A type of *khoomii* that is sung in a high *register* with clear *overtones* that sound like whistling.

syllabic text setting *Vocal* music in which each syllable of text is sung to one pitch.

syncopation A *rhythmic* effect that provides an unexpected accent, often by temporarily unsettling the *meter* through a change in the established pattern of stressed and unstressed *beats*.

synthesizer Any *radioelectric instrument* or *digital electronic instrument*; a modern synthesizer is generally self-contained with a performance interface, sound-editing controls, and sound-generation circuitry.

tail See *nduah*.

tan nhac A Westernized *Vietnamese* popular song tradition of the French colonial period that used Western instruments and Vietnamese lyrics, and occasionally drew on Vietnamese *folk melodies*.

tango An Argentinian-derived style of song and dance.

Tet Vietnamese New Year.

text setting The way in which a text is sung or "set" to music. See *syllabic* and *melismatic*.

texture The perceived interrelationship of simultaneous musical sounds.

theme A short *melody* that is prominently stated and that recurs one or more times in a piece of music.

throat singing See *khoomii*.

Tibetan Buddhist chant See *dbyang*.

tizita A category of *tuning* and *melody*, based on a *pentatonic scale*, that is widely used in secular music of the Ethiopian highlands.

tonal music Music in which a single *pitch* and its associated *harmonies* serve as the point of departure and return.

toque The *rhythmic* patterns played by the *batá* drum in *Santería* ceremonies.

traditional music See *folk music*.

transcription The writing down of music in *notation*.

tremolo A regular fluctuation or "trembling" of a sound, produced by varying the *intensity* of the sound.

triangle A small, triangular *struck idiophone* made of solid cylindrical metal and struck with a metal bar.

triple meter A rhythmic organization based on groupings, or *measures*, of three *beats*.

trumpet An *aerophone* in which the player's compressed lips cause the air in the instrument to vibrate.

tshig Tibetan term for sung syllables with actual meaning. Contrast with *vocables*.

tuning (1) The act of adjusting the frequencies produced by one or more instruments so that they sound at the same *pitch*; (2) any ordered collection of *intervals* that are organized around a system used in a given cultural context.

'ud Plucked five-stringed Middle Eastern *lute* with a short neck and a large body with a rounded back.

uilleann pipes Irish *smallpipes* with three *drones*, a keyed *chanter*, and a bellows to fill the bag.

ukulele A small, four-stringed Hawaiian *chordophone* that became popular in the twentieth century.

ululation A vocal sound of joy or celebration commonly produced by women in Africa and the Middle East.

union pipes See *uilleann pipes*.

unison The playing or singing of exactly the same *pitch* at the same time by two or more performers.

universalism The belief that certain musical traditions or practices are found in all *cultures*.

vernacular music Music linked to the commonplace aspects of life. See also *folk music*.

verse A variable strophe of text that is sung to a fixed, repeating melody in a *strophic* song.

vibrato A regular fluctuation of a sound, produced by varying the *pitch* of the sound.

vihuela A small, strummed *folk guitar*, a key instrument in the *mariachi ensemble*.

violin A small bowed *lute* with a hollow wooden body and a solid neck to which the fingerboard is attached. See also *fiddle*.

vocables An alternative word for "nonsense syllables."

vocal Music produced by the voice, whether by one person or many.

vocal style A particular, idiosyncratic manner of singing that features particular tone *qualities*, *articulations*, or uses of *vibrato*.

vocalise Untexted *vocal* music.

war dance A Native American dance performed by men. See *fancy war dance*.

washboard See *rub board*.

Western classical music The varied musical styles and practices derived from elite European and American musics of the eighteenth and nineteenth centuries. See also *classical*.

Western harmonic system See *harmony*.

Western music Most broadly, music found in the Western Hemisphere (and thus all of the musics discussed in this book); musics of Euro-American origins, especially *Western classical music*.

Western orchestra The major *instrumental ensemble* of *Western classical music* from the late eighteenth century to the present. Commonly consists of bowed *chordophones* with the addition of *aerophones*, *idiophones*, and *membranophones*.

whole tone The *interval* made of two *semitones* in *Western classical music*.

wind instruments *Aerophones* such as *trumpets*, *flutes*, and *reed instruments*, that rely on the vibration of an enclosed column of air for their *pitch* and *quality*.

world music A cover term for a variety of musical styles from around the globe, increasingly referring to "world pop."

yang-yig A songbook of Tibetan *dbyang*. See also *dbyangs-yig*.

zema Ethiopian Christian *chant*: the music of the *Ethiopian Christian liturgy*.

zither A *chordophone* without a neck or yoke and whose strings are stretched parallel to the soundboard.

zydeco Dance music that emerged in the 1950s among the *Creoles* of the Gulf Coast. The name *zydeco* is said to derive from a French expression, *les haricots* (literally, "the beans"), alluding to a metaphor popular among *Creole* peoples of color that "the beans are not salty," that is, they are unflavored by expensive salted meat.

Sources

Preface and Acknowledgments

BOOKS AND ARTICLES

Appadurai, Arjun. "Global Ethnoscapes: Notes and Queries for a Transnational Anthropology." In *Recapturing Anthropology: Working in the Present,* edited by Richard G. Fox. Santa Fe: School of American Research Press, 1991, 191–210.

Schafer, A. Murray. *The New Soundscape. A Handbook for the Modern Music Teacher.* Scarborough, Ontario and New York: Berandol Music Limited and Associated Music Publishers, Inc., 1969.

Slobin, Mark. "Micromusics of the West: A Comparative Approach." *Ethnomusicology,* 36, no. 1 (1992): 1–87.

———. *Subcultural Musical Sounds. Micromusics of the West.* Hanover, N.H.: Wesleyan University Press, 1993.

Strohm, Reinhard. *Music in Late Medieval Bruges.* Oxford: Clarendon, 1985.

Chapter One

In Chapter One, I drew on the expertise and publications of the ethnomusicologist Theodore Levin, whose work forms the backbone of the discussion in this chapter about the sig-nificance of Tuvan music. The different styles mentioned that reflect the contours of the Tuvan landscape ("steppe" and "mountain," "nose" and "chest," and so on) are described in detail and can be heard on the easily available CD *Tuvanian Singers and Musicians,* No. 21 of the World Network Series.

The text, transliteration, and translation for *Vuoi tu venire in Merica* were provided by Andrea Malaguti.

BOOKS AND ARTICLES

Levin, Theodore C. Program notes for Huun-Huur-Tu concert, World Music, Sanders Theatre, Cambridge, Mass., March 2, 1997.

Levin, Theodore C., and Michael E. Edgerton. "The Throat Singers of Tuva." *Scientific American.* 281, no. 2 (September 1999): 80–87.

Myers, Helen, ed. *Ethnomusicology: Historical and Regional Studies.* New York: Norton, 1993.

Nettl, Bruno. *Theory and Method in Ethnomusicology.* London: Free Press of Glencoe, 1964.

Chapter Two

The case studies for this chapter are based on a combination of sources. Jim Farrington, formerly of the Wesleyan University Olin Library, helped me to locate the recording heard here of *Come O Sleep* within the uncatalogued Commins

Collection; Commins's source remains unclear. I thank Richard Wolf and Charles Capwell for aiding my efforts to trace the source of this recording. Julie Rohwein brought *All the Pretty Little Horses* and its widespread circulation to my attention. Caprice Corona and Norma Cantú provided some helpful information on the *quinceañera*. Robin Carruthers brought the lullaby study by Trehub et al. to my attention.

The bagpipe is a formidable instrument for those who do not play it, but it is remarkably well documented in the written sources listed below. Robert J. Hogan of New York City generously supplied piping manuals and recordings as well as his own extensive experience as a piper and band leader. Charles Starrett, who commenced dissertation research on American bagpipe bands during the summer of 1999, sorted out the MacCrimmons' complicated history and added many details that deepened my discussion of the pipes and the many settings in which they are played. In this chapter as in those to follow, I have drawn on the *New Grove Dictionary* and the *New Grove Dictionary of Musical Instruments* for discussion of musical instruments.

BOOKS AND ARTICLES

Adam, Barbara. "Perceptions of Time." *Companion Encyclopedia of Anthropology,* edited by Tim Ingold. London and New York: Routledge, 1994.

"Bagpipe." *New Harvard Dictionary of Music,* edited by Don Randel. Cambridge, Mass.: Belknap Press of Harvard University Press, 1986.

Baines, Anthony. *Bagpipes.* Oxford: Oxford University Press, 1960.

Bodley, Séóirse, and Breandan Breathnach. "Ireland." *The New Grove Dictionary of Music and Musicians,* edited by Stanley Sadie. London: Macmillan, 1980.

Breaking the Waves. Written and directed by Lars von Trier. London: Faber, 1996. (film)

Buckley, Martin J. *Scarlet and Tartan.* Sydney: Red Hackle Association, 1986.

Campsie, Alistair Keith. *The MacCrimmon Legend: The Madness of Angus MacKay.* Edinburgh: Canongate, 1980.

Cannon, Roderick D. *The Highland Bagpipe and Its Music.* Edinburgh: John Donald, 1988.

Cantú, Norma. "*La Quinceañera:* Toward an Ethnographical Analysis of a Life-Cycle Ritual." *Southern Folklore* 56, no. 1 (April 1999): 73–101.

Cocks, William A., Anthony C. Baines, and Roderick D. Cannon. "Bagpipe." *The New Grove Dictionary of Music and Musicians,* edited by Stanley Sadie. London: Macmillan, 1980.

———. "Bagpipe." *The New Grove Dictionary of Musical Instruments,* edited by Stanley Sadie. London: Macmillan, 1984.

Collinson, Francis M. *The Bagpipe: The History of a Musical Instrument.* London: Routledge and Kegan Paul, 1975.

Commins, Dorothy Berliner. *Lullabies of the World.* New York: Random House, 1967.

Copland, Aaron. "The Little Horses" (lullaby). *Old American Songs, Second Set.* London: Boosey & Hawkes, 1962.

Cullen, Kevin. "Gaelic Column Bags Top Award in Ireland." *Boston Globe,* March 18, 1997, B2.

Dunbar, John Telfer. *History of Highland Dress.* Edinburgh and London: Oliver & Boyd, 1962.

Dunbar, J. Telfer. "Early Tartans." In *Old Irish and Highland Dress,* 2d ed., edited by H. F. McClintock. Dundalk, Scotland: Dundalgan Press, 1950.

Ewart, David, and May Ewart. *Scottish Ceilidh Dancing.* Edinburgh and London: Mainstream Publishing, 1996.

Fabbri, Franco. "A Theory of Musical Genres: Two Applications." In *Popular Music Perspectives,* edited by David Horn and Philip Tagg. Papers from the First International Conference on Popular Music Research, Amsterdam, June, 1981. Göteborg and Exeter: International Association for the Study of Popular Music, 1982.

Finnegan, Ruth H. *The Hidden Musicians.* Cambridge: Cambridge University Press, 1989.

Hobsbawm, Eric. "Introduction: Inventing Traditions." In *The Invention of Tradition,* edited by Eric Hobsbawm and Terence Ranger. Cambridge: Cambridge University Press, 1983.

Hogan, Robert J. *The Irish-American Manual of Bagpiping Instruction.* New York: Robert J. Hogan, 1996.

Kramer, Aaron, ed. and trans. *The Last Lullaby: Poetry from the Holocaust.* Syracuse, N.Y.: Syracuse University Press, 1998.

Lomax, John A., and Alan Lomax. *American Ballads and Folksongs.* New York: Macmillan, 1934.

———. "Hush-You-Bye." *Folk Song USA: The 111 Best American Ballads.* New York: Duell, Sloan, and Pearce, 1947.

Moloney, Mick. "Notes" for *Fathers and Daughters: Irish Traditional Music in America.* Ho-Ho-Kus, New Jersey: Shanachie Records Corp., 1985.

Monaghan, Peter. "Simon Fraser's Pipers Blow Away Competition." *Chronicle of Higher Education,* July 18, 1997.

Neher, Andrew. "A Physiological Explanation of Unusual Behavior in Ceremonies Involving Drums." *Human Biology* 4: 151–60.

Nicol, Angus. "Highland Laments Ring Out." *Times* (London), August 10, 1999.

Podnos, Theodor H. *Bagpipes and Tunings.* Detroit: Information Coordinators, Inc., 1974.

Radano, Ronald M. "Interpreting Muzak: Speculations on Musical Experience in Everyday Life." *American Music* 7 (Winter 1989): 448–60.

Rodriguez, Cindy. "Coming of Age, Latino Style." *Boston Globe,* January 5, 1997, C1.

Rouget, Gilbert. *Music and Trance: Relationship Between Music and Possession.* Trans. from French, revised by Brunhilde Biebuyck in collaboration with the author. Chicago and London: University of Chicago Press, 1985.

Saaduddin, Abul H. "Bangladesh." *The New Grove Dictionary of Music and Musicians,* edited by Stanley Sadie. London: Macmillan, 1980.

Seton, Sir Bruce Gordon, and Pipe-Major John Grant. *The Pipes of War* (new introduction by Major General Frank Richardson). East Ardsley, England: EP Publishing; New York: British Book Centre, 1920 and 1974.

Sheehy, Daniel. "Mexican Mariachi Music: Made in the U.S.A." In *Musics of Multicultural America,* edited by Kip Lornell and Anne K. Rasmussen. New York: Schirmer Books, 1997, 131–54.

Shepherd, Robbie. *Let's Have a Ceilidh: The Essential Guide to Scottish Dancing.* Edinburgh: Cannongate, 1992.

Tanenbaum, Susie J. *Underground Harmonies: Music and Politics in the Subways of New York.* Ithaca: N.Y.: Cornell University Press, 1995.

Terry, Don. "Mariachi Musicians Sustaining Their Traditions." *New York Times,* October 31, 1997, A14.

Tick, Judith. *Ruth Crawford Seeger: A Composer's Search for American Music.* Oxford and New York: Oxford University Press, 1997.

Trehub, Sandra, Anna M. Unyk, and Laurel J. Trainor. "Maternal Singing in Cross-Cultural Perspective." *Infant Behavior and Development* 16 (1993): 185–95.

Trevor-Roper, Hugh. "The Invention of Tradition: The Highland Tradition of Scotland." In *The Invention of Tradition,* edited by Eric Hobsbawm and Terence Ranger. Cambridge: Cambridge University Press, 1983.

Vander, Judith. *Songprints: The Musical Experience of Five Shoshone Women.* Urbana: University of Illinois Press, 1988.

Web Sites

Ana's *Quinceañera* Web Page:
    http://clnet.ucr.edu/research/folklore/quinceaneras
Montie's List of Pipe Band Web Pages:
    http://incolor.inebraska.com/derby/bagpipe/thelist
Bagpipes:
    news://rec.music.makers.bagpipe
    http://www.hotpipes.com

Chapter Three

For my discussion of Chinese *muk'yu,* I have drawn on Su Zheng's materials published in Zheng (1992), and forthcoming in Zheng (2000). For the discussion of Arab-American migration, I have drawn on the recording and articles of Anne Rasmussen (1991, 1992), as well as my own long-time fieldwork with Syrian Jews from Aleppo now living in the United States. Ronald Radano provided helpful advice regarding spirituals.

For the Vietnamese case study, in addition to a brief trip of my own to Houston's Little Saigon and the superb resources provided by the *Gale Encyclopedia* and the *Penguin Atlas of Diaspora* (specifically the information on Vietnamese migration), I am indebted to the publications and advice of Adelaida Reyes, Pham Duy, and Deborah Wong. Pham Duy supplied scores and readings of *The National Road,* and Andrew Talle gathered and translated information on Vietnamese instruments. Terry Miller graciously provided copies of *Nhac Viet.*

Books and Articles

Allen, William Francis, Charles Pickard Ware, and Lucy McKim Garrison. *Slave Songs of the United States.* New York: Books for Libraries Press, 1971 (first published by A. Simpson & Co., 1867).

Arana, Miranda. "Modernized Vietnamese Music and Its Impact on Musical Sensibilities." *Nhac Viet: The Journal of Vietnamese Music* 3 (1994) 1, 2: 91–110.

Bankston, Carl L. "Vietnamese Americans." *Gale Encyclopedia of Multicultural America,* edited by Judy Galens, Anna Sheets, and Robyn V. Young. Detroit: Gale Research, 1995.

Chaliand, Gérard, and Jean-Pierre Rageau. *The Penguin Atlas of Diasporas,* translated by A. M. Berrett. New York: Viking, 1995.

Dictionary of the Vietnamese Language 1997 (Tu Dien Tieng Viet 1997) Hanoi and Da Nang: Nha Xuat Ban Da Nang [Da Nang Publishing House], 1997.

Dorson, Richard. "Is There Folk in the City?" In *The Urban Experience and Folk Tradition,* edited by Américo Paredes and Ellen J. Stekert. Austin: University of Texas Press, 1971.

Epstein, Dena J. *Sinful Tunes and Spirituals: Black Folk Music to the Civil War.* Urbana: University of Illinois Press, 1977.

Faison, Seth. "Despite Dissonance China Sticks to Its Refrain: Fix That Opera." *New York Times,* June 21, 1998.

———. "Arts Abroad: After the Drama, a Shanghai 'Peony'? Yes, with Changes." *New York Times,* November 25, 1999.

Gall, Susan, ed. *The Asian American Almanac.* Detroit: Gale Research, 1995.

Gargan, Edward A. "Trading Fame for Freedom: Chinese Opera Stars Find Haven, and Hardship, in U.S." *New York Times,* June 21, 1998.

Gibbs, Jason. "Reform and Tradition in Early Vietnamese Popular Song." *Nhac Viet: The Journal of Vietnamese Music* 6 (Fall 1997): 5–33.

Haiek, Joseph R., publisher. *Arab American Almanac 1992* (fourth ed.). Glendale, Calif.: News Circle Publishing House, 1992.

Henretta, James A. *America's History to 1877.* Chicago: Dorsey Press, 1987.

Kartomi, Margaret J. *On Concepts and Classifications of Musical Instruments.* Chicago: University of Chicago Press, 1990.

Loan, Nguyen Thuy. *Lich su Am nhac Viet Nam* (History of Vietnamese Music). Hanoi: Nha Xuat Ban Am Nhac Viet Nam (Music Publishing House of Vietnam), 1990.

MacFarquhar, Neil. "This Pop Diva Wows 'Em in Arabic." *New York Times,* May 18, 1999.

Miller, Ruby M., and Willard E. Miller. *United States Immigration.* Santa Barbara: ABC-CLIO, Inc., 1996.

Naff, Alixa. *Becoming American: The Early Arab Immigrant Experience.* Carbondale: Southern Illinois University Press, 1985.

Nguyen, Phong T. *Searching for a Niche: Vietnamese Music at Home in America.* Kent, Ohio: Viet Music Publications, 1995.

Nguyen, Phong Thuyet, and Patricia Shehan Campbell. *From Rice Paddies and Temple Yards: Traditional Music of Vietnam.* Danbury, Conn.: World Music Press, 1990.

Norton, Mary Beth. *A People and a Nation: A History of the United States, Fourth Edition.* Boston: Houghton Mifflin, 1994.

Oestreich, James R. "Lincoln Center to Revive Opera Thwarted by China." *New York Times,* March 16, 1999.

Oliver, Paul. "Spirituals. II. Black." *The New Grove Dictionary of Music and Musicians,* edited by Stanley Sadie. London: Macmillan, 1980.

Pham Duy. *Musics of Vietnam.* Edited by Dale R. Whiteside. Carbondale and Edwardsville: Southern Illinois University Press, 1975.

Poché, Christian. "'Ud." *The New Grove Dictionary of Musical Instruments,* edited by Stanley Sadie. London: Macmillan, 1984.

Radano, Ronald M. "Soul Texts and the Blackness of Folk." *Modernism/Modernity* 2, no. 1 (1995): 71–95.

———. "Denoting Difference: The Writing of the Slave Spirituals." *Critical Inquiry* 22, no. 3 (1996): 506–44.

Rasmussen, Anne K. "Individuality and Social Change in the Music of Arab Americans." Ph.D. dissertation, University of California at Los Angeles, 1991.

Rasmussen, Anne K. "An Evening in the Orient: The Middle Eastern Nightclub in America." *Asian Music* 23, no. 2 (1992): 61–88.

Reyes Schramm, Adelaida. "Tradition in the Guise of Innovation." *Yearbook for Traditional Music* 18 (1986): 91–101.

———. *Songs of the Caged, Songs of the Free: Music and the Vietnamese Refugee Experience.* Philadelphia: Temple University Press, 1999.

Seeger, Charles. "Versions and Variants of *Barbara Allen*" (with "Comment on the Words," by Edward Cray) *Selected Reports* 1, no. 1 (1966): 120–67.

Slobin, Mark. "Music in Diaspora." *Diaspora* 3, no. 3 (1994): 243–51.

Sowell, Thomas. *Migrations and Cultures: A World View.* New York: Basic Books, 1996.

Van Giang. *The Vietnamese Traditional Music in Brief.* Saigon: Ministry of State in Charge of Cultural Affairs, c. 1970?.

Vecoli, Rudolph J., et al., eds. *Gale Encyclopedia of Multicultural America.* Detroit: Gale Research, 1995.

Wickmann-Walczak, Elizabeth. "Ma Bomin and the Question of Creative Authority in the *Peony Pavillion* Controversy." *ACMR Reports: Journal of the Association for Chinese Music Research,* 11 (Fall 1998): 107–10.

Wong, Deborah. "'I Want the Microphone': Mass Mediation and Agency in Asian American Popular Music." *Drama Review* 38, no. 2 (1994): 152–67.

———. "Pham Duy at Home: Vietnamese American Technoculture in Orange County." In *Music and Technoculture,* edited by René T. A. Lysloff and Leslie Gay. Hanover, N.H.: Wesleyan University Press, forthcoming.

Wong, Isabel. "The *Peony Pavillion.*" *ACMR Reports: Journal of the Association for Chinese Music Research* 11 (Fall 1998): 111.

Zheng, Su De San. "Music and Migration: Chinese American Traditional Music in New York City." *The World of Music* 32, no. 3 (1990): 48–67.

———. "From Toisan to New York: *Muk'yu* Songs in Folk Tradition." *CHINOPERL Papers* no. 16 (1992/3). New York: Conference on Chinese Oral and Performing Literature.

Zheng, Su. *Claiming Diaspora: Music, Transnationalism, and Cultural Politics in Chinese/Asian America.* Oxford: Oxford University Press, forthcoming.

RECORDINGS

The Music of Arab Americans: A Retrospective Collection. Research and documentation by Anne K. Rasmussen. Rounder CD 1122 (1997). Compact disc.

Seeger, Charles, ed. *Versions and Variants of Barbara Allen.* Washington, D.C.: Library of Congress, 1964. L.P.

CD-ROM

Pham Duy. *Truong Ca Con Duong Cai Quan* (*Voyage through the motherland*). San Jose, Calif.: Coloa, Inc., 1995.

Chapter Four

For the overview of music in Boston, I have drawn on a combination of ethnographic research, documentary sources, and internet websites.

It was my own experience in confronting the very different musical profile of Boston—after thirteen years of intensive fieldwork in New York City—that sparked my interest and guided my fieldwork in Boston, including research with members of the local Ethiopian community.

Much of the material on campus musical life was gathered with the help of students in my 1996 Harvard University seminar "Music of the City." The overview of early music derives in large part from a research seminar on the Early Music Movement I jointly taught with my Harvard colleagues Carol Babiracki and Thomas Forrest Kelly. I also acknowledge our teaching assistant, Jen-Yen Chen, and the five students whom I advised in a project documenting the Voice of the Turtle: Judah Cohen, Caprice Corona, Hubert Ho, David Lyczkowski, and Judith Quiñones. I thank Millie Rahn and Betsy Siggins Schmidt for advice and materials on Club Passim and the folk-music movement. Michael Washington and Lara Pellegrinelli provided useful insights on the Boston jazz scene.

The work of the urban geographers Downs and Stea provided a wealth of insights in their publications and useful maps of greater Boston on which I have drawn. Michael Tenzer and Evan Ziporyn generously provided information on the Balinese gamelan.

For the overview of Houston, I drew on my familiarity as a native of that city, as well as insights gained from my research with the Houston Jewish community, carried out in the 1980s, and a brief field trip to Houston in May, 1999. Coverage of Houston metropolitan area musical events in the *Houston Chronicle* provided an invaluable resource. I thank Inez and Maurice Eskowitz and Asmara Tekle for their research assistance.

I gathered materials on music in Juneau via interviews with musicians and attendance at musical events in July 1999. I thank Jocelyn, Jim, and Susan Clark; Stefan Hakenberg; Judge Tom Stewart; Sally Schlichting; Steve Tada; the Fiery Gypsies; Betsy Sims; and Buddy Tabor, for information given in interviews.

BOOKS AND ARTICLES

Alarik, Scott. "Folk Kicks Up Its Heels." *Boston Globe,* April 27, 1999.

Barfield, Thomas, ed. *The Dictionary of Anthropology.* Oxford Malden, Mass.: Blackwell Publishers, 1997.

Berman, Sam. "With a Politician's Passing, Memories of 'Charlie on the MTA.'" *Boston Globe,* July 9, 1998.

Block, Adrienne Fried. *Amy Beach, Passionate Victorian.* New York: Oxford University Press, 1998.

Broyles, Michael. *Music of the Highest Class: Elitism and Populism in Antebellum Boston.* New Haven: Yale University Press, 1992.

Buchholdt, Thelma. *Filipinos in Alaska, 1788–1958.* Anchorage: Aboriginal Press, 1996.

Byrne, David. "I Hate World Music." *New York Times,* October 3, 1999.

Diagram Group. *Musical Instruments of the World: An Illustrated Encyclopedia.* New York: Facts on File, 1976.

Diamond, Jody. "Out of Indonesia: Global Gamelan." *Ethnomusicology* 42, no. 1 (1998): 174–83.

Downs, Roger M., and David Stea. *Maps in Minds: Reflections on Cognitive Mapping.* New York: Harper & Row, 1977.

Erlmann, Veit. *Nightsong: Performance, Power, and Practice in South Africa.* Chicago: University of Chicago Press, 1996.

Fink, Mitchell, ed. *Off the Record: (Stories told to) Joe Smith, An Oral History of Popular Music.* New York: Warner Books, 1988.

Finnegan, Ruth H. *The Hidden Musicians.* Cambridge: Cambridge University Press, 1989.

Foerster, Robert Franz. *Italian Emigration of Our Times.* Cambridge, Mass.: Harvard University Press, 1919.

Fuld, James J. *The Book of World-Famous Music,* 4th ed. New York: Dover, 1995.

Guerra, Joey. "Rappin' with South Park Mexican." *Houston Chronicle,* February 11, 1999.

———. "Mariachi: Music to Celebrate." *Houston Chronicle,* February 25, 1999.

Handlin, Oscar. *Boston's Immigrants: A Study in Acculturation.* Cambridge, Mass.: Belknap Press of Harvard University Press, 1979.

Kartomi, Margaret J. "Gamelan." *The New Grove Dictionary of Musical Instruments,* edited by Stanley Sadie. London: Macmillan, 1984.

McPhee, Colin. *A House in Bali.* New York: John Day, 1946.

———. *Music in Bali: A Study in Form and Instrumental Organization.* New Haven: Yale University Press, 1966.

Mitchell, Rick. "Lovett Lovingly Recalls His Roots." *Houston Chronicle,* November 30, 1998.

———. "Straight-Up Gospel." *Houston Chronicle,* February 7, 1999.

———. "Pushing All the Right Buttons." *Houston Chronicle,* May 6, 1999.

Murray, Jean, ed. *Music of the Alaska-Klondike Gold Rush.* Fairbanks: University of Alaska Press, 1998.

O'Connor, Thomas H. *The Boston Irish: A Political History.* Boston: Northeastern University Press, 1995.

Pellegrinelli, Lara. "A Guided Tour of America's Most Fascinating Jazz Clubs." *New Music Box* 9 (January 2000). Available at www.newmusicbox.org/archive/index

Plotkinoff, David. "Joan Baez: A Legend in Search of Listeners." *Philadelphia Inquirer,* January 24, 1993.

Reyes Schramm, Adelaida. "Explorations in Urban Ethnomusicology: Hard Lessons From the Spectacularly Ordinary." *Yearbook for Traditional Music* 14 (1982): 1–14.

Rubin, Cynthia, and Jerome Rubin. *Comprehensive Guide to Boston.* Newton, Mass.: Emporium Publications, 1972.

Schmidt, John C. *The Life and Works of John Knowles Paine.* Ann Arbor: UMI Research Press, 1980.

Tenzer, Michael. *Balinese Music.* Berkeley: Periplus Editions, 1991.

————. *Gamelan Gong Kebyar: The Art of Twentieth-Century Balinese Music.* Chicago and London: University of Chicago Press, 2000.

Tommasini, Anthony. "Even at Birth, Opera Wed the Stirring and the Silly." *New York Times,* June 14, 1997.

Turner, Martha Anne. *The Yellow Rose of Texas: Her Saga and Her Song.* Austin: Shoal Creek Publishers, Inc., 1976.

Ward, Charles. "Ars Lyrica Brings Home 'Early Music.'" *Houston Chronicle,* February 23, 1999.

Vecoli, Rudolph J., et al., eds. *Gale Encyclopedia of Multicultural America.* Detroit: Gale Research, 1995.

WEB SITES

Joan Baez:

www.vanguardrecords.com/Baez/Home

www.vanguardrecords.com/Baez/Sings

Berklee College of Music:

www.berklee.edu

Boston Camerata:

members.aol.com/Boscam/cambio

Boston College:

www.bc.edu/cwis/aboutbc

The Boston Early Music Festival:

www.bemf.org/background

Boston Lyric Opera:

www.blo.org

Boston Pops, Esplanade Concerts:

www.pbs.org/wgbh/pages/pops/background/history

Boston Symphony Orchestra:

www.bso.org/newdesign/fsbso

Boston University:

www.bu.edu/admissions/aboutbu/history

Brandeis University:

www.brandeis.edu/overview/historical

Club Passim:

www.clubpassim.org/CPHistory

Gamelans:

www.sei.com/users/kk/swarasanti/gamelan

Gamelan Galak Tika at M.I.T.:

web.mit.edu/afs/athena/mit.edu/org/g/galak-tika/www

Handel and Haydn Society:

www.handelandhaydn.org/about

New England Conservatory of Music:

www.newenglandconservatory.edu

Opera Company of Boston:

www.blo.org

New Music Box:

www.newmusicbox.org

Tufts University:

www.tufts.edu/source/about

Voice of the Turtle:

http://home.att.net/~derekburrows/lhomepagers

RECORDINGS

The Confederacy, Based on Music of the South during the years 1861–65. Liner notes by Richard Bales. New York: Columbia Masterworks SL-220, ML 4927, XLP 30159. (LP and liner notes).

Paris by Night. Houston. 1/36. Westminster, Calif.: Thuy Nga Productions, 1996 (videotape).

Solomon Linda's Original Evening Birds. *Mbube Roots, Zulu Choral Music from South Africa, 1930s–1960s.* Cambridge, Mass.: Rounder Records, 1987.

Chapter Five

For Chapter Five, I have depended on the work of Walter Kauffman and consulted the recordings by Lewisohn and Hart for the Tibetan case study. The discussion of Santería draws on María Teresa Vélez's article in *Diaspora* and her recently published book. My own long-term fieldwork with Ethiopian Christian musicians in Ethiopia and in the United States are the sources for the major case study, much of which was originally drafted for the 1999 Ethel V. Curry Distinguished Lecture in Musicology at the University of Michigan. Interviews with Hailegebriot Shewangizou and Tilahun Gebrehiwot were of great help in clarifying the sources of new directions in Ethiopian diaspora church music. Monica Devens and Thomas Kane provided sage advice on translation.

Books and Articles

Amira, John, and Steven Cornelius. *The Music of Santería: Traditional Rhythms of the Batá Drums.* Crown Point, Ind. and New York: White Cliffs Media, 1992.

Comaroff, Jean, and John Comaroff. "Introduction." In *Modernity and its Malcontents: Ritual and Power in Postcolonial Africa.* Chicago: University of Chicago Press, 1993.

Cox, Harvey Gallagher. *Fire from Heaven: The Rise of Pentacostal Spirituality and the Reshaping of Religion in the Twenty-First Century.* Reading, Mass.: Addison-Wesley, 1995.

Crossley-Holland, Peter. Review of *Tibetan Buddhism: Tantras of Gyuto: Mahakala,* edited by David Lewiston. *Ethnomusicology* 18, no. 2 (1974): 339–41.

Dalai Lama. *Freedom in Exile: The Autobiography of the Dalai Lama.* New York: Harper Perennial, 1991.

Eck, Diana. "Neighboring Faiths." *Harvard Magazine* 99, no. 1 (Sept.–Oct. 1996): 38–44.

Gregory, Steven. *Santería in New York City: A Study in Cultural Resistance.* New York: Garland, 2000.

Harrison, Frank Llewellyn. *Time, Place, and Music: An Anthology of Ethnomusicological Observation.* Amsterdam: Frits Knuf, 1973.

Helffer, Mireille. Review of *The Music of Tibet. The Tantric Rituals. Ethnomusicology* 16, no. 1 (1972): 152–54.

Leach, Edmund Ronald. *Rethinking Anthropology.* London: Athlone Press, 1961.

Mercier, Jacques. *Ethiopian Magic Scrolls.* New York: George Braziller, 1979.

Nomachi, Kazuyoshi. *Bless Ethiopia.* Tokyo: Odyssey Publications, 1998.

Powers, John. *An Introduction to Tibetan Buddhism.* Ithaca, N.Y.: Snow Lion Publications, 1995.

Rappaport, Roy A. "The Obvious Aspects of Ritual." In *Ecology, Meaning, and Religion.* Richmond, Calif.: North Atlantic Books, 1979.

Shelemay, Kay Kaufman. "The Musician and Transmission of Religious Tradition: The Multiple Roles of the Ethiopian *Dabtara*." *Journal of Religion in Africa* 22, no. 3 (1992): 242–60.

———. "Zema: A Concept of Sacred Music in Ethiopia." *The World of Music* 24, no. 3 (1982): 52–67.

Shelemay, Kay Kaufman, and Peter Jeffery. *Ethiopian Christian Liturgical Chant: An Anthology.* vols. 1-3. Madison, Wisc.: A-R Editions, 1994–1998.

Shelemay, Kay Kaufman, Peter Jeffery, and Ingrid Monson. "Oral and Written Transmission in Ethiopian Chant." *Early Music History* 12 (1993): 55–117.

Smith, Huston, Kenneth N. Stevens, and Raymond S. Tomlinson. "On an Unusual Mode of Chanting by Certain Tibetan Lamas." *Journal of the Acoustical Society of America* 41 (May 1967): 1262–1264.

Tucci, Giuseppe. *Religions of Tibet.* Translated from the German and the Italian by Geoffrey Samuel. Berkeley: University of California Press, 1980.

Turner, Victor. *The Ritual Process.* Ithaca, N.Y.: Cornell University Press, 1977.

Van Gennep, Arnold. *The Rites of Passage.* Translated by Monika B. Vizedom and Gabrielle L. Caffee. Chicago: University of Chicago Press, 1960.

Vélez, María Teresa. "Eya Aranla: Overlapping Perspectives." *Diaspora* 3, no. 3 (1994): 289–304.

———. "The Trade of an Afro-Cuban Religious Drummer, Felipe García Villamil." 2 vols. Ph.D. dissertation, Wesleyan University, 1996.

———. *Drumming for the Gods: The Life and Times of Felipe García Villamil, Santero Palero and Abakua.* Philadelphia: Temple University Press, 2000.

Recordings

Jenkins, J., ed. "Ethiopia I. Copts." *An Anthology of African Music.* Recorded 1965. UNESCO Collection. Kassel: Bärenreiter Musicaphon BM 30 L 2304.

Lewiston, David, ed. *Tibetan Buddhism: Tantras of Gyuto: Mahakala.* Nonesuch, H-72055 (1973).

CD-ROM

Eck, Diana. *On Common Ground: World Religions in America* (Pluralism Project). New York: Columbia University Press, 1997. CD-ROM.

Web Sites

The Pluralism Project Website:
   www.fas.harvard.edu/~pluralism

Tibetan Music in North America:
   www.tibet.org/chaksampa

Chapter Six

In addition to the many secondary sources listed below, I am grateful to Samantha Chaifetz and Mike Bortnick of the Harvard Ballroom Club and Team for lessons, demonstrations, and explanations regarding the competition tango today. Research assistants David Lyczkowski and Sarah Morelli helped mine a wide range of secondary sources on the dance and found contacts in the world of tango and bhangra. A seminar on bhangra and a performance by the MIT bhangra team

provided a useful introduction to bhangra on American college campuses, as did experiencing a Boston Bhangra
Blowout in 1999. For information on Morris dancing, I drew
on my own observations of groups such as the Newtowne
Morris Men who frequently dance in Harvard Square and
earlier encounters with Morris dancers in locales as diverse
as Bath, England and New Haven, Connecticut.

BOOKS AND ARTICLES

Banerji, Sabita. "Ghazals to Bhangra in Great Britain." *Popu-
    lar Music* 7, no. 2 (1988): 207–13.

Barrand, Anthony G. "But America for a Morris Dance!" *Sing
    Out!* 33, no. 4 (1988): 14–21.

Barrella, Humberto. *El Tango después de Gardel, 1935–1959.*
    Buenos Aires: Corregidor, 1999.

Baumann, Gerd. "The Re-Invention of Bhangra: Social
    Change and Aesthetic Shifts in a Punjabi Music in
    Britain." *The World of Music* 32, no. 2 (1990): 81–95.

Béhague, Gerard. "Tango." *The New Grove Dictionary of
    Music and Musicians,* edited by Stanley Sadie. London:
    Macmillan, 1980.

Bessman, Jim. "Bhangra Beat Transforms Indipop Scene."
    Billboard 3, no. 39 (1999): 100–1.

Carroll, Dennis J. "In Wisconsin, the Polka Beat Goes On."
    Boston Globe, November 29, 1996.

Černušák, Gracian, and Andrew Lamb. "Polka." *The New
    Grove Dictionary of Music and Musicians,* edited by
    Stanley Sadie. London: Macmillan, 1980.

Cohen, Judah. "Bhangra, Asian Beat Music of the Asian Di-
    aspora: An Exploration of a Transforming Gender
    Space." Unpublished paper, 1998.

Collier, Simon. *Tango! The Dance, the Song, the Story.* New
    York: Thames and Hudson, 1995.

Connerton, Paul. *How Societies Remember.* Cambridge:
    Cambridge University Press, 1989.

De Buenosaires, Oscar. *Tango: A Bibliography.* Albuquerque:
    FOG Publications, 1991.

Flores, Rafaelo. *El Tango, desde el Umbral Hacía Dentro.*
    Madrid: Euroliceo, 1993.

Gorin, Natalio, ed. *Astor Piazzolla: A Manera de Memorias.*
    Buenos Aires: Editorial Atlantida, 1990.

Gronow, Pekka. "Ethnic Records: An Introduction." In *Eth-
    nic Recordings in America.* Washington, D.C.: American
    Folklife Center, Library of Congress, 1982.

Hall, Edward T. *The Hidden Dimension.* Garden City, N.Y.:
    Doubleday, 1969.

Hanna, Judith Lynne. *Dance, Sex and Gender.* Chicago: Uni-
    versity of Chicago Press, 1988.

———. "Dance." In *Ethnomusicology. An Introduction,*
    edited by Helen Myers. London and New York: Macmil-
    lan Press and W. W. Norton, 1992.

Harrington, Richard. "Piazzolla and the Newfangled Tango:
    An Argentine Composer's 30-Year Quest for Respect."
    Washington Post, May 7, 1988, C1.

Huq, Rupa. "Asian Kool? Bhangra and Beyond," In *Dis-
    Orienting Rhythms: The Politics of the New Asian Dance
    Music,* edited by Sanjay Sharma, John Hutnyk, and Ash-
    wani Sharma. London, and Atlantic Highlands, N.J.:
    Zed Books, 1996.

Kaeppler, Adrienne L. "American Approaches to the Study of
    Dance." *Yearbook for Traditional Music* 10 (1991): 11–21.

Keil, Charles, Angeliki V. Keil, and Dick Blau. *Polka Happi-
    ness.* Philadelphia: Temple University Press, 1992.

Lomax, Alan. "Brief Progress Report: Cantometrics-Choreo-
    metrics Projects," *Yearbook of the International Folk
    Music Council* 142 (1972): 142–44.

McLane, Daisann. "In the Footsteps of the Conga and the
    Alley Cat." *New York Times,* August 18, 1996.

Peña, Manuel. *The Texas-Mexican Conjunto: History of a Work-
    ing-Class Music.* Austin: University of Texas Press, 1985.

Romani, G., and Ivor Beynon. "Accordion." *The New Grove
    Dictionary of Musical Instruments,* edited by Stanley
    Sadie. New York: Macmillan, 1984.

Savigliano, Marta E. *Tango and the Political Economy of Pas-
    sion.* Boulder, Colo.: Westview Press, 1995.

Sharma, Ashwani. "Sounds Oriental: The (Im)Possibility of
    Theorizing Asian Musical Cultures." In *Dis-Orienting
    Rhythms: The Politics of the New Asian Dance Music,*
    edited by Sanjay Sharma, John Hutnyk, and Ashwani
    Sharma. London and Atlantic Highlands, N.J.: Zed
    Books, 1996.

Sharma, Sanjay. "Noisy Asians or 'Asian Noise.'" In *Dis-
    Orienting Rhythms: The Politics of the New Asian Dance
    Music,* edited by Sanjay Sharma, John Hutnyk, and Ash-
    wani Sharma. London and Atlantic Highlands, N.J.: Zed
    Books 1996.

Sharma, Sanjay, John Hutnyk and Ashwani Sharma, eds. *Dis-
    Orienting Rhythms: The Politics of the New Asian Dance
    Music.* London and Atlantic Highlands, N.J.: Zed
    Books, 1996.

Spottswood, Richard. "The Sajewski Story: Eighty Years of
    Polish Music in Chicago." In *Ethnic Recordings in
    America. A Neglected Heritage.* Washington: American
    Folklife Center, Library of Congress, 1982.

Taylor, Julie M. "Tango: Theme of Class and Nation." *Ethno-
    musicology* 20, no. 2 (1976): 273–91.

Thomas, Helen, ed. *Dance, Gender, and Culture.* Bas-
    ingstoke, England: Macmillan, 1993.

Walker, Caroline. *The Modern Dances: How to Dance Them.*
    Chicago: Saul Brothers, 1914.

Walser, Robert. "The Polka Mass: Music of Postmodern Eth-
    nicity." *American Music* 10, no. 2 (Summer 1992):
    183–202.

RECORDINGS

Secteto Mayro Orchestra. *A Passion for Tango.* Angel/Columbia Records CDC554857. Compact disc with liner notes.

Squeeze Play: A World Accordion Anthology. Produced and edited by Richard Spottswood. Rounder CD 1090, compact disc.

WEB SITES

Bhangra:

http://www.bhangrablowout.com

Astor Piazzolla:

http://www.piazzolla.org

Includes "A Sad, Current, and Conscious Tango" (*Un Tango Triste, Actual, Consciente*), an interview (translated into English) by Gonzola Saavedra with Astor Piazzolla, July 1989, Barcelona, Spain, shortly before Piazzolla's death.

Morris dance:

http://www.compulink.co.uk/~ant/morris

http://ucowww.ucsc.edu/~sla/morris/biblio

http://www.cdss.org

http://www.mit.edu/people/ijs/blackjokers

http://www.sheldonbrown.com/banbury

Tango and la Cumparsita:

http://totango.net/cumpar.html

Chapter Seven

Much of the introductory material on music and memory for this chapter as well as the case study on the *pizmonim* is further developed in my book *Let Jasmine Rain Down*, which is based on more than a decade of fieldwork among Syrian Jews in New York, Mexico, and Israel. Americo Paredes's classic study of the *corrido* provided substantial documentation on the famous ballad *Gregorio Cortez*. Vernel Bagneris' extraordinary images and sounds of the little-seen jazz funeral made available rare primary materials on that subject. Robert Rumbolz and Ingrid Monson provided details that enhanced the information Roe-min Kok had gathered on the jazz band. Details regarding the "Wheat Song" came from Nabil Azzam; I am, in addition, grateful to Moses Tawil, Louis Massry, Joseph Saff, Sheila Schweky, and the late Sophie Cohen for information given in interviews about the *pizmon Ramah Everai*; for translations I thank James Robinson and Joshua Levisohn; for gathering information on the *'ud*, I thank Roe-min Kok and Mark Kligman.

BOOKS AND ARTICLES

Azzam, Nabil Salim. "Muhammad 'Abd al-Wahhab in Modern Egyptian Music." Ph.D. dissertation, University of California, Los Angeles, 1990.

Bagneris, Vernel, ed. *Rejoice When You Die.* Baton Rouge: Louisiana State University Press, 1998.

Bergreen, Laurence. *Louis Armstrong: An Extravagant Life.* New York: Broadway Books, 1997.

Bragg, Rick. "Jazzy Final Sendoff for Chicken Man." *New York Times,* February 1, 1999.

Brunn, H. O. *The Story of the Original Dixieland Jazz Band.* Scranton, Penn.: Louisiana State University Press, 1960.

Collier, James Lincoln. "Armstrong, Louis." *The New Grove Dictionary of Jazz,* edited by Barry Kernfeld. London: Macmillan, 1998.

———. "Bands." *The New Grove Dictionary of Jazz,* edited by Barry Kernfeld. London: Macmillan, 1998.

———. "Jazz." *The New Grove Dictionary of Jazz,* edited by Barry Kernfeld. London: Macmillan, 1998.

Chase, Gilbert. *America's Music,* 3rd ed. Urbana: University of Illinois Press, 1987.

Dean, Roger T. "Jazz, improvisation and brass." *The Cambridge Companion to Brass Instruments,* edited by Trevor Herbert and John Wallace. Cambridge: Cambridge University Press, 1997.

Dweck, Francine, and Sheila Haber. *Festival of Holidays Recipe Book.* Brooklyn, N.Y.: Sephardic Community Center, 1987.

Farmer, H. G. "Qanun." *The New Grove Dictionary of Musical Instruments,* edited by Stanley Sadie. London: Macmillan, 1984.

Fuld, James J. "Twinkle, Twinkle, Little Star (ABCDEFG; Baa, Baa, Black Sheep; Schnitzelbank)." *The Book of World Famous Music: Classic, Popular, and Folk,* 4th ed. New York: Dover, 1995.

Gushee, Lawrence. "A Preliminary Chronology of the Early Career of Fred 'Jelly Roll' Morton." *American Music iii* (1985): 389–412.

———. "Oliver, King." *The New Grove Dictionary of Jazz,* edited by Barry Kernfeld. London: Macmillan, 1998.

Hazen, Margaret Hindle, and Robert M. Hazen. *The Music Men: An Illustrated History of Brass Bands in America, 1800–1920.* Washington, D.C. and London: Smithsonian Institution Press, 1987.

Idelsohn, A. Z. "Die arabische Musik." In *Hebraisch-Orientalischer Melodienschatz,* Vol. 4: *Gesänge der Orientalischen Sefardim.* Jerusalem-Berlin-Vienna: Benjamin Hart Verlag, 1923.

Marco, Guy A., ed. *Encyclopedia of Recorded Sound in the United States.* New York: Garland, 1993.

Par, C. F. "The Alphabet." In *The New Blue Book of Favorite Songs,* edited by John W. Beattie. Chicago: Hill and McCreary, 1941.

Rubin, David C. *Memory in Oral Traditions: The Cognitive Psychology of Epic, Ballads and Counting-out Rhymes.* New York and Oxford: Oxford University Press, 1995.

Schacter, Daniel L. *Searching for Memory: The Brain, the Mind, and the Past.* New York: Basic Books, 1996.

Schafer, William J. *Brass Bands and New Orleans Jazz.* Baton Rouge: Louisiana State University Press, 1977.

———. "Brass Band." *The New Grove Dictionary of Jazz,* edited by Barry Kernfeld. London: Macmillan, 1998.

Schuller, Gunther. *Early Jazz: Its Roots and Musical Development.* New York: Oxford University Press, 1968.

Shelemay, Kay Kaufman. "Recording Technology, the Record Industry, and Ethnomusicological Scholarship." In *Comparative Musicology and the Anthropology of Music,* edited by Bruno Nettl and Philip Bohlman. Chicago: University of Chicago Press, 1991.

———. *Let Jasmine Rain Down: Song and Remembrance among Syrian Jews.* Chicago: University of Chicago Press, 1998.

Tick, Judith. *Ruth Crawford Seeger: A Composer's Search for American Music.* New York: Oxford University Press, 1997.

Vecoli, Rudolph J., et al., eds. *Gale Encyclopedia of Multicultural America.* Detroit: Gale Research, 1995.

Wilkie, Curtis. "A Funeral for the 'Chicken Man': Shrunken Heads, Incense and Jazz." *Boston Sunday Globe,* January 31, 1999, A5.

Williams, Martin, ed. *The Smithsonian Collection of Classic Jazz.* 3rd ed. Notes booklet. Washington, D.C.: Smithsonian Institution, 1973.

Williams, Martin. *The Smithsonian Collection of Classic Jazz,* rev. ed. Washington, D.C.: Smithsonian Institution, 1987.

WEB SITE

Shaare Zedek Pizmon Page:

www.bsz.org/bszframe-music

Chapter Eight

For this chapter, I drew on the sources listed below as well as the help of a number of individuals. Gil Rose of the Boston Modern Orchestra Project and Reza Vali provided information, recordings, and scores for the Flute Concerto.

For advice and translation on the *enka* example, I thank Takashi Koto and Tomie Hahn. Christine Yano's research on *karaoke* provided a wealth of historical and ethnographic detail.

Ronald Emoff's work on Cajun poetics provided valuable insights. For help with the Creole repertories, I thank Asmara Tekle. The writings of Tisserand on zydeco have been a particularly valuable resource.

Barry Jean Ancelet kindly provided information concerning several photographs.

The note on the orchestra reflects the *New Grove Dictionary of Music and Musicians* entry of this title.

BOOKS AND ARTICLES

Ancelet, Barry Jean, and Elemore Morgan, Jr. *Cajun and Creole Music Makers.* Jackson: University Press of Mississippi, 1999.

Arceneaux, George. *Youth in Acadie: Reflections on Acadian Life and Culture in Southwest Louisiana.* Baton Rouge: Claitor's Publishing Division, 1974.

Bernard, Shane K. *Swamp Pop: Cajun and Creole Rhythm and Blues.* Jackson: University Press of Mississippi, 1996.

Borwick, John. "Sound Recording, Transmission, and Reproduction. 6. Recording." *The New Grove Dictionary of Music and Musicians,* edited by Stanley Sadie. London: Macmillan, 1980.

Brasseaux, Carl A. *Acadian to Cajun: Transformation of a People, 1803–1877.* Jackson: University Press of Mississippi, 1992.

———. "Creoles of Color in Louisiana's Bayou Country 1766–1877." In *Creoles of Color of the Gulf South,* edited by James H. Dorman. Knoxville: University of Tennessee Press, 1996.

Broven, John. *South to Louisiana: The Music of the Cajun Bayous.* Gretna, La.: Pelican Publishing Company, 1983.

Conrad, Glenn R. *The Cajuns: Essays on their History and Culture.* Lafayette: Center for Louisiana Studies, University of Southwestern Louisiana, 1978.

Crowley, Larry. "Queen Ida Still Cookin' On, Offstage." *Arizona Republic,* May 15, 1997, C1.

Diagram Group. *Musical Instruments of the World: An Illustrated Encyclopedia.* New York: Facts on File, 1976.

Dorman, James H. *Creoles of Color of the Gulf South.* Knoxville: University of Tennessee Press, 1996.

———. "Ethnicity and Identity: Creoles of Color in Twentieth-Century South Louisiana." *Creoles of Color of the Gulf South.* Knoxville: University of Tennessee Press, 1996.

Emoff, Ron. "A Cajun Poetics of Loss and Longing." *Ethnomusicology* 42, no. 2 (Spring/Summer 1998): 283–301.

Evans, David. *Big Road Blues: Tradition and Creativity in the Folk Blues.* Berkeley: University of California Press, 1982.

Gleason, Philip. "Identifying Identity: A Semantic History." In *Theories of Ethnicity: A Classical Reader,* edited by Werner Sollors. New York: New York University Press, 1996.

Gronow, Pekka. "Ethnic Recordings: An Introduction." In *Ethnic Recordings in America.* Washington, D.C.: Library of Congress, 1982.

Hanger, Kimberly S. "Origins of New Orleans Free Creoles of Color." In *Creoles of Color of the Gulf South,* edited by James H. Dorman. Knoxville: University of Tennessee Press, 1996.

Hildebrand, Lee. "Queen Ida Cookin' in More Ways than One." *San Francisco Chronicle,* May 20, 1990, Sunday Datebook, 39.

Hobsbawn, Eric. "Introduction: Inventing Traditions." In *The Invention of Tradition,* edited by Eric Hobsbawm and Terence Ranger. Cambridge: Cambridge University Press, 1983.

Jennings, Dana. "In Bayou Country, Music is Never Second Fiddle." *New York Times,* November 22, 1998.

Keil, Charles. "Music Mediated and Live in Japan." *Ethnomusicology* 28, no. 1 (1984): 91–96.

Lawson, Kyle. "She's Still Ruling Zydeco's Roost; Queen Ida Plays a Mean Accordion But She's No Lawrence Welk." Minneapolis–St. Paul *Star Tribune,* July 9, 1995, 8F.

Lum, Casey Man Kong. *In Search of a Voice: Karaoke and the Construction of Identity in Chinese America.* Mahwah, N.J.: Lawrence Erlbaum Associates, 1996.

Minton, John. "Houston Creoles and Zydeco: The Emergence of an African American Urban Popular Music." *American Music* 14, no. 4 (Winter 1996): 480–526.

Mitsui, Toru, and Shuhei Hosokawa, eds. *Karaoke Around the World: Global Technology, Local Singing.* London and N.Y.: Routledge, 1998.

Monson, Ingrid. *Saying Something: Jazz Improvisation and Interaction.* Chicago and London: University of Chicago Press, 1996.

"More Good Stuff; Saturday." *The Phoenix Gazette.* May 19, 1994, Z2.

Nash, Manning. *The Cauldron of Ethnicity in the Modern World.* Chicago: University of Chicago Press, 1989.

Nettl, Bruno. "Streets." In *The Western Impact on World Music: Change, Adaptation, and Survival.* New York: Schirmer Books, 1985.

Post, Lauren C. *Cajun Sketches.* Baton Rouge: Louisana State University Press, 1977.

Proulx, E. Annie. *Accordion Crimes.* New York: Scribner, 1996.

Ratliff, Ben. "Frank Yankovic, Long-Reigning Polka King, is Dead at 83." *New York Times,* October 15, 1998.

Reyes Schramm, Adelaida. "Ethnic Music, the Urban Area, and Ethnomusicology." *Sociologus* 29 (1979) new series: 1–18.

Rushton, William Faulkner. *The Cajuns: From Acadia to Louisiana.* New York: Farrar Straus Giroux, 1979.

Savigliano, Marta E. "Exotic Encounters." In *Tango and the Political Economy of Passion.* Boulder, Colo.: Westview Press, 1995.

Shane, Bernard K. *Swamp Pop: Cajun and Creole Rhythm and Blues.* Jackson: University of Mississippi Press, 1996.

Spottswood, Richard Keith. *Ethnic Music on Records: A Discography of Ethnic Recordings Produced in the United States, 1893 to 1942,* 7 vols. Urbana: University of Illinois Press, 1990.

Sollors, Werner. "Foreword: Theories of Ethnicity." In *Theories of Ethnicity: A Classical Reader.* New York: New York University Press, 1996.

Strachwitz, Chris A. "Cajun Country." *The American Folk Music Occasional* [no. 2], edited by Chris Strachwitz and Pete Welding. New York: Oak Publications, 1970.

Tisserand, Michael. *The Kingdom of Zydeco.* New York: Arcade Publishing, 1998.

Titon, Jeff Todd. *Early Downhome Blues: A Musical and Cultural Analysis.* Urbana: University of Illinois Press, 1977.

Trevor-Roper, Hugh. "The Invention of Tradition: The Highland Tradition of Scotland." In *The Invention of Tradition,* edited by Eric Hobsbawm and Terence Ranger. Cambridge: Cambridge University Press, 1983.

Valdés, Alisa. "Fresh Squeezed." *Boston Globe,* January 3, 1998, D1.

Vali, Mahmood-Reza. "Breaking the Sound Barrier." Program notes for Concerto for Flute and Orchestra, Boston Modern Orchestra, February 13, 1998.

Vecoli, Rudolph J., et al., eds. *Gale Encyclopedia of Multicultural America,* vols. 1–2. New York: Gale Research, 1995.

Westrup, Jack, with Neal Zaslow and Eleanor Selfridge-Field. "Orchestra." *The New Grove Dictionary of Musical Instruments,* edited by Stanley Sadie. London: Macmillan, 1984.

Whitfield, Irene Thérèse. *Louisiana French Folk Songs.* Baton Rouge: Louisiana State University Press, 1939.

Yeh, Nora. Review of *In Search of a Voice: Karaoke and the Construction of Identity in Chinese America,* by Casey Man Kong Lum. *Ethnomusicology* 41, no. 3 (1997): 565–7.

Yano, Christine. "The Floating World of Karaoke in Japan." *Popular Music and Society* 20 (1996): 1–17.

WEB SITES

Hawaii Star Bulletin:

http://www.starbulletin.com/96105/16/features/story2

Includes "Queen Ida Gets Down on the Bayou Sound," by Ann Marie Swan, *Hawaii Star Bulletin,* May 16, 1996.

Chapter Nine

The case study on *Nkosi Sikelel' iAfrika* was compiled with the assistance of members of Kuumba, who provided details of their experience learning the new South African national anthem in September 1998. Veit Erlmann's discussion of *mbube* was an additional resource. The reggae case study was compiled from the secondary sources listed below and was improved by suggestions from anonymous readers.

The Shoshone case study depends heavily on research published by the ethnomusicologist Judith Vander, although the interpretations of the music's significance in Shoshone public life are my own. I gathered additional materials on the Shoshone powwow during a brief field trip to the Wind River Reservation during the summer of 1998, and am grateful for the generous assistance of Judith Vander.

BOOKS AND ARTICLES

Brownell, F. G. *National Symbols of the Republic of South Africa.* Melville, South Africa: Chris Van Rensburg Publications, 1995.

Burton, Bryan. *Moving Within the Circle.* Danbury, Conn.: World Music Press, 1993.

Chang, Kevin O'Brien, and Wayne Chen. *Reggae Rousters: The Story of Jamaican Music.* Philadelphia: Temple University Press, 1998.

Dunning, Jennifer. "A Culture's Age-Old Rituals Made Fresh in a Journey Through Time." *New York Times,* August 10, 1998, E5.

Erlmann, Veit. *Nightsong: Performance, Power, and Practice in South Africa.* Chicago: University of Chicago Press, 1996.

———. *Music, Modernity, and the Global Imagination: South Africa and the West.* New York, Oxford University Press, 1999.

Goldberg, Carey. "Powwows Change, but Drummer is the Same." *New York Times,* August 24, 1997, Week in Review, 4.

Foster, Roy. "What Is Political History?" In *What Is History Today?,* edited by Juliet Gardiner. Atlantic Highlands, N.J.: Humanities Press International, 1988.

Harlan, Theresa. "Creating a Visual History: A Question of Ownership." *Aperture* 139 (Summer 1995): 20–33.

Haynes, George Edmund. "Negroes and the Ethiopian Crisis," *The Christian Century* 52, no. 27 (November 20, 1935): 1485.

Hebdige, Dick. *Subculture: The Meaning of Style.* New York: Routledge, 1988.

Hobsbawm, Eric. "Inventing Traditions." In *The Invention of Tradition,* edited by Eric Hobsbawm and Terence Ranger. Cambridge: Cambridge University Press, 1983.

Hutton, Ronald. "What is Political History?" In *What Is History Today?,* edited by Juliet Gardiner. Atlantic Highlands, N.J.: Humanities Press International, 1988.

Jackson, Zig. "Social Identity: A View from Within." *Aperture* 139 (Summer 1995): 34–38.

Kaur, Raminder and Virinder S. Kalra. "New Paths for South Asian Identity and Musical Creativity." In *Dis-Orienting Rhythms: The Politics of the New Asian Dance Music,* edited by Sanjay Sharma, John Hutnyk, and Ashwani Sharma. London and Atlantic Highlands, N.J.: Zed Books, 1996.

Lipsitz, George. *Dangerous Crossroads: Popular Music, Postmodernism, and the Poetics of Place.* London and New York: Verso, 1994.

Madsen, Brigham D. *The Northern Shoshoni.* Caldwell, Idaho: Caxton Printers Ltd., 1980.

———. *The Shoshoni Frontier and the Bear River Massacre.* Salt Lake City: University of Utah Press, 1985.

Morgan, Kenneth O. "What Is Political History Today?" In *What Is History Today?,* edited by Juliet Garner. Atlantic Highlands, N.J.: Humanities Press International, 1988.

Norton, Mary Beth. *A People and A Nation: A History of the United States,* 4th ed. Boston: Houghton Mifflin Company, 1994.

Powers, William K. "Ogala Song Terminology." In *Selected Reports in Ethnomusicology* 3, no. 2, edited by Charlotte Heth. Los Angeles: Program in Ethnomusicology, University of California, Los Angeles, 1980.

———. "Plains Indian Music and Dance." In *Anthropology on the Great Plains,* edited by W. Raymond Wood and Margot Liberty. Lincoln: University of Nebraska Press, 1980.

Pow Wow Time, a *Ranger* special edition. *Ranger,* Riverton, Wyoming, Thursday, May 21, 1998.

Reckford, Verena. "From *Burru* Drums to Reggae Ridims; The Evolution of Rasta Music." *Chanting Down Babylon: The Rastafari Reader,* edited by Nathaniel Samuel Murrell, William David Spencer, and Adrian Anthony McFarlane. Philadelphia: Temple University Press, 1998.

Rickard, Jolene. "Sovereignty: A Line in the Sand." *Aperture* 139 (Summer 1995): 51–60.

Rose, Tricia. *Black Noise: Rap Music and Black Culture in Contemporary America.* Hanover, N.H.: Wesleyan University Press, 1994.

Scott, James C. *Domination and the Arts of Resistance: Hidden Transcripts.* New Haven: Yale University Press, 1990.

Shabalala, Joseph Bekhizizwe. "Joseph Bekhizizwe Shabalala: A Unifying Force." In *Nightsong: Performance, Power and Practice in South Africa,* edited by Veit Erlmann. Chicago: University of Chicago Press, 1996.

Singer, Norman J. "Symbols of Ethiopian Culture in Jamaica Beyond Rastafarianism." *Proceedings of the Ninth International Congress of Ethiopian Studies, Moscow,*

August 26–29, 1986. Moscow: USSR Academy of Sciences, Africa Institute, 1988.

Smith, Huston, and Reuben Snake, eds. *One Nation Under God: The Triumph of the Native American Church.* Santa Fe: Clear Light Publishers, 1996.

Smyth, Willie, ed. *Songs of Indian Territory: Native American Music Traditions of Oklahoma.* Oklahoma City: Center of the American Indian, 1989.

Vander, Judith. "The Song Repertoire of Four Shoshone Women: A Reflection of Cultural Movements and Sex Roles." *Ethnomusicology* 26, no. 1 (1983): 73–83.

———. *Ghost Dance Songs and Religion of a Wind River Shoshone Woman.* Los Angeles: Program in Ethnomusicology, UCLA, 1986.

———. *Songprints: The Musical Experience of Five Shoshone Women.* Urbana: University of Illinois Press, 1988.

———. *Shoshone Ghost Dance Religion: Poetry, Songs, and Great Basin Context.* Urbana: University of Illinois Press, 1997.

Web Site

Biography of Enoch Mankayi Sontonga, by Genevieve Walker:

http://www.polity.org.za/people/sontonga

Chapter Ten

The addition of the Hawaiian case study was suggested by a brief discussion of the Moe family in James Clifford's *Routes* and a memorable night I spent at a performance by the traveling Ukelele Hall of Fame. Yo-Yo Ma's exploration of the tango provided a provocative "real-world" follow-up to our exploration of the tango, as did Evan Ziporyn's creative elaborations on Balinese gamelan music.

I first became interested in David Hykes's explorations of chant "harmonic chant" during the late 1970s when I sang with his Harmonic Choir in New York City. I have followed his career ever since with interest and thank him and Theodore Levin for an update on recent developments.

Charles Starrett contributed to the discussion of electroacoustic instruments, and Reece Michaelson drafted the brief biography of Yo-Yo Ma. I thank Deborah Wong for providing the translation of *A Tango for You* and to Inez and Maurice Eskowitz for helping me locate video and sound recordings of this piece.

Books and Articles

Appadurai, Arjun. "Introduction: Commodities and the Politics of Value." In *The Social Life of Things: Commodities in Cultural Perspective.* Cambridge: Cambridge University Press, 1986.

Beloff, Jim. *The Ukulele: A Visual History.* San Francisco: Miller Freeman Books, 1997.

Clifford, James. *Routes: Travel and Translation in the Late Twentieth Century.* Cambridge, Mass.: Harvard University Press, 1997.

Davies, Hugh. "Hawaiian Guitar." *The New Grove Dictionary of Musical instruments,* edited by Stanley Sadie. London: Macmillan, 1984.

Farhi, Paul. "See It, Hear It, Read It—Buy It?" *Washington Post,* November 28, 1995, D1.

Hafner, Katie. "In Love with Technology, as Long as It's Dusty." *New York Times,* March 25, 1999, G1.

Harris, Ron. "New Technology Could Reshape Music Industry." *Star Tribune* (Minneapolis), December 12, 1998, 1D.

Hinsley, Curtis M. "The World as Marketplace: Commodification of the Exotic at the World's Columbian Exposition, Chicago, 1893." In *Exhibiting Cultures: The Poetics and Politics of Museum Display,* edited by Ivan Karp and Steven D. Lavine. Washington: Smithsonian Institution Press, 1991.

Hood, Mantle. "Musical Ornamentation as History: The Hawaiian Steel Guitar." *Yearbook of Traditional Music* 15 (1983): 141–8.

Horner, Bruce. "On the Study of Music as Material Social Practice." *Journal of Musicology* 16, no. 2 (1998): 159–99.

Hykes, David. "In Concert: The Harmonic Choir." Program notes, March 20, 1981.

Kanahele, George S., ed. *Hawaiian Music and Musicians.* Honolulu: University Press of Hawaii, 1979.

Kirshenblatt-Gimblett, Barbara. "Objects of Ethnography." In *Exhibiting Culture: The Poetics and Politics of Museum Display,* edited by Ivan Karp and Steven D. Lavine. Washington: Smithsonian Institution Press, 1991.

McManus, Jim. "Sorting Out the Proposals for Improving Digital Sound." *New York Times,* May 7, 1998, G11.

Meintjes, Louise. "Paul Simon's *Graceland,* South Africa, and the Mediation of Musical Meaning." *Ethnomusicology* 34, no. 1 (1990): 37–73.

Morgan, Christine. "Business Technology: 3D Listening from Only Two Speakers." *Daily Telegraph* (London), November 8, 1993, 34.

Nettl, Bruno. "The Dual Nature of Ethnomusicology in North America." In *Comparative Musicology and the Anthropology of Music,* edited by Bruno Nettl and Philip Bohlman. Chicago: University of Chicago Press, 1991.

Odell, Jay Scott. "Ukulele." *The New Grove Dictionary of Musical Instruments,* edited by Stanley Sadie. London: Macmillan, 1984.

Pareles, Jon. "Think Globally, Listen Locally." *New York Times,* February 4, 2000.

Pressing, Jeff. *Synthesizer Performance and Real-Time Techniques*. Madison, Wisc.: A-R Editions, 1992.

Roberts, David, and Hugh Davies. "Synthesizer." *The New Grove Dictionary of Musical Instruments*, edited by Stanley Sadie. London: Macmillan, 1984.

Slobin, Mark. *Subcultural Sounds: Micromusics of the West.* Hanover, N.H.: Wesleyan University Press, 1993.

Snider, Mike. "CD Sound Reaches New Heights." Detroit *News,* May 17, 1999, 81.

Tassel, Janet. "Yo-Yo Ma's Journeys." *Harvard Magazine,* March–April 2000: 43–51, 207.

Wallace, Arminta. "Death of Vinyl." *Irish Times,* City Edition, June 30, 1992, News Features, Reviews, 9.

Wallis, Roger, and Krister Malm. *Big Sounds from Small Peoples.* New York: Pendragon Press, 1984.

RECORDING

Brozman, Bob. *Traditional Hawaiian Guitar.* Woodstock, N.Y.: Homespun Video, 1993. Videocassette.

Epiloque

Takaki, Ronald. *From Different Shores: Perspectives on Race and Ethnicity in America,* 2d ed. New York and Oxford: Oxford University Press, 1994.

Wong, Deborah. "I Want the Microphone: Mass Mediation and Agency in Asian-American Popular Music." *TDR: The Drama Review* 38, no. 3 (T143, Fall 1994): 152–67.

© Appendix: Classifying Musical Instruments

Based on Curt Sachs, "Terminology," in *The History of Musical Instruments* (New York: W. W. Norton, 1940).

Credits

Every effort has been made to contact the copyright holder of each of these selections. If proper acknowledgment has not been made, please contact us.

translated by A. M. Berrett, copyright © 1995 by Gerard Chaliand and Jean-Pierre Rageau. Used by permission of Viking Penguin, a division of Penguin Putnam Inc.; p. 73: AP/Wide World Photos; p. 74 (top): Courtesy Mrs. Russell Bunai (research by Anne Rasmussen); p. 74 (bottom): Jonathan Friedlander; p. 76: Photo © 2000 Jack Vartoogian; p. 77 (top): Courtesy Johnny Sarweh; p. 77 (bottom): Courtesy MGM Grand Hotel and Casino, Las Vegas, Nevada; p. 79: Courtesy Kay Kaufman Shelemay; p. 80: Sarah G. Partridge/Bettmann/Corbis; p. 81: "The Slave Trade" from The Penguin Atlas of Diasporas by Gerard Chaliand and Jean-Pierre Rageau, translated by A. M. Berrett, copyright © 1995 by Gerard Chaliand and Jean-Pierre Rageau. Used by permission of Viking Penguin, a division of Penguin Putnam Inc.; p. 82 (left): Courtesy New York Public Library, Schomburg Center for Research in Black Culture; p. 82 (right): © Hulton-Deutsch Collection/CORBIS; p. 84: AP/Wide World Photos; p. 85: © P. J. Griffiths/Magnum Photos; p. 86: Photo by Huynh Tam, Paris, 1989; p. 87 (top): From Rice Paddies and Temple Yards: Traditional Music of Vietnam by Phong Nguyen and Patricia Shehan Campbell © 1990 World Music Press; p. 87 (bottom): Photo by Adelaida Reyes; p. 89: Courtesy Bui Huu Nhut; p. 92: Courtesy Ngan Khoi Chorus, Music Director Tran, Chuc; p. 97: Sketches for Francesco Cavalli's "Ercole Amante" by Robin Linklater, BEMF 1999. Designer costumes (left to right): Bellezza, Cintia, and Ercole. Design & typography by Siobhan Kelleher & Robert Torres. Used with permission of BEMF; p. 101: Courtesy Harvard Map Collection, Harvard College Library; p. 105 (top): © Kindra Clineff/Index Stock Imagery; p. 105 (bottom): From Harper and Row: Maps in Minds by Roger M. Downs and David Stea, 1977; p. 106: Courtesy Greater Boston Convention & Visitors Bureau, Inc.; p. 110: Photo by John Bohn/The Boston Globe. Republished with permission of Globe Newspaper Company, Inc., from July 16, 2000, issue of The Boston Globe, © 2000; p. 111: © Kevin Fleming/CORBIS; p. 112: © Peter Wallace; p. 113: Photo by Lisa Luciano; p. 114 (bottom): Courtesy of the artist, Rafael Kayanan, and First Night Inc., Boston; p. 116: Photo by Tom Herde/The Boston Globe; p. 119: Photo by Kim Furnald, Courtesy Furnald/Gray, Boston; p. 122 (top): © Bill Polo; p. 122 (bottom): Photo by Takashi Koto. Copyright © 1998 by Takashi Koto; p. 126 (bottom): Photo by Susan Wilson; courtesy of the Klezmer Conservatory Band; p. 127: Courtesy Kay Kaufman Shelemay; p. 129: Photo Courtesy of Gamelan Galak Tika and The Boston Globe; p. 130: Photo by Susan Wilson/Courtesy Club Passim; p. 132: © 1962 TIME Inc. Reprinted by permission; p. 133: Bettmann/Corbis; p. 135 (top): © 1999 MBTA; p. 135 (bottom): Courtesy King's Noyse; p. 139: Courtesy Joanne Rile Management, Inc.; p. 141: Courtesy Harvard Map Collection, Harvard College Library; p. 142: Courtesy of Moores School of Music, University of Houston;

p. 144: Courtesy Zydeco Dots; p. 146: Photo by Inez Eskowitz; p. 147: Courtesy Kay Kaufman Shelemay; p. 150: Courtesy Kay Kaufman Shelemay; p. 151: © Michael Penn; p. 153: Collection Kay Kaufman Shelemay; p. 156: Courtesy Kay Kaufman Shelemay; p. 157 (top): © Nik Wheeler/Corbis; p. 157 (bottom): Photo by Bob Seidemann; p. 159: AP/Wide World Photos; p. 160: Photo by Adriana Groisman; p. 161: Photo © Terry Sanders; p. 162: Courtesy Kay Kaufman Shelemay; p. 164 (top): Courtesy Harvard Map Collection, Harvard College Library; p. 164 (bottom): © Kazuyoshi Nomachi/PPS; p. 165 (top): Photo by Gorffu Kassa, Courtesy Saint Gebriel Church; p. 165 (bottom): Courtesy Kay Kaufman Shelemay; p. 167: Courtesy Kay Kaufman Shelemay; p. 168: From Jacques Mercier, Ethiopian Magic Scrolls, Braziller, 1979; p. 169 (top): From Walter Kaufmann, The Tibetan Buddhist (Tantric) Song Book, Indiana University Press; p. 169 (bottom): From Ethiopian Christian Liturgical Chant, edited by Kay Kaufmann Shelemay and Peter Jeffery. Used with permission of A–R Editions, Inc.; p. 170: From Ethiopian Christian Liturgical Chant, edited by Kay Kaufman Shelemay and Peter Jeffery. Used with permission of A–R Editions, Inc.; p. 173: © Kazuyoshi Nomachi/PPS; p. 174: Courtesy Kay Kaufman Shelemay; p. 176: Photo © Jack Vartoogian; p. 179: Photo by Diana L. Eck, the Pluralism Project at Harvard University; p. 181: © Wally McNamee/CORBIS; p. 185: © Michael S. Yamashita/CORBIS; p. 186: Margaret Riegel/NTY Pictures; p. 187 (top): From Folk Dances of Pamjab, by Iqbal Singh Dhillon, Delhi, India, National Book Shop, 1998. Reproduced with permission of the author; p. 187 (bottom): Photo by Jessie Singh Birring/Courtesy of 4x4 Dancers; p. 190: © Lindsay Hebberd/CORBIS; p. 191: Courtesy ISHQ Records; p. 192 (top): Courtesy Kate Koperski; p. 192 (bottom): Courtesy Pekka Gronow Collection; p. 194: Courtesy Hohner; p. 195: Courtesy Roderick Cannon; p. 197 (top): Photo by Dick Blau; p. 197 (bottom): Reuters Newsmedia Inc./Corbis; p. 199 (top): Corbis; p. 199 (bottom): From Zoe Ingalls, "The Tango: A Scholarly History of a 'Very Passionate Dance,'" April 18, 1997. Copyright 2000, The Chronicle of Higher Education. Reprinted with permission. This article may not be posted, published, or distributed without permission from The Chronicle; p. 204 (top): Courtesy Adriana Groisman; p. 204 (bottom): From Asahi Graph, June 1, 1987. Reproduced with permission of Asahi Graph, Tokyo; p. 205: Courtesy Natalio Gorin; p. 208 (top): Kevin Fleming/Corbis; p. 208 (bottom): AP/Wide World Photos; p. 211: Courtesy Aleppo Heritage Society, Tel Aviv; p. 217: Courtesy Alan Paredes; p. 221: Bettmann/Corbis; p. 223: Bettmann/Corbis; p. 224 (top): © Philip Gould/CORBIS; p. 226: Courtesy Kay Kaufman Shelemay; p. 232: Photo courtesy Tawil family; p. 236 (left): Bettmann/Corbis; p. 236 (right): Courtesy Joe Bush; p. 237: Courtesy Sephardic Community Center, Brooklyn,

New York; **p. 238** *(top)*: Photograph courtesy Tawil family; **p. 238** *(bottom)*: Photo courtesy Maria Garcia; **p. 242** *(left)*: Courtesy EMI, Arabia; **p. 242** *(right)*: Photograph courtesy Tawil family; **p. 244**: Courtesy of Sephardic Community Center, Brooklyn, New York; **p. 247**: Photo by Irene Young; **p. 250**: © Philip Gould/CORBIS; **p. 252**: Courtesy Reza Vali; **p. 253**: © Richard Hamilton/Corbis; **p. 255** *(left)*: © 1997 MMB Music, Inc., Saint Louis. Used by permission. All Rights Reserved; **p. 255** *(right)*: © Jack Vartoogian; **p. 257** *(top)*: Courtesy of FLECO Corporation, Chino, CA; **p. 257** *(bottom)*: © Charles Gupton/Stock, Boston/Picture-Quest; **p. 258** *(top)*: Courtesy Kay Kaufman Shelemay; **p. 258** *(bottom)*: Sony Music Enterprises, Inc.; **p. 263** *(top)*: From *South to Louisiana: The Music of the Cajun Bayou* by John Broven, © 1983 used by permission of the licenser, Pelican Publishing Company, Inc.; **p. 263** *(bottom)*: Philip Gould/Corbis; **p. 264**: From *Cajun Sketches: From the Prairies of Southwest Louisiana* by Lauren C. Post. Copyright © 1974 by Louisiana State University Press. Reprinted by permission of Louisiana State University Press; **p. 268**: From *South to Louisiana: The Music of the Cajun Bayou* by John Broven, © 1983 used by permission of the licenser, Pelican Publishing Company, Inc.; **p. 269**: Philip Gould/Corbis; **p. 270**: From *Histoires de l'Accordeon* by Francois Billard and Didier Roussin, Climat, I.N.A., 1991. Collection Philippe Krumm; **p. 271** *(top)*: From *Histoires de l'Accordeon* by Francois Billard and Didier Roussin, Climat, I.N.A., 1991. Collection Didier Roussin; **p. 271** *(bottom)*: Courtesy Musikinstrumenten-Museum, Markneukirchen; **p. 272** *(top)*: © Lynn Goldsmith/Corbis; **p. 272** *(bottom)*: © Jack Vartoogian; **p. 274** *(top)*: Philip Gould/CORBIS; **p. 274** *(bottom)*: Photo by Bacque; **p. 277**: Photo © Jack Vartoogian; **p. 284** *(top)*: © Neal Preston/Corbis; **p. 284** *(bottom)*: © Corbis; **p. 285**: Portrait of E. M. Sontonga by courtesy of the Amathole Museum, King William's Town; **p. 286**: Photo by Andrea Mandel, Courtesy of Gallo Records

and Right Side Management; **p. 290**: © Charles O'Rear/CORBIS; **p. 291** *(top)*: Pictorial Press Limited; **p. 291** *(bottom)*: Photo by Carlos Reyes, Andes Press Agency, London; **p. 292**: Corbis; **p. 294**: © Rene Burri/Magnum Photos; **p. 295**: © 2000 Rahav 'Cosi' Alfasi/Photopass.com; **p. 296**: Courtesy Beatrice Crofts; **p. 297**: © Baldwin H. Ward & Kathryn C. Ward/Corbis; **p. 300**: Courtesy Kay Kaufman Shelemay; **p. 301**: Courtesy Shoshone Tribal Cultural Center; **p. 302**: "Calendar" cover of May 14, 1998, *The Boston Globe*; **p. 303**: © Mike Zens/Corbis; **p. 304**: Courtesy Kay Kaufman Shelemay; **p. 306**: Courtesy Kay Kaufman Shelemay; **p. 308**: © Owen Franken/Corbis; **p. 309** *(top)*: Courtesy VFW Post 3628, Riverton, WY; **p. 309** *(bottom)*: Photo by Judith Vander, from *Songprints: The Musical Experience of Five Shoshone Women* (pl. 21); **p. 312** *(top)*: © Wayne Nicholls; **p. 312** *(bottom)*: Artwork by Raymond Nordwall. Courtesy of the SOAR Corporation (www.soundofamerica.com); **p. 313**: Courtesy Kay Kaufman Shelemay; **p. 315**: Courtesy Hohner; **p. 318** *(middle)*: Courtesy Blix Street Records; **p. 318** *(bottom)*: Corbis; **p. 319**: © Bettmann/Corbis; **p. 320**: AP/Wide World Photos; **p. 322**: Smithsonian Institution, Washington, D.C.; **p. 324**: Courtesy Kay Kaufman Shelemay; **p. 325**: From Wallis and Malm, *Big Sounds from Little Peoples*, 1984. Pendragon Press. Reproduced with the permission of the publisher; **p. 326**: Courtesy Kay Kaufman Shelemay; **p. 327** *(bottom)*: © Douglas Peebles/CORBIS; **p. 327** *(top)*: Photo by Haley S. Robertson; **p. 328**: Courtesy Ukulele Hall of Fame; **p. 330** *(second from right)*: Courtesy Cairdin Accordians, Limerick, Ireland; **p. 331**: Corbis; **p. 333**: © Roger Ressmeyer/CORBIS; **p. 334**: Courtesy Toyota Motor North America, Inc.; **p. 335**: AP/Wide World Photos; **p. 337**: Courtesy Gamelan Son of Lion; **p. 338** *(top)*: Courtesy Arcturus Records, Tenafly, N.J.; **p. 338** *(bottom)*: Photo © 2000 Doron Chmiel; **p. 339**: Courtesy Kay Kaufman Shelemay.

Index

Page numbers in *italics* refer to illustrations; numbers in **boldface** refer to definitions. **Boldface text** indicates special features such as Listening Guides.

379